Get the eBook FREE!

(PDF, ePub, Kindle, and liveBook all included)

We believe that once you buy a book from us, you should be able to read it in any format we have available. To get electronic versions of this book at no additional cost to you, purchase and then register this book at the Manning website.

Go to https://www.manning.com/freebook and follow the instructions to complete your pBook registration.

That's it!
Thanks from Manning!

DSLs in Action

DSLs in ACTION

DEBASISH GHOSH

MANNING

Greenwich
(74° w. long.)

M Manning Publications Co.
180 Broad St.
Suite 1323
Stamford, CT 06901

Development Editor: Cynthia Kane
Copyeditor: Joan Celmer
Typesetters: Dennis Dalinnik
Cover designer: Marija Tudor

ISBN 9781935182450
Printed in the United States of America

To my grandfather, who taught me my first alphabet

brief contents

contents

foreword

I have always enjoyed working with compilers, the engineering part of it as much as the creative process, on crafting my own language. Programming languages in general and Domain Specific Languages (DSLs) in particular are something I'm very passionate about.

The concept of DSLs is nothing new. For example, Lisp developers have developed and used "little languages" for a long time. But in recent years DSLs have become more widely used and adopted in the industry in general. The tools and techniques have matured, and it has never been easier to start exploring the wonderful world of language design.

DSLs, as most languages, are about communication. A well-crafted DSL communicates the essence and means of the domain it represents in a way that feels and is so natural that you don't even think about its underlying technology. It helps to bridge the gap between business and technology and between stakeholders and programmers—a skill more important than ever and well worth acquiring.

Debasish is a highly regarded expert in both the Scala and open source communities. I have been reading his intellectually challenging but highly enjoyable blog for years and I got to know Debasish more closely about a year ago when he started contributing to the Akka project. It immediately became evident that he was not only a deep thinker, but also a pragmatic hacker who gets things done. I have enjoyed discussing programming languages, design, and more with him ever since.

I'm excited about this book. It covers a lot of ground and it is not only wide but also deep. It will take you on a journey through the state-of-the-art in the DSL landscape today, and along the way you will learn how to think when designing flexible and natural DSLs. As a bonus you'll also get a tour through some of the most interesting programming languages today such as Scala, Groovy, Clojure, and Ruby and learn how each one makes you think about and approach a problem differently. Enjoy the ride. I sure did.

JONAS BONÉR
SCALABLE SOLUTIONS
http://jonasboner.com

preface

In spring 2001 the company I work for, Anshinsoft (http://www.anshinsoft.com), made a foray into enterprise application development for one of the largest securities brokers and asset management firms in the Asia-Pacific region. The process stimulated my interest in the challenges of modeling a specific problem domain and translating the model into real-world implementation artifacts. Since then, it's been a long journey through the pages of Eric Evans' domain-driven design book (*Domain-Driven Design: Tackling Complexity in the Heart of Software*), the teachings of Josh Bloch on designing good APIs (How to Design a Good API & Why it Matters; http://www.infoq.com/presentations/effective-api-design) and Martin Fowler's preaching on domain-specific languages (DSLs).

The purpose behind a well-designed DSL is to provide a humane interface to your target users. The best way to do that is to have a programming model that speaks the language of the domain. For way too long we've been developing applications that are like a black box to business users. Believe me, every user would love to have a look at the business rules that you model in your code base rather than having to scramble through the boxes and arrows on a whiteboard.

The rules embedded in your code need to be comprehensible to the user. They need to be presented in a language that the user understands. This is what I realized in the 10 years I have spent working in domain modeling. When the rules are comprehensible, a DSL shines, communication between the development team and the business users becomes more effective, and your software becomes more expressive to your users.

An implementation language plays an important role any time you want to provide expressive syntax and semantics to your users. We've seen the phenomenal growth of an ecosystem that fosters expressive language development. Ruby, Groovy, Scala, and Clojure have been forerunners in encouraging developers to write more succinct yet expressive code. I've been programming in all these languages and I feel that idiomatic code written in any of them can be much more domain-friendly than most of their predecessors.

Writing a book on DSLs has been a challenge. I tried to focus on everything that's *real-world* about DSLs. That's why I chose a specific domain upfront. As the book progresses, you'll feel how the domain models grow in complexity as business requirements add up. This helps you appreciate how a DSL-driven development approach scales up with the added complexity of the problem domain. There's nothing radical in the approach; a DSL only encourages you to add an extra dimension to your thought process of API design. Remember, it's your users who'll be using the DSL. Please keep them in mind and you'll be successful!

acknowledgments

Unusual as it may seem, I'd like to start with a self-acknowledgment. I had no idea that I could keep myself focused for so long on a specific topic of interest. The process of writing this book taught me the values of perseverance, self-determination, and self-belief.

Thanks to my team at Anshinsoft for creating a workplace where ideas are nurtured and given wings to fly. The late-night brainstorming sessions helped me to carve out many a complex domain model and ignited in me a love of DSLs.

Thanks to our client manager, Watanabe san (Mr. Tohru Watanabe), who taught me the domain model of the securities trading business. This book is filled with examples of what he's taught me over the many years that we've interacted.

Thanks to the following reviewers for helping me improve the quality of the manuscript: Sivakumar Thyagarajan, Darren Neimke, Philipp K. Janert, James Hatheway, Kenneth DeLong, Edmon Begolli, Celso Gonzalez, Jason Jung, Andrew Cooke, Boris Lenzinger, David Dossot, Federico Tomassetti, Greg Donald, John S. Griffin, Sumit Pal, and Rick Wagner. Special thanks to reviewers Guillaume Laforge and John Wilson for teaching me nuances of writing Groovy DSLs; Michael Fogus for his suggestions on improving the contents of chapters 5 and 6; and Sven Efftinge for his suggestions on Xtext and external DSLs in chapter 7. And to Franco Lombardo for doing a final technical proofread of the manuscript shortly before it went to press.

During the course of writing *DSLs In Action*, the Twitter community was an invaluable source of assistance and inspiration, offering many words of wisdom.

I've had an excellent team to work with at Manning Publications. Cynthia Kane, my development editor, was tireless in assisting me with grammar, style, and taking a reader-centric view of every chapter that I wrote. If you find the text easy to read and understand, it's thanks to the many iterations of each chapter that Cynthia went through and made me do as well. Thanks to Karen Tegtmeyer for organizing the peer reviews, Maureen Spencer for all the help she extended during the course of manuscript development, Joan Celmer for being so responsive during copyediting, and the rest of the Manning crew who provided support during production. I also want to express my thanks to publisher Marjan Bace for having confidence in me.

Very special thanks to my wife, Mou, who's been the quintessential source of inspiration to me throughout this journey. Her words of encouragement at every step of this long and arduous process made all the difference in making it a meaningful and fruitful one.

about the book

Every time you design a domain model on your whiteboard, it seems to get lost in translation within the complex code base you started with. When you design your implementation model in your favorite programming language, it no longer speaks the dialect that the domain expert can understand. If your implementation on the whiteboard doesn't conform exactly to the specifications you agreed on with the domain user, there's no way it can be verified by the person who understands the domain rules.

DSLs in Action addresses this core issue by suggesting a DSL-driven application development model. Design your domain APIs around the syntax and semantics that the domain user understands. Then, even during the development of the code base, the user can do incremental verifications of the domain rule implementations. If your code speaks the language of the domain, it becomes clearer to the person who develops it, to the one who maintains it, and to a nonprogrammer domain expert who understands the business.

This book addresses the issues of *using* a DSL as well as *implementing* one. It talks about a DSL as a thin veneer of linguistic abstraction on top of an underlying semantic model. The semantic model is the implementation that manages the core structure of the domain, while the language layer speaks the dialect of the domain user.

You will learn how to design and implement DSLs using modern languages like Ruby, Groovy, Scala, and Clojure. The book discusses the strengths and weaknesses of the paradigms that these languages support in designing a DSL. By the time you've finished reading the book, you'll have a thorough understanding of the concepts that you need to master in order to design beautiful domain abstractions that your user can understand and appreciate.

Who should read this book?

If you want to design good APIs that are expressive enough for your domain users as well as for your fellow programmers, this book is for you. If you're a domain user and would like to improve your communication with the application development team, this book is for you. If you're a programmer who feels the pain of trying to verify with your domain users whether the implementation of their business rules is correct, this book is for you as well.

Roadmap

Figures 1, 2, and 3 will give you an idea of how the book is organized and of what you can expect as you read it. The book has three parts:

- Using DSLs
- Implementing DSLs
- Future trends in DSL development

In part 1 (chapters 1-3), you'll get a detailed overview of how a DSL-driven development environment fits into your application architecture. If you're a programmer or an architect, this part of the book will help you adapt your current development stack

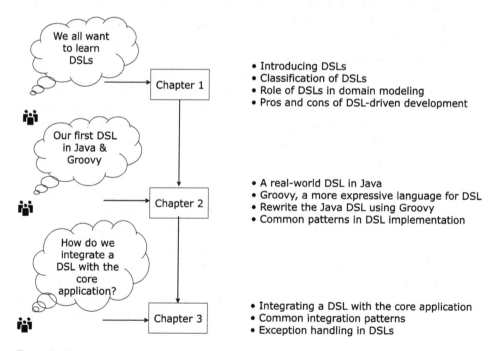

Figure 1   Your journey through chapters 1 through 3

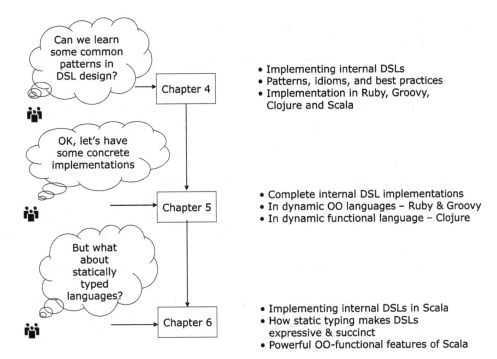

Figure 2   Your journey through chapters 4 through 6

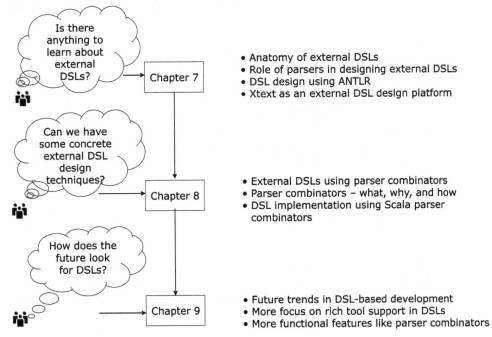

Figure 3   Your journey through chapters 7 through 9

with the new paradigm. The book is centered on languages that run on the Java Virtual Machine (JVM). If you're a Java programmer, you'll quickly determine how you can integrate your current Java-based project with DSLs that you develop in other, more expressive JVM languages.

Behind the user-friendly syntactic structures of a DSL is an underlying semantic model. Part 2 and chapters 7 and 8 focus on how to design the semantic model so that it acts as a good host for the linguistic abstractions of the DSL above it. This part of the book is more appropriate for developers who want to build beautiful abstractions as part of their domain model. Chapters 4 through 8 contain lots of DSL implementation snippets in languages like Ruby, Groovy, Clojure, and Scala. If you're using one of these languages or planning to use them for your DSL implementation in the near future, you'll find these chapters extremely useful. I start with basic DSL implementation techniques, then cover advanced techniques like metaprogramming, parser combinators, and frameworks like ANTLR and Xtext.

Part 3 (chapter 9) focuses on the future and techniques like parser combinators and DSL workbenches.

DSLs in Action is targeted at real practitioners. It contains theory, but only when it's required for the purpose of understanding the implementation that follows. I wrote the book with the full and honest intention that it be useful to the developer community in the real world.

Typographical conventions

The book has a number of callouts and sidebars used to call your attention to important information.

In most cases, I've used the following sidebar template to present information related to the domain of securities trading and settlement:

 Financial brokerage system

Information that's accompanied by this icon contains something you should know to understand the domain that's the focus of the DSL discussion. Special terms and concepts that you need some background information about are presented in these sidebars.

I've also included a number of callouts in the book that use the following template and icon:

These callouts contain information that stands out from the rest of the text in the section. The callouts might contain special idioms of DSL design, highlights from a discussion that we've recently had, or other nuggets that I want to emphasize.

I use one more icon in the book to attract your attention:

> **ℹ Information about individual languages**
>
> When you see this icon, you'll know that the sidebar contains tidbits of information about the language used in the current examples. In order to fully understand the examples, you'll need to be familiar with these specific concepts.

Be sure to read the extra information highlighted with these icons. It will help you to fully understand the ideas being discussed.

Code conventions and downloads

This book includes numerous example DSLs, many of which are substantial enough to explain complete domain rule implementations. The code is written in Java, Ruby, Groovy, Scala, and Clojure. Source code in listings or in text is in a `fixed-width font` to separate it from ordinary text. Method names, parameters, object properties, other scripts like those of ANTLR or Xtext, and XML elements and attributes in text are also presented in `fixed-width font`.

Source code can be verbose and detailed in order to provide a meaningful explanation of the semantics and the context. In many cases, the original source code has been reformatted, adding line breaks and reworking indentation, to accommodate the available page space in the book. In rare cases, this was not enough, and some listings include line continuation markers.

Code annotations accompany many of the source code listings, highlighting important concepts. In some cases, numbered bullets link to explanations that follow the listing.

I acknowledge that not all of you will be familiar with all the programming languages that I've used to implement the DSL structures. Keeping this in mind, I've included short reference cards (or cheat sheets) for the languages I discuss in appendixes C through G. These are not meant to be a complete reference for the language, but only brief pointers to the language features used in explaining the DSL implementations. References are provided to complete texts that you should read to supplement the cheat sheets.

Most of today's IDEs are mature enough to let you develop projects in multiple languages. But, for those readers who aren't familiar with the polyglot development environment, appendix G is a good starting point.

The source code for all examples in this book is available from Manning's website, http://www.manning.com/DSLsinAction, which also contains relevant instructions on how to build and run them in your environment. Be sure to keep a copy of these listings when you go through the text.

Author Online

The purchase of *DSLs in Action* includes free access to a private web forum run by Manning Publications, where you can make comments about the book, ask technical questions, and receive help from the author and from other users. To access the forum and subscribe to it, point your web browser to www.manning.com/DSLsinAction. This page provides information on how to get on the forum once you are registered, what kind of help is available, and the rules of conduct on the forum.

Manning's commitment to our readers is to provide a venue where a meaningful dialogue between individual readers and between readers and the author can take place. It is not a commitment to any specific amount of participation on the part of the author, whose contribution to the forum remains voluntary (and unpaid). We suggest you try asking the author some challenging questions lest his interest stray! The Author Online forum and the archives of previous discussions will be accessible from the publisher's website as long as the book is in print.

About the author

Debasish Ghosh (@debasishg on Twitter) is the chief technology evangelist at Anshinsoft (http://www.anshinsoft.com), where he specializes in leading the delivery of enterprise-scale solutions for clients ranging from small to Fortune 500 companies. His research interests are OO and functional programming, DSLs, and NoSQL databases. He's a senior member of the ACM and authors a programming blog at *Ruminations of a Programmer* (http://debasishg.blogspot.com). He can be reached at dghosh@acm.org.

About the cover illustration

The figure on the cover of *DSLs in Action* is captioned "A man from Durdevac, near Osijek, Slavonija, Croatia." The illustration is taken from a reproduction of an album of Croatian traditional costumes from the mid-nineteenth century by Nikola Arsenovic, published by the Ethnographic Museum in Split, Croatia, in 2003. The illustrations were obtained from a helpful librarian at the Ethnographic Museum in Split, itself situated in the Roman core of the medieval center of the town: the ruins of Emperor Diocletian's retirement palace from around AD 304. The book includes finely colored illustrations of figures from different regions of Croatia, accompanied by descriptions of the costumes and of everyday life.

The village of Durdevac is near the town of Osijek in Slavonia, a geographical and historical region in eastern Croatia. Men in Slavonija traditionally wear red caps, white shirts, blue waistcoats, and pants with embroidered ornamentation. The final accessories are a wide woolen or leather belt and thick woolen socks, topped off with a jacket made from brown sheepskin, just like the figure on the cover of this book is wearing.

Dress codes and lifestyles have changed over the last 200 years, and the diversity by region, so rich at the time, has faded away. It is now hard to tell apart the inhabitants of different continents, let alone of different hamlets or towns separated by only a few miles. Perhaps we have traded cultural diversity for a more varied personal life—certainly for a more varied and fast-paced technological life.

Manning celebrates the inventiveness and initiative of the computer business with book covers based on the rich diversity of regional life of two centuries ago, brought back to life by illustrations from old books and collections like this one.

Part 1

Introducing domain-specific languages

What are domain-specific languages (DSLs)? What value do they have for an application developer? What value do they add for the business user who'll use the application? Does DSL-driven development improve communication between the development team and the team of domain experts? What are the pros and cons of DSL-driven development? These are some of the questions that you'll find answers to in part 1 of this book.

Chapters 1, 2, and 3 form part 1 of *DSLs In Action*. I'll introduce many of the commonly used DSLs and talk about general design principles so you can get an idea of what to look for when you design a DSL of your own.

Chapter 1, is as usual, an introduction to DSLs.

In chapter 2, you'll design what might be your first DSL. As you work along, you'll get a taste of how expressive DSLs evolve iteratively from the user requirements. First, you'll implement the DSL in Java; then you'll see how it can be more expressive using Groovy, another language on the JVM.

In chapter 3, you will learn integrating internal and external DSLs in a core application and how to manage errors and exceptions.

Part 1 will be equally appealing to programmers and nonprogramming domain users. I've kept implementation details out of part 1 so you can get a broad overview of the DSL landscape.

Learning to speak the language of the domain

This chapter covers

- What a DSL is
- The benefits a DSL offers, both to business users and to solution implementers
- The structure of a DSL
- Using well-designed abstractions

Every morning on your way to the office, you pull your car up to your favorite coffee shop for a Grande Skinny Cinnamon Dolce Latte with whip. The barista always serves you exactly what you order. She can do this because you placed your order using precise language that she understands. You don't have to explain the meaning of every term that you utter, though to others what you say might be incomprehensible. In this chapter, you'll look at how to express a problem in the vocabulary of a particular domain and subsequently model it in the solution domain. The implementation model of this concept is the essence of what is called a *domain-specific language (DSL)*. If you had a software implementation of the coffee shop example where a user could place an order in the language that they use every day, you would have a DSL right there.

Every application that you design maps a problem domain to the implementation model of a solution domain. A DSL is an artifact that forms an important part of this mapping process. You'll look more closely at the definition of what a DSL is a bit later. First, you need to understand the process that makes this mapping possible. For this mapping to work, you need a common vocabulary that the two domains share. This vocabulary forms one of the core inputs that lead to the evolution of a DSL.

A good abstraction is essential to a well-designed DSL implementation. If you want to dig deep into the subject of well-designed abstractions, appendix A has a detailed discussion about the qualities to look for. A good plan of attack is to skim the appendix now, then continue reading this chapter. Section 1.7 contains basic information about abstractions, but appendix A is much more detailed.

1.1 The problem domain and the solution domain

Domain modeling is an exercise that helps you analyze, understand, and identify the participants involved in a specific area of activity. You start with the problem domain and identify how the entities collaborate with each other meaningfully within the domain. In the earlier example of the coffee shop, you placed your order in the most natural language of the domain, using terminology that mapped closely to what the barista understands. Terminology forms the core entity of the problem domain. The barista could easily figure out exactly what she needed to serve you to fulfill your request because you're both familiar with the required terminology.

1.1.1 The problem domain

In a domain modeling activity, the *problem domain* is the processes, entities, and constraints that are part of the business that you're analyzing. Domain modeling, also known as *domain analysis* (see [1] in section 1.9), involves the identification of all the major components of the domain and how they collaborate. In the example you began with, the barista knew all the entities like coffee, whipped cream, cinnamon, and nonfat milk that formed her problem domain model. When you analyze a more complex domain like a trading and settlement system for financial brokers, securities, stocks, bonds, trade, and settlement are some of the components that belong to the problem domain. Along with these components, you'll also study how securities are issued, how they're traded in stock exchanges, settled between various parties, and updated in books and accounts. You identify these collaborations and analyze and document them as artifacts of your analysis model.

1.1.2 The solution domain

You implement a problem domain analysis model in terms of the tools and techniques offered by the *solution domain*. The barista could map your order to the procedure that she needed to follow to serve your Grande Skinny Cinnamon Dolce

Latte. The process she followed and the tools she used formed parts of her solution domain. When you're dealing with a larger domain, you might need more support from your solution domain in terms of the tools, methodologies, and techniques that it needs to offer. You need to *map* the problem domain components into appropriate solution domain techniques. If you use an object-oriented methodology as the underlying solution platform, then classes, objects, and methods form the primary artifacts of your solution domain. You can compose these artifacts to form larger ones, which might serve as better representations of higher-level components in your problem domain. Figure 1.1 illustrates this first step in domain modeling. As you move along, you'll flesh out the process of how to get to the solution domain by using techniques that domain experts can understand throughout the lifecycle of transformation.

The primary exercise involved in domain modeling is mapping the problem domain to artifacts of the solution domain, so that all components, interactions, and collaborations are represented correctly and meaningfully. To do this, you first need to classify domain objects at the proper level of granularity. When you correctly classify domain objects, each object of the problem domain is visible in the solution domain, with its proper structure and semantics. But your map can be only as good as the language of interaction between the domains. A solid interaction requires that the problem domain and the solution domain share a common vocabulary.

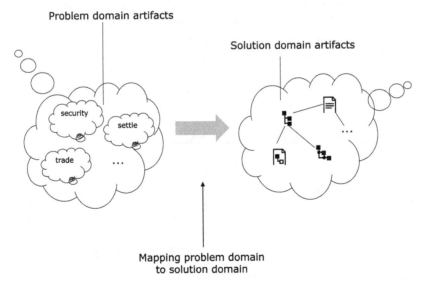

Figure 1.1 Entities and collaborations from the problem domain must map to appropriate artifacts in a solution domain. The entities shown on the left (security, trade, and so on) need corresponding representations on the right.

1.2   Domain modeling: establishing a common vocabulary

When you start an exercise in domain modeling, you start with the problem domain that you're going to model. You need to understand how the various entities of the domain interact among themselves and fulfill their responsibilities. While you're figuring all this out, you collaborate with domain experts and with other modelers. Domain experts know the domain. They communicate using the domain vocabulary, and use the same terminology when they explain domain concepts to the outside world. The modelers know how to represent an understanding of the model in a form that can be documented, shared, and implemented by software. The modelers must also understand the same terminology and reflect the same understanding in the domain model that they're designing.

Sometime back I started working on a project that involved modeling the back-office operations of a large financial brokerage organization. I wasn't a domain expert, and I didn't know much about the details and complexities involved in the practices of the securities industry practices. Now, after working in that domain for quite a while, I think it's similar enough to other domains that you might deal with to model most of my examples and annotations in this book on that domain. The sidebar in this section gives a brief introduction to the domain of securities trading and financial brokerage, which you'll use as running examples for implementing DSLs. As you progress, I'll define new concepts wherever applicable and focus on the relevant details only when necessary. If you're not familiar with what goes on in a stock exchange, don't panic. I'll give you enough background in the sidebars to help you understand the basic concepts of what you model.

On the first day of our requirements analysis meeting, the domain specialists of the financial industry started talking about coupon bonds, discount bonds, mortgages, and corporate actions. These terms were part of the usual terminology that a

Financial brokerage systems: a background

The business of financial brokerage starts with a trading process. This process involves the exchange of securities and cash between two or more parties, referred to as the *counterparties* of the trade. On a certain date, the counterparties promise to make the trade (this date is referred to as the *trade date*) at a place known as the *stock exchange*, based on an agreed upon price, known as the *unit price*. The securities, which form one leg of the exchange process (the other being cash), can be of several types, such as stocks, bonds, mutual funds, and a host of other types that can have a hierarchy of their own. There are, for example, several types of bonds, like coupon bonds and discount bonds.

Within a certain number of days of the promise to trade, the exchange is made by transferring the ownership of funds and securities between the counterparties; this exchange is known as the *settlement* process. Each security type has its own life-cycle of trade, execution, and finalization, and passes through a series of state changes in the course of the trading and settlement process.

brokerage specialist uses to communicate, but I didn't know what they meant. Also, lots of terms were being used synonymously. The terms discount bond and zero coupon bond are synonymous, and they were being used interchangeably by different domain experts in different contexts. But because these terms were unknown to me, confusion reigned. Not all of us were specialists in the financial industry, and we soon realized that we needed to share a common vocabulary to make the knowledge-sharing sessions more meaningful. Not only did we collaborate in terms of the common domain vocabulary, we also made sure that the model we designed and developed spoke the same language—the natural language of the domain.

1.2.1 *Benefits of a common vocabulary*

A common vocabulary, shared between the stakeholders of the model, serves as the binding force that unifies all artifacts that are part of the implementation. More importantly, with the common vocabulary in place, you can easily follow the path of features, functions, and objects across all phases of the project delivery cycle. The same terms that the modeler uses for documenting use-cases appear as module names in programs, entity names in data models, and object names in test cases. In this way, a common vocabulary bridges the gap between the problem domain and the solution domain. Creating a common vocabulary might take more time up-front than you're initially willing to spend, but I can almost guarantee that you'll save yourself a lot of redoing in the long run. Let's look at some of the tangible benefits that a common vocabulary offers.

SHARED VOCABULARY AS THE GLUE

During the requirements analysis phase, a shared vocabulary serves as the common bridge of understanding between the modelers and the domain experts. All your discussions are more succinct and effective. When Bob (who's a trader) talks about interest accrual for bonds, Joe (who's a modeler) knows that Bob is referring specifically to coupon bonds.

COMMON TERMINOLOGY IN TEST CASES

The common vocabulary can also serve as the basis for developing test cases. Then, the domain expert group can verify these test cases. A sample test case from my earlier project on brokerage system implementation reads: *For a zero coupon bond issued by Trampoline Securities with a face value of USD 10,000 and a primary value date of 15th May 2001 at a price of 40%, the investor will have to pay USD 4,000 at issue launch.* The test case makes perfect sense to the modeler, the tester, and the domain specialist who's reviewing it, because it uses terminology that forms the most natural representation of the domain language.

COMMON VOCABULARY DURING DEVELOPMENT

If the development team is using the same vocabulary to represent program modules, the resulting code is also going to speak the same domain language. For example, if you talk about modules like bond trading and settlement of securities, when you write code, you'll use the same vocabulary to name domain entities.

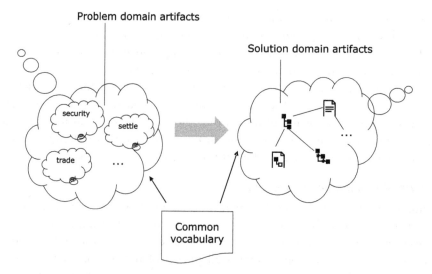

Figure 1.2   The problem domain and the solution domain need to share a common vocabulary for ease of communication. With this vocabulary, you can trace an artifact of the problem domain to its appropriate representation in the solution domain.

Developing and sharing a common vocabulary between the problem and solution domains is the first step in our march toward the solution domain. Let's update figure 1.1 with this common glue that binds the domains together to come up with figure 1.2.

You know that the developers and the domain experts need to share a common vocabulary, but how will the language be mapped? How does the domain expert understand the model that the developers are generating? This communication problem is a common one in any software development ecosystem.

Looking at figure 1.2, you'll realize that the domain experts are in no way equipped to understand the technical artifacts that currently populate the solution-domain model. As systems increase in complexity, the models get bloated and the communication gap keeps on widening. The domain experts don't need to understand the complexities that surround an implementation model; they need to verify whether the business rules being implemented are correct. Ideally, the experts themselves would write test scripts to verify the correctness and comprehensiveness of the domain rules' implementation, but that's not a practical solution.

What if you could offer the experts a communication model that builds on the common vocabulary and rolls off everyone's tongue with the same fluidity that a domain person uses in his everyday business practice? You can. This is the moment when the DSL enters the picture!

1.3   Introducing DSLs

Joe, the IT head for the hypothetical company Trampoline Securities, had no idea what Bob, the trader, was up to as he leaned over Bob's shoulders and took a sneak peek at his console. To his amazement, Joe discovered that Bob was busy typing commands and statements in a programming environment that he thought belonged exclusively to the members of his development team. Here's the fly-on-the-wall record of their conversation:

- Joe: Hey Bob, can you write programs?
- Bob: Yeah, sort of, in our new TrampolineEasyTrade system.
- Joe: But, but, you're a trader, right?
- Bob: So? We use this software for that, too.
- Joe: You're supposed to be *using* the software, not *programming* in it! The product isn't even out of the development labs.
- Bob: But I thought it'd be great if I could write some tests for the software that I'll be using later. That way, I can pass on my inputs to the development team way early in the sprint. Being part of this exercise makes me feel like I'm contributing more. I have a much better feel for what's being developed. And I can check to see if my use cases are working, too.
- Joe: But that's the responsibility of the development team! I sit with them every day. I've got tools in place to check code coverage, test coverage, and a bunch of other metrics that'll guarantee that what we deliver is the best it can be.
- Bob: As far as knowing about financial brokerage systems is concerned, who do you think understands the domain better? Me? Or your set of tools?

Ultimately Joe had to admit that Bob, who's an expert in the domain of financial brokerage systems, was better equipped to verify whether their new offering of the trading platform covered the functional specs adequately and correctly. What Joe couldn't understand is how Bob, who isn't a programmer, could write tests using their testing framework.

As a reader, you must also be wondering. Look at the following listing, which shows what Bob had up on his console.

Listing 1.1 Order-processing DSL

```
place orders (
  new Order to buy(100 sharesOf "IBM")
    limitPrice 300
    allOrNone
    using premiumPricing,
  new Order to buy(200 sharesOf "CISCO")
    limitOnClosePrice 300
    using premiumPricing,
  new Order to buy(200 sharesOf "GOOGLE")
    limitOnOpenPrice 300
    using defaultPricing,
  new Order to sell(200 bondsOf "SUN")
    limitPrice 300
    allOrNone
```

```
using {
  (qty, unit) => qty * unit - 500
}
)
```

Looks like a code snippet, right? It is, but it also contains language that Bob usually speaks when he's at his trading desk. Bob's preparing a list of sample order-creation scripts that place orders on securities using various pricing strategies. He can even define a custom pricing strategy on his own when he places the order.

What's the language that Bob's programming in? It doesn't matter to him, as long as he gets his work done. To him, it's the same language that he speaks at his trading desk. But let's determine how what Bob is doing differs from the run-of-the-mill coding that we do every day in our programming jobs:

- The vocabulary of the language that Bob is using seems to correspond closely with the domain that he belongs to. In his day job at his trading desk, he places orders for his clients using the same terminology that he's writing directly into his test scripts.
- The language that he's using, or the subset of the language that you see on his console, doesn't seem to apply outside the domain of financial brokerage business.
- The language is expressive, in the sense that Bob can clearly articulate what he wants to do as he steps through the process of creating a new order for his client.
- The language syntax looks succinct. The syntactic complexities of the high-level languages you usually program in have magically disappeared.

Bob is using a *domain-specific language,* tailor-made for financial brokerage systems. It's immaterial at this point what the underlying language of implementation is. The fact that the underlying language isn't obvious from the code in listing 1.1 indicates that the designer successfully created an expressive language for a specific domain.

1.3.1 *What's a DSL?*

A DSL is a programming language that's targeted at a specific problem; other programming languages that you use are more general purpose. It contains the syntax and semantics that model concepts at the same level of abstraction that the problem domain offers. For example, when you order your Cinnamon Latte, you use the domain language that the barista readily understands.

> **DEFINITION** Abstraction is a cognitive process of the human brain that enables us to focus on the core aspects of a subject, ignoring the unnecessary details. You'll talk more about abstractions and DSL design in section 1.7. Appendix A is all about abstractions.

Programs that you write using a DSL must have all the qualities that you expect to find in a program that you write in any other computer language. A DSL needs to give you the ability to design abstractions that form part of the domain. In the same way that you can build a larger entity out of many smaller ones in the problem domain, a well-designed DSL gives you that flexibility of composition in the solution domain. You should be able to compose DSL abstractions just like you compose your functionalities in the problem domain.

Now you know what a DSL is. Let's talk about how it differs from other programming languages you've been using.

How's a DSL different from a general-purpose programming language?

The answer to the difference is in the definition itself. The two most important qualities of a DSL that you need to remember are:

- A DSL is targeted at a *specific problem area*
- A DSL contains syntax and semantics that model concepts at the *same level of abstraction as the problem domain* does

When you program using a DSL, you deal only with the complexity of the problem domain. You don't have to worry about the implementation details or other non-essential elements of the solution domain. (For more discussion about nonessential complexity, see appendix A.) More often than not, people who aren't expert programmers can use DSLs—if the DSL has the appropriate level of abstraction. Mathematicians can easily learn and work with Mathematica, UI designers feel comfortable writing HTML, hardware designers use VHDL (very-high-speed integrated circuit hardware description language; a DSL used in electronic design automation) to name a few such use cases. Because nonprogrammers need to be able to use them, DSLs must be more intuitive to users than general-purpose programming languages need to be.

You write a program only once, but you manage its evolution for many years. For a program to evolve, it needs to be nurtured by people, many of whom may not have been involved in designing the initial version. The key issue is communication, the ability for your program to communicate with its intended audience. In the case of a DSL, the direct audience is neither the compiler nor the CPU, but the human minds that need to understand its behavior. The language needs to be communicative to its audience and allow code snippets that are expressive enough to map to the thought process of the domain modeler. For this to happen, the DSL that you design has to offer the correct level of *syntactic* as well as *semantic* abstractions to the user.

What's in a DSL for business users?

As you've learned from the discussion so far, DSLs stand out from normal high-level programming languages in two ways:

- DSLs offer a higher level of abstraction to the user. This implies that you don't have to be concerned about the nuances of identifying specific data structures or other low-level details. You can focus on solving the problem at hand.
- DSLs offer a limited vocabulary that's specific to the domain it addresses. The fact that it contains nothing extra helps you focus on the problem that you're

modeling. A DSL doesn't have the horizontal, spread-out focus of a general-purpose programming language.

Both these qualities make DSLs a friendlier tool for the nonprogramming domain expert. Your business analysts understand the domain, which is what a DSL abstracts.

With more and more programming languages offering higher levels of abstraction design, DSLs are poised to be a major component in today's application development ecosystem. Nonprogramming domain analysts will surely have a major role to play here. With a DSL implementation in place, they'll be able to write test scripts correctly from day one. The idea isn't to run the scripts immediately, but to ensure that you've adequately covered the possible business scenarios in your implementation. When the DSL is designed at an effective level of abstraction, it's not unusual for domain experts to browse through source code that defines the business logic. They'll be able to verify the business rules, and provide immediate feedback to developers based on their observations.

Now that you've seen some of the values that a DSL offers to you as a developer and as a domain user, let's take a look at some of the commonly used DSLs in the industry today.

1.3.2 *Popular DSLs in use*

DSLs are everywhere. Whether or not you brand them as DSLs, I'm sure you're using a lot of them in every application that you develop. Table 1.1 lists a few of the most commonly used DSLs.

Table 1.1 Commonly used DSLs

DSL	Used for
SQL	Relational database language used to query and manipulate data
Ant, Rake, Make	Languages for building software systems
CSS	Stylesheet description language
YACC, Bison, ANTLR	Parser-generator languages
RSpec, Cucumber	Behavior-driven testing language in Ruby
HTML	Markup language for the web

There are a lot more DSLs that you use on a regular basis. Can you identify some of the common characteristics that these languages have? Here are a few:

- All DSLs are specific to the domain. Each language is of *limited expressivity*; you can use a DSL to solve the problem of that particular domain only. You can't build cargo management systems using only HTML.

  DEFINITION Martin Fowler used the term limited expressivity to describe the most important characteristic of a DSL. In his 2009 DSL Developer's

Conference keynote talk ([3] in section 1.9), Martin mentioned that it's this *limited expressivity* that differentiates a DSL from a general-purpose programming language. You can model anything and everything with a general-purpose programming language. With a DSL, you can model only one specific domain, but in a more expressive way.

- For each of the languages listed in table 1.1 (and the other popular ones being used), you usually need to use the *abstractions* that they publish. Barring specific exceptions, you don't even need to know the underlying *implementations* of these languages. Every DSL offers a set of contracts that you can use to build your solution domain model. You can compose multiple contracts to build more complex models. But you don't need to step out of the offered contracts and get down to the implementation level of the DSL.
- Every DSL is expressive enough to make its intentions clear to the nonprogramming user. The DSL isn't merely a collection of APIs that you use; every API is concise and speaks the vocabulary of the domain.
- For every DSL, you can go back to your source file months after you wrote them and immediately be able to figure out what you meant.

It's a fact that DSL-based development encourages better communication between developers and domain experts. This is its greatest virtue. By using a DSL, a nonprogramming domain expert won't transform himself into a regular programmer. But with the expressiveness and explicitly communicative APIs that DSLs offer, the domain expert will be able to understand which business rules the abstraction implements and whether it adequately covers all possible domain scenarios.

Let's look at one motivating example of a DSL snippet selected from the list in table 1.1. Consider the following snippet from a Rakefile, which is mainly used to build Ruby-based systems:

```
desc "Default Task"
task :default => [ :test ]

Rake::TestTask.new { |t|
  t.libs << "test"
  t.pattern = 'test/*_test.rb'
  t.verbose = true
  t.warning = false
}
```

This code snippet creates a number of unit tests that can be run as the default task. Even if you don't know Ruby, this snippet means the same thing to you; it's just as expressive to you. How can that be? The snippet has explicit hotspots that match vocabulary you're familiar with and provides an easy-to-use interface to the user of the DSL. In this case, Rake will be used by the developer. The language of the code uses semantics that match the level of abstraction that a developer expects and understands. Similarly, if you develop a DSL for the trader community, you need to keep in mind the level of expressiveness that suits the expectations and experiences of a trader

Financial brokerage systems: trade and settlement

A trade is performed between two parties (*counterparties*) and involves an exchange of securities and currencies that's subject to the regulations of the market where it takes place. The trade is only a promise, and needs to be settled within a fixed number of days after the trade is made. This date, referred to as the *settlement date*, depends on a number of factors like the specific market where the trade is executed, life cycle of the security, the nature of the trade, and the date when the trade was made (*trade date*).

Each trade has an associated cash value. The cash value is the amount of money that's due from the party that bought the security. This cash value depends on things like the principal value, stamp duty, and brokerage fees and commissions, to name a few.

After the trade is completed in the stock exchange, the trade details are entered into the back office of the trading organization. This process is called *trade enrichment*. The system computes all the details: the settlement date, trade tax, commission, and the final cash value.

at the dealing desk. This section contains a sidebar that has a short introduction to some of the basic terminology of the trading system. Have a look at the definitions because you'll be using many of them in the example DSLs that you'll develop over the course of the book.

When you design a DSL, keep your target users in mind. A DSL needs to be as expressive and granular as necessary for the user to understand it. In the following chapters, you'll learn how to design DSLs at the level of abstraction that feels most natural to users. Meanwhile, let's fill in some of the missing links in figure 1.2 so you'll have a more complete picture of how DSLs enable a better mapping between the problem and the solution domain.

1.3.3 Structure of a DSL

Look at figure 1.3, which shows how a DSL script binds the common vocabulary to the underlying implementation model of the solution domain.

The following describes the three principles that a well-designed DSL embodies to make your software more communicative to domain users:

- A DSL provides a direct mapping to the artifacts of the problem domain. If the problem domain has an entity named *Trade*, the DSL script must contain the same abstraction that plays the same role.
- The DSL script must use the common vocabulary of the problem domain. The vocabulary becomes the catalyst for better communication between developers and business users. When business users interact with the software domain model, the DSL script is their interface, as shown in figure 1.3.

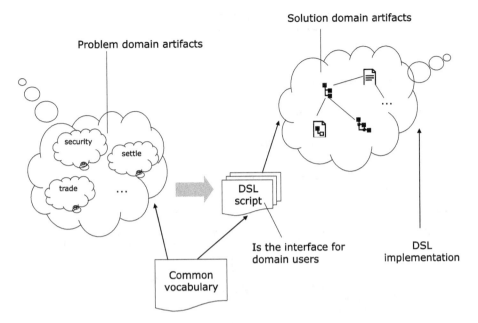

Figure 1.3 A DSL script provides a representation of the domain language to the implementation model. It uses the common vocabulary as the underlying dictionary that makes the language feel more natural to users.

- The DSL script must abstract the underlying implementation. This principle is an important part of good abstraction design, and it applies to DSLs as well. The DSL script cannot contain accidental complexities that deal with implementation details.

In figure 1.3, the relationships shown between the node labeled DSL script and the other nodes illustrate these three principles. If you keep these principles in mind as you design your DSL, your software will communicate effectively to domain users. In the next section, you'll look at the execution model of a DSL—how the DSL script and its implementation model is realized when you run your application.

1.4 Execution model of a DSL

Domain experts use the DSL script to understand the domain model and business rules. You, as a developer, need to implement the DSL in terms of an underlying technology platform. In most cases, a DSL is nothing but a layer of abstraction over the host language that presents a domain-friendly interface to the business users. (It's not always the host language. See section 1.5 for details about DSL classification.) You're kind of extending the host language to implement another language on top of it. This concept is sometimes referred to as a *metalinguistic abstraction*. You'll also come across DSLs that don't use an embedded language for implementation. Maybe it uses a custom language that the team designed specifically for implementing the DSL. In

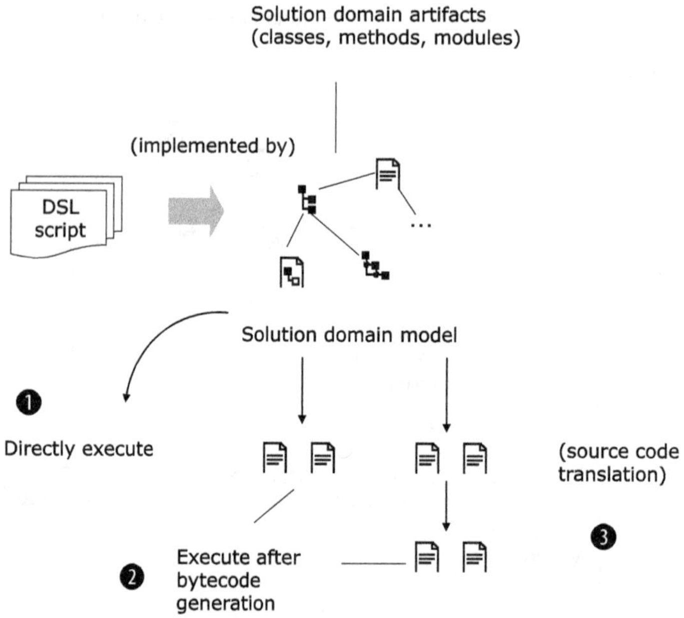

Solution domain artifacts
(classes, methods, modules)

(implemented by)

DSL
script

Solution domain model

❶

Directly execute

(source code
translation)

❸

Execute after
bytecode
generation

❷

Figure 1.4   Three execution models for a DSL script. You can directly execute the program that implements the solution domain model ❶. Alternatively you can instrument bytecodes and then execute the script ❷. Or you can do a source code translation (as with Lisp macros) and then generate bytecodes for execution ❸.

section 1.5, you'll look more closely at how DSL implementations are classified. For now, let's talk about how you execute a DSL script.

Figure 1.4 shows the three most common ways to execute a DSL script.

1   The script can directly execute the underlying model without any more code generation or manipulation. There might be an interpreter that directly interprets the script and runs it. The UNIX little programming languages awk and sed are examples of DSLs that execute directly.

2   A DSL script that's developed on a virtual machine follows the second model. The semantic model underlying any Java DSL script generates bytecodes that are executed on the JVM.

3   Some languages offer compile-time metaprogramming. When you're developing a DSL using this kind of language, you build metastructures as part of your source code, which get translated to the normal forms of the language before it runs. Lisp supports this technique through *macros* that get expanded to normal Lisp forms during the macro expansion phase (I discuss this in more detail in appendix B). For these languages, there's an intermediate stage where you have source code translation before the byte code is generated for the virtual machine.

Now that you're comfortable with the three common models of execution for a DSL script, revisit the DSL in listing 1.1 that Bob was playing with. Irrespective of the language of implementation, you'll discover that it also needs a semantic model as its underlying implementation. That model might be a host language like Ruby or Scala, or it might be a custom language that the developers at Trampoline Securities designed to implement the trading DSL.

Consider Ant, the popular build tool, and the XML-based DSL that it presents to the user. As a developer, when you look at the following XML snippet in Ant, you'll find that it expresses familiar concepts. The code clearly spells out that it'll build a `jar` as the target and that this task has a dependency on the task `compile`.

```
<target name="jar" depends="compile">
  <mkdir dir="${build.dist}"/>
  <jar jarfile="${build.dist}/${name}-${version}.jar">
    <fileset dir="${build.classes}" includes="**"/>
    <fileset dir="${src.dir}">
      <include name="*"/>
    </fileset>
  </jar>
</target>
```

This DSL script has an underlying semantic model; the implementation is in the form of Java classes, methods, and packages that create interfaces for tasks and dependencies. The developer doesn't have to cross the boundaries of the DSL interface and dig down into the implementation in order to use Ant. Of course, there might be an exceptional situation when the developer might need to do so, because Ant is an extensible framework. But that's only the exception.

So far, we've mostly been talking about DSL scripts that are designed as extensions of a host language, but that's not the only kind of DSL script there is. You can also classify DSLs based on the way you implement them. The next section lays down a taxonomy of DSLs.

1.5   Classifying DSLs

A DSL speaks the language of the domain. The richer the domain, the more expressive the DSL needs to be. To the domain user, a DSL makes him understand the story of the domain that the developers have implemented as the underlying model. It doesn't matter to him how the underlying model has been implemented, so long as he has coherent access to the domain abstractions through the DSL script.

The most popular way to classify DSLs is related to the way you implement them. Martin Fowler made this broad classification some time back and it's recognized and followed by almost all practitioners in the industry today. He classifies a DSL as *internal* or *external*, depending on whether it's been implemented on top of an existing host language. Internal DSLs are also known as *embedded* DSLs because they're implemented as an embedding within a host language. (Internal DSLs will be discussed further in chapters 5 and 6 where you'll implement DSLs using JVM languages like Ruby, Groovy,

Scala, and Clojure.) External DSLs are also called *standalone* DSLs because they're developed ground-up as an independent language, without using the infrastructure of an existing host language. Chapters 7 and 8 deal more with external DSLs.

Besides these two broad classifications, you're also looking at newer paradigms of DSL development. Companies like Intentional Software (http://www.intentsoft.com/) have come out with tools you can use to create nontextual DSLs. Such developments and growing trends are subjects in chapter 9. For now, you will focus on the two main classifications and use examples to discuss some of their characteristics.

1.5.1 Internal DSLs

An *internal* DSL is one that uses the infrastructure of an *existing* programming language (also called the host language of the DSL) to build domain-specific semantics on top of it. One of the most popular internal DSLs used today is Rails, which is implemented on top of the Ruby programming language. When you write Rails code, you're programming in Ruby, based on the semantics that Rails implements for developing web applications. In most cases, an internal DSL is implemented as a library on top of the existing host language. In section 2.1, you'll develop an order-processing DSL as an example of an internal DSL, based on Java and Groovy as the host language. Figure 1.5 illustrates the structure of an internal DSL.

As you see in figure 1.5, the internal DSL script is a thin veneer over the abstractions of an underlying host language. Now let's see what an external DSL looks like.

1.5.2 External DSLs

An *external* DSL is one that's developed ground-up and has separate infrastructure for lexical analysis, parsing techniques, interpretation, compilation, and code generation. Developing an external DSL is similar to implementing a new language from scratch with its own syntax and semantics. Build tools like make, parser generators like YACC, and lexical analysis tools like LEX are examples of popular external DSLs. Of course, the complexity of an external DSL implementation depends on how rich you

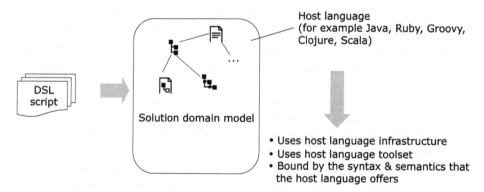

Figure 1.5 You implement an internal DSL using an existing host language and the infrastructure that it offers.

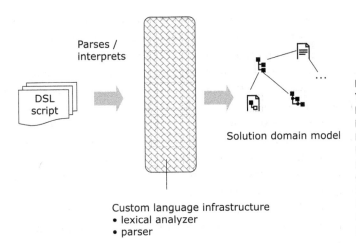

Parses / interprets

DSL script

Solution domain model

Custom language infrastructure
• lexical analyzer
• parser

Figure 1.6
You need to develop your own language-processing infrastructure for an external DSL. The infrastructure includes lexical analyzers, parsers, and code generators commonly found in high-level language implementations. Note that the complexities of each of them depend on how detailed your language is.

want it to be. In most cases, you'll find that the external DSL doesn't need to have all the complexities of a full-blown language. You'll see many examples in chapters 7 and 8. Figure 1.6 shows how an external DSL is structured on top of a custom language infrastructure.

Figure 1.6 shows the generic components of an external DSL. In real-life examples, you might not need all of them or you might decide to combine components, depending on the complexity of your language.

Do you need to create a DSL in the form of a textual representation? Not always; a graphical representation can often be more self-explanatory. Let's see how.

1.5.3   *Nontextual DSLs*

Besides internal and external DSLs, there's a growing trend in the industry toward developing richer ways of modeling the domain. A DSL needs to be a representation of the domain but the definition doesn't mandate that this representation or language needs to be a textual one. In fact, many claim that software code is too narrow a medium to adequately express domain knowledge. Some of the reasons that are often cited are:

- Text allows only limited notational freedom to express a domain problem.
- Many domain problems are better visualized by the domain user in the form of rich artifacts like spreadsheets or graphical models.
- In a text-based script, domain logic is often scattered within the maze of syntactic structures that are accidentally too complex.
- A domain expert is always more comfortable manipulating visual models than source code.

In response to these reasons, one other type of DSL is fast becoming the next-generation way to model and harvest domain knowledge. The domain user gets to see and process a representation of the domain knowledge through an editor called the Projection Editor. The Projection Editor can project the appropriate view of the domain to the user, which he can then manipulate without writing a single line of code. At the back end, the Projection Editor can generate code that models the users' intentions. Intentional's DSL Workbench (http://www.intentsoft.com) and JetBrains' Meta Programming System (MPS) (http://www.jetbrains.com/mps) are two examples of rich DSL modeling tools. In chapter 9, you'll see more such examples and the features that they offer in the discussion of future trends of DSL-based development.

Classifying DSLs as internal, external, and nontextual is only one broad way of looking at the types of implementations that DSLs can have. For all practical purposes, you can consider the nontextual DSLs as external DSLs only, because the underlying infrastructure that you use to develop DSL APIs isn't a host language.

Now that you have a pretty good idea of what DSLs are and how you can use them to improve communication between developers and domain users, what do you think are some of the valid use cases for writing a DSL? Do you need to write a DSL for every piece of code that you develop? Or are there specific circumstances that make a more compelling case for DSL-based development?

1.6   When do you need a DSL?

Every application has business rules that need to be explicit, readable, and declarative. A DSL is an ideal way to model these kinds of rules. It doesn't take a lot of effort to develop a DSL that expresses a time period as `2.weeks.ago` instead of `time()` − `1209600`. But the impact that it has on users can be huge.

Should you use DSL-based development in your next project? Before you decide, you need to weigh the pros and cons. As with any other technology, DSLs can have pitfalls. As a developer, you're the best person to judge whether you need a DSL for modeling the current problem. For that, you need to be aware of some of the common advantages and disadvantages that DSLs offer.

1.6.1   The advantages

DSL-based development gets you more return on your investment when the complexity of the domain is high. As I mentioned before, you're going to use small DSL engines in almost every project that you implement. When you're planning for a complex modeling project, you need to make a conscious decision and weigh your options before making the final call. Following are some points that will help you weigh in on your decision toward DSL-based development.

DSLs ARE EXPRESSIVE
They tend to provide a small, focused surface area for the APIs and deal with abstractions that speak the precise semantics of the domain. Users love them.

DSLs ARE CONCISE
Because they're concise, DSLs are easy to *look at, see, think about,* and *show.* Dan Roam (see [2] in section 1.9) calls these the four steps to visual thinking. It's the conciseness of a DSL that reduces the semantic distance between the program and the problem.

DSLs ARE DESIGNED AT A HIGHER LEVEL OF ABSTRACTION

DSLs don't have to deal with lower-level language constructs, optimizing data structures, and other implementation techniques. Instead, DSLs embody domain knowledge at a level where it can be conserved, validated, and reused more easily than an implementation that's based on a general-purpose programming language. This makes DSLs suitable for many nonprogramming domain experts.

DSLs CAN GIVE HIGHER PAYOFF

DSL-based development tends to produce a higher payoff in the long run of your development lifecycle.

DSL-BASED DEVELOPMENT IS SCALABLE

If the project team has an imbalance of expertise in a specific programming language, expert programmers can focus initially on the implementation of the DSL. The rest of the team can then use the DSL. The DSL, because it's at a higher level of abstraction, becomes easier to learn and can be used as the vehicle to scale up the development team.

As is the case with any other technology paradigm, DSL-based development has its share of advantages when you use it in a development cycle. We'll talk more about DSL-based development in chapter 3. Next are some of the common pitfalls of DSLs that might cause heartache for your development project.

1.6.2 The disadvantages

All the disadvantages of DSLs relate to implementation overheads that incur additional cost in the software development lifecycle.

LANGUAGE DESIGN IS HARD

DSL implementation is language design, and language design is a complex task that doesn't scale. Instead of starting anew with the complexities of the lexers and grammars of your language, most DSLs are implemented as an embedding within a higher-level language. Still, it's complex enough and is definitely not an exercise to be undertaken by nonexpert programmers. Later chapters cover language features and their suitability for implementing embedded DSLs.

DSLs HAVE AN UPFRONT COST

DSL-based development has an upfront cost that you'll incur in your project. Accepting this cost makes sense only when the model is at least moderately complex. You'll eventually benefit when the cost factors level off during the later stages of the development cycle.

USING DSLs CAN LEAD TO PERFORMANCE CONCERNS

DSLs sometimes can cause performance concerns for your application. After all, it's yet another layer of indirection. As a project manager, you need to consider factors like scale of deployment and scope of reusability when you're deciding whether to use DSL-based development.

DSLs SOMETIMES LACK ADEQUATE TOOL SUPPORT

Any development methodology needs rich tool support to scale out to the community of programmers. Tool support includes availability of IDE integrations, unit testing support, language workbenches, and profiling support to name a few. If your DSL generates multiple target languages for execution, interoperability between all the languages can also be a potential concern.

YET-ANOTHER-LANGUAGE-TO-LEARN SYNDROME

Any external DSL has to be learned separately by the developers. With internal DSLs, all you have to learn is the interface that it publishes on top of the existing host language. But developers are often disturbed to find that not only do they have to learn yet another new language, but it's one that has limited applicability.

DSLs CAN LEAD TO LANGUAGE CACOPHONY

Typically, when you develop an application, you need to use multiple DSLs. When you have multiple languages, there's always the concern that when you combine them you won't get a unified model for the domain. DSL composition isn't easy, because individual DSLs tend to evolve independently of each other. Unless you manage it carefully, language multiplicity can lead to anarchy.

As you saw in figure 1.3, a DSL is a linguistic abstraction that's on top of an underlying implementation model. The better you abstract your domain model, the easier it is to build a natural language on top of it. Let's look at the qualities that the underlying model needs to have in order to be a strong foundation for an expressive DSL.

1.7   *DSLs and abstraction design*

In earlier sections of this chapter, I've used the term *abstraction* to loosely mean any artifact from the domain that exhibits a coherent set of behavior. *An abstraction focuses on the essential attributes of the subject, removing any unnecessary details from the user.* But what constitutes the essential parts depends on the perspective from which you view the abstraction. In this section, you'll look at how abstraction is related to designing a DSL and what role it plays in making your DSL expressive.

As you'll see in chapters 5 and 6, a well-designed abstraction is the foundation on which you build the linguistic layer of the DSL. But how do you make your abstractions well-designed?

From the criteria that make an abstraction optimal, I've identified four as the essential qualities that the design should support. Table 1.2 summarizes these qualities.

Designing good abstractions is a separate topic. In this chapter, I won't digress into the details. Instead, I discuss abstraction design extensively in appendix A. There I discuss each of the qualities described in table 1.2 in much more detail and with lots of real-world examples. Go through the appendix before you dive into the next chapters. When you're comfortable distinguishing well-designed abstractions from the poorly designed ones, you'll better appreciate how they contribute to more effective DSL design techniques.

Table 1.2 Qualities of a well-designed abstraction

Quality of abstraction	Effect on design
Minimalism	Publish only those behaviors that you promise to your clients. Publishing more leads to exposing the implementation of your abstraction, which can lead to difficulty later.
Distillation	Keep your abstraction's implementation free of all nonessential details.
Extensibility	Design your abstractions so that they can grow in a piecemeal manner without impacting existing clients.
Composability	Your abstractions should be able to compose with other abstractions, leading to higher-order abstractions.

1.8 Summary

You've reached the end of a long introduction to the rationale behind DSLs. When you model a specific domain, your implementation needs to speak the vocabulary of the domain. When you have the common vocabulary in place, the DSL brings the domain syntax and semantics into your solution model.

Be sure your DSL is expressive enough by using well-designed abstractions that use the power of the host language. Designing abstractions is an iterative process, and so is designing a good DSL. You can't achieve a well-designed DSL in the first iteration. It always evolves through a collaborative effort between the developer and the domain expert. Involve the team of domain experts early in the development process. If they can understand what your abstraction promises and verify the implementation of their business rules, that's proof that your model is both correct and sufficiently expressive.

Laying the groundwork for an unfamiliar paradigm of development is always an arduous process. Kudos to you for successfully undertaking that task. Now you'll start the journey into the real-world pragmatics of DSL design and implementation. In chapter 2, the focus is more on actual DSLs that have been implemented using modern languages on the JVM. The adventure starts with Java, then continues into the expressiveness of Groovy, Scala, and Ruby. You'll notice how the expressiveness of our

Key takeaways & best practices

- *A DSL is a communication medium between developers and business practitioners.* Always involve your domain expert while you're designing a DSL.
- *A DSL might not be suitable for every occasion.* Weigh the pros and cons before you decide to design and invest in one.
- *DSL design is always iterative.* Give it the diligence and effort that it deserves.
- *Keep in mind that the syntax of the DSL needs to be expressive enough for the end user.* Don't overengineer your DSL. Doing that only makes the syntax cluttered and increases the complexity of the implementation.

models increases as you use some of today's state-of-the-art programming languages. Stay tuned!

1.9   References

1   Coplien, James O. 1998. *Multiparadigm Design in C++*. Addison-Wesley Professional.

2   Roam, Dan. 2009. *The Back of the Napkin: Expanded Edition*. Portfolio Hardcover.

3   Fowler, Martin. Introducing Domain-Specific Languages. 2009 DSL Developer's Conference (http://msdn.microsoft.com/en-us/data/dd727707.aspx).

The DSL in the wild

In the previous chapter, you saw how DSLs improve communication between the development team and the domain experts. We discussed the overall architecture of DSLs and the various execution models that they support. But what good are those DSLs without a meaningful, real-world use case? Given a real-world problem, how can you judge whether designing a DSL would be a better solution than using the traditional model of software development? In this chapter, we dive into these real-world pragmatics of DSL design.

We'll start with a motivating example of the ground-up design, implementation, and refinement of a real-world DSL from our preferred domain of the financial brokerage business. We'll look at a couple of implementations, then proceed to explain some of the general patterns that you'll come across when you design DSL implementations. Figure 2.1 shows a visual roadmap of how we're going to explore real-world DSLs in this chapter.

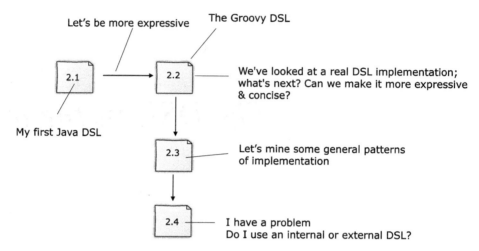

Figure 2.1   Roadmap for chapter 2

In every section, we'll discuss a real-world application of DSLs, either in the form of an implementation use case or as a collection of patterns that you can use in your own model. At the end of this chapter, you'll know how to think in terms of modeling your problem domain using DSL-based paradigms. I'll show you a typical, API-based model and a DSL-based model side-by-side and you'll learn to appreciate how the latter makes a more expressive presentation to your domain users.

2.1   *Building your first Java DSL*

An example is worth a thousand words. As I hinted in chapter 1, the examples we'll be working with are primarily from the financial securities domain, with specific references and explanations to set up the context of the implementation. (Be sure to read the sidebars for details about this domain.) Not only will the explanations help you understand the specific domain, you can refer to them when we discuss examples of DSL implementations that are related to these concepts. Because the examples use the same domain as a basis, you'll be able to improve and add to the DSL snippets as we move along.

In section 1.3, we saw Bob, the trader, working on snippets of the DSL that processes client orders before placing them in the stock exchange for the trade transaction. Let's build on that scenario as you develop your first DSL.

Suppose you're in charge of implementing a DSL that processes orders using domain vocabulary similar to what Bob was using. As you saw in chapter 1, one of the primary forces that drives DSL development is the involvement of a domain expert. With a sufficiently expressive DSL, he can comprehend the business rules and logic that your development team implements. He can verify the logic before the code base gets out of the development labs. You can even involve him in writing functional test

Financial brokerage system: processing client orders

As we discussed in chapter 1, the trading process involves buying and selling securities in the market place, guided by the rules of the stock exchange. These transactions take place in response to *orders* placed by investors through registered agents. These agents can be brokers, clearing banks, or financial advisers. A typical order from a client consists of information like the security to be transacted (buy or sell), quantity, and the unit price details. All these elements specify any constraint that the counterparty wants to impose on the price of execution. The following steps are performed from when the order is placed until the execution notice of trades is generated:

1 The investor places the order with the agent.
2 The agent records the order and forwards it to the stock exchange.
3 The order is executed and the *notice of execution* comes back to the agent.
4 The agent records the execution details and passes the notice to the investor.

suites as a user of your DSL. Not only do you get comprehensive test coverage using the domain knowledge of an expert, your DSL also gets to pass a real-world usability check. As the leader of the project, it's extremely important that you orchestrate the involvement of the Bobs of your team early on in the process.

Let's assume that the DSL snippet you implement builds new orders for a specific client request. The language, needless to say, speaks the vocabulary of the domain and allows the user (Bob on our team) to manipulate all combinations of order processing rules within the semantic constraints of valid business rules. Don't get hung up on the best syntax to use for this DSL right at the beginning. As I mentioned in chapter 1, DSLs always need to evolve iteratively and are never done right the first time. In the following sections, you'll learn how the order-processing DSL evolves gradually, how its expressivity increases depending on the implementation language you select, and how the example culminates in an expressive enough language that makes Bob happy. The important thing is to start the process with a limited scope and a moderate expectation. But, as you learned in chapter 1, any exercise in DSL building starts with setting up the common vocabulary across the stakeholders of the project.

2.1.1 Setting up the common vocabulary

Bob looked at the problem domain, identified the core requirements, and immediately came up with the necessary language constructs for the order-processing DSL. They are shown in table 2.1.

Now that the vocabulary is in place, we'll start the initial implementation in the dominant language of our programming community—Java. Java has the highest number of developers in the industry. Anything you can build with Java as the backbone

Table 2.1 Preliminary vocabulary for a DSL that processes orders

Domain concept	Details
1 New order	• Must specify an instrument name. • Quantity should be mandatory. • Whether to *buy* or *sell* needs to be specified. • An order can be specified as *all-or-none*, indicating that either the whole order needs to be completed or that none of it is completed. No partial orders should be fulfilled.
2 Order pricing	• *Unit price* needs to be mentioned. • Examples of unit price are *limit-price*, *limit-on-close-price*, and *limit-on-open-price*.
3 Order valuation	• The full order needs to be valued based on a *pricing scheme*. • The pricing scheme can be predetermined or the user can specify an *ad-hoc scheme* inline

has huge potential for seamless acceptance within the community. Let's start the exercise and explore the limits of expressiveness that Java offers as an implementation language. Our goal is to make Bob feel comfortable as he steps in to write the functional tests and validate the business rules.

2.1.2 *Your first Java implementation*

Java is an object-oriented (OO) language. As the first step in designing the DSL, you need an object representation of the Order abstraction that encapsulates the various attributes of a client order.

BUILDING THE ORDER ABSTRACTION

The following listing is the Order class in Java that Bob will use to process new orders.

Listing 2.1 Order abstraction for Java DSL

```
public class Order {
  static class Builder {
    private String security;
    private int quantity;
    private int limitPrice;
    private boolean allOrNone;
    private int value;
    private String boughtOrSold;

    public Builder() {}
    public Builder buy(int quantity, String security) {
      this.boughtOrSold = "Bought";
      this.quantity = quantity;
      this.security = security;
      return this;
    }
    public Builder sell(int quantity, String security) {
      this.boughtOrSold = "Sold";
```

❶ Builder design pattern

❷ Fluent interface through method chaining

```
      this.quantity = quantity;
      this.security = security;
      return this;
    }
    public Builder atLimitPrice(int p) {
      this.limitPrice = p;
      return this;
    }
    public Builder allOrNone() {
      this.allOrNone = true;
      return this;
    }
    public Builder valueAs(OrderValuer ov) {
      this.value = ov.valueAs(quantity, limitPrice);
      return this;
    }
    public Order build() {
      return new Order(this);
    }
  }

  private final String security;
  private final int quantity;
  private final int limitPrice;
  private final boolean allOrNone;
  private int value;
  private final String boughtOrSold;

  private Order(Builder b) {
    security = b.security;
    quantity = b.quantity;
    limitPrice = b.limitPrice;
    allOrNone = b.allOrNone;
    value = b.value;
    boughtOrSold = b. boughtOrSold;
  }

  // getters
}
```

Immutable
❸ **properties**

The implementation of the class shown in this listing uses some of Java's common idioms and design patterns to make the published API more expressive. The builder design pattern ❶ lets the user of the API construct orders incrementally. The pattern uses fluent interfaces ❷ that provide an easy-to-read representation of the domain problem. (I discuss fluent interfaces more in chapter 4.) By using the builder as the mutable object, you ensure the immutability of the Order data members ❸ for easier concurrency. One of the effects of using a builder to construct an object is that the core abstraction becomes immutable.

DEFINITION The Builder design pattern is commonly used to build objects incrementally. It separates the process of constructing the object from its representation, so that multiple representations can use the same process. For more information, see [5] in section 2.6.

That's the implementation part of the Builder pattern. We'll come back to some of the issues in the code. First, let's find out how the DSL shapes up in real world when Bob uses it.

USING THE ORDER BUILDER

The following usage snippet has sufficient domain vocabulary density; almost all the keywords that we noted in table 2.1 are in the published API language:

```
Order o =
  new Order.Builder()
    .buy(100, "IBM")
    .atLimitPrice(300)
    .allOrNone()
    .valueAs(new StandardOrderValuer())
    .build();
```

❶ Order valuation algorithm

But even though we've used the right vocabulary, the DSL is also Java, so it has to abide by the syntax restrictions and verbosity that Java requires as a programming language. The call to valueAs ❶ takes as input an implementation artifact that you have to specify nonlocally to the current context. Java doesn't support higher-order functions out of the box, so we can't specify a pretty inline valuation strategy. For the Java implementation, the user of the DSL can define only concrete implementations for each of the order valuation strategies. In the DSL implementation, we define the contract for order valuation as an interface:

```
public interface OrderValuer {
  int valueAs(int qty, int unitPrice);
}
```

Simulating higher-order functions in Java

Though Java doesn't support higher-order functions out of the box, some libraries simulate them by using objects. See lambdaJ (http://code.google.com/p/lambdaj), Google Collections (http://code.google.com/p/guava-libraries), and Functional Java (http://functionaljava.org) for samples. If you're stuck with Java, these libraries provide options for modeling higher-order functions. The drawback is that these options are quite verbose and definitely not as elegant as those offered by languages like Groovy, Ruby, or Scala.

The DSL user defines separate concrete implementations for specific valuation strategies:

```
public class StandardOrderValuer implements OrderValuer {
  public int valueAs(int qty, int unitPrice) {
    return unitPrice * qty;
  }
}
```

Now Bob can't define his valuation policies inline, which was one of his original requirements. He thinks that's a major deterrent, given that we've claimed that DSLs can help nonprogramming domain experts write meaningful functional tests. He has other observations about the order-processing DSL:

- *Verbosity in syntax*—The language contains lots of unnecessary parentheses and other extra flourishes that interrupt the flow and get in the way of a nonprogrammer domain expert.

- *Extra nondomain complexity in syntax*—Bob's referring to the `Builder` class that had to be explicitly used by the DSL user. The DSL could have been implemented without using the complexities of the `Builder` class. We could have used chained setter methods of the `Order` class itself to build fluent interfaces. But the `Builder` class encourages immutable abstraction design without mutable properties. Can we get rid of this additional syntax from our language? Using more abstraction power, we can hide the explicit builder from the surface syntax and make it even more succinct:

```
new Order.toBuy(100, "IBM")
        .atLimitPrice(300)
        .allOrNone()
        .valueAs(new StandardOrderValuer())
        .build();
```

This solution only pushes the complexity from the syntax to the implementation. The bottom line is that the verbosity remains at the implementation level, if not at the usage level of the DSL.

ANALYZING THE JAVA DSL

We as Java programmers can fully appreciate the concerns that an explicit Builder pattern addresses and that make APIs fluent. The Java-based DSL that we designed looks pretty good when Java programmers are using the DSL. But there's no denying the fact that we can overcome the verbosity of Java by using an implementation language that's more expressive to its users, yet results in a more concise code base. Let's analyze the Java code in more detail and look at the Java features that lead to the syntactic complexities that Bob complained about. Table 2.2 lists the Java features that map to Bob's reported issues.

In the following sections, we'll explore options that can honor Bob's suggestion of making the DSL friendlier to the domain experts.

Table 2.2   Mapping issues reported against Java's limitations

Issue reported	Responsible Java feature
Verbose (unnecessary parentheses and syntax)	▪ Part of basic Java syntax. ▪ Parentheses are mandatory for functions. Dots are mandatory for method dispatch on objects and classes.

Table 2.2 Mapping issues reported against Java's limitations *(continued)*

Issue reported	Responsible Java feature
Nondomain complexity	• Java is not a malleable language. Many common idioms need to be expressed through additional layers of indirection, also known as design patterns. • Additional class structures need to be constructed as part of the abstraction design. Some bubble up as surface syntax in the final published API. The `Builder` class is an example of such unnecessary syntactic barriers that came up in our earlier DSL. • Java is not an interpreted language. Executing any snippet of Java code requires you to define a class with a `public static void main` method. Ultimately these are perceived as added syntactic noise by the DSL user.
Inability to express inline valuation strategy function	• Java doesn't offer higher-order functions as first-class features of the language.

2.2 *Making friendlier DSLs*

The expressiveness of a DSL is judged by your user. In this case, Bob has identified areas in your Java-based solution that need to be more closely aligned to the problem domain. Let's try to make the DSL friendlier for Bob to use. One of the strategies you'll look at introduces an additional layer in the form of XML that externalizes the domain language in a more human-readable form. The second strategy discusses implementing the DSL in an entirely new and more expressive programming language, Groovy.

2.2.1 *Externalizing the domain with XML*

XMLs are frequently used for business markups, so why not use XML for designing the domain language in our application? XML has rich tooling support, is recognized by all browsers and IDEs, and has a slew of frameworks and libraries for parsing, processing, and querying purposes.

True, XML is externalizable in the sense that a domain expert can write XML structures that are separate from the programming machinery. But XML is completely declarative, inordinately verbose, and doesn't easily support the expression of control structures. The following snippet shows sample XML for the order-processing DSL shown in listing 2.1. I've intentionally elided parts of it to avoid showing the ugliness that arbitrary expressions can bring to an XML structure.

```
<orders>
  <order>
    <buySell>buy</buySell>
    <quantity>100</quantity>
    <instrument>IBM</instrument>
    <limitPrice>300</limitPrice>
    <allOrNone>true</allOrNone>
```

```
        <valueAs>...</valueAs>
      </order>
    ...
</orders>
```

The idea behind XML is not to do programming, but to express document structures in a completely portable way. DSLs often contain control structures that can't be expressed elegantly in XML. Many Java EE and XML (Java Platform, Enterprise Edition) frameworks use XML to provide declarative configuration parameters. But if you try to write business logic and domain rules using XML, you'll soon hit the same bottleneck of expressivity that our Java implementation faced before. Try a more direct approach, without going beyond the boundaries of your natural programming language. Remember, the language is the most powerful programming tool that you have.

2.2.2 *Groovy: a more expressive implementation language*

By now you must have realized that you're trying to design a DSL that fits within the confines of the underlying implementation language. The DSL that clients will be using is the same language that the DSL is implemented in. In your first attempt, all the problems that Bob mentioned are the innate limitations of the Java programming language, which you couldn't work around in your implementation of the DSL. The technique used is called *embedding* the DSL within the host language, which you've already seen in section 1.7 when we discussed the taxonomy of internal and external DSLs.

Now let's now try to embed our DSL in a language that's more expressive than Java. Groovy is a language that runs on the JVM, is more expressive than Java, is dynamically typed, and supports higher-order functions.

A GROOVY SOLUTION

As you progress through this book, you'll look at the features of Groovy that can help you design better DSLs. You are going to implement the order-processing DSL using Groovy, but first, here's a sample of that DSL in Groovy that has the same functions as the earlier Java example:

```
newOrder.to.buy(100.shares.of('IBM')) {
  limitPrice    300
  allOrNone     true
  valueAs       {qty, unitPrice -> qty * unitPrice - 500}
}
```

This snippet creates a new client *order* for buying 100 shares of IBM at a *limit price* of 300 dollars in an *all-or-none* mode. The *order valuation* is computed using the specified formula. The end result is the same as the earlier Java example; the difference is the expressivity that the higher-order abstractions of Groovy bring to the implementation. DSL constructs like 100.shares.of('IBM') are possible only because Groovy offers fabulous metaprogramming capabilities. This makes the language more natural to the domain user. The following listing is the complete implementation of the DSL in Groovy.

Listing 2.2   Order processing DSL in Groovy

```
class Order {
  def security
  def quantity
  def limitPrice
  def allOrNone
  def value
  def bs

  def buy(su, closure) {
    bs = 'Bought'
    buy_sell(su, closure)
  }

  def sell(su, closure) {
    bs = 'Sold'
    buy_sell(su, closure)
  }

  private buy_sell(su, closure) {
    security = su[0]
    quantity = su[1]
    closure()
  }

  def getTo() {
    this
  }
}
def methodMissing(String name, args) {                         ❶ Hook to intercept
  order.metaClass.getMetaProperty(name).setProperty(order, args)    nonexistent
}                                                                    method calls

def getNewOrder() {
  order = new Order()
}                                                              ❷ Closure for inline
                                                                 valuation strategy
def valueAs(closure) {                                           specification
  order.value = closure(order.quantity, order.limitPrice[0])
}                                                             ❸ Metaprogramming
                                                                to inject new
Integer.metaClass.getShares = { -> delegate }                   methods
Integer.metaClass.of = { instrument -> [instrument, delegate] }
```

In the following sections, I'm going to be a cheerleader for DSL-based implementations. I'm going to only touch on the features of Groovy that stand out with respect to this specific implementation. In chapters 4 and 5 will cover in detail all the features that make Groovy a great language for DSL implementation. For now, let's look at specific Groovyisms that make this expressivity possible.

METHOD SYNTHESIS USING METHODMISSING

You can invoke nonexistent methods in Groovy; methodMissing offers the hook to intercept all such invocations ❶. In the order-processing DSL, every invocation of methods like limitPrice and allOrNone is intercepted by methodMissing and converted to calls of property setters on the `Order` object. The `methodMissing` hook provides conciseness in the code base and flexibility when you're adding method calls without explicit definitions.

GROOVY METAPROGRAMMING TECHNIQUES FOR DYNAMIC METHOD INJECTION
Using metaprogramming techniques, we've injected methods into built-in classes like `Integer` that add to the expressivity of the language. The method `getShares` adds a property named `shares` to the class `Integer` that makes a great combinator for forming the natural flow of the DSL ❸.

FIRST-CLASS SUPPORT FOR HIGHER-ORDER FUNCTIONS AND CLOSURES
This support is possibly the most important feature that makes languages like Groovy shine over Java in offering expressive DSLs. The difference this makes is huge; just look at the `valueAs` method ❷ invocations in the Groovy and Java versions of the language.

Now you've got your DSL implementation in Groovy and a DSL usage snippet. But you still need the mechanism to integrate the two and set up an execution environment that can execute any instance of the DSL supplied to it. Let's see how to do that.

2.2.3 *Executing the Groovy DSL*

Groovy has scripting abilities. Any Groovy code can be executed through the interpreter and you can use this Groovy power to set up an interactive execution environment for your order-processing DSL. Enter the DSL implementation (listing 2.2) in a file called `ClientOrder.groovy`. Enter the usage snippet in another text file named order.dsl. Make sure that both are in `classpath`, then submit the following script to the Groovy interpreter:

```
def dslDef = new File('ClientOrder.groovy').text
def dsl = new File('order.dsl').text
def script = """
  ${dslDef}
  ${dsl}
"""
new GroovyShell().evaluate(script)
```

Integrating a DSL into your core application

The example in this section shows only one way of integrating DSL implementation along with the DSL invocation. We'll talk about more integration methods in chapter 3 when we discuss integrating DSLs into your core application.

The example uses string concatenation to build the final script that gets executed. One disadvantage of this approach is that if there are any errors in execution, the line numbers in the stack trace won't match the line numbers in the source file order.dsl. As I've mentioned, building a DSL and integrating it with your application is an iterative process. We'll improve on this strategy in chapter 3 when we discuss yet another method of integrating a Groovy DSL into your application.

Congratulations! You've successfully designed and implemented a DSL that'll make any domain person happy. The Groovy-based order-processing DSL that you've implemented fulfils expressivity criteria that puts it way ahead of the earlier Java version. More importantly, you know that DSL design is an iterative process. Had we not developed the Java version, you wouldn't have realized the importance of using a more expressive language as the base of the implementation.

> In part 2 of this book (chapters 4-8), we'll look at other DSL implementations, not only in Groovy, but in other JVM languages like Scala, Clojure, and JRuby. This comparison will help you realize how DSL implementation techniques can vary depending on the features that the underlying host language offers.

Now that you've seen a complete implementation of a DSL that solves a real-life use case, you've got an inside-out view of how an implementation evolves through the stages of successive refinement. The Groovy implementation turned out to be expressive to the users. But what are some of the underlying implementation techniques that contributed to its expressiveness?

Depending on the language you choose for implementing an internal DSL, you get some of these techniques for free. Building a well-designed DSL is the art of mixing the idioms of the host language and these techniques in a way that transforms that host language into the shape of your DSL. You used some of the techniques that Groovy offers when you designed your implementation. But not all DSLs are alike. Like every other language, there are definite patterns in DSL design that depend on the platform of your implementation, the core skill set of your team members, the overall architecture of your application, and other constraints related to your development ecosystem.

Up next, we'll take a look at some of the implementation patterns of DSLs. Patterns are like ready-made packages of reusable design knowledge that you can use in your own implementations. They teach you how to make friendlier DSLs using the power of the host language. In the next section, you'll learn about the variations in patterns that internal and external DSLs exhibit under the constraints of a particular implementation. You can't implement all these patterns in every language, but you need to understand all the patterns so that you can make the optimal choice within your implementation platform.

2.3   *DSL implementation patterns*

Classifying DSLs as *internal* or *external* is too broad a definition, considering the multitude of architectural patterns that these languages implement in practice. All internal DSLs share the common trait of being built on top of a host language. The common trait of all external DSLs is that they build their language infrastructure from scratch. It's not only the *commonality* of their origin that characterizes the entire taxonomy of DSLs. As we saw in chapter 1, a DSL is an embodiment of good abstraction design principles. To design a good abstraction, you need to consider not only the commonality of forms between the participating components but also the *variabilities* that each exhibits.

In the next two sections, we'll explore some of these patterns of variability. When you have an idea of the patterns that exist even within the same family of DSLs, you'll be able to map your own DSL requirements to the concrete implementation architecture more easily. The more you identify such recurring patterns, the easier it'll be for you to reuse your abstractions. As you learned from our discussions in appendix A about designing abstractions, when you can reuse your abstraction, the language that you design becomes more extensible. In case you haven't read appendix A yet, do that now. The information it contains will help you during your journey through the rest of this book.

2.3.1 Internal DSL patterns: commonality and variability

Internal DSLs are everywhere. With languages like Ruby and Groovy offering flexible and concise syntax and a powerful metaprogramming model, you can find DSL development that piggybacks these capabilities in almost every piece of software. The common pattern across all internal DSLs is that they are always implemented on top of an existing host language. I tend to use the term *embedded* more when I talk about *internal* DSLs, because it makes one aspect of their architecture explicit. You can use the infrastructure of an existing language in a number of ways, each of which results in DSL implementations that vary in form, structure, flexibility, and expressivity.

Internal DSLs manifest primarily in two forms:

- *Generative*—Domain-specific constructs are transformed to generate code through compile-time macros, preprocessors, or some form of runtime metaobject protocol (MOP).
- *Embedded*—Domain-specific types are embedded within the type system of the host language.

Even this micro-classification is not entirely without its share of ambiguity. Consider Ruby and its accompanying web framework Rails, written as an internal DSL in Ruby. From that point of view, Rails is *embedded* within Ruby. But Rails also uses Ruby's metaprogramming power to generate lots of code during runtime. From this point of view, it's *generative* as well.

Let's consider some of the statically typed languages that purely embed DSLs within the type system of the host language. Haskell and Scala are the dominant players in this category; the DSL that you design inherits all the power of the host type system. Finally, there are language extensions to Haskell (Template Haskell) that add generative capabilities to the language through macros.

We have numerous variations even within the classification of internal DSLs, including instances when a single language offers multiple paradigms of DSL development. Figure 2.2 shows a diagrammatic view of the taxonomy and some languages that implement these variations.

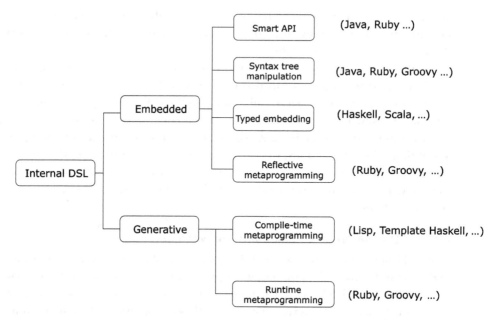

Figure 2.2 An informal micro-classification of patterns used in implementing internal DSLs

In this section, we'll look at these common variations found among some of the internal DSL implementation techniques, using figure 2.2 as a reference.

Chapters 4 and 5 are supplements to the material in this section. In those chapters, we'll discuss DSL patterns and implementations in much more detail.

SMART API

Smart API is possibly the simplest and most frequently used implementation of internal DSLs you'll encounter. This technique is based on chaining methods in sequence similar to the Builder pattern implementation (see [1] in section 2.6). Martin Fowler calls the Smart API a *fluent interface* (http://www.martinfowler.com/bliki/FluentInterface.html). For this pattern, you create APIs that get wired up in the natural sequence of the domain action that you're trying to model. This process makes it *fluent,* and the domain-based method names make it readable and meaningful to the DSL user. The following code snippet is from the Guice API (http://code.google.com/p/google-guice/), which is the dependency injection (DI) framework from Google. If you're the user trying to wire up a Java interface with an implementation as a declarative module of your application, the following use of the API seems to flow naturally and expresses the intent of your use case:

```
binder.bind(Service.class).to(ServiceImpl.class).in(Scopes.SINGLETON)
```

Figure 2.3 illustrates how the APIs chain forward through repeated invocations on the returned object.

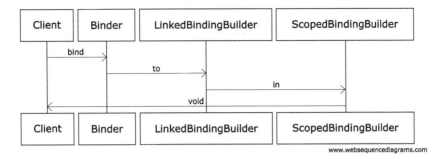

Figure 2.3 Smart API using method chaining. Note how the method calls progress forward and return only at the end to the client.

With method chaining, you use the infrastructure of the host language and build Smart APIs that speak the vocabulary of your domain. The drawback of this technique is that it can lead to the proliferation of many small methods that might not make much sense on their own. Also, not all use cases can be implemented using fluent interfaces. Typically, using the Builder pattern to incrementally construct and configure objects is most effective when you use method chaining to model the process; the Java implementation of the order-processing DSL in section 2.1 is an example. In languages like Groovy or Ruby that offer named arguments, the Builder pattern and fluent interfaces become somewhat redundant. (Named arguments with defaults are also available in Scala 2.8.) For example, the previous Java snippet turns into a more concise yet expressive Groovy code using a mix of normal and named parameters:

```
binder.bind Service, to: ServiceImpl, in: Scopes.SINGLETON
```

Smart API is a common pattern used in internal DSLs. The exact implementation of it depends on what language you're using. The main takeaway from this discussion is: Always choose the most idiomatic implementation technique when you're using DSL patterns. I'll come back to this topic with more examples and implementation variations when I talk about fluent interfaces in the context of internal DSL implementation in chapter 4. For now, let's move on to another pattern.

SYNTAX TREE MANIPULATION
Syntax tree manipulation is yet another option that's used for implementing internal DSLs. The design follows the interpreter pattern (see [1] in section 2.6) and uses the infrastructure of the host language to create and manipulate the abstract syntax tree (AST) of the language. After you've generated the AST, it's your responsibility to traverse the AST and do the manipulations that will generate the necessary code for the domain logic. Groovy and Ruby have developed this infrastructure through library support that can generate code by manipulating the AST.

   Come to think of it, this is what Lisp offers you out of the box with its language infrastructure. In Lisp, every program is a list structure, which is the AST

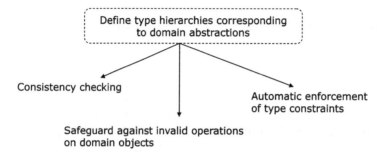

Figure 2.4   An embedded typed DSL comes with lots of implicit guarantees of consistency. Use a type to model your DSL abstraction. The constraints that you define within your type are automatically checked by the compiler, even before the program runs.

that the programmer has access to. Manipulating the AST to generate code is the basis of the Lisp macros. You can extend the core language syntax by manipulating the AST.

TYPED EMBEDDING

DSL patterns based on metaprogramming rely on code generation techniques to keep the interface of the DSL precisely at the level of abstraction that the domain demands. But what if your host language doesn't support any form of metaprogramming? When you're designing a DSL, it's extremely important to be minimal in what you offer to your users as the syntax of the language. The more support the host language infrastructure provides for abstraction, the easier it is for you to achieve this minimalism.

Statically typed languages offer *types* as one of the means to abstract domain semantics and make the surface syntax of your DSLs concise. Instead of generating code to express the domain behavior you want, you can define domain-specific types and implement them in terms of the types and operations offered by your host language. These types will form the language interface of your DSL that the user will be working with; he won't care about their concrete implementations. Typed models come with a guarantee of some level of implicit consistency in your programming model. Figure 2.4 is a snapshot of what types can offer to your DSL.

The biggest advantage of this technique is that because your DSL's type system is embedded in the type system of the host language, your type system is automatically type-checked by the language compiler. Your DSL users will be able to take full advantage of the IDE integration capabilities of the host language like smart assist, code completion, and refactoring.

Consider the following example in Scala that models the abstraction of a `Trade`. In this example, `Trade`, `Account`, and `Instrument` are *domain-specific types* ❶ that have business rules encapsulated within them ❷. With Ruby or Groovy we generated additional code to implement domain behavior; in Scala we implement similar semantics within *types* and leave it to the compiler to check for consistency.

```
trait Trade {
  type Instrument                                              Abstract
  type Account                                           1     domain types

  def account: Account
  def instrument: Instrument                               2   Abstract domain
                                                               operations
  def valueOf(a: Account, i: Instrument): BigDecimal
  def principalOf: BigDecimal
  def valueDate: Date
  //..
}
```

Languages like Haskell and Scala that offer advanced static typing let you design purely typed embedded DSLs without resorting to code generation techniques, preprocessors, or macros. As a DSL user, you can compose typed abstractions using combinators that are implemented in the language itself. The type systems that these languages offer provide advanced capabilities like type inferencing and support of higher-order abstractions that make your language concise yet sufficiently expressive. Paul Hudak demonstrated this with Haskell in 1998 (see [2] in section 2.6), when he used the techniques of monadic interpreters, partial evaluation, and staged programming to implement purely embedded DSLs that can be evolved incrementally over time. Christian Hofer, et al discuss similar implementations with Scala in [3] in section 2.6. They also discuss how you can polymorphically embed multiple implementations within a single DSL interface using the techniques of Scala traits, virtual types, higher-order generics, and family polymorphism. In chapter 6, I'll use sample implementations to explain how static typing in Scala helps you to design pure, embedded domain-specific languages (EDSLs).

> **DEFINITION** Monads figure in a model of computation popularized by Haskell. Using monads, you can compose abstractions, following predefined rules. I discuss monadic structures in chapter 6 when I talk about DSL implementations in Scala. For more information, go to http://en.wikipedia.org/wiki/ Monad_(functional_programming).

Now we're going to talk about several metaprogramming patterns that we use frequently in DSL implementations. Languages that support them can't thrive without them. In the world of DSLs, metaprogramming offers one of the richest techniques to design custom syntax for your DSL.

REFLECTIVE METAPROGRAMMING

You can apply patterns at a local level of implementation; Smart API was an example of that. But when you design a DSL, you might need to adopt patterns as general implementation strategies. They shape the way you structure your whole implementation and they're one of the key features of your host language. In our discussion of implementation patterns for internal DSLs (refer to our roadmap in figure 2.1), metaprogramming is one such concept that manifests itself in various forms when you design a DSL. Reflective metaprogramming is the pattern that we'll discuss in this section.

Suppose you're designing a DSL where you need to read stuff from configuration files and invoke methods dynamically, depending on the contents of the file. Here's a real-life example in Ruby that reads from a YAML file, composes the method name, and dynamically invokes the method using arguments read from the file:

```
YAML.load_file(x_path).each do |k, v|
  foo.send("#{k}", v) unless foo.send(k)
end
```

Because the method name isn't known until runtime, we'll use the metaprogramming abilities of Ruby to do a dynamic dispatch on the object using `Object#send()`, instead of the usual dot notation of invoking methods statically. This coding technique is reflective metaprogramming; Ruby discovers methods at runtime and does the invocation. DSL implementations that deal with dynamic objects use this technique to delay method invocations until the last moment when it gets the complete information, maybe from configuration files.

RUNTIME METAPROGRAMMING

Unlike reflective metaprogramming, which discovers existing methods at runtime, you can use other forms of metaprogramming that can generate code dynamically during runtime. Runtime metaprogramming is another way by which you can achieve small surface syntax for your DSL. It makes your DSL look lightweight on the surface; the heavy lifting of code generation is transferred to the backend infrastructure of your host language.

Some languages expose their runtime infrastructure components as meta-objects that programmers can manipulate. In Ruby or Groovy, you can use such components in your programs to dynamically change the behavior of meta-objects during runtime and inject new behavior to implement your domain constructs. Figure 2.5 shows a brief overview of the runtime behavior of metaprogramming in Ruby and Groovy.

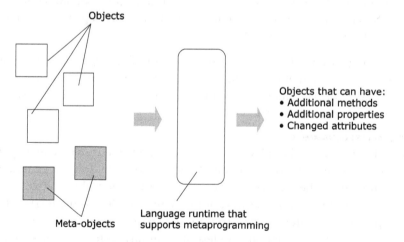

Figure 2.5   Languages that support runtime metaprogramming let users generate code on the fly. This code can add behaviors dynamically to existing classes and objects.

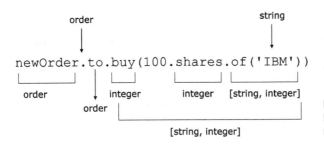

Figure 2.6
Enriching the domain syntax through runtime metaprogramming

In the order-processing DSL that we developed in section 2.1, we used this same technique in Groovy to generate additional methods like shares and of in built-in classes like Integer. These methods don't have any meaningful role to play in the semantics of the action that the DSL performs. Rather, they serve as useful glue to make the language more natural to the domain we're modeling. Figure 2.6 annotates the return types of each method that's called in sequence for a section of the Groovy-based DSL. You can see how the power of metaprogramming generates code during runtime to string together the new methods and adds to the expressivity of the language.

Rails and Grails are two of the most powerful web development frameworks that use the power of runtime metaprogramming. In Rails, when you write the following snippet, the Ruby metaprogramming engine generates all the relevant code for the relational model and validation logic, based on the definition of the Employees table.

```
class Employee < ActiveRecord::Base {
  has_many :dependants
  belongs_to :organization
  validates_presence_of :last_name, :title, :date_of_birth

  # ..
}
```

Runtime metaprogramming makes your DSL dynamic by generating code during runtime. But there's another form of code generation that takes place during compilation and doesn't add any overhead during runtime. Our next DSL pattern is compile-time metaprogramming, which is mostly found in the Lisp family of languages.

COMPILE-TIME METAPROGRAMMING
With compile-time metaprogramming, you can add custom syntax to your DSL, much like you can with the pattern you just learned about (runtime metaprogramming). Although these patterns are similar, there are some crucial differences between the two, as table 2.3 makes clear.

In typical implementations of compile-time metaprogramming, the user interacts with the compiler and generates program fragments during the *compilation* phase.

Macros are the most common way to implement compile-time metaprogramming. In section 4.5 we'll delve into the details of how compile-time metaprogramming works, with specific examples from Clojure.

Table 2.3   Comparison of compile-time and runtime metaprogramming

Compile-time metaprogramming	Runtime metaprogramming
You define syntax that gets processed before runtime, during the compilation phase.	You define syntax that gets processed through the MOP of the language during runtime.
No runtime overhead because the language runtime has to deal only with valid forms.	Some runtime overhead because meta-objects are processed and code is generated during runtime.

Preprocessor-based macros in C and templates in C++ are some examples of language infrastructure that can generate code during the compilation phase. But in the long history of programming languages, Lisp is the granddaddy of compile-time metaprogramming. C macros operate at the lexical level through textual substitution. Lisp macros work with ASTs and offer significant power in designing abstractions at the syntax level. Figure 2.7 shows a schematic diagram of how the custom syntax that you define in your DSL gets transformed through the macroexpansion phase into valid program forms, which are then forwarded to the compiler.

That was the last of the internal DSL implementation patterns that we'll discuss in this chapter. We've discussed various flavors of metaprogramming that you'll find mostly in dynamic languages like Ruby, Groovy, and Clojure. We also talked about static typing and the benefits that it brings when you're designing type-safe DSL scripts. In chapters 4, 5, and 6, we'll get back to all these patterns and discuss each of them, with specific examples in each of the languages.

We started the chapter with the promise that we'd talk about real-world DSL design. We discussed DSL implementations in Java and Groovy, and we just now

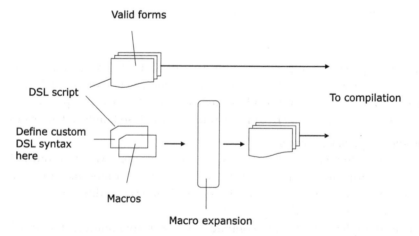

Figure 2.7   You use macros to do compile-time metaprogramming. Your DSL script has some valid language forms and some custom syntax that you've defined. The custom syntax is in the form of macros, which get expanded during the macroexpansion phase into valid language forms. These forms are then forwarded to the compiler.

finished looking into the patterns that come up in internal DSL implementation. Each pattern is a snippet of experience that you, as a practitioner, should feel free to reuse. All of them have been used successfully in building real-world DSL implementations.

Now we'll move on to the next obvious sequel of this discussion. What do you do when your host language doesn't support the syntax that you're looking for in your DSL? You need to get out of the confines of your host language and search for alternatives that you'll need to build from scratch. You need to use external DSLs. In the next section, we'll look at some of the implementation patterns that external DSLs offer.

2.3.2 *External DSL patterns: commonality and variability*

External DSL design follows the same lifecycle and principles of general-purpose language design. I know this statement is inherently repulsive and might drive you away from thinking about designing external DSLs in your next project. Although the statement is true in theory, it's not all that grim when you consider that your DSL isn't necessarily as complex in syntax and semantics as a general-purpose programming language can be. In reality, you can process some external DSLs by manipulating strings using regular expressions. But the only common trait of all external DSLs is that they aren't implemented using the infrastructure of a host language.

External DSL processing consists of the following two broad phases, as figure 2.8 explains:

❶ *Parse*—where you tokenize the text and use a parser to recognize valid inputs

❷ *Process*—where you do the business processing on valid inputs that were recognized by the parser in the first phase

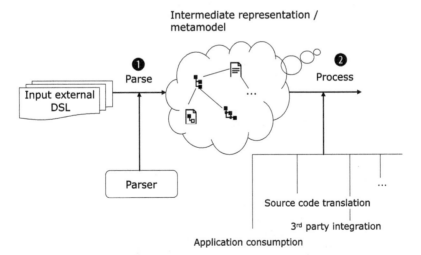

Figure 2.8 The processing stages of an external DSL. Note that unlike internal DSLs, the parser is now part of what you need to build. In internal DSLs, you use the parser of the host language.

If you're designing a simple DSL in which the parser itself processes the inputs inline, the two phases might be combined. The more common and realistic approach is one in which the parser generates an intermediate representation of the input text. In various scenarios and for varying complexities of the DSL, this intermediate representation can be an AST or a more sophisticated metamodel of the language you're designing. The parser can also vary in complexity, ranging from simple string processing to detailed *syntax-directed translation* (a parsing technique discussed more in chapter 8) using parser generators like YACC and ANTLR. The processing phase works on the intermediate representation and either generates the target output directly or can itself transform into an internal DSL that gets processed using the infrastructure of the host language.

In the following sections, we'll briefly discuss each of the patterns that you're likely to encounter in external DSL implementations. In chapter 7, we'll have a more detailed discussion about the implementation aspects of each of them. Figure 2.9 lists some of the common patterns found in real-world external DSL implementations.

Each pattern shown in figure 2.9 provides a way to describe the syntax of your DSL using a form that's external to the host language of implementation. This means that the DSL script that you'll write won't pass as valid syntax in the implementation language. For each of these patterns, you'll see how you can transform the custom DSL syntax into an artifact that can be consumed by your host language.

CONTEXT-DRIVEN STRING MANIPULATION

Suppose you need to process business rules, but instead of traditional APIs you want to provide a DSL interface to your users. Consider the following example:

```
commission of 5% on principal amount for trade
                      values greater than $1,000,000
```

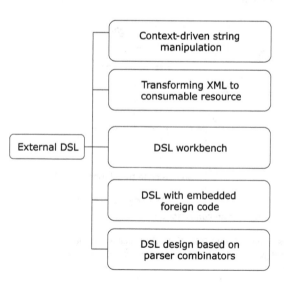

Figure 2.9

An informal micro-classification of common patterns and techniques of implementing external DSLs

This is a string that doesn't make sense in any programming language. With appropriate pre-processing and scrubbing, you can coerce it into valid Ruby or Groovy code. The parser will be a fairly simple one that tokenizes the string and does simple transformations through regular expression manipulations. The resulting form will be Ruby or Groovy code that can be executed right away as an implementation of the business rule.

TRANSFORMING XML TO A CONSUMABLE RESOURCE

Many of you have probably worked with the Spring DI framework. (If you're unfamiliar with Spring, go to http://www.springframework.org.) One of the ways you can configure the DI container is through an XML-based specification file. You need to put all your dependencies of abstractions and implementations into this file. During runtime, the Spring container bootstraps the specification file and wires up all dependencies into a `BeanFactory` or `ApplicationContext`, which remains alive during the lifecycle of the application and serves up all the necessary context information. The XML specification that you write is an external DSL that gets parsed and persisted as a resource to be consumed by the application.

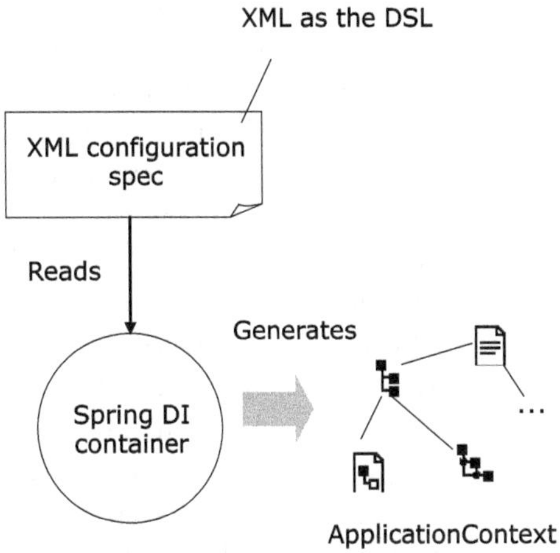

Figure 2.10 shows a schematic overview of how Spring uses XML as the external DSL to bootstrap its `ApplicationContext` abstraction.

Figure 2.10 XML is being used as the external DSL to abstract Spring configuration specification. The container reads and processes XML during startup and produces the `ApplicationContext` that your application uses.

Another similar example is the Hibernate mapping file that maps the database schema with your entity description files. (For more information about Hibernate, go to http://hibernate.org.) Both examples follow the parse and process stages of execution, albeit with different lifecycles and persistence strategies. They exhibit the commonality of external DSLs, but differ from the pattern we discussed earlier (context-driven string manipulation) in the form and complexity of the parser and the lifetime of the intermediate representation.

DSL WORKBENCH

The core concepts of metaprogramming that we discussed in the context of internal DSLs have been extended to another level by some of the language workbenches and metaprogramming systems that are currently available. When you write code in text form, the compiler needs to parse the code to generate the AST. What if the system already maintains the code that you write in the form of an AST? If a system could do that, the result would be easier transformation, manipulation, and subsequent code generation from the intermediate representation.

Eclipse Xtext (http://www.eclipse.org/Xtext) is a great example of a system that offers a complete solution for end-to-end development of external DSLs. Instead of storing your DSL in plain text form, it stores a higher-order representation of your DSL grammar in the form of metamodels. These metamodels can then be integrated seamlessly with a number of other frameworks like code generators, rich editors, and so on. Tools like Xtext are called DSL workbenches because they offer a complete environment for developing, managing, and maintaining their external DSLs. We'll discuss designing DSLs based on Xtext with a detailed case study in chapter 7.

JetBrains' Meta Programming System (http://www.jetbrains.com/mps/index.html) supports nontextual representations of program code that eliminate the need for code parsing. The code is always available as the AST, with all its annotations and references, and allows you to define generators that generate code in numerous programming languages. It's as if you're designing your external DSL in a metalanguage offered by the metaprogramming system of the workbench. You can define business rules, types, and constraints like you would do through your programming language. The difference is in the external presentation, which is much friendlier, might be graphical, and is easier for you to manipulate.

Looking back at figure 2.9, you've just learned about three of the commonly used techniques for external DSL implementation. We'll discuss two others that might be the two most prominent techniques that you'll use in your real-world applications. We're almost to the end of our third milestone of the chapter. By now, you have a good appreciation for all the techniques of internal and external DSL implementations that we've discussed so far. I'm sure that you're anxiously waiting to see some of them being used in the larger context of modeling a domain. We'll be taking that journey soon.

MIXING DSL WITH EMBEDDED FOREIGN CODE

Parser generator tools like YACC and ANTLR let programmers use syntax notation that's similar to Extended Backus-Naur Form (EBNF) to declare the grammar of the language. The tool processes the production rules and generates the parser of the language. When you implement a parser, you usually want to also define some actions that your parser should take when it recognizes a fragment of input. One example of such an action is building up an intermediate representation of the input language string, which will be used in later stages by your application.

Tools like YACC and ANTLR let you embed host language code for action definitions within the production rules. Associated with each rule, you can write code fragments in C, C++, or Java that get bundled into the final parser code that the tool generates. This is a pattern of external DSL design in which you can extend the native DSL with foreign embedding in some other high-level language. We'll discuss a complete DSL design using this pattern with ANTLR as the parser generator in chapter 7. Now let's move on to our final classification.

DSL DESIGN BASED ON PARSER COMBINATORS

This classification is the final unit shown in figure 2.9. Now we get to discuss one of the most innovative ways to design an external DSL. In the last section, you saw how you can use external tools along with embeddings of a programming language in YACC or ANTLR to generate a parser for your DSL. These tools generate efficient parsers of the grammar that you feed them. The drawback is that they aren't exactly the friendliest of tools to use. Many of today's languages offer a better alternative in the form of *parser combinators*.

In combination with a powerful type system, you can design parser combinators to be an expressive DSL that's implemented as a library within the language itself. You can develop parsers using the full power of your host language artifacts like classes, methods, and combinators, without resorting to an external tool set.

Scala offers a parser combinator library as part of its standard library. Using Scala's power of higher-order functions, we can define combinators that make the parser DSL look like declarative EBNF production rules. Check out the following grammar that's declared using Scala parser combinators. It defines the grammar for a small order-processing language using pure Scala.

```
object OrderDSL extends StandardTokenParsers {
  lexical.delimiters ++= List("(", ")", ",")
  lexical.reserved += ("buy", "sell", "shares", "at",
    "max", "min", "for", "trading", "account")
  def instr = trans ~ account_spec
  def trans = "(" ~> repsep(trans_spec, ",") <~ ")"
  def trans_spec = buy_sell ~ buy_sell_instr
  def account_spec = "for" ~> "trading" ~> "account" ~> stringLit
  def buy_sell = ("buy" | "sell")
  def buy_sell_instr = security_spec ~ price_spec
  def security_spec = numericLit ~ ident ~ "shares"
  def price_spec = "at" ~ ("min" | "max") ~ numericLit
}
```

If you can't get into the details of the above snippet, that's totally OK. I threw in this sample implementation only to demonstrate the power of declarative parser development within the confines of a host language. Using this technique, you'll be able to develop your external DSL parser fully in Scala.

 I'll revisit the topic of parser combinators in chapter 8, which contains a comprehensive external DSL that's built using Scala parser combinators.

We've come to the end of this road. We've covered all the DSL implementation patterns and techniques that were listed earlier in the chapter. These descriptions were sort of thumbnails aimed at providing the bigger picture in the context of real-world DSL implementation. In chapters 4 through 8, you'll see in detail how to use each of these in various forms when we take up real-world domain problems and implement DSLs for each of them.

Before we end the chapter, we need to take a realistic view of a topic you'll find useful every time you step out to design a DSL: how to decide on the pragmatics of *which form of DSL* to use in your application. In chapter 1, we discussed when to use a DSL. Now I'm going to explain how to choose between internal and external DSLs when you're designing an application. DSLs make perfect sense when they're used to model specific problems of the domain. But you need to do a balancing act in choosing the engineering aspects of it. Whether you choose to design an internal DSL or an external one can depend on a lot of factors; not all of them will necessarily be driven by technology choices.

2.4   *Choosing DSL implementations*

As programmers, we're always faced with many options, be it in design methodology, programming paradigms, or using idioms in specific implementations. We've been talking about designing DSLs, the virtues of well-designed abstractions, and a multitude of options to make your language expressive enough to your user community. Now we have to talk about some other options that you'll face.

Suppose you've decided to adopt a DSL-based development approach for your project and you've already identified a couple of business domain components that make good candidates for expressive DSL design. How do you decide on your DSL implementation strategy? Do you want to use the host language and model your problem as an internal DSL? Or would you prefer to design an external DSL to get to the level of expressivity that your users need? As with most problems in software engineering, there's no universal choice. It all depends on the set of constraints that the problem domain presents and the set of options your solution domain offers. In this section, let's review some of the factors you need to consider before jumping in to decide on the DSL implementation technique.

REUSING EXISTING INFRASTRUCTURE
Internal DSLs piggyback on the host language infrastructure, syntax, semantics, module system, type system, method of error reporting, and the complete tool chain that it integrates with. This piggybacking is possibly the most definitive advantage of implementing internal DSLs. For external DSLs, you need to build all these from the ground up, which is never an easy proposition. Even within internal DSLs, you have lots of implementation patterns to choose from, as we saw in the last section. Your choice here will mostly depend on the capabilities of your host language and the level of abstraction that it supports.

If you use a language like Scala or Haskell that offers rich type systems, you can decide to use them to encode your domain types and have a purely embedded DSL. But embedding might not always be the most appropriate option available. The language that you're trying to embed needs to have concrete syntax and semantics similar to that of the host language for embedding to work. A mismatch in either will make your DSL look foreign to the ecosystem of the host language and will never compose with its native control structures. In such cases, you might want to resort to metaprogramming techniques, if they're offered by your host language. As I discussed earlier, metaprogramming lets you extend the base language with your own domain constructs and can often lead to the design of more expressive surface syntax for your DSL compared to the embedded variant.

LEVERAGING EXISTING KNOWLEDGE

There are situations when your decision to use an implementation paradigm is driven by the available knowledge base of your team members. Internal DSLs are more likely to score on this point. The important point to consider is that being familiar with the language doesn't imply that the programmers are aware of the DSL-friendly idioms that it offers. Fluent interfaces are commonly used in Java and Ruby, but they have their pitfalls too. And there are situations when you need to consider aspects like mutability of abstractions, context sensitivity of the fluent API, and the *finishing problem* of finalizing the chain (see [4] in section 2.6) to make your DSL semantically consistent. All these things involve subtle idiomatic usage of the language, which contributes to the consistency of your DSL.

Leveraging existing knowledge is certainly an important consideration. As the leader of the team, judge the expertise of your team members, based on the context of DSL implementation, not on their familiarity of the surface syntax of the language. I've seen instances when a team decided to use XML as the external DSL and gained a lot in productivity and user acceptance instead of trying to shoehorn internal DSLs into Java.

LEARNING CURVE WITH EXTERNAL DSLs

Maybe you're afraid to choose external DSLs because you think that designing them is just as complex as designing a general-purpose programming language. If that's what you're thinking, I don't blame you. Just having to deal with terms like *syntax-directed translation, recursive descent parsers, LALR* and *SLR* seems to remind you of how complex the whole thing can be.

In reality, most of the external DSLs required in application development don't need to be as complicated as a full-blown programming language. Then again, some external DSLs will be complex, and there is an associated learning curve as part of the cost of development. The advantage is that you can customize almost everything, including how you handle errors and exceptions, instead of being confined within the constraints of an underlying host language.

THE RIGHT LEVEL OF EXPRESSIVITY

Although internal DSLs score a lot of points by reusing existing infrastructure, it's also true that the constraints that the base language forces on you can make it difficult to achieve the right level of expressivity for your domain users. More often than not, modules are identified as candidates for DSL long after the development environment and the tool chain have been finalized. It's not always possible to switch to an alternate language that might have been a better candidate for the DSL design.

When this happens, you need to consider external DSLs as part of your application infrastructure. The main advantage of modeling a problem with an external DSL is that you can design it precisely to the level of sophistication that you need for the problem at hand. It also gives you ample room for tweaking, based on user feedback. This isn't always possible with internal DSLs, because you have to abide by the basic constraints of syntax and semantics that the base language enforces.

COMPOSABILITY

In a typical application development scenario, you need to compose DSLs with each other and also with the host language. Composing internal DSLs with the host language is easy. After all, the DSL uses the same language and is mostly implemented as a library that embeds into your host language.

But let's talk a bit about combining multiple DSLs, even when they're implemented using the same host language. If you're using statically typed languages for implementation and you've designed embedded DSLs, you need the support of the host language's type system to ensure seamless composability between them. Languages that support functional programming paradigms encourage you to design internal DSLs based on functional combinators. The internal DSL and the combinators can be completely composable, if they're designed properly. External DSLs are harder to design in this manner, particularly if they were designed separately and without considering composability as an upfront criterion.

2.5   *Summary*

From the rationale of DSLs in chapter 1 to the real-world pragmatics of DSL use, implementation, and classification, you've come a long way in a short time. If chapter 1 gave you a precursor to DSL-based development paradigms, this chapter has exposed you to the pragmatics of real-world usage.

I started the chapter with an example to emphasize how DSL-based program development focuses on making abstractions more expressive. A Java-based implementation of the order-processing DSL was expressive enough for the programmer as a user. But when we speak of DSLs as being an effective vehicle for non-programming domain experts, you need to have an implementation language that helps you express more in the language of the domain. The Groovy implementation did precisely that; the level of expressiveness increased considerably when we moved from Java to Groovy.

In the next section, we changed gears from the specifics of an implementation to the broader topic of DSL patterns. You learned about the patterns in DSL implementations that exist even within the broad classification of internal and external DSLs. DSLs can be of varying complexity. As a DSL designer, you need to decide on the strategy of implementation that best suits the problem at hand. We discussed all of those patterns in section 2.3 to give you an overall idea of the implementation techniques.

In this chapter, you've seen how DSLs vary in form and structure. It's the architect's responsibility to give it the final shape that models the domain. Before we talk about that, we need to discuss how you integrate DSLs with your development environment.

Key takeaways & best practices

- *Java offers features that make your DSL expressive enough.* If you feel limited with Java, target other languages on the JVM that have good interoperability with Java.
- *When you're using a specific language for DSL implementation, keep an eye on the patterns that it offers to make your DSL idiomatic.* If you're using Groovy or Ruby, metaprogramming is your friend. With Scala, the rich type system can form the backbone of your DSL implementation.
- *Keep an open mind when you're selecting the type of DSL you're going to design.* External DSLs might seem difficult, but most likely you won't require the sophistication needed to build a full-blown language from the ground up.

So far, you've seen the macromodel of DSLs in action. Now it's time to think in terms of the micromodeling artifacts of DSL-based development. If you're on the JVM and your core application is in Java, how do you integrate your Groovy DSL so that it can talk to the Java components and still maintain its own identity as a separately evolving entity? There are quite a few options you can adopt, and a few pitfalls to avoid. But that's for the next chapter.

In all the following chapters, you'll implement DSL snippets from the securities trading domain, and Bob will always be there with us as the all-seeing eye to help us make our DSLs more expressive.

2.6   References

1   Gamma, E., R. Helm, R. Johnson, and J. Vlissides. 1995. *Design Patterns: Elements of Reusable Object-Oriented Software.* Addison-Wesley Professional.

2   Hudak P. 1998. Modular Domain-Specific Languages and Tools, *Proceedings of the 5th International Conference on Software Reuse.*

3   Hofer, Christian, Klaus Ostermann, Tillmann Rendel, and Adriaan Moors. 2008. Polymorphic Embedding of DSLs, *Proceedings of the 7th International Conference on Generative Programming and Component Engineering*, pp 137-148.

4   Ford, Neal, *Advanced DSLs in Ruby,* http://github.com/nealford/presentations/tree/master.

DSL-driven application development

This chapter covers

- Integrating internal and external DSLs in a core application
- Managing errors and exceptions
- Optimizing performance

In the two previous chapters, we've looked at many of the user- and implementation-level perspectives of DSLs. You've seen how expressive abstractions lead to an easier understanding of the code base and reduce the feedback cycle from the domain experts. But at the end of the day, however expressive the DSL is that you design, you need to integrate it with the model of your core Java application. (Your application might not be in Java; I'm using that as an example.) You're also going to need to take care of certain aspects related to the integration upfront. In this chapter, we'll talk about those issues, as well as others that you need to address when you consider developing a whole application that uses DSLs.

You develop your main application using a primary language of the platform, like Java. For some of the business rules or configuration specifications, you might decide to use DSLs written in languages that can be more expressive than Java. How can you integrate them seamlessly within your core application? Because DSLs tend

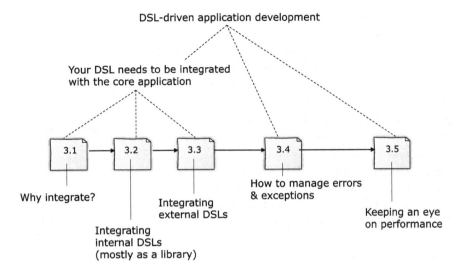

Figure 3.1 **How you'll progress through the chapter and learn the issues related to DSL-driven application development**

to evolve *independently* of the main application, your architecture needs to be flexible enough to compose the changing DSLs with minimal impact on the running application. Figure 3.1 shows how I'm going to address these issues as you progress through the chapter.

We're going to consider three main aspects of DSL-driven application development:

- Integration issues
- Handling exceptions and errors
- Managing performance

DSLs don't work in isolation. When you're integrating them with your application, you need to consider numerous issues, including the fact that both the DSLs and your core application can raise exceptions that manifest as errors to the DSL users. How do you handle them? (We'll discuss this in section 3.4.) The chapter concludes with an overview of performance concerns that might arise when you use a DSL.

By the end of the chapter, you'll understand how you should architect your application so that it integrates seamlessly with DSLs written in a different language.

3.1 *Exploring DSL integration*

Like all beautiful abstractions, a DSL needs to integrate with the other components of your application architecture. In most common use cases, a DSL models the changing artifacts of your applications, like business rules and configuration parameters. It's important that you design your DSL and the application such that they can evolve independently of each other and yet be able to integrate seamlessly with the workflow.

In this section, we'll explore various ways to make DSL integration seamless. Remember, a DSL might address the concerns of *one,* specific domain, but it can be used across *multiple,* larger domains. Whether the DSL is used in this way depends on how generic the domain that it addresses is. A DSL that manipulates date and time can be used across all applications that need to handle date calculations, but a DSL that deals with corporate tax regulations might be useful within a more limited context. The date-manipulation DSL must be more malleable so that it can integrate with multiple application contexts.

Before we go into the details of integrating DSLs into your application, look at figure 3.2, which shows how your DSL-driven application architecture looks.

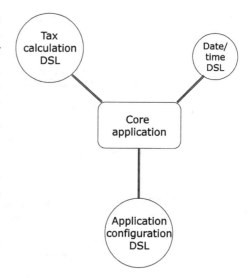

Figure 3.2   A macroscopic view of DSL-based application architecture. Note the decoupling of the DSLs from the core application. They have different evolution timelines.

In a typical layered architecture, a DSL can be used at any level so long as it publishes the right context for integration with that layer of the application. Integrating internal DSLs is easier because they're designed primarily as libraries in the same language as your application. External DSL integration is trickier and needs to plug in through published, specific end points that your application can subscribe to. Before we delve any deeper into the integration aspects of internal and external DSLs with specific use cases for your application architecture, here are some reasons why you should care about DSL integration.

3.1.1   Why you should care about DSL integration

Just as you need to care about wiring the components of your core application, you need to think about integrating the whole application with externally pluggable DSL scripts. A DSL can evolve independently of your application, so you need to have the right amount of coupling between them.

> When you use an expressive language like Groovy, Ruby, or Scala as the main language of your core application, you might not have any integration issues; you'll never feel the need to plug in DSL scripts written in any other language. The issues that I describe in the following sections mostly relate to integrating DSL scripts with a Java application.

Developers tend to be aggressive using DSLs of multiple languages within the same application without thinking beforehand about how to integrate them. If you choose the wrong language for DSL implementation, the perfectly healthy looking

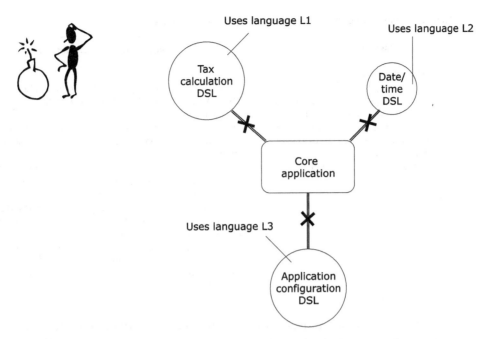

Figure 3.3 Our application architect is having a nightmarish time thinking about how to integrate DSLs written in various languages with the core application. It's a time bomb that's waiting to explode. Can you help him out?

architecture in figure 3.2 could very well turn out to be a nightmare for the application developer. No one wants to be in the position of our friend in figure 3.3.

Table 3.1 describes which aspects you need to consider to ensure that the DSL you develop integrates seamlessly with your application and to avoid being in the situation of the poor guy in figure 3.3.

Table 3.1 Integrating DSLs into your core application

Issue to address	As an architect you should . . .
Separation of concerns How do you ensure that the DSL has clearly defined boundaries between the core problem that it addresses and the application context that it interacts with?	Define the bounded context of the DSL correctly and think about how it might be used in situations different from the current application. Look at the principle of distillation of abstraction design that I discuss as one of the core qualities in appendix A.
Evolution of the DSL API The DSL API needs to evolve independently of the application context	Make sure the evolution of the API maintains backward compatibility. If the DSL is a third-party one, raise a red alert the moment you notice incompatible changes being made in the DSL APIs. If you don't, these changes will come back to bite you later.

Table 3.1   Integrating DSLs into your core application *(continued)*

Issue to address	As an architect you should . . .
Avoid language cacophony Using too many languages in DSLs leads to chaos in the development and maintenance of the whole architecture. This isn't only a technology issue, but a personnel issue as well. People might not be cooperative if they have to maintain code that uses too many languages.	Ensure that the language you choose for implementing DSLs has seamless interoperability with the host language of your application. Compromise on the flexibility of your DSL's syntax, rather than use a language that doesn't offer the best integration abilities with the core application ecosystem. Just because languages are running on the same virtual machine (VM) doesn't imply seamless interoperability. Consider this a warning. If the language that you're using to implement a DSL offers multiple ways to interoperate with the host language of the application, choose the one that offers the most natural form of integration rather than using generic sandbox-based scripting environments. We'll discuss such options in section 3.2 in the context of Groovy and Java interoperability.

Now that you have an understanding of why you need a definite strategy for integrating DSLs into core applications, let's look at some of their use patterns. We'll start with internal DSLs, where integration is done mostly in the form of APIs that are available in the DSL library.

3.2   *Internal DSL integration patterns*

You design an internal DSL as a library either in the same language that your application is implemented in or in one that offers a seamless interoperability with it. In both cases, the integration doesn't need any external infrastructure; it's like yet another API call between the boundaries of the DSL and the core application. I call this *homogeneous integration* because the languages involved interoperate well enough within the constraints of the underlying VM. Look at figure 3.4, which illustrates how DSLs developed using Java, Groovy, and Spring configuration integrate homogeneously on the JVM. You could deploy each of the DSLs as a jar file that the main application can refer to.

Suppose you're developing an application using Java as the primary programming language. But because you're a polyglot, you choose to use the power of Groovy to implement your XML Builder functionality. (Builders offer a great way to process XML in Groovy. Go to http://www.ibm.com/developerworks/java/library/j-pg04125/.) Then you discover a third-party JRuby-based DSL that you can use to load all your Spring beans to manage application configurations. How should you integrate your DSLs with your core application? The integration has to be such that it shouldn't incur too much complexity for the user, but at the same time you need to keep the DSL sufficiently decoupled from the core application so that it can manage its own

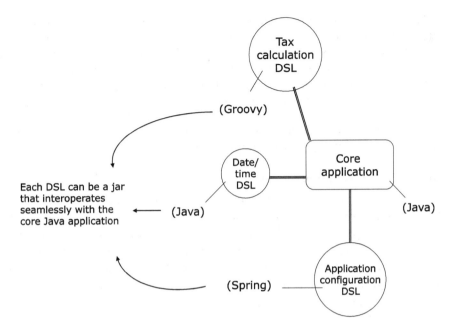

Figure 3.4 All three DSLs integrate homogeneously with the core application. Each DSL can be deployed as jar files that interoperate seamlessly in the JVM.

evolution and lifecycle over time. You can integrate your DSL written in these JVM languages with the Java application in a number of ways.

When you consider the collection of languages on the JVM, most offer a number of ways to integrate with Java. Table 3.2 lists the ways you can use each of them. But you need to be aware of the pros and cons of each and use the option that best suits your problem.

Table 3.2 Integration points published by internal DSLs

Internal DSL pattern	Published integration point
Java 6 Scripting Engine (discussed in section 3.2.1)	Use the corresponding scripting engine that comes with Java 6 to integrate DSLs written in scripting languages like Groovy.
DSL wrapper (discussed in section 3.2.2)	Wrap Java objects with smarter APIs written in languages like JRuby, Scala, or Groovy and use the Java integration capabilities of these languages.
Language-specific integration features (discussed in section 3.2.3)	Directly integrate with Java through abstractions that can load and parse scripts directly. Groovy offers such direct integration.
Spring-based integration (discussed in section 3.2.4)	Use Spring to load beans written in dynamic languages directly into your application through declarative configuration.

> When we talk about integration in the following sections, we're assuming that the core application is developed using Java. This use case is the one that's used most frequently today. Another point to note is that even though all these languages offer varying degrees of integration capabilities with Java, integration among them is at an immature stage. You won't find a Groovy application using Ruby for a DSL.

Let's look at the patterns listed in table 3.2 and see how some of the JVM languages use them to integrate with a Java-based application.

3.2.1   Using the Java 6 scripting engine

Java as a platform has become ubiquitous. For some time, programmers have been talking about a unification layer that allows interoperability across all the languages that the platform embraces. Using Java 6 scripting, you can embed scripting languages within Java applications by using the appropriate engines. Now you can even integrate DSLs that were implemented using languages like Groovy or JRuby through the Java APIs defined in the `javax.script` package. Let's look at an example of this kind of integration, using our order-processing DSL from chapter 2 as a case study.

PREPARING THE GROOVY DSL

In section 2.2.2, we implemented a Groovy script that executed the DSL for order creation. In this section, we'll look at the same DSL, integrated and invoked from within a Java application. This example will give you an idea of the power of Java scripting as an enabler of DSL integration.

Let's assume that we have the Groovy DSL implementation for processing client orders (`ClientOrder.groovy`) shown in the following listing (the content of this listing is repeated from section 2.2.2).

Listing 3.1   ClientOrder.groovy: order-processing DSL in Groovy

```
ExpandoMetaClass.enableGlobally()

class Order {
  def security
  def quantity
  def limitPrice
  def allOrNone
  def value
  def bs

  def buy(su, closure) {
    bs = 'Bought'
    buy_sell(su, closure)
  }

  def sell(su, closure) {
    bs = 'Sold'
```

```
      buy_sell(su, closure)
  }

  def getTo() {
    this
  }

  private buy_sell(su, closure) {
    security = su[0]
    quantity = su[1]
    closure()
  }
}

def methodMissing(String name, args) {
  order.metaClass.getMetaProperty(name).setProperty(order, args)
}

def getNewOrder() {
  order = new Order()
}

def valueAs(closure) {
  order.value = closure(order.quantity, order.limitPrice[0])
  order
}

Integer.metaClass.getShares = { -> delegate }
Integer.metaClass.of = { instrument -> [instrument, delegate] }
```

The `Order` abstraction in this code that we developed on the Groovy side captures the order details that the user enters. In another script file, order.dsl in listing 3.2, the DSL user does the scripting (also in Groovy) that uses the implementation in listing 3.1 to place orders for the client. Note that this script is based purely on the DSL that we designed in listing 3.1 and assumes minimal understanding of the workings of the programming language. In addition to creating the orders, the script accumulates them into a collection that's returned to the caller. But who's the caller? Don't worry, you'll find out soon.

> **Listing 3.2   order.dsl: Groovy script for placing orders**

```
orders = []
newOrder.to.buy(100.shares.of('IBM')) {
  limitPrice    300
  allOrNone     true
  valueAs       {qty, unitPrice -> qty * unitPrice - 500}
}                                                               ❶ Add order to the
orders << order                                                    collection

newOrder.to.buy(150.shares.of('GOOG')) {
  limitPrice    300
  allOrNone     true
  valueAs       {qty, unitPrice -> qty * unitPrice - 500}
}
orders << order
```

```
newOrder.to.buy(200.shares.of('MSOFT')) {
  limitPrice    300
  allOrNone     true
  valueAs       {qty, unitPrice -> qty * unitPrice - 500}
}
orders << order                                              ❷ Return collection
orders                                                          to caller
```

In listing 3.2, the user uses newOrder to create a new Order abstraction that gets filled up with attributes like buy or sell, the share to transact, limit price, valuation strategy, and so on. Every order that gets created is appended to a collection ❶. The collection is returned at ❷.

Now we come to the interesting part of the story: you are going to integrate the DSL implementation and the script with the main Java application.

INTEGRATING THE DSL IMPLEMENTATION AND THE SCRIPT

The code fragment in listing 3.3 shows a snippet of code from the main application. This snippet expects the collection of orders to be returned from the DSL execution so that it can further process the orders. The Java code in the snippet uses the scripting engine for Groovy. Similarly, implementations of scripting engines are available for other JVM languages like JRuby, Clojure, Rhino, and Jython that can be integrated into your Java application as seamlessly as this Groovy one (go to https://scripting.dev.java.net/ for more information).

Listing 3.3   Java application code that invokes the Groovy DSL

```
ScriptEngineManager factory = new ScriptEngineManager();      Get factory for
ScriptEngine engine = factory.getEngineByName("groovy");    ❶ ScriptEngine

List<?> orders  = (List<?>)                                    Get Groovy
  engine.eval(new InputStreamReader(            List of orders ❷ ScriptEngine
    new BufferedInputStream(                  ❸ returned
      new SequenceInputStream(
        new FileInputStream("ClientOrder.groovy"),     ❹ Evaluate
        new FileInputStream("order.dsl")))));             DSL script

System.out.println(orders.size());
for(Object o : orders) {                        ❺ Process
  System.out.println(o);                           orders
}
```

Let's look at the steps that led to the integration. Figure 3.5 shows a sequence diagram, annotated with the actions that listing 3.3 performs on the DSL script and implementation.

As you can see, Java 6 scripting APIs provide a viable option for integrating your DSL into your Java application using almost any JVM language. javax.script also offers APIs that let you set up bindings of variables at various scopes to exchange information between your DSL and the Java components.

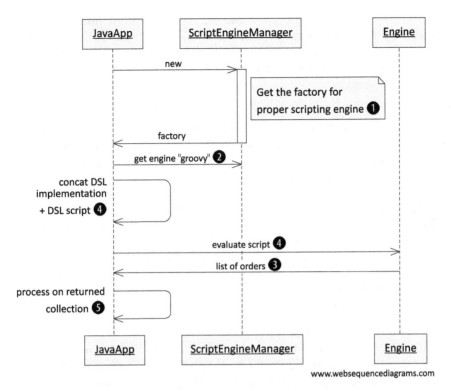

Figure 3.5   Integrating the Groovy DSL through the Java 6 scripting engine. The interaction diagram shows all the steps involved in evaluating the Groovy DSL script within the sandbox of the `ScriptEngine`.

PROBLEMS WITH JAVA 6 SCRIPTING

Java 6 scripting is one of the most generic ways to get JVM languages to interoperate. And like any generic strategy, there's always a better option for the specific language that you're working with. Because the DSL script gets loaded in a separate `ClassLoader` and executes in its own sandbox, you face problems of interoperability between the Groovy and Java abstractions. Note how we get a list of `Objects` from the Groovy DSL script within Java in listing 3.3, as opposed to a list of `Order` abstractions. The only way you can invoke `Order` methods on it is by using reflection. Also, because the script executes in the sandbox of the `ScriptEngine`, when there's an exception, the line numbers mentioned in the stack trace don't match the line numbers in the source file. This situation can make it difficult to debug exceptions thrown from the DSL script. Let's explore some better options for integrating an internal DSL.

> Scripting engines were introduced in Java 6 as a generic way to handle script execution from within Java programs. The design principles of the Java 6 `ScriptEngine`-based APIs cater to all JVM languages that implement an infrastructure that's compliant with Java Specification Request (JSR) 233.

If the language that you plan to use for DSL implementation offers its own specific ways of integrating with Java, review it carefully before deciding in favor of implementations that are JSR 233 compliant. Using the language-specific solution is probably best practice because it's likely to be simpler and more idiomatic.

You just saw how the scripting APIs of Java 6 work to enable polyglotism on the JVM. I picked up the example in Groovy because we implemented a Groovy DSL in chapter 2 that could be seamlessly plugged into the Java application without much of a fuss. You can use similar techniques to plug DSLs written in other JVM languages like JRuby, Clojure, or Rhino into your Java applications.

Polyglotism encourages use of multiple languages even within a single solution domain. The languages need to have good interoperability and well-published integration points. Usually such a family of languages operates on a common runtime like the JVM that hosts languages like Java, Scala, Ruby, Groovy, and so on. One of the main ideas behind DSLs is to use the most suitable language to design your domain API and integrate it with the core application through the common runtime.

You can integrate your DSL at various levels. The Java scripting option we discussed in section 3.2.1 lets you embed your DSL within the execution framework of the `Script-Engine` and invoke the DSL scripts. It has the advantage that your DSL is totally decoupled from the application and executes within the sandbox of the `ScriptEngine` context. The disadvantage of this approach is that it's not intuitive to have the DSL components interact easily with the environment of the main application.

Let's look at another approach to DSL integration that operates at a different level than script engines and integrates more closely with the host language of your application.

3.2.2   *Using a DSL wrapper*

In this integration approach, you build the DSL as a wrapper layer on top of the main application components using the rich features that the DSL host language offers. You can adopt this approach to make your legacy applications publish smarter APIs. Using the rich language features of yet another JVM language, you can make more expressive domain components based on the legacy abstractions. Not only will your domain experts love them, but your fellow API users will also enjoy using them.

SETTING UP THE EXAMPLE

In this example, we'll use Scala, the statically typed language for the JVM that also has nice interoperability features with Java. Suppose your main application is written in Java and all your domain objects are implemented as part of the application. Your client is aware of the hype and fun of DSL-based development and asks you to implement some smart DSL features on top of their existing legacy Java trading application. This scenario is perfect for you to *integrate by wrapping*.

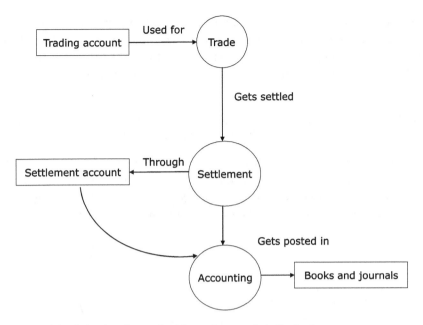

Figure 3.6 Role of trading and settlement accounts in the trade process

To help explain the concept of integrating by wrapping, I'm going to use another example from the world of securities trading. Figure 3.6 shows an overview of the trade process. Don't forget to read the sidebar; it provides enough background information for you to follow along.

Financial brokerage systems: client account

In order to trade, a client needs to open an account (called the *trading account*) with the Stock Trading Organization (STO). All trades for the client are booked in that account and recorded by the STO. When the trade is done, the settlement process has to be initiated. That process does the final balancing of the securities and currencies that were exchanged between the two parties.

For example: client XXX buys 100 shares of SONY @50 USD per share through STO Nomura Securities. The STO gets those securities from the stock exchange where a broker does the sell. After the trade is made, there's a settlement process during which 100 shares of SONY and approximately 5000 USD are exchanged between the two counterparties. This settlement is done through an account (the *settlement account*), which can be same as the trading account of the client or it can be a different account.

To review, the trading account is used for doing the trade, and the settlement account is used for settling the trade. They can be the same account or different ones. Figure 3.6 shows an overview of the process.

Consider the `Account` domain model, an entity from our friendly domain of securities trading operations. An account is an entity through which the firm, its clients, and the brokers manage trading and settlement activities. The sidebar in this section gives a brief explanation of the role of accounts and their types in trading and settlement operations.

 If you've forgotten what trading and settlement mean in the context of our domain, review the callouts in chapters 1 and 2.

Listing 3.4 contains a simplified view of the domain model for the `Account` entity that we'll use to discuss the wrapper approach to DSL integration. `Account` is a Java class on which we'll implement Scala wrappers. Ultimately, you're going to find out how the usage patterns in client APIs become more succinct and expressive when you use a wrapper.

Listing 3.4 Account domain object in Java

```java
public class Account {
    public enum STATUS { OPEN, CLOSED }

    public enum TYPE { TRADING, SETTLEMENT, BOTH }

    private String number;
    private String firstName;
    private List<String> names = new ArrayList<String>();
    private STATUS status = STATUS.OPEN;
    private TYPE accountType = TYPE.TRADING;
    private double interestAccrued = 0.0;

    public Account(String number, String firstName) {
        this.number = number;
        this.firstName = firstName;
    }

    public Account(String number, String firstName, TYPE accountType) {
        this(number, firstName);
        this.accountType = accountType;
    }

    //.. getters ommitted

    public double calculate(final Calculator c) {
        interestAccrued = c.calculate(this);
        return interestAccrued;
    }

    public boolean isOpen() {
        return status.equals(STATUS.OPEN);
    }

    public Account addName(String name) {
        names.add(name);
        return this;
    }
}
```

If you've been programming in Java, I'm sure you're neither amused nor surprised by the verbosity and boilerplate stuff that the model in listing 3.4 uses. Let's try to figure out how you can make the abstraction smart enough so your client can get some APIs that let him express his intents in a more domain-rich vocabulary. At the end of this exercise, you'll have a DSL that'll integrate nicely into the guts of your Java application.

BUILDING THE DSL

Let's start with the abstraction `AccountDSL` in Scala that acts as an adapter to the `Account` Java class, and implement something called smart domain APIs. Remember, your ultimate goal is to make the `Account` class so smart that the client can apply the language on existing instances of the `Account` class, no matter what DSL you design. In the following code snippets, I'll show you how to enrich the `AccountDSL` abstraction incrementally. I'll also discuss potential uses of the DSL so that you get a feel for the enrichment as it occurs in the domain abstraction.

The following listing shows the DSL layer in Scala that we'll use seamlessly with the Java `Account` class.

Listing 3.5   AccountDSL in Scala

```scala
class AccountDSL(value: Account) {
  import scala.collection.JavaConversions._        // ❶ Convert Java
  def names =                                      //    collection to Scala
    value.getNames.toSeq.toList ::: List(value.getFirstName)

  def belongsTo(name: String) = {
    (name == value.getFirstName) || (names exists(_ == name))   // ❷ Domain API
  }

  def <<(name: String) = {                         // ❸ New operator syntax
    value.addName(name)                            //    on collection
    this
  }
  //..
}
```

The code in the listing uses some of the typical Scala idioms that I describe briefly in the sidebar "Scala 101". For more Scala details, see [1] in section 3.7.

In listing 3.5, `AccountDSL` is an adapter to the Java `Account` class and wraps it as an underlying implementation. At ❶ we convert the Java collection to a Scala one, which we'll use subsequently with higher-order functions. (Scala collections are always semantically richer than Java collections in the sense that you can apply higher-order functions to make operations on them more expressive.) This code uses Scala 2.8 `implicit` conversions between Java and Scala collections. If you're still working on a Scala version that's earlier than 2.8, you can use the `jcl` conversion APIs like this:

```scala
def names =
  (new BufferWrapper[String] {
    def underlying = value.getNames
  }).toList ::: List(value.getFirstName)
```

Scala 101

In the method `belongsTo`, we use a predicate as:

```
>> (names exists(_ == name))
```

This predicate is a succinct way to express the following in Scala:

```
>> (names.exists(n => n == name))
```

1 In Scala, the dot (.) is optional when you invoke methods on a receiver.
2 The underscore (_) that we use is shorthand for anything substitutable in Scala. In listing 3.5, _ is the placeholder for supplying the parameter to the higher-order function that `exists` accepts.
3 The Scala type inferencer does an inferencing of the parameter type of the function that `exists` takes.
4 In Scala, operators are methods. We can define << as the method that adds the `name` to the order object. Using symbolic operators like << might be visually appealing to some, but as a cautionary note, this is a matter of personal choice and can lead to unreadable code if you use it too much.

In listing 3.5, we define a domain API `belongsTo` ❷ using our new Scala collection and higher-order functions. Note the succinctness of implementation that Scala offers. Finally, we define an operator-like syntax using << to make our DSL more expressive and concise at ❸.

With the new Scala APIs wrapping our original Java implementation, the client can express his domain intents more succinctly, as we'll see shortly. Being expressive and concise is one of the major benefits of DSL-driven development. This example clearly demonstrates this power of DSL.

USING SCALA IMPLICITS

Before we talk more about the client, we need to take care of one other thing that I promised earlier. You need to make `Account` interoperable with `AccountDSL`, so that all the smartness you implement on top of `AccountDSL` can be applied to `Account` instances as well. Scala offers *implicits* that you can use to make any feature that's already available on `AccountDSL` work on instances of the `Account` class too. All you have to do is ensure that an implicit definition of the conversion is available in the lexical scope of execution:

```
implicit def enrichAccount(acc: Account): AccountDSL =
    new AccountDSL(acc)
```

Now that you have transparent conversion from `Account` to `AccountDSL`, you can use the new DSL APIs on `Account` instances too. Let's create some instances of our Java class `Account`:

```
val acc1 = new Account("acc-1", "David P.")
val acc2 = new Account("acc-2", "John S.")
val acc3 = new Account("acc-3", "Fried T.")
```

Implicits in Scala

In our definition of the `enrichAccount` method, there's an `implicit` modifier in front of the method definition `enrichAccount`. In Scala, the `implicit` modifier for a method is used to define an automatic conversion from one type to another. In this case, the method `enrichAccount` converts an `Account` to an instance of `AccountDSL`. Instead of using

```scala
scala> enrichAccount(acc1) belongsTo("David P."),
```

you can directly use an instance of `Account` to invoke methods of `AccountDSL`:

```scala
scala> acc1 belongsTo("David P.")
```

It's like all methods of `AccountDSL` have been injected into the class `Account`. Sound familiar? It's similar to what we do with Ruby monkey patching that lets you split open any class and extend it with additional methods.

But there's a difference. In Scala, implicits are *lexically scoped*. The automatic conversion between `Account` and `AccountDSL` is available only in the lexical scope of the method `enrichAccount`. Ruby *open classes* that allow modifications of existing classes on a global scope are significantly different. For some more insights on the virtues of Scala implicits, see [3] in section 3.7.

Now add a few more account holder names to acc1 using the new operator <<:

```scala
acc1 << "Mary R." << "Shawn P." << "John S."
```

Note how concise yet expressive the previous snippet looks as compared to what we would have done with our original Java APIs:

```java
acc1.addName("Mary R.").addName("Shawn P.").addName("John S.");
```

Let's form a collection of accounts and print the first names (firstName) of those accounts that include John S. as one of the owners:

```scala
val accounts = List(acc1, acc2, acc3)
accounts filter(_ belongsTo "John S.") map(_ getFirstName) foreach(println)
```

Expressive indeed! In fact, the code is much more expressive than what you would get with the original Java APIs. The reason for the difference is that the richness of Scala as a language helps you craft rich semantics in a reduced surface area of the API. In the previous snippet, we use combinators like filter, map, and foreach that operate on higher-order functions. These combinators make the code much more concise than what you would get with an imperative Java syntax. Are you having fun? Let's party on!

Get the list of accounts belonging to John S. and compute the sum of accrued-Interest for all accounts for which the accumulated interest is greater than a pre-defined threshold:

```scala
accounts.filter(_ belongsTo "John S.")
  .map(_.calculate(new CalculatorImpl))
```

```
.filter(_ > threshold)
.foldLeft(0.0)(_ + _)
```

This snippet contains applications of the Scala idiom that I explained in an earlier sidebar. The _ is a placeholder for the type-inferenced argument that the predicate in filter takes as input. This snippet expresses the domain problem with more clarity than what you would get out of a language that has more verbose syntax like Java. As I discussed in chapter 1, it's all thanks to the richness in abstraction design that a more powerful language like Scala offers, by reducing the *accidental complexity* of your code.

Note the CalculatorImpl object that calculate() takes as input. We defined Calculator as an interface in Java with CalculatorImpl as its implementation:

```
public interface Calculator {
    double calculate(Account account);
}

public class CalculatorImpl implements Calculator {

    @Override
    public double calculate(Account account) {
        //.. implementation
    }
}
```

Most of the time, you'll have the same implementation of the Calculator interface being passed into the Account#calculate() method. One way to avoid this repetition is to use DI to inject the implementation dynamically during runtime. Scala offers a better alternative: you can make this parameter implicit in all calls of calculate.

```
class AccountDSL(value: Account) {

//.. as above

  def calculateInterest(
    implicit calc: Calculator): Double = {
    value.calculate(calc)
  }
}
```

❶ Implicit Calculator instance

You define an implicit argument to the method calculateInterest and have the implicit default set up in the scope of execution of the DSL ❶. Now you have an implicit default value for the implementation of Calculator; you don't need to pass Calculator repeatedly to invocations of calculateInterest. Look at the final version of the calculation of accrued interest for all accounts that belong to John S:

```
implicit val calc = new CalculatorImpl

accounts.filter(_ belongsTo "John S.")
  .map(_.calculateInterest)
  .filter(_> threshold)
  .foldLeft(0.0)(_ + _)
```

With support for features like closures and higher-order functions, Scala offers you the power to define control abstractions that look like syntax that's built into the language. Using Java objects as underlying implementations, you can design powerful control constructs that make your DSL succinct and expressive.

BENEFITS TO USERS

As we discussed in chapter 1, the point is not that a nonprogramming domain expert will be able to program in any DSL that you design. It's the explicit communicability of the API that matters for a well-designed DSL. In the previous snippet, you'll notice functional combinators like `map`, `filter`, and `foldLeft` that don't qualify as very meaningful to the domain person. But the domain person will be able to figure out the following hotspots easily from that snippet:

- Filter the account belonging to John S
- `calculateInterest` on it
- Filter only those that are > the threshold value
- Add up the interest values

When you offer all these hotspots in a localized surface area of the code base, it becomes easier for the domain expert to comprehend and verify the business logic. With an imperative approach, the same logic would have been spread across a larger code segment, making it much more difficult for someone who doesn't know programming.

Let's define a control abstraction using our `Account` Java object and the `Account-DSL` that we implemented in listing 3.5:

```
object AccountDSL {
  def withAccount(trade: Trade)(operation: Account => Unit) = {
    val account = trade.account
    //.. initialization
      try {
        operation(account)
      } finally {
        //.. clean up
      }
  }
}
```

The underlying abstractions used in this snippet, `Account` and `Trade`, are Java classes that might have been enriched using Scala wrappers. Now it's the turn of your DSL users to use such abstractions to perform useful domain operations. The following DSL code fragment is possible using the control abstraction `withAccount` and a wrapper to integrate Scala and Java. It's so much more expressive and closer to the domain syntax than what would have been possible with an only-Java paradigm.

```
withAccount(trade) {
  account => {
    settle(
      trade using
        account.getClient
              .getStandingRules
```

```
            .filter(_.account == account)
            .first)
    andThen journalize
  }
}
```

This sequence of API invocation does exactly what you see in figure 3.7.

withAccount does all this in only a few lines of clear domain-specific code. Show this snippet to your domain expert. I'm sure he'll be able to explain to you what it does. I did the same thing with one of the Bob's on our project team. (Remember Bob? He's our friendly domain expert from Trampoline Securities who joined us in section 1.4.) Can you imagine what happened? Bob looked over the code and here's the conversation that followed:

- *Bob:* You're picking up the first of the selected standing rules after filtering, right?
- *Me:* Yeah!
- *Bob:* But sometimes there's going to be more than one match for the same account.
- *Me:* Then how do you decide which rule to pick up?
- *Bob:* When that happens, every rule has a priority tagged onto it. You need to pick up the one with the highest priority.
- *Me:* Great!

The next time your manager talks about a big up-front investment for DSL implementation, tell him about what you've learned. It's a myth that every integration effort using a DSL requires a huge outlay of money. The wrapper technique we discussed in this section is a real-life testimony to this. In fact, this technique builds on your current investment in the Java domain model, and you get the added benefit of code that's smarter and more useful to the domain experts.

You can use the DSL wrapper technique whenever you use Scala as the DSL implementation language on top of Java. You probably noticed you can make your Java objects smarter using the power of Scala type system. The implicits feature is the secret sauce that lets you do it. In the next section, we'll look at how to use some

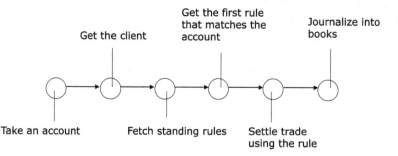

Figure 3.7 The flow as depicted in the preceding code snippet takes an account and describes the sequence until the end of the transaction.

language-specific integration features to implement DSLs on top of Java. We'll again take Groovy as an example and revisit the DSL that we discussed in section 3.2.1.

3.2.3 *Language-specific integration features*

Let's revisit the original order-processing DSL that you integrated with your core Java application in section 3.2.1. Moving away from the `ScriptEngine` approach, we'll use a technique that loads Groovy classes dynamically in your Java application. Loading the classes dynamically ensures better manageability of your Groovy objects, even within the core Java application.

 To get more Groovy information about metaprogramming, closures, and delegates, check out [2] in section 3.7.

COMMUNICATING BETWEEN JAVA CODE AND GROOVY DSL

Suppose that in your trading application you've used Java 6 `ScriptEngine` to integrate your order-processing DSL with the Java application. Things were running fine until one day the client came back with a new requirement: additional processing needs to be done on the collection of orders that the script returns to your Java application. Specifically, he needs to compute the total valuation of all orders that have been placed so far, and he needs custom displays of order attributes for the customer.

Up to this point, you've been loading the DSL implementation (`Client-Order.groovy`) and the user-defined script (`order.dsl`) as a single Groovy script that's executed in the sandbox of the `ScriptEngine`. The Groovy DSL is completely opaque to the Java code; the script is loaded using a different classloader than your Java classes, which makes them invisible in your main application. You need to buy some time from your client to try to implement alternate ways to integrate the DSL that make Groovy classes more visible to your Java application.

BETTER INTEGRATION WITH GROOVY CLASSLOADER

In this section, we're going to treat Groovy classes as reusable abstractions in the Java application and use `GroovyClassLoader` to load only the order-processing script that your user writes. The following listing shows the changes you need to make to your DSL to make things more Groovy.

> **Listing 3.6   RunScript.java: DSL integration using `GroovyClassLoader`**

```
public class RunScript {
    public static void main(String[] args)
            throws CompilationFailedException, IOException,
                InstantiationException, IllegalAccessException {

        final ClientOrder clientOrder =
            new ClientOrder();                           ❶ Set up the
                                                            metaclass
        clientOrder.run();                               ❷ Load the
                                                            Groovy class
        final Closure dsl =
            (Closure)((Script) new GroovyClassLoader().parseClass(
                new File("order.dsl")).newInstance()).run();
```

```
        dsl.setDelegate(clientOrder);
        final Object result = dsl.call();

        List<Order> r = (List<Order>) result;
        int val = 0;
        for(Order x : r) {
            val += (Integer)(x.getValue());
        }
        System.out.println(val);
    }
}
```

Set up delegate ❸ for the closure

Execute ❹ DSL

Process result ❺ collection

Let's recap how this listing makes DSL integration more meaningful in Groovy. We've separated the abstraction ClientOrder.groovy and precompiled it to make the Order class available to the Java application. In the Java class, we execute an instance of ClientOrder to set up the metaclass ❶. The DSL script order.dsl returns a Closure that contains the DSL code ❷. Next, we set up ClientOrder as the delegate of the Closure to resolve the symbols that the script uses ❸. Then, we call the DSL script to return a list of Order objects ❹. Finally, we can find out the total order valuation by iterating over individual orders ❺.

As soon as we come out of the execution of the DSL script, we get back a list of Order objects that we can use for other business processing. We couldn't have done this with the code in listing 3.3, where we used a Java 6 scripting API to integrate our DSL with the Java application. Now your client is happy, and you've learned a new way to integrate your Groovy DSL into your Java application.

THE FINAL RESULT

Here's the DSL script order.dsl, changed to return a Closure to the Java application.

Listing 3.7   order.dsl: the DSL script now returns a Closure

```
{->
orders = []
ord1 =
newOrder.to.buy(100.shares.of('IBM')) {
  limitPrice    300
  allOrNone     true
  valueAs       {qty, unitPrice -> qty * unitPrice - 500}
}
orders << ord1

ord2 =
newOrder.to.buy(150.shares.of('GOOG')) {
  limitPrice    300
  allOrNone     true
  valueAs       {qty, unitPrice -> qty * unitPrice - 500}
}
orders << ord2

ord3 =
newOrder.to.buy(200.shares.of('MSOFT')) {
  limitPrice    300
```

```
    allOrNone     true
    valueAs       {qty, unitPrice -> qty * unitPrice - 500}
}
orders << ord3

println "Orders ..."
orders.each { println it }
}
```

This Groovy DSL is better than the earlier version of the order-processing DSL that you saw in chapter 2. It also offers better Java integration than what you saw with the `ScriptEngine`-based approach in section 3.2.1.

From a language-specific integration feature, let's move on to a framework-based integration approach that you can use to integrate internal DSLs with a Java application. Spring offers a suitable platform; the next section shows how to use it.

3.2.4 *Spring-based integration*

We've come to the final integration technique that I summarized in table 3.2. It's one level up in terms of abstraction because it offers integration through a framework, as opposed to through a language, as discussed earlier. How often have you fantasized about how helpful it would be if some of the business rules that you've implemented in Java could have been changed dynamically without having to restart your application?

SPRING'S DYNAMIC LANGUAGE SUPPORT
Since version 2.0, Spring has supported bean implementation using expressive, dynamic languages like Ruby and Groovy. (For more information about Spring, go to http://www.springframework.org.) These beans are also *refreshable*. A refreshable bean is one that allows itself to reload dynamically when its underlying implementation changes. Let's consider an example from our financial brokerage domain where an implementation of a `TradingService` needs to look up rules for computing the accrued interest on coupon bonds.

```
public class TradingServiceImpl implements TradingService {
    private AccruedInterestCalculationRule accIntRule;          ◁─┐   Calculation
                                                                  │   rule injected
    @Override                                                   ❶   by Spring
    public void doTrade(Trade trade) {
        // .. implementation
    }
}
```

In this snippet, the business rules for accrued interest calculation are injected at runtime through DI using Spring ❶. Using the dynamic language support that Spring offers, you can implement these rules using expressive languages like JRuby or Groovy or Jython. This is an area where a small, rich DSL is a great fit. The benefits are twofold:

- The code is more expressive because the languages themselves are more rich.
- You can auto-reload the runtime instance of the bean when the underlying implementation changes.

In the current example, we can use a Java interface for the rule contract:

```
public interface AccruedInterestCalculationRule {
    BigDecimal calculate(Trade trade);
}
```

And the backing implementation of the rule can be done using a DSL written in Ruby:

```
require 'java'

class RubyAccruedInterestCalculationRule {
  def calculate(trade)
    //.. implementation
  end
end

RubyAccruedInterestCalculationRule.new
```

Now there's just one thing left to do.

WIRING UP THE IMPLEMENTATION

You can then wire up the whole implementation using the following XML configuration snippet in Spring. Now, when you ask for an instance of AccruedInterestCalculationRule from within your Java program, you get an instance that is implemented using the Ruby DSL.

```
<lang:jruby
  id="accIntCalcRule"
  refresh-check-delay="5000"
  script-interfaces=
    "org.springframework.scripting.AccruedInterestCalculationRule "
  script-source="classpath:RubyAccruedInterestCalculationRule.rb">
</lang:jruby>
```

Congratulations! Using Spring, you've successfully integrated a Ruby DSL into your Java application. This model of DSL integration is nonintrusive and keeps the DSL component decoupled from the context where it is used. If you are using Spring as the DI framework in your application, consider this integration pattern as an option for dynamically reloading business-rule DSLs.

Now that you've seen the homogeneous integration patterns related to internal DSLs, let's look at patterns for integrating external DSLs. External DSLs can be any form. You can implement them using a custom language infrastructure. In the next section, we'll revisit all the external DSL implementation patterns we discussed in section 2.3.2 and see how each publishes explicit integration points for your core application. Note that external DSLs are custom-made for specific applications only; our discussion on integration patterns for external DSLs will be limited to a few common techniques that are currently being used.

3.3 *External DSL integration patterns*

How do you integrate XML with your application? Did you just scream *"Using the XML parser!"* If you did, you are correct! Because XML isn't part of the host language you're using to implement the application, you need separate machinery to parse and process

XML. XML is so commonly used that you get a slew of tools like XPath, XQuery, and a huge number of XML parsers bundled with almost every enterprise solution. Integrating XML with your application is a no-brainer. Unfortunately, the external DSLs that you'll design for your applications aren't lucky enough to inherit such a repertoire of tools. Integrating your external DSL with your application is likely to rely on specific techniques that can't be generalized as a pattern.

Judging from what I said in the last paragraph, you must be thinking that integrating external DSLs is a nightmare in the application development lifecycle. It all depends on how complex the DSL is and the technique that you're using to develop it. If you use standard tools like ANTLR or YACC to develop parsers for your external DSL, integration is pretty straightforward; read section 2.3.2 again. For every external DSL pattern that we discussed in that section, you can see that the integration points are quite obvious after you've designed the DSL.

Let's look at the patterns of external DSL that we discussed in section 2.3.2 again and try to figure out the integration points that each of them publish. Table 3.3 lists a summary of thoughts for how you can integrate external DSLs with your core application.

Table 3.3 Integration points published by external DSLs

External DSL pattern	Published integration point
Context-driven string manipulation	The string is converted to the host language through a tokenization process, using techniques like regular expression matching and dynamic code evaluation. The resultant code snippet is the integration point with the application.
Transforming XML to a consumable resource	XML parsers are the most natural form of integration point. After parsing, XML is converted to data structures of the host language that can be directly used by the application.
Nontextual representation	The nontextual representation is converted to an AST. You can use the AST as the basis for generating multiple forms of concrete syntax trees. You can target one of the concrete syntax trees to generate the host language of the application, which then becomes the integration point.
Mixing DSL with embedded foreign code	The DSL processing engine transforms the DSL into appropriate data structures in the language of the embedded code and plugs in the embedded code snippets as callbacks. The result is a set of data structures in the embedded code that can be directly used in the core application, using the same language.
DSL design-based on parser combinators	Parser combinators are implemented as a library in languages like Scala. The rules that you write to parse the external DSL are combinators in the host language. Using embedded snippets of the host language, you build up data structures that get populated by the rules. When the rules reduce to the topmost node of the tree, you have the complete semantic model of the DSL.

Why didn't I go into the details of integration patterns for external DSLs like I did for internal DSLs? Internal DSL integration takes place through a host language, but external DSLs often require a more elaborate stack that depends on the specific application domain. Designing a language-processing infrastructure is a more open-ended problem than designing APIs in a host language. It's difficult to have a generic discussion of external DSL integration patterns without delving into the specific details of what it needs to achieve and the infrastructure involved. We'll take up these techniques in detail with examples in chapters 7 and 8.

> In chapter 7, we'll discuss external DSL design using ANTLR, a commonly used parser generator. We'll also look at tools that help you generate an external DSL through a workbench. For both ANTLR and the DSL Workbench, we'll also discuss how to integrate the external DSL with your core application.
>
> Chapter 8 has a detailed discussion about external DSL design using Scala parser combinators.

We've just covered all the integration patterns for internal and external DSLs. Now you can handle most of the problems you'll encounter when you're integrating your DSL with your core application. Throughout this discussion, I've assumed that your core application is developed in Java and that you're trying to integrate DSLs that were designed in more expressive languages with that application. This use case is the most common one that you'll encounter in real-world programming, so it is imperative that you have a solid understanding of the integration issues related to the problem.

Figure 3.1 illustrates the most important issue related to DSL-driven application development: integrating the DSL with the core application. This issue is sometimes considered late in the development cycle, as an afterthought, rather than being addressed up front. Now we'll look at yet another concern that's often ignored by programmers at the beginning of the DSL development lifecycle. Deciding on a strategy for handling errors and exceptions is something that needs to be high on your priority list, particularly if your DSL has a fairly large user base.

3.4   *Handling errors and exceptions*

It's superimportant to be as friendly to your user with error reporting as you are with the expressiveness of your syntax. Because a DSL is a language of limited applicability, your error messages should also speak the language of the domain. Error and exception reporting in a DSL-based environment needs to be disciplined so you never mislead the user, leaving them in a state of confusion. You need to clearly articulate the exact condition that the system is in. This concept is called domain-driven exception reporting, which we'll discuss in section 3.4.1. We'll also talk about the two main types of error states that your DSL user will have to face. Together, these comprise the three-pronged view of error and exception handling strategies that you, as a DSL designer, need to consider. This view is shown in figure 3.8.

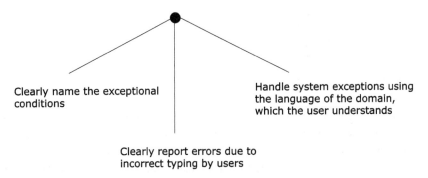

Clearly name the exceptional
conditions

Handle system exceptions using
the language of the domain,
which the user understands

Clearly report errors due to
incorrect typing by users

Figure 3.8   The three-pronged strategy for dealing with errors and exceptional states in a DSL

Depending on the type of DSL (internal or external) you have and the implementation language you're using, the ways in which the error conditions manifest themselves will vary. Table 3.4 contains an overview of the error and exception issues and your responsibilities as a DSL designer.

Table 3.4   What you need to know about errors and exceptions in DSLs

Issue	How to handle as a DSL designer
You need to clearly state the exceptional conditions within a DSL.	An exceptional state is also a domain abstraction. Always use the domain language to express any exception that might occur during processing. See section 3.4.1.
You need to handle errors that might result when the user types method names, object names, and other things incorrectly.	The exact strategy depends on the implementation language you're using. See section 3.4.2.
You need to handle exceptions that might arise when the system enters an invalid business state. What will happen, for example, when someone tries to transfer funds between accounts and the communication line to the bank is down?	When you report such an exception, be sure to supply all relevant details to the user in the language they understand. See section 3.4.3.

Let's look at each of these issues in detail.

3.4.1   *Naming an exception*

When you name an exceptional condition in the DSL, use the language that the domain uses to describe the situation. The exception might not be an infrastructure fault—it can also be an alternate path of a business use case. The idea is to present such situations in the language of the domain. Here's an example from a system that settles trades between counterparty accounts:

```
val fromBalance = fromAccount.getSecurityBalance
if (fromBalance <= tradeQuantity)
    throw new SettlementFailedException(
        " Insufficient security balance in " +
        "account " + counterpartyAccount.getName +
        " for settlement completion")
settle(..)
```

The system has reached an exceptional state; the settlement will fail when the seller doesn't have a sufficient security balance in his account. This state of affairs is expressed by the exception name `SettlementFailedException`, the common verbiage that describes the situation in a real-world settlement system. When the user gets this exception, he's going to know exactly what has happened. He is also going to see the accompanying message, which you've written, that clearly states the details of why it failed.

3.4.2   *Handling incorrect typing errors*

No matter how expressive your DSL, your user is going to make mistakes. It's human nature. When you're programming in a statically typed language like Java or Scala, the compiler promptly notifies you of such mistakes as soon as you make them. Anytime you go against the rules of the type system of the language you're using, the compiler acts as the policeman for you, as in figure 3.9.

If the user is sufficiently knowledgeable in the host language that implements the DSL, error messages reported by the compiler can be helpful. Modern

Figure 3.9   The compiler is the policeman!

IDEs that provide code assist and autocompletion facilities can also be helpful with such typing errors. But what can you do when that help is not available?

WHEN THE TYPE SYSTEM CAN'T HELP YOU

A dynamically typed language like Ruby or Groovy doesn't come with compiler help for type errors. In these languages, most such mistakes are manifested as runtime errors after they're processed through the usual method dispatch pipeline that the language implements. Without compile-time error checking, well-designed DSLs in dynamic languages take advantage of features like `methodMissing` to install user-friendly error handlers. A DSL user can get information from these handlers that help them rectify the error.

`methodMissing` is a useful technique when you're designing DSLs in a dynamic language. In the following example in Ruby I've added just enough context information to make the runtime exception more meaningful to the user:

```
class Trade
  //..
  def method_missing(method, *args, &block)
    raise NoMethodError, <<ERRORINFO
method: #{method}
args: #{args.inspect}
on: #{self.to_yaml}
ERRORINFO
  end
  //..
end
```

If the user supplies a method name that's not implemented on a trade object, Ruby raises a NoMethodError by default. The snippet contains an implementation of method_missing that provides a custom error handler, adding more context information for the user. (For an example of how to use methodMissing to synthesize new methods in Groovy, see section 2.2.2.)

THE ROLE OF PARSERS

For an external DSL, when you use parsers to parse the input script, ensure that you report the exact line number and the position in the input string where the error occurred. Such user-friendly error reporting depends a lot on what you're using to generate the parser of your DSL syntax. Top-down parsers generated by ANTLR offer better support for error reporting than the bottom-up ones generated by YACC. We'll discuss more of these in chapter 7 when we talk about designing external DSLs using parser generators.

OK. Now you know how to deal with the inevitable typos or erroneous input that a user is bound to try to sneak in. What can you do about business conditions that make some actions impossible?

3.4.3 *Handling exceptional business conditions*

Your DSL should be able to report the precise exceptional state, using domain-driven exception reporting, which we discussed earlier in section 3.4.1. More importantly, the DSL should have handlers in place that take care of all domain exceptions raised while the DSL is running. This includes all clean-up actions, resource releases, and transaction rollbacks.

Proper exception handling and reporting is also related to the strategy you choose for integrating your DSL script with the core application. Integration strategies that rely on the ScriptEngine-based approach like the one we saw in section 3.2.1 are usually poor at exception reporting. Consider the following example from the section where we discussed embedding Groovy scripts within a Java application:

```
ScriptEngineManager factory = new ScriptEngineManager();
ScriptEngine engine = factory.getEngineByName("groovy");

try {
  List<?> orders = (List<?>)
  engine.eval(new InputStreamReader(
```

```
     new BufferedInputStream(
       new SequenceInputStream(
         new FileInputStream("ClientOrder.groovy"),
         new FileInputStream("order.dsl")))));
} catch (javax.script.ScriptException screx) {                    ❶ Handle
  // handle                                                          exception
}
```

In this example, we didn't handle the exception explicitly within the Groovy method. We assumed that it would be handled by the caller function ❶. The class `javax.script.ScriptException` has methods like `getFileName()` and `getLineNumber()` that'll help you locate exactly where the exception occurred. The important point here is to be careful about handling exceptions that originate from inside your DSL and provide enough context information to the user. For code running in the sandbox of the `ScriptEngine`, the right context for handling the exception is not always intuitive. This is yet another reason why you should opt for better language-specific ways to integrate your DSL, and fall back on the scripting option only if necessary

DSLs are designed for readability and expressiveness in the domain. Always try to keep the user in mind when designing DSLs. At the same time, be aware of the performance considerations that a DSL can impose on your design. What's the trade-off?

3.5   *Managing performance*

Performance is an important criterion, but, believe it or not, I don't think it's the most important one. You can improve the performance of an underperforming application by scaling up or scaling out resources. But when you've implemented a spaghetti system without any concern for expressivity or maintainability, you're going to be stuck with it for the rest of its life.

Even so, you need to consider performance factors when you design an application. Let's face it—a properly designed DSL usually isn't a hindrance to the optimal performance of your application. Some of the dynamic languages like Groovy or Ruby are slower compared to Java. But as an application developer or architect, you need to make a trade-off between the raw speed that the application offers and the aspects of making your code base maintainable, expressive, and adaptive to future changes.

Not all parts of your application need to be blazing fast. Portions of it require more ease of maintenance than speed. Consider the configuration parameters of your application. They need to be processed once, possibly when the application starts up. It's more important for some of the configuration parameters to be externalized and presented to the user in a form that's more readable than pure code, than for your application to start super quickly. The advantages of added expressiveness far outweigh the problems that might result from an increase in the startup time of the application.

Lots of initiatives are underway to make dynamic languages perform better on the JVM. It makes more sense to invest in using these languages to design expressive DSLs.

If you have an expressive code base today, tomorrow you'll automatically get the benefits of improved performance when Groovy and Ruby language runtimes become more performant on the JVM.

Why do you think people use languages like Groovy and Ruby for designing a DSL, knowing full well that their code base will be less performant than equivalent Java code? It's because these languages are maintainable, readable, and adaptive to changes. It's much easier to grow your DSL when you have an inherently expressive host language underneath. With respect to performance, these factors are equally as important as the raw speed of execution. All of these together determine the evolution path and lifeline of the language that you design for the domain.

Statically typed languages like Scala are almost as performant as native Java. The wrapper model of DSL integration that you saw in section 3.2.2 is unlikely to cause any difference in performance compared to your native Java application.

Script engines that operate in a sandbox environment are somewhat slower, but then again, you don't use scripts for performance-intensive tasks anyway. Scripting DSLs are mostly used for processing lightweight domain logic that's usually exposed to end users and domain experts. Embedded DSLs or internal DSLs are mainly implemented as libraries in the host language and don't incur any performance penalty whatsoever. External DSLs are free standing and implement their own language machinery. In most pragmatic applications, you don't need to design external DSLs that have the complexity of a full-blown high-level language. In the real world, tools like parser generators (YACC, ANTLR) and parser combinators (as in Scala and Haskell) can be used effectively to easily build the necessary language infrastructure.

Finally, remember the golden rule for performance tuning: benchmark extensively before going for optimization.

3.6   *Summary*

In this chapter, we discussed all aspects of DSL-driven application development. You learned how to select the right strategy for integrating your DSL with the core application. The patterns of integration we discussed have given you a good idea about when

---

Key takeaways & best practices

- *DSLs never stand alone.* They have to be integrated with your core application. Let this be your golden rule when you're planning a DSL design, beginning at day one.
- *When you design an internal DSL, choose the language that has the best integration capabilities with the core language of your application.*
- *External DSLs often need additional infrastructure, like parser generators.* Keep this in mind when you're planning the implementation phase so that you have appropriate development resources on your team.
- *Follow established best practices while you integrate your DSL with your core application.*

to use the wrapper-based integration approach over the one based on `ScriptEngine`. The exact strategy depends a lot on the implementation language that you're using. We also talked about how to handle errors and exceptions and how to report them to users in a language that's natural to the domain you're modeling. Finally, we concluded the chapter with a discussion about the trade-offs you might have to make between the performance and manageability of your DSL code.

With this chapter, we come to the end of the Getting Started section of the book. In the following chapters, we'll dive deep into all the implementation aspects of DSLs. We'll cover many of the JVM languages, design and implement DSL snippets using each of them, and then discuss the virtues and gotchas of every approach that they offer. It's going to be a fascinating ride. Be prepared, stay calm, and buckle up for the trip ahead.

3.7   *References*

1 Odersky, Martin, Lex Spoon, and Bill Venners. 2008. *Programming in Scala.* Artima.

2 König, Dierk, Paul King, Guillaume Laforge, and Jon Skeet, 2009. *Groovy in Action,* Second Edition. Manning Early Access Program Edition. Manning Publications.

3 Ghosh, Debasish. Why I like Scala's Lexically Scoped Open Classes. *Ruminations of a Programmer.* http://debasishg.blogspot.com/2008/02/why-i-like-scalas-lexically-scoped-open.html.

Part 2

Implementing DSLs

On the surface, DSL syntax appears to be aligned to the dialect that the domain user speaks in his daily life. Part 1 focused mainly on the importance of making your software speak the language of the domain. But even when you've accomplished this, behind the syntax of the DSL is an underlying semantic model that you need to develop, following principles of well-designed abstractions. Unless you have a semantic model that is extensible, malleable, and composable, it'll be difficult to have an expressive syntax on top.

Part 2 (chapters 4 through 8) discusses all the idioms and best practices that make a good semantic model.

When you design a DSL, it is important to use the most appropriate language that offers the level of abstraction that you need to program in. In this part of *DSLs in Action* I discuss DSL implementation using Groovy, Ruby, Scala, and Clojure. Each of these languages has its own strengths and weaknesses and each offers features that you can use to model the components of your DSL. As a developer seeking to use DSL-based development, you need to be aware of the idioms that these languages offer and the ways they integrate with your main application stack.

Part 2 also covers external DSL development using modern frameworks like ANTLR and Xtext (from Eclipse). ANTLR is a parser generator that helps you write custom parsers for the DSL that you're developing. Xtext is an environment that gives you a full stack for developing and managing external DSLs.

I cap off part 2 with a discussion of parser combinators, the beautiful functional abstractions for developing external DSLs.

Internal DSL
implementation patterns

This chapter covers

- Embedded DSL patterns with metaprogramming
- Embedded DSL patterns with typed abstractions
- Generative DSL patterns with runtime metaprogramming
- Generative DSL patterns with compile-time metaprogramming

In part 1, you were inducted into the DSL-driven development paradigm. You saw DSLs in all their glory and the issues that you need to address to use DSLs in a real-world application. This chapter marks the beginning of the discussion about the implementation-level issues of DSLs.

Every architect has their own toolbox that contains tools for designing beautiful artifacts. In this chapter, you'll build your own toolbox to hold architectural patterns that you can use to implement DSLs. Figure 4.1 depicts the broad topics that I plan to cover.

As a DSL designer, you need to be aware of the idioms and best practices in DSL implementation. We'll start with how to build a collection of patterns that you can

Why you need a toolbox
of implementation patterns
for DSLs

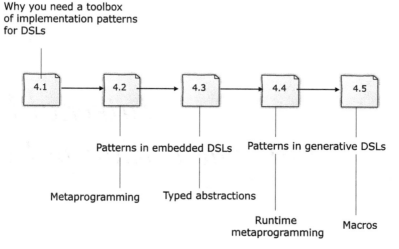

Figure 4.1   Roadmap of the chapter

use in real-life application development. Internal DSLs are most often embedded in a host language. Many of these languages support a meta-object protocol that you can use to implement dynamic behaviors onto your DSL. Most of these languages are dynamically typed, like Ruby and Groovy; we'll discuss several patterns that use the metaprogramming power of these languages in section 4.2. Statically typed languages offer abstraction capabilities to model your DSL with embedded types, which we'll look at in section 4.3 in the context of using Scala as the implementation language. In sections 4.4 and 4.5, we'll look at code-generation capabilities of languages you can use to implement concise internal DSLs. These are called generative DSLs because they have a concise syntax on the surface, but implement domain behaviors by generating code either during compile time or runtime. At the end of the chapter, you'll feel good knowing that now you have a bag full of tricks, patterns, and best practices that you can use to model real-life problem domains.

4.1   *Filling your DSL toolbox*

A master craftsman always has a packed toolbox. He starts filling up his toolbox with an initial seed that he inherited from his master, then enriches it over the years of practicing his art. We're talking about DSLs in this book, specifically about filling up your own toolbox for implementing internal DSLs.

Let's start with the common patterns of internal DSLs we discussed in section 2.3.1. These are patterns of implementation that you can apply in various scenarios when you're doing DSL-based design. The discussion in section 2.3.1 also contained code snippets that illustrated how the patterns manifest themselves in certain commonly used languages. In this chapter, we'll build on that discussion, provide examples from our problem domain of financial brokerage systems, and map the examples onto implementations that realize their solution domains. As you read, make sure you collect all the things you need to enrich your toolbox. Sometimes I'll show you multiple implementation techniques for the same pattern, often in different languages, and highlight the trade-offs that each involves.

Before we move on to the details, look at figure 4.2, which picks up a few of the patterns that we identified in chapter 2 and annotates each of them with example artifacts that we'll discuss in this chapter. To clarify one of the annotations in the figure: look at the box "Reflective metaprogramming", which is a pattern for embedded DSL. In the examples that I'll discuss in this chapter, you'll see how to use this pattern to implement *implicit context* in Ruby and Groovy and *dynamic decorators* in Ruby. Both of these implementation artifacts make DSLs that help users express the intent clearly without any unnecessary complexity.

As figure 4.2 indicates, internal DSLs fall into two categories:

- *Embedded*—The DSL is inside the host language, which implies that you, the programmer, write the entire DSL explicitly
- *Generative*—Part of the DSL code (mostly repetitive stuff) is generated by the compile-time or runtime machinery of the language

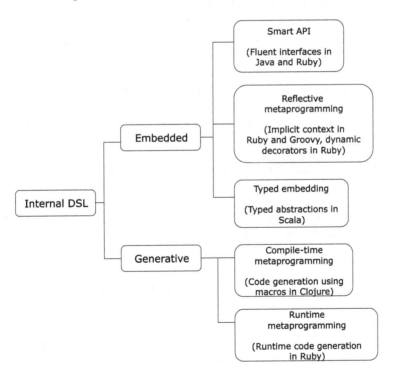

Figure 4.2 Internal DSL implementation patterns, along with example artifacts. I'll discuss each of these artifacts in this chapter, and provide sample implementations in the languages specified in the figure.

In any real-world application, patterns don't occur in isolation. Patterns manifest themselves in the form of cooperating forces and solutions in every use case that you'll be working with. The effects that one pattern generates are handled by another pattern; the entire system evolves as a coherent pattern language. In the following sections, I've chosen to follow the style that you'll encounter in your role as a DSL designer. Instead of providing a geometrically structured description of each of the patterns in isolation, I'll take sample DSL fragments from our financial brokerage systems domain and deconstruct each of them to explore these pattern structures. This method will not only give you an idea of how each of the patterns can be implemented in real-life use cases, but you'll also appreciate how these structures can be synergistically stitched together to create a greater whole.

Let's start with the pattern structures that you'll use to implement embedded DSLs.

4.2 *Embedded DSLs: patterns in metaprogramming*

Metaprogramming is writing programs that write programs. OK, that's what you find in textbooks, and more often than not you're misled into thinking that metaprogramming is yet another code generator with an embellished name. Practically speaking, metaprogramming is programming with the meta-objects that the compile-time or the runtime infrastructure of your environment offers. I won't go into the details of what that means; I'm sure you know all about it by now, after having gone through the detailed discussion that we had in section 2.5.

In this section, we'll look through examples in our domain that can be modeled using metaprogramming techniques. In some cases, I'll start with implementations in a language that doesn't offer the power of metaprogramming. Then you'll see how the implementation transforms to a more succinct one when we use a language that lets you program at a higher level of abstraction using metaprogramming.

> **CODE ASSISTANCE**   In all of the following sections that have rich code snippets, I include a sidebar that contains the prerequisites of the language features that you need to know in order to appreciate the implementation details. These sidebars are just the feelers for the language features used in the code listing that follow. Feel free to read the appropriate language cheat-sheet that's in the appendixes for more information about a particular language.

Every subsection that follows contains a theme that manifests itself as an instance of a metaprogramming pattern implementation, all of which are shown in figure 4.2. We'll start with a sample use case, look at the DSL from the user's point of view, and deconstruct it to unravel the implementation structures. It's not that each use case implements only one pattern instance. In fact, all the following themes comprise multiple pattern instances working toward the fulfillment of realizing the solution domain.

4.2.1 *Implicit context and Smart APIs*

Let's begin with a brief refresher from the earlier chapters. Clients register themselves with stock trader firms; these firms trade the clients' holdings for them and keep them safe. For more information about client accounts, refer to the callout *Financial brokerage systems: client account* in section 3.2.2.

With that out of the way, let's talk about designing a DSL that registers client accounts with the trader. You can judge for yourself how applying metaprogramming techniques under the hood can make your APIs expressive without users knowing anything about the implementation.

JUDGING THE EXPRESSIVITY OF A DSL

Look at the following DSL script. This DSL creates client accounts to be registered with the stock broker firm.

ℹ Ruby tidbits you need to know

- *How classes and objects are defined in Ruby.* Ruby is OO and defines a class in the same way that any other OO language does. Even so, Ruby has its own object model that offers functionalities to the users to change, inspect, and extend objects during runtime through metaprogramming.
- *How Ruby uses blocks to implement closures.* A closure is a function and the environment where the function will be evaluated. Ruby uses block syntax to implement closures.
- *Basics of Ruby metaprogramming.* The Ruby object model has lots of artifacts like classes, objects, instance methods, class methods, singleton methods, and so on that allow reflective and generative metaprogramming. You can dig into the Ruby object model at runtime and change behaviors or generate code dynamically.

Listing 4.1 DSL that creates a client account

```
Account.create do                                    ◄┐
    number      "CL-BXT-23765"                          ❶ Create account
    holders     "John Doe", "Phil McCay"
    address     "San Francisco"
    type        "client"
    email       "client@example.com"

end.save.and_then do |a|                             ◄┐
    Registry.register(a)                                ❷ Save account
    Mailer.new
        .to(a.email_address)
        .cc(a.email_address)
        .subject("New Account Creation")
        .body("Client account created for #{a.no}")     ❸ Send mail
        .send                                        ◄┐    after open
end
```

This code listing shows how the client *uses* the DSL. Note how it hides the implementation details and makes the account creation process expressive enough for the client. It not only creates the account, it does other stuff as well. Can you identify what else it does by looking at listing 4.1, without looking at the underlying implementation? If you can figure out all the actions that the code does you have a smart DSL implementation.

You can easily identify the actions that the DSL performs from the code. It creates the account ❶ and saves it (possibly to the database) ❷. Then it, among other things, registers the account and sends a mail to the account holder ❸.

As far as expressivity is concerned, the DSL does a fairly good job of offering intuitive APIs to the user. Show this DSL snippet to a domain expert and they'll also be able to identify the sequence of actions that it does because the DSL honors the vocabulary of the domain. Now let's look at the underlying implementation.

DEFINING THE IMPLICIT CONTEXT

The `Account` object is an abstraction that implements the methods called while an instance is created. This is the plain old Ruby way to define the instance methods of a class. The script is shown in the following listing.

> Listing 4.2 Expressive domain vocabulary in implementation of `Account`

```ruby
class Account
  attr_reader :no, :names, :addr, :type, :email_address

  def number(number)
    @no = number
  end

  def holders(*names)
    @names = names
  end

  def address(addr)
    @addr = addr
  end

  def type(t)
    @type = t
  end

  def email(e)
    @email_address = e
  end

  def to_s()
    "No: " + @no.to_s +
    " / Names: (" + @names.join(',').to_s +
    ") / Address: " + @addr.to_s
  end
end
```

Now let's look beyond the obvious method definitions of the abstraction and gaze into some of the subtle aspects that you can identify as the implementation patterns that we talked about earlier.

With any code snippet, you need to define the context under which that code will run. The context can be an object that you defined earlier or an execution environment that you set up explicitly or declared implicitly. Some languages mandate that the context be explicitly wired with every invocation of the corresponding methods. Consider the following Java code:

```
Account acc = new Account(number);
acc.addHolder(hName1);
acc.addHolder(hName2);
acc.addAddress(addr);
//..
```

All invocations of methods that operate on the `Account` object need to have the context object passed explicitly as the dispatcher. Explicit context specification makes verbose code that doesn't help make DSLs readable and succinct. It's always a plus if a language allows implicit context declaration; it results in terse syntax and a concise surface area for the API. In listing 4.1, we invoke methods like `number`, `holders`, `type`, `email`, and others on an *implicit context* of the `Account` that gets created.

How do you make the context implicit? Here's the relevant code, implemented in Ruby as part of the `Account` class that does exactly that through a clever bit of metaprogramming:

```
class Account
  attr_reader :no, :names, :addr, :type, :email_address

  ## rest as in listing 4.1                              ❶ create takes
                                                              a block
  def self.create(&block)
    account = Account.new
    account.instance_eval(&block)                        ❷ eval block in
    account                                                 Account context
  end
end
```

Look at ❷, where `instance_eval` is a Ruby metaprogramming construct that evaluates the block that's passed to it in the context of the `Account` object on which it's invoked. It's as if the newly constructed `account` were implicitly passed to every invocation of the method that you pass around in the Ruby block ❶. This code is an example of *reflective metaprogramming*. The context of evaluation is determined through reflection during runtime by the Ruby execution environment.

You can perform the same trick in Groovy as well, which is another language with strong metaprogramming capabilities.

The previous Ruby code snippet becomes the code shown in the following listing in Groovy.

ℹ Groovy tidbits you need to know

- How to *create a closure in Groovy* and set up a context for method dispatch.

Listing 4.3   Implicit context set up for method dispatch in Groovy

```groovy
class Account {

  // method definitions

  static create(closure) {
    def account = new Account()
    account.with closure
    account
  }
}

Account.create {
  number      'CL-BXT-23765'
  holders     'John Doe', 'Phil McCay'
  address     'San Francisco'
  type        'client'
  email       'client@example.com'
}
```

Note how the implementations differ, yet we have APIs of similar expressivity in both the languages.

USING SMART APIS TO IMPROVE EXPRESSIVENESS

Readability is an inevitable consequence of expressiveness in a DSL. Implementing *fluent interfaces* is one way to improve readability and make Smart APIs. You can implement method chaining so that the output from one method flows naturally as the input of another. This technique makes your series of API invocations feel more natural, and it's closer to the sequence of actions that you would perform in the problem domain. This makes the APIs smart in the sense that you don't need to include any boilerplate code in their invocation.

Consider the sequence of method calls that causes mail to be sent in ❸ of listing 4.1. The API invocation flows in the same sequence of actions that you would do when you're working with a mail client.

Watch out for fluency issues when you design DSLs on your own. The next listing shows the snippet of code that implements the `Mailer` class that we used in the DSL in listing 4.1.

Listing 4.4   Mailer class with fluent interfaces

```ruby
class Mailer
  attr_reader :mail_to, :mail_cc, :mail_subject, :mail_body

  def to(*to_recipients)
    @mail_to = to_recipients
    self                           ◁─┐  Return self
  end                                ❶  for chaining

  def cc(*cc_recipients)
    @mail_cc = cc_recipients
    self
  end
```

```
  def subject(subj)
    @mail_subject = subj
    self
  end

  def body(b)
    @mail_body = b
    self
  end

  def send
    # actual send
    puts "sending mail to (#{@mail_to.join(",")})"
  end
end
```

The `Mailer` instance is returned to the caller ❶ to be used as the context for the next invocation. The `send` method is the final method of the chain that finishes the entire sequence and sends the email.

In listing 4.1, which shows how to use the account-creation DSL, the three steps involved in creating the account are quite explicit. Let's look at an even more explicit view in figure 4.3, which shows the steps that apply the patterns that give the DSL its shape.

The steps for applying a pattern are: create an instance of the account, save it to the database, and do other actions as part of the follow up. The third step in the sequence has been explicitly modeled as a closure, or a Ruby block. Note that the block takes the

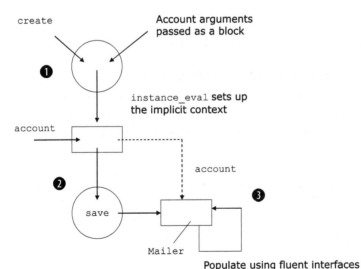

Figure 4.3 The steps of pattern application: ❶ **The account is created through the implicit context that is set up using** `instance_eval`. ❷ **The account is saved.** ❸ **The Mailer is set up using fluent interfaces and gets the account from a block.**

created account instance as an input and uses it to perform the other actions. The instance remains unchanged; this is called a side-effecting action.

Managing side effects is an extremely subtle issue in program design. You need to decouple them to make abstractions pure. Abstractions that are free from side effects make your world a better place. Always shoot for explicit separation of side-effecting actions when you're designing DSLs. In listing 4.1, all the side-effecting code is decoupled in a separate block. Doing this is not specific to internal DSL design; you should this in mind when you're designing any abstractions.

In this section, we discussed two of the implementation patterns that are used extensively in DSL-based design paradigms. The key takeaways from this section are listed in the sidebar.

Key takeaways from this section

Implement Smart APIs with fluent interfaces using method chaining (`Mailer` class in listing 4.4).

Implicit context makes DSLs less verbose and incurs less surface area for the APIs, leading to better expressivity (the create class method in the Ruby snippet and the static create method in the Groovy code in listing 4.3).

Isolate side effects from pure abstractions (the Ruby block in listing 4.1 that registers the account and sends mail to the account holder).

Next we'll look at other implementation structures that use reflective metaprogramming to implement dynamic behaviors in your DSL.

4.2.2 *Reflective metaprogramming with dynamic decorators*

During our explorations of metaprogramming techniques, you saw in section 4.2.1 how you can use them to make your DSL expressive and succinct. In this section, we'll explore yet another aspect of runtime metaprogramming: manipulating class objects dynamically to decorate other objects.

The Decorator design pattern is used to add functionalities to objects dynamically during runtime. (In appendix A, I talk about the role of decorators as a design pattern for enabling composability between abstractions.) In this section, we're going to look at this topic more from an implementation perspective and see how the power of metaprogramming can make more dynamic decorators.

DECORATORS IN JAVA

Let's start with the abstraction for `Trade`, a domain entity that models the most fundamental entity involved in the trading process. For the purpose of this example, we'll consider the contract from the point of view of composing a `Trade` object with decorators that affect its *net value*. For basic information about how a trade's net cash value is computed, take a look at the accompanying sidebar.

Financial brokerage systems: the cash value of a trade

Every trade has a cash value that the counterparty receiving the securities needs to pay to the counterparty delivering the securities. This final value is known as the *net settlement value* (NSV). The NSV has two main components: the gross cash value and the tax and fees. The gross cash value depends on the unit price of the security that was traded, the type of the security, and additional components like the yield price for bonds. The additional tax and fee amounts include the taxes, duties, levies, commissions, and accrued interest involved in the trading process.

The gross cash value calculation depends on the type of the security (equity or fixed income), but is fundamentally a function of the unit price and the quantity traded.

The additional tax and fee amounts vary with the country of trade, the exchange where the trading takes place, and the security that's traded. In Hong Kong, for example, a stamp duty of 0.125% and a transaction levy of 0.007% are payable on equity purchases and sales.

Consider the Java code in the following listing.

Listing 4.5 Trade and its decorators in Java

```java
public class Trade {                                      // <--1 Trade abstraction
    public float value() {                                //   Compute and return
        // ..                                             //  2 the trade value
    }
}

public class TaxFeeDecorator extends Trade {
    private Trade trade;

    public TaxFeeDecorator(Trade trade) {                 //  Decorators  3
        this.trade = trade;
    }
    @Override
    public float value() {
        return trade.value() + //..;                      //  Details of tax
    }                                                     //  and fee
}                                                         //  4 computation
public class CommissionDecorator extends Trade {
    private Trade trade;

    public CommissionDecorator(Trade trade) {
        this.trade = trade;
    }
    @Override
    public float value() {
        return trade.value() + //..;                      //  Details of commission
    }                                                     //  5 computation
}
```

The code in this listing implements the contract for the `Trade` abstraction **❶** and two of the decorators **❸** that can be composed with `Trade` to impact the net value of the execution **❷**, **❹**, **❺**. The usage of this decorator pattern is as follows:

```
Trade t =
    new CommissionDecorator(
        new TaxFeeDecorator(new Trade()));
System.out.println(t.value());
```

You could go on adding additional decorators from the outside over the basic abstraction of `Trade`. The final value that's computed will be the net effect of applying all the decorators on the `Trade` object.

If Java is your language of implementation, listing 4.5 is your DSL for computing the net value of a given trade. Now it's obvious that the code is almost the best that we can do with Java as the implementation language. It makes perfect sense to a programmer, and if they are familiar with the design patterns that the Gang of Four has taught us (see [1] in section 4.7), they must be satisfied with a domain-specific realization of the sermon. But, can we do better?

IMPROVING THE JAVA IMPLEMENTATION

With the reflective metaprogramming capabilities of Ruby or Groovy, we can make the DSL more expressive and dynamic. But before we look into the corresponding implementation, let's identify some of the areas that are potential candidates for improvement. See table 4.1.

Dynamically typed languages like Ruby and Groovy are more concise in syntax than Java. Both offer *duck typing*, which can make more reusable abstractions at the expense of static type safety that languages like Java and Scala give you out of the box. (You can also implement duck typing in Scala. We'll talk about that in chapter 6.) Let's explore more of the dynamic nature of Ruby to get the knowledge you need to improve on the points mentioned in table 4.1.

Table 4.1   Possible improvement areas for decorators in the Java DSL

Can we improve?	How?
Expressivity and domain friendliness.	Be less verbose, but the sky's the limit here.
Hardwired relationship between `Trade` and the decorators.	Get rid of static inheritance relationships, which will make the decorators more reusable.
Readability. The Java implementation reads outside in, from the decorators to the core `Trade` abstraction, which isn't intuitive.	Put `Trade` first, and then the decorators.

DYNAMIC DECORATORS IN RUBY

The following listing is a similar `Trade` abstraction in Ruby, slightly more fleshed out than the Java implementation in terms of real-life contents.

> ℹ **Ruby tidbits you need to know**
> - *How modules in Ruby can help implement mixins* that you can tag on to other classes or modules.
> - *Basics of Ruby metaprogramming* that generate runtime code through reflection.

Listing 4.6 Trade abstraction in Ruby

```ruby
class Trade
  attr_accessor :ref_no, :account, :instrument, :principal

  def initialize(ref, acc, ins, prin)
    @ref_no = ref
    @account = acc
    @instrument = ins
    @principal = prin
  end

  def with(*args)
    args.inject(self) { |memo, val| memo.extend val }
  end

  def value
    @principal
  end
end
```

❶ **Dynamic module extension**

Apart from the `with` method ❶, there's not much to talk about in terms of implementation differences with this code's Java counterpart. I'll get back to the `with` method shortly. First, let's look at the decorators. I've designed the decorators as Ruby modules that can be used as *mixins* in our implementation(for more information about mixins, see appendix A, section A.3):

```ruby
module TaxFee
  def value
    super + principal * 0.2
  end
end

module Commission
  def value
    super - principal * 0.1
  end
end
```

Even without examining the details too closely, you can see that the decorators in the snippet aren't statically coupled to the base `Trade` class. Wow, we've already successfully improved one of the issues that were listed in table 4.1.

Remember we mentioned duck typing? You can mix in the modules of the above snippet with *any* Ruby class that implements a `value` method. And it so happens that our `Trade` class also has a *value* method. But how exactly does the `super` call work in

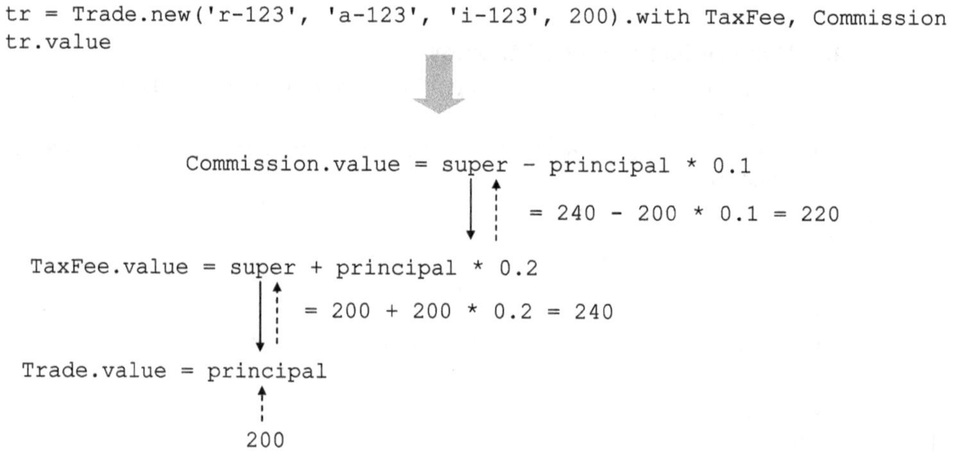

```
tr = Trade.new('r-123', 'a-123', 'i-123', 200).with TaxFee, Commission
tr.value
```

Commission.value = super - principal * 0.1

= 240 - 200 * 0.1 = 220

TaxFee.value = super + principal * 0.2

= 200 + 200 * 0.2 = 240

Trade.value = principal

200

Figure 4.4   How the super call wires up the value() method. The call starts with Commission.value(), Commission being the last module in the chain, and propagates downward until it reaches the Trade class. Follow the solid arrow for the chain. Evaluation follows the dotted arrows, which ultimately results in 220, the final value.

these module definitions? In Ruby, if you specify a super call without any arguments, Ruby sends a message to the parent of the current object to invoke a method of the same name. This is where reflective metaprogramming comes in as the sweet spot of implementation. In this case, it happens to be the value method. Notice how we're invoking a super class method without statically wiring up any specific super class. Figure 4.4 illustrates how the super calls of the Trade class and the decorators chain together at runtime to give us the desired effect.

But where is the metaprogramming magic going on? And how does it make our DSL more expressive? For the answers, let's go back to the with method in listing 4.6. What it does is take all the decorators that are passed as arguments to the method and creates an abstraction, *dynamically* extending the Trade object with all of them. Look at figure 4.5, which shows how the decorators get wired dynamically with the subject class.

The dynamic extension in the figure is equivalent to the effect that we could have had with static extension of Ruby classes. But the fact that we can make it happen during runtime makes things much more reusable and decoupled. Here's how you apply decorators to the Trade object using the implementation in listing 4.6.

```
tr = Trade.new('r-123', 'a-123', 'i-123', 20000).with TaxFee, Commission
puts tr.value
```

Using metaprogramming techniques, we wired objects during runtime and implemented the DSL in the previous snippet. Now it reads well from the inside out, as you would expect with the natural domain syntax. The syntax has less accidental complexity than the Java version and is certainly more expressive to the domain person. (See appendix A, section A.3.2 for a discussion of accidental complexity.) There you have

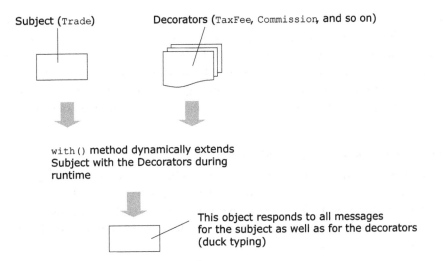

Figure 4.5   The subject (`Trade` class) gets all the decorators (`TaxFee` and `Commission`) and extends them dynamically using the `with()` method.

Key takeaway from this section

The Decorator design pattern helps you attach additional responsibilities to objects. If you can make decorators dynamic like we did with Ruby modules in this section, you get the added advantage of better readability for your DSL.

---

it. We've successfully addressed all three items for improvement from table 4.1. Wasn't that easy?

It's not all coming up roses though. Any pattern based on dynamic metaprogramming has pitfalls that you need to be aware of. Read the accompanying sidebar for that mild note of exception that might come back to bite you in the end.

When you use runtime metaprogramming in dynamically typed languages, the conciseness of your syntax is improved, the expressivity of the domain language is greatly enhanced, and you can dynamically manipulate the abilities of class structures. All these pluses come at the price of diminished type safety and slower execution speed. I'm not trying to discourage you from using these techniques in designing DSLs for your next project. But, as always, designing abstractions is an exercise in managing trade-offs. In the course of using DSL-based development, you'll encounter situations where static type safety might be more important than offering the best possible expressiveness to your DSL users. And as you'll see in course of this chapter, even with static type checking there are options with languages like Scala for making your DSL as expressive as its Ruby counterpart. Weigh all the options, then decide whether to take the plunge.

In this section, you saw how you can use metaprogramming to help you implement dynamic decorators. It's so different and much more flexible than what you would do in a statically typed language like Java or C#. Most importantly, you saw how you can use dynamic decorators to implement a real-world DSL snippet for our domain. In the next section, we'll continue our journey through the world of reflective metaprogramming techniques and implement yet another variant of one of the most popular design patterns in Java.

4.2.3   Reflective metaprogramming with builders

Remember our order-processing DSL that we built as part of a motivating example in chapter 2? We started with an example in Java where we used the Builder design pattern (see [1] in section 4.7) to make the order-processing DSL expressive to the user. As a quick recap, here's how the client uses the Java implementation of the DSL, replicated from section 2.1.2:

```
Order o =
  new Order.Builder()
    .buy(100, "IBM")
    .atLimitPrice(300)
    .allOrNone()
    .valueAs(new OrderValuerImpl())
    .build();
```

This code uses the fluent interfaces idiom to build a complete Order. But with Java, the entire building process is static; all the methods that the builder supports need to be statically invoked. Using patterns of dynamic metaprogramming in Groovy, we can make builders much more minimalistic, but still expressive (see [2] in section 4.7; I also discuss the minimalism property of abstraction design in appendix A, section A.2). The user has to write less boilerplate code, and that makes the final DSL more precise and easier to manage. The language runtime uses reflection (that's why it's called reflective metaprogramming) to do what would otherwise have to be done statically, using lots of boilerplate code.

ℹ Groovy tidbits you need to know

- *How classes and objects* are defined in Groovy.
- *Groovy builders* let you create hierarchical structures using reflection. The syntax that it offers is concise and ideal for a DSL.

THE MAGIC OF GROOVY BUILDERS

Consider the skeleton components in listing 4.7 for modeling a Trade object in Groovy. Once again, as a side note, the Trade abstraction we're developing here is much simpler than what you would use to develop a production-quality trading system and is only for the purpose of demonstrating the concept that we're addressing in this section.

Listing 4.7   Trade abstraction in Groovy

```groovy
package domain.trade

class Trade {
  String refNo
  Account account
  Instrument instrument
  List<Taxfee> taxfees = []
}

class Account {
  String no
  String name
  String type
}

class Instrument {
  String isin
  String type
  String name
}

class Taxfee {
  String taxId
  BigDecimal value
}
```

Here we have a plain old abstraction for Trade that contains an Account, an Instrument, and a list of Taxfee objects. First let me introduce the builder script that will magically introspect into the guts of the classes and create the correct objects with the values that you supply for them.

Listing 4.8   Dynamic builders for Trade objects in Groovy

```groovy
def builder =
  new ObjectGraphBuilder()

builder.classNameResolver = "domain.trade"
builder.classLoader = getClass().classLoader           ❶ Building the
                                                            builder
def trd = builder.trade( refNo: 'TRD-123') {
  account(no: 'ACC-123', name: 'Joe Doe', type: 'TRADING')
  instrument(isin: 'INS-123', type: 'EQUITY', name: 'IBM Stock')
  3.times {
      taxfee(taxId: 'Tax ${it}', value: BigDecimal.valueOf(100))
  }
}
                                                       Dynamically
                                                    created methods ❷
assert trd != null
assert trd.account.name == 'Joe Doe'
assert trd.instrument.isin == 'INS-123'
assert trd.taxfees.size == 3
```

If you're from a Java background, the code in this listing looks magical indeed. The DSL user writes methods, like trd ❶, that construct the builder that creates trade objects. Within the trd method, the user calls methods like account and instrument

❷, which we don't have as part of the `Trade` class. Yet somehow the code runs, as if these methods were created magically by the language runtime. It's the power of Groovy metaprogramming that does the trick.

INSIDE GROOVY BUILDERS

In fact, it's the combination of metaprogramming techniques, named parameters, and closures that make the DSL snippet in listing 4.8 work so wonderfully. You've seen quite a few examples in earlier chapters of how closures work in Groovy. Let's dig into some of the details of how the runtime discovers the class names, builds the correct instances, and populates with the data that you've supplied to the builder. The salient points are listed in table 4.2.

Table 4.2 Builders and metaprogramming

Runtime discovery	How it works
Matching the method name	For any method invoked on the `ObjectGraphBuilder`, Groovy matches the method name with a `Class` using a `ClassName-Resolver` strategy that gives it the `Class` to instantiate.
Customizing `ClassNameResolver`	You can customize the `ClassNameResolver` strategy with your own implementation.
Creating the instance	When Groovy has the `Class`, it uses another strategy, `NewInstanceResolver`, that calls a no-argument constructor to create a default instance of the class.
Working with hierarchical structures	The builder gets more sophisticated when you have references within your class that set up a parent/child relationship (like we have in `Trade` and `Account` in listing 4.8). In these cases, it uses other strategies like `RelationNameResolver` and `ChildPropertySetter` to locate the property classes and create instances.

For more details about how Groovy builders work, refer to [2] in section 4.7.

You've seen enough of metaprogramming techniques and how you can use them to design expressive DSLs. It's now time to take stock of what we did in this whole section and review the patterns from figure 4.2 that we've implemented so far. After all, you want to use them as the tools in your repertoire to build a world of DSLs.

> **Key takeaway from this section**
>
> *You can use builders to construct an object incrementally* within your *DSL*. When you make the builders dynamic, you cut down on the boilerplate code that you have to write. Dynamic builders like the ones in Groovy or Ruby smooth out the implementation aspect of your DSL by constructing methods dynamically through the meta-object protocol of the language runtime.

4.2.4   *Lessons learned: metaprogramming patterns*

Don't think about the patterns we've covered as isolated entities, shut away by themselves. When you work on a domain, you'll find that each results in *forces* that you need to *resolve* by applying other patterns (see [5] in section 4.7). Figure 4.6 is a reminder of what we've implemented so far. In the figure, the DSL patterns from figure 4.2 are listed on the left and the implementation instances of each of them that have been used in the code examples in this chapter are listed on the right.

We discussed a few important patterns that you would frequently use in implementing internal DSLs. These are primarily targeted for dynamically typed languages that offer strong metaprogramming capabilities.

From reflective metaprogramming we're going to move on to another category of patterns that you'll use when you're implementing internal DSLs in statically typed

---

Key takeaway from this section

The patterns we discussed in this section help you make your DSLs less verbose and more dynamic. We used the metaprogramming capabilities of the language to do stuff during runtime that would you would otherwise have to do statically, using boilerplate code.

It's not only the specific implementation in Ruby or Groovy that matters. You need to think through the context that leads to these implementations. Indeed, there are lots of other ways to make your DSL dynamic when you're using powerful implementation languages.

When you get a feel for the problem that this technique solves in real-life domain modeling, you'll be able to identify many such instances and come up with solutions of your own.

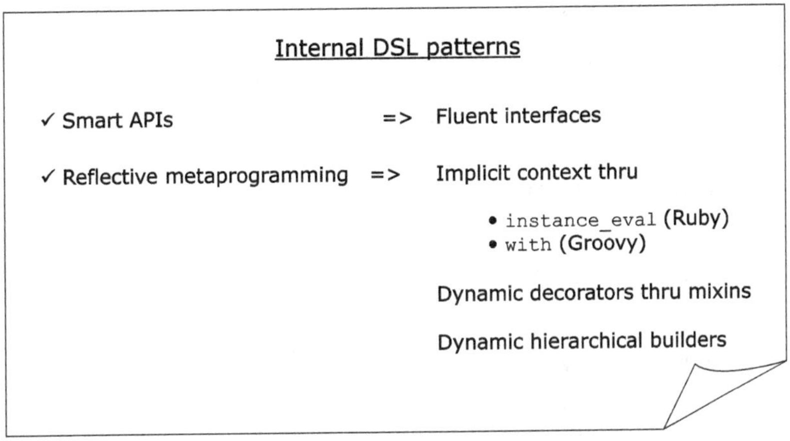

Figure 4.6   Internal DSL patterns checklist up to this point. In this chapter, you've seen implementations of these patterns in Ruby and Groovy.

languages like Scala. When you model your DSL components as typed abstractions, some of your business rules are implemented for free as part of the language's type system. This is yet another way to make your DSL concise, yet expressive.

4.3   *Embedded DSLs: patterns with typed abstractions*

In the patterns we've discussed so far, you've learned how to get concise code structures in your DSL, not only in how they're used, but also as part of the implementation.

In this section, we move away from dynamic languages and try to find out if we can make DSLs expressive using the power of a type system. For these examples, we're going to be using Scala. (All Scala code that I demonstrate in this section is based on Scala 2.8.) We'll focus on how types offer an additional level of consistency to our DSL, even before the program can run. At the same time, types can make a DSL as concise as some of the dynamic languages that we've already discussed. Refer to figure 4.2 frequently, which is our frame of reference for all the patterns that we'll be discussing in this chapter.

4.3.1   *Higher-order functions as generic abstractions*

So far in our discussions about domains, we've concentrated on the operations of the financial brokerage system, like maintaining client accounts, processing trades and executions, and placing orders on behalf of its clients. In this section, let's look at a client document that determines all trading activities that the broker does during the work day. A daily transaction activity report for a client account is something that the trading organization generates for some of its clients and dispatches to their respective mailing addresses.

GENERATING A GROUPED REPORT

Figure 4.7 shows a sample client activity report that contains the instruments traded, the quantity, the time of the trade, and the amount of money involved in the trade.

A/C Name: _____ Address: _____			
Trading Activity for 12/12/2009			
Instrument	Quantity	Time	Amount
Google	2000	08:20	
IBM	1200	11:30	
Google	350	11:45	....
Verizon	350	12:10	
IBM	2100	12:20	
Google	1200	12:50	
....	....	....	

Figure 4.7
A simplified view of a sample client activity report statement

Instrument	Quantity	Time	Amount
Google	2000 1200 350	08:20 11:45 12:50	
IBM	1200 2100	11:30 12:20	....
Verizon	350	12:10	
		....	
....	....		

A/C Name: _____ Address: _____

Trading Activity for 12/12/2009

Figure 4.8
Sample view of the account activity report sorted and grouped by the instruments traded during the day. Note how the instruments are sorted and the quantities grouped together under each instrument.

Many organizations offer their clients a flexible way to view daily transactions. They can view it sorted on specific elements, or grouped. If I have a trading account, I might want to see all my transactions sorted and grouped by the individual instruments traded during the day. Figure 4.8 shows that view.

Maybe I also want a view that groups all my transactions based on the quantities traded in each of them, as in figure 4.9.

In reality, the report can contain lots of other information. We're going to focus only on what is useful for the context we're going to implement. In this example, we'll construct a DSL that lets a client view his trading activity report based on a custom grouping function. We'll start with a DSL that implements separate functions for each

A/C Name: _____ Address: _____

Trading Activity for 12/12/2009

Quantity	Instrument	Time	Amount
350	Google Verizon	12:50 12:10	
1200	Google IBM	11:45 11:30	....
2000	Google	08:20	
2100	IBM	12:20	
....	....	.....	

Figure 4.9
Sample view of the account activity report sorted and grouped by the quantity of instruments traded during the day.

grouping operation. Then, we'll improve the verbosity of our implementation by designing a generic `groupBy` combinator that accepts the grouping criterion as a higher-order function.

> **DEFINITION**   As a reminder, a combinator is a higher-order function that takes another function as input. Combinators can be combined to implement DSL structures as we'll see here and also in chapter 6. Appendix A also contains details about combinators.

You'll see the power of Scala's type system that makes the operation statically type safe, combined with its ability to handle higher-order functions. To that end, let's jump right in with code examples.

> **ℹ Scala tidbits you need to know**
> - *Case classes define immutable value objects.* A case class is a concise way to design an abstraction where the compiler gives you a lot of goodies out of the box.
> - *Implicit type conversions* allow you to extend an existing abstraction in a completely noninvasive way.
> - *For-comprehensions* offer a functional abstraction of an iterator over a collection.
> - *Higher-order functions* let you design and compose powerful functional abstractions.

SETTING UP THE BASE ABSTRACTIONS

Let's start bottom up with the final view of how your DSL will look. Then we'll work toward implementing the same thing using Scala. Here's how users will use your DSL:

```
activityReport groupBy(_.instrument)
activityReport groupBy(_.quantity)
```

In the code snippet, the first invocation generates the activity report grouped by instrument, and the second one generates it grouped by the quantity traded. The following snippet implements the basic abstraction of a client activity report. Let's take a more detailed look at some of the features that the abstraction offers.

```
type Instrument = String                                        ◁─┐  ❶ Concrete type
                                                                     definition
case class TradedQuantity(instrument: Instrument,
  quantity: Int)                                                ◁─┐  ❷ Value object

implicit def tuple2ToLineItem(t: (Instrument, Int)) =
  TradedQuantity(t._1, t._2)                                    ◁─┐  ❸ Implicit Tuple2
                                                                     to LineItem
case class ActivityReport(account: String,
  quantities: List[TradedQuantity]) {                           ◁─┐  ❹ The main
  //..                                                               abstraction
}
```

This isn't a Scala book. Even so, for your understanding, I'm going to highlight some of the features that this code fragment offers. It'll help you compare it with an equivalent Java fragment, and demonstrate some of the expressive power that it has.

Keeping in mind that we need to be expressive in our DSL, we start with a type definition that models a domain artifact **❶**. This keeps the code self-documented by avoiding opaque native data types. It also makes the code more meaningful to a domain user and keeps the type of `Instrument` flexible enough for future changes.

The case class `TradedQuantity` **❷** models a value object. Value objects are supposed to be immutable and Scala *case classes* are a succinct way to represent them. A *case class* offers automatically immutable data members, syntactic convenience for a built-in constructor, and out-of-the-box implementations of `equals`, `hashCode`, and `toString` methods. (Case classes are a great way to model value objects in Scala. For more details, see [4] in section 4.7.)

The implicit declaration **❸** is the Scala way to provide automatic conversion between data types. Implicits in Scala are *lexically scoped*, which means that this type conversion will be functional only in the module where you explicitly import the implicit definition. In this example, the tuple (`Instrument`, `Int`) can be implicitly converted to a `TradedQuantity` object through this declaration. Note that (`Instrument`, `Int`) is the Scala literal representation for a tuple of two elements. A more verbose representation is `Tuple2[Instrument, Int]`. (In section 3.2.2, I discussed how Scala `implicits` work. If you need to, make a quick visit back to refresh your memory.)

Finally, we come to the main abstraction of the client activity report. `Activity-Report` **❹** contains the account information and the list of all tuples that represent the quantities and instruments traded during the day.

Now we're going to step through the following iterative modeling process and implement the grouping function that'll give the client the custom views they like to have for their daily transaction report. Table 4.3 shows how we'll improve our model using an iterative process.

Table 4.3 Iterative improvement of the DSL

Step	Description
Create a DSL for the client to view the trading activity report. Support grouping operations by `Instrument` and `Quantity`.	Implement specialized grouping functions: `groupByInstrument` and `groupByQuantity` Reduce repetitive boilerplates by implementing a generic grouping function: `groupBy{T <% Ordered[T]]`

First we'll implement the `groupBy` functions.

FIRST ATTEMPT: A SPECIALIZED IMPLEMENTATION

If we build specialized implementations of the `groupBy` function for the `Activity-Report` abstraction, the DSL user is going to get quite an expressive API. But we're discussing *implementations* here; expressive *usage* can't be the only yardstick for judging the completeness of our DSL. The following listing shows the specialized implementation for grouping by `Instrument` and `Quantity`. Notice how we need to define specialized functions for each kind of grouping that we want to give to the user.

> **Listing 4.9 Activity report with specialized implementations of `groupBy`**

```scala
type Instrument = String

case class TradedQuantity(instrument: Instrument,
  quantity: Int)

implicit def tuple2ToLineItem(t: (Instrument, Int)) =
  TradedQuantity(t._1, t._2)

case class ActivityReport(account: String,
  quantities: List[TradedQuantity]) {
  import scala.collection.mutable._

  def groupByInstrument = {
    val m =
      new HashMap[Instrument, Set[TradedQuantity]]          ❶ MultiMap
        with MultiMap[Instrument, TradedQuantity]              with mixin

    for(q <- quantities)
      m addBinding (q.instrument, q)                        ❷ For
                                                               comprehension
    m.keys.toList
          .sortWith(_ < _)
          .map(m.andThen(_.toList))                         ❸ Grouping by
  }                                                            Instrument

  def groupByQuantity = {
    val m =
      new HashMap[Int, Set[TradedQuantity]]
        with MultiMap[Int, TradedQuantity]

    for(q <- quantities)
      m addBinding (q.quantity, q)

    m.keys.toList
          .sortWith(_ < _)
          .map(m.andThen(_.toList))
  }
}
```

Can you identify the drawbacks of this implementation? Before we look into them, let me briefly explain some of the Scala idioms that we're using in this listing.

In the implementation of `ActivityReport` in listing 4.9, `quantities` can contain multiple entries for the same `Instrument`, so we define a multimap in ❶ using Scala's mixin syntax. With `HashMap`, we mix in the *trait* `MultiMap` to get a concrete instance of the `MultiMap`. For more details about Scala traits and mixins, refer to [4] in section 4.7.

We iterate over `quantities` and populate the `HashMap` using *for comprehensions* of Scala ❷. This is quite different from a `for` loop that we have in imperative languages. (I'll discuss `for` comprehensions in detail when we talk about monadic structures in

Scala in section 6.9.) In ❸ we sort the keys of the MultiMap and forms a List grouped by Instrument. Each member of the List is a Set containing the quantities that correspond to a single Instrument. The underscores have their usual meaning that we discussed in section 3.2.2.

The main drawback of the implementation in listing 4.9 is the number of boilerplate repetitions that the code contains. groupByInstrument and groupByQuantity have the same overall structure; only the attribute based on which the grouping is to be done is different. Do you hear a familiar voice from the past, crying out against a violation of well-designed abstraction principles? If not, turn to appendix A, where I discuss how the process of *distillation* keeps your abstractions free from all accidental complexities. The problem with this code is that the specialized groupBy implementation encourages boilerplate code. Not only that, if we add more grouping criteria later to the ActivityReport class, we'll need to write more boilerplate code to implement customized grouping. What can we do about that? What we need is a more generic implementation.

THE GENERIC IMPLEMENTATION
Let's make the implementation more generic and subsume the specialized methods.

Listing 4.10   Generic implementation of `groupBy`

```scala
type Instrument = String

case class TradedQuantity(instrument: Instrument,
  quantity: Int)

implicit def tuple2ToLineItem(t: (Instrument, Int)) =
  TradedQuantity(t._1, t._2)

case class ActivityReport(account: String,
  quantities: List[TradedQuantity]) {
  import scala.collection.mutable._

  def groupBy[T <% Ordered[T]](f: TradedQuantity => T) = {   ◁
    val m =
      new HashMap[T, Set[TradedQuantity]]
        with MultiMap[T, TradedQuantity]
    for(q <- quantities)
      m addBinding (f(q), q)
    m.keys.toList.sort(_ < _).map(m.andThen(_.toList))
  }
}
```

❶ Parameterized by what to group

Now the implementation is reduced in size. Did you see how the density increased when we implemented the generic groupBy ❶ to create more powerful abstractions? Table 4.4 provides a summary of how you implement the generic groupBy.

Now let's look at the invocation of groupBy by the DSL user and follow the sequence of implementation steps that's executed. This exercise will help you understand how the type system of Scala works behind the scenes to create an expressive DSL structure.

Table 4.4   Implementing a generic `groupBy`

Step	Description
Implement a generic `groupBy`	Needs to be parameterized with the type that we'll use for grouping the activity report. It will accept a function `f` as its argument, which models the criteria of grouping. `groupBy` is an example of Scala's support for *higher-order functions*. You can pass around functions like any other data type as parameters and return types. You can use this ability to abstract the criteria and replace specialized implementations of grouping as in listing 4.9. Look at figure 4.10 to understand how such a generic function works under the hoods

Examining what goes on behind the scenes is an important step in DSL design and if you're an implementer, you should be extremely sure to understand every bit of it. Read this section several times if you need to, until you have a clear understanding of how the method dispatch works in Scala. Quite a few idioms are hidden in the 15 lines of implementation shown in listing 4.10 that need careful consideration. When you're confident you see how the various idioms are wired to fulfill the contract that the API publishes, you'll be able to make it a part of your toolbox.

```
val activityReport =
  ActivityReport("john doe",
    List(("IBM", 1200), ("GOOGLE ", 2000), ("GOOGLE", 350),
      ("VERIZON", 350), ("IBM", 2100), ("GOOGLE", 1200)))

println(activityReport groupBy(_.instrument))
println(activityReport groupBy(_.quantity))
```

Instead of trying to explain that code textually, let me explain the sequence of actions that take place for the invocation `activityReport groupBy(_.instrument)` in figure 4.10.

Higher-order functions aren't specific only to typed abstractions. All modern languages offer higher-order functions and closures, irrespective of whether or not they're statically typed. You can use the pattern implementations I discuss here in different ways and languages. Keep an eye on the context in which the patterns are being used, and use your implementation language to get things done.

Remember, we're trying to explore all internal DSL implementation patterns across the languages that you use on the JVM. You can use a statically typed language or a dynamically typed one; either way, your goal should be to use the appropriate tool for the power you need in modeling your DSL.

In the next section, we're going to discuss how to use explicitly typed constraints to express domain logic and behavior. This is something that dynamically typed languages can't support. But given an expressive and rich type system, using explicitly typed constraints can be a potent tool in your toolbox. They can make your DSLs unbelievably succinct.

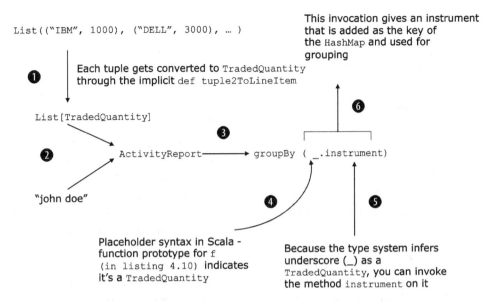

Figure 4.10 Activity report computation grouped by instrument (`groupBy(_.instrument)`). Follow the steps in the figure and correlate them with listing 4.10 and the snippet that follows it, which uses the DSL to compute the `ActivityReport` for "john doe".

4.3.2 *Using explicit type constraints to model domain logic*

When you design a domain model, you implement abstraction behaviors that must honor the rules and constraints that the domain imposes on you. Languages like Ruby and Groovy are dynamically typed, so all such domain rules need to be encoded as runtime constraints. In section 4.2, you saw how reflective metaprogramming works toward implementing DSL structures that model these domain rules in Ruby and Groovy. In this section, I'll start with an example of runtime validation implementation in Ruby. Then I'll demonstrate how you can implement similar constraints more succinctly using the static type system of Scala.

RUNTIME VALIDATION IN RUBY

Consider the simple example from our domain of a `Trade` abstraction in Ruby, which we partially modeled in listing 4.7. A `Trade` object needs an `Account` object, which we call the *trading account* of the client. In listing 4.7, the account object is well represented with the `attr_accessor` class methods. In the domain of trading systems, there can be multiple types of accounts (discussed in the sidebar titled *Financial brokerage systems: client account* in section 3.2.2). But the account that we specify in a `Trade` abstraction is constrained to be a *trading account* only; it can't be a *settlement-only account*. This domain rule needs to be validated every time we build a `Trade` object with an `Account` object. How do you do this in Ruby? You can insert the usual validation check as in the following snippet:

```
class Trade
  attr_accessor :ref_no, :account, :instrument, :principal

  def initialize(ref, acc, ins, prin)
    @ref_no = ref
    raise ArgumentError.new("Has to be a trading account")
      unless trading?(acc)
    @account = acc
    ## ..
```

Wherever you expect to have a trading account passed in your domain model, you need to do this same validation over and over *during runtime*. (You can make the validation more declarative using class methods, as used in Rails; but still, it remains a runtime validation.) You also need to write explicit unit tests for each of these cases to check whether the particular domain behavior fails as it should when supplied with a nontrading account. All this requires additional code, which you can avoid if your language supports explicit specification of typed constraints.

In statically typed languages, you can specify constraints over specific types that'll be checked during compile time. When you have a program that compiles successfully, at least one level of consistency of domain behaviors is already enforced within your model.

EXPLICITLY TYPED CONSTRAINTS IN SCALA

Let's try to model a `Trade` object in Scala that has some domain constraints over accounts and instruments. At the end of this exercise, you'll realize how explicit type constraints can make your DSL abstractions promise an extra level of consistency that the dynamically typed ones can't, even before you execute it. You'll definitely want this trick in your toolkit when you're using a statically typed language in your application.

> **ℹ Scala tidbits you need to know**
> - The *power of type-based programming*. You can use types to express many constraints the domain in your DSL. Generic type parameters and abstract types are your friends.
> - *Abstract vals* let you keep the abstraction open until the last stage of instantiation.

Every trade object needs a `Trading` account. Here's how we model this behavior in Scala. The following listing shows only this one aspect of a `Trade` object and is meant only as an example.

Listing 4.11 Trade object with typed constraints in Scala

```
trait Account
trait Trading extends Account
trait Settlement extends Account
```
 Two Account types

```
trait Trade {
    type A <: Trading

    val account: A
    def valueOf: Unit
}
```

❷ **Account subtype of Trading**

❸ **Account instance**

This listing is an example of how types can enforce implicit business rules. In the listing, we've modeled `Account` and `Trade` objects using Scala traits (see [4] in section 4.6). We've used separate types for `Trading` and `Settlement` accounts ❶. As a programmer, you can't pass a `Settlement` account to a method that expects a `Trading` account. The compiler enforces this rule; a business rule that expects a `Trading` account doesn't have to explicitly check to determine whether you passed a valid account type.

We've also defined some of the business rules explicitly. We've abstracted type `A` with constraints (`<: Trading`) in `Trade` ❷. You can't instantiate a `Trade` object with any account type other than `Trading` ❸. You don't have to write any extra code to enforce the validation; again, the compiler does it for you.

A trade is a contract between two parties that involves an exchange of instruments. If you need a little brush up on some of the attributes of a trade, see the sidebar that's in section 1.4. Depending on the instruments that are traded, the behavior, lifecycle, and calculations of the trade vary. An *equity trade* is one that involves an exchange of equities with currencies. When a fixed income is the instrument type that's being exchanged in a trade, we call it a *fixed income trade*. For more details about equities, fixed incomes, and other instrument types, see the sidebar in this section.

> ### Financial brokerage systems: instrument types
>
> Instruments that are traded can be of various types designed to meet the needs of the investors and issuers. Depending on the type, every instrument follows a different lifecycle in the trading and settlement process.
>
> The two main classifications are equity and fixed income.
>
> Equities can again be classified as common stock, preferred stock, cumulative stock, equity warrants, or depository receipts. The types of fixed income securities (also known as bonds) include straight bonds, zero coupon bonds, and floating rate notes. For the purpose of our discussion, it's not essential to be familiar with all these details. What is important is that the `Trade` abstractions will vary, depending on the type of instrument that's being traded.

Let's specialize our definition of `Trade` to model an `EquityTrade` and a `FixedIncomeTrade` in the following listing.

Listing 4.12 `EquityTrade` and `FixedIncomeTrade` model

```
trait Instrument
trait Stock extends Instrument
```

```
trait FixedIncome extends Instrument

trait EquityTrade extends Trade {                    ❶ EquityTrade works
  type S <: Stock                                       on Stock
                                                                    ❷ Instrument
  val equity: S                                                        types
  def valueOf {
    //..
  }                                                    ❸ Implementation of
}                                                         trade valuation

trait FixedIncomeTrade extends Trade {               ❹ FixedIncomeTrade
  type FI <: FixedIncome                                  works on FixedIncome

  val fi: FI                              ❺ Instrument
  def valueOf {                             types
    //..                                            ❻ Implementation of
  }                                                    trade valuation
}
```

Like the explicit constraints on `Account` that we used in listing 4.11, in this listing we're constraining the traded instrument type. Again, business rules are enforced implicitly by the compiler.

We've specified separate types for `EquityTrade` and `FixedIncomeTrade` ❶ and ❹. As a programmer, you can't pass a `FixedIncomeTrade` to a method that expects an `EquityTrade`. The compiler enforces this rule; a business rule that expects a particular type of `Trade` doesn't have to explicitly check to determine whether you passed a valid trade type.

An `EquityTrade` trades a `Stock` ❶ and a `FixedIncomeTrade` trades a `FixedIncome` ❹. The basic business rule is completely enforced at the compiler level without a single line of validation from the programmer. Accordingly, you constrain the abstract vals `equity` ❷ and `fi` ❺.

The `valueOf` method is polymorphic and typed. You can provide separate implementations of the `valueOf` method ❸ and ❻, assuming that your `Trade` abstraction gets an appropriate type, either `Account` or `Instrument`.

Using typed abstractions and explicit constraints on the values and types, we implemented quite a bit of domain behavior without a single line of procedural logic. Not only is our main code base smaller, the number of unit tests that you need to write and maintain has also been reduced. When you need to maintain a code base, don't you feel more comfortable when you have a declarative type annotation that expresses some critical semantics of the domain being modeled?

This discussion was on a different path from what we've been doing with dynamic language-based DSL implementations in the earlier sections. Now let's look back at what you've learned about the *statically typed way of thinking* and how it differs from the Ruby or Groovy way.

4.3.3   *Lessons learned: thinking in types*

In this section, you've learned how types can play a significant role in designing expressive domain abstractions. The main difference from the earlier Groovy and Ruby examples is that with the safety net of static type checking, you already have one level of correctness built into your implementation. A typed code that compiles correctly guarantees that you'll satisfy many of the constraints of the domain. We'll explore this further in chapter 6 when we design more DSLs using Scala. Figure 4.11 is an updated checklist of internal DSL patterns that you learned about in this section.

We've discussed a few important patterns that you'll use frequently when you're implementing internal DSLs with statically typed languages. Although metaprogramming is the secret sauce for dynamic languages, typed abstractions offer concise DSL development mechanisms when you're using statically typed languages.

> **Key takeaways from this section**
>
> The main purpose of this section was to make you *think in types*. For each abstraction that's in your domain model, make it a typed one and organize the related business rules around that type. Many of the business rules will be automatically enforced by the compiler, which means you won't have to write explicit code for them. If your implementation language has a proper type system, your DSL will be as concise as ones written using dynamic languages.

So far you've seen implementation patterns that make concise internal DSLs, either by abstracting domain rules within a powerful type system or through reflection using the metaprogramming power of the host language. In the next section, we'll look at patterns that will make the language runtime write code for you. You're going to make concise DSLs by using generated code.

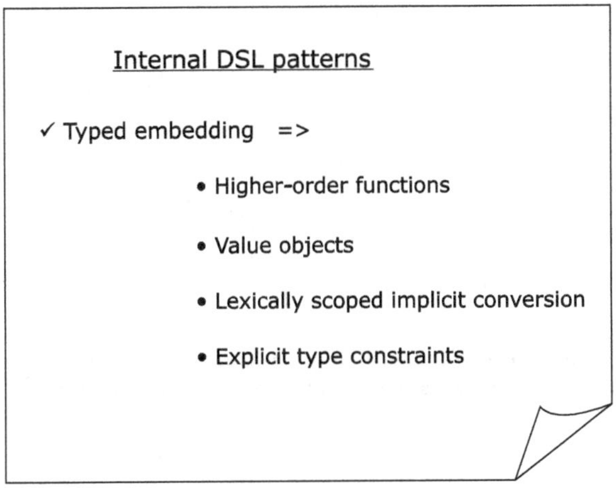

Internal DSL patterns

✓ Typed embedding   =>

      • Higher-order functions

      • Value objects

      • Lexically scoped implicit conversion

      • Explicit type constraints

Figure 4.11
Program structures for *typed embedding* of internal DSLs. These patterns teach you how to think with types in a programming language.

4.4   *Generative DSLs: boilerplates for runtime generation*

Metaprogramming has many facets. In the previous sections, you saw numerous examples of reflective metaprogramming. The VM introspects on meta-objects during runtime, discovers objects that can be applied to the current context, and magically invokes it. But you can look at metaprogramming in a different way. In fact, the classic definition of metaprogramming is *writing code that writes code*.

This definition has specific semantics when we talk about it in the context of different languages. Languages like Lisp offer compile-time metaprogramming, as we saw in detail in section 2.5.2. Languages like Ruby and Groovy offer runtime metaprogramming and can generate code during runtime using eval and dynamic dispatch methods. In this section, we'll examine a specific example of how you can reduce the surface area of your DSL abstractions by writing less *explicit* code, instead relying on the language runtime to generate the rest for you. You might be asking yourself, why is this important?

4.4.1   *How generative DSLs work*

When you design a generative DSL, you'll write less boilerplate code. Instead, the language generates that code for you through metaprogramming. Figure 4.12 offers a visual explanation.

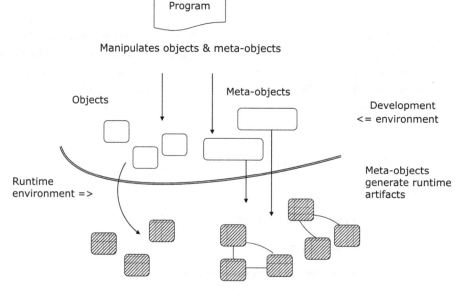

Figure 4.12   Runtime metaprogramming generates code from meta-objects during runtime. The meta-objects generate more objects, which reduces the amount of boilerplate code that you need to write.

Besides the objects that you develop, you also manipulate meta-objects that generate more artifacts for you when the program runs. These additional artifacts represent the code that the language runtime writes for you. It's as if you're giving subtle instructions to your assistant so you can concentrate on the more important aspects of your job. The assistant takes care of all the routine operations that your instructions advised him to perform. But what are these meta-objects? Where do they live and how do they do what you ask them to do? Join me as we explore designing generative DSLs in Ruby.

4.4.2   *Ruby metaprogramming for concise DSL design*

In our domain of securities trading and settlement, we've been talking about trades in this chapter. In a real-world application, a `Trade` module is a complex one with lots of domain objects and associated business rules, constraints, and validations. Some of these validations are generic and apply to all similar attributes in the same context, but others are specific to the context and need to be explicitly coded within the class definition. Nonetheless, the general flow of validation checks is the same and can be centralized or generated using appropriate techniques.

Let's see how Ruby metaprogramming can make things simpler for you.

USING CLASS METHODS TO ABSTRACT VALIDATION LOGIC

Assume that you're developing your trading application in Rails using `ActiveRecord` for persistence handling. Here's an idiomatic code snippet for the `Trade` model.

```
class Trade < ActiveRecord::Base
  has_one                :ref_no
  has_one                :account
  has_one                :instrument
  has_one                :currency
  has_many               :tax_fees

  ## ..

  validates_presence_of    :account, :instrument, :currency
  validates_uniqueness_of  :ref_no

  ## ..
end
```

If you have experience using Rails in a project, you know what the last two lines in the class definition do. The two Ruby *class methods*, `validates_presence_of` and `validates_uniqueness_of`, encapsulate the validation logic for the attributes that we supply as arguments. Note how the domain constraints for these attributes are nicely abstracted away from the surface area of the exposed API (a good example of distilled model design). I discuss the principles of distillation in abstraction design in section A.3. During runtime, these methods generate the appropriate code snippets that validate these attributes.

> **ℹ Ruby tidbits you need to know**
>
> - Basics of Ruby *metaprogramming*. The Ruby object model has many artifacts like classes, objects, instance methods, class methods, singleton methods, and so on, that let you use reflective and generative metaprogramming. You can dig into the Ruby object model at runtime and change behaviors or generate code dynamically.
> - *Modules* and how they let you implement mixins for extending your existing abstractions.

MIXINS FOR DYNAMIC METHOD GENERATION

Let's do something similar for the Trade abstraction that we developed in Ruby in listing 4.6. What we'll do is put inline validation logic into the class definition of Trade, but we'll hide the details of invocation and the exception-reporting machinery of the validation behind the scenes; all that boilerplate code is going to be generated during runtime. Here's how we want the abstraction to look:

```
class Trade
  include ...

  attr_accessor :ref_no, :account, :instrument
  trd_validate :principal do |val|
    val > 100
  end

  ## ..
end
```

❶ What to include?

❷ Validation logic as block

In this snippet, something appears to be missing in ❶ (I'll clarify this shortly). Also, trd_validate is the validation machinery that can generate runtime code for invoking the validation logic that we pass as the block in ❷.

But, where does trd_validate come from? It must be something that we've defined elsewhere and needs to be linked to the code that defines the main class. Possibly the elided portion in ❶ is the place to look at. Let's unravel the code a bit more. Before we go into the details of how this Trade model gets the trd_validate method, here's a Ruby module TradeClassMethods that defines our class method trd_validate:

```
module TradeClassMethods
  def trd_validate(attribute, &check)
    define_method "#{attribute}=" do |val|
      raise 'Validation failed' unless check.call(val)
      instance_variable_set("@#{attribute}", val)
    end

    define_method attribute do
      instance_variable_get "@#{attribute}"
    end
  end
end
```

❶ Generate setter for attribute

❷ Generate getter for attribute

What does this snippet do? It generates setter ❶ and getter ❷ methods during runtime for the attribute that's passed to the method trd_validate, using Ruby's dynamic method definition capabilities. In the process of defining them, this code also generates more code for invoking the validation logic that the user passed to it in the form of a block. Nice! Just imagine the amount of boilerplate code that we didn't have to write by using this metaprogramming feature. This savings is multiplied for every attribute that you use to invoke trd_validate.

THE FINAL GLUE

Now it's time to assemble things. Let's define another module that glues TradeClass-Methods with the Trade class and makes trd_validate available within Trade. The following listing is the final version of the code that glues everything together and makes all the above magic happen.

Listing 4.13 Trade with domain validation

```
## enable_trade_validation.rb
require 'trade_class_methods'
module EnableTradeValidation
  def self.included(base)
    base.extend TradeClassMethods
  end
end

## trade.rb
require 'trade_class_methods'
require 'enable_trade_validation'

class Trade
  include EnableTradeValidation

  attr_accessor :ref_no, :account, :instrument
  trd_validate :principal do |val|
    val > 100
  end

  ## ..
end
```

You just saw how to avoid writing boilerplate validation logic explicitly by using metaprogramming techniques to generate it. This code is generated *during runtime* when the Ruby VM executes your program.

Key takeaways from this section

Most of the patterns we discussed in this chapter *focus on making your DSL less verbose* and yet more expressive. Ruby and Groovy offer strong support for runtime metaprogramming that generates code for you. Whenever you feel that the code you're writing for implementing a DSL looks repetitive, think metaprogramming. Instead of writing the code yourself, let the language runtime write it for you.

What a long, exciting chapter this is. We've been discussing lots of tricks that you need up your sleeve when you're writing DSLs. Don't worry if everything isn't sinking in the first time you read it. After you get an overall idea of these techniques, you'll be able to think through your problem and carve out your solution domain in the best way possible. If you need a light refreshment to recharge your programming batteries, go get it now. What we'll be discussing next relates to a new development on the JVM of an age-old paradigm of program development. It's Lisp metaprogramming, packaged on the JVM, and it's called Clojure. Ruby and Groovy metaprogramming is primarily based on runtime code generation, but Clojure does it during compile time using macros. We're going look at how macros shape the way you think about designing internal DSLs.

4.5   Generative DSLs: macros for compile-time code generation

Finish up your snack, because now we're going to talk about how generative metaprogramming in Ruby and Groovy generates code during runtime. Your DSL surface syntax will still be concise; you don't have to write the boilerplate stuff that the language runtime generates for you. With Clojure (the Lisp on the JVM), you get all the benefits of code generation, minus the runtime overhead of it that Groovy and Ruby incur. (For information about Clojure, go to http://clojure.org.) Invented by Rich Hickey, Clojure offers the syntax and semantics of Lisp, along with seamless integration with the object system that Java offers. For a more detailed introduction to the language and the runtime, refer to [3] in section 4.7.

4.5.1   Metaprogramming with Clojure

Clojure is a dynamically typed language that implements duck typing and offers powerful functional programming capabilities. In this section, we'll focus more on the generative capabilities of Clojure that are available through its system of macros.

Code generation using Clojure macros is a form of *compile-time metaprogramming*, which we discussed briefly in section 2.3.1. If you're not familiar with the basic concepts of how compile-time macros work in Lisp or Clojure, now's a good time to review the concepts that I discuss in appendix B. As a brief refresher, look at figure 4.13, which outlines the basic flow of events in a compile-time metaprogramming system. The program that you write defines higher-order abstractions as macros that get expanded to valid Clojure forms during the compilation phase.

Before we dive into the implementation details, let's look at a snippet of the problem domain that we're going to cover. When a client places an order to the broker for trading an instrument (either buy or sell), the following sequence of actions take place:

1 The broker places the order in the exchange
2 Street-side trades are done between brokers according to the placed order and results in execution
3 Executions get allocated to client accounts and results in generation of client trade

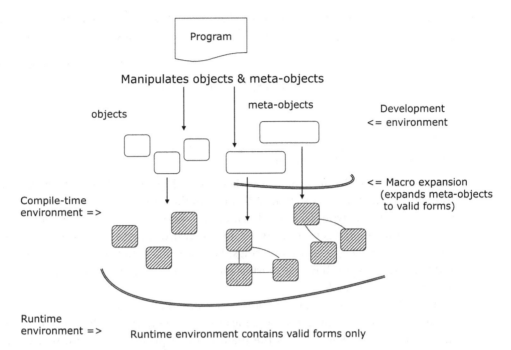

Program

Manipulates objects & meta-objects

meta-objects

objects

Development
<= environment

Compile-time
environment =>

<= Macro expansion
(expands meta-objects
to valid forms)

Runtime
environment =>   Runtime environment contains valid forms only

Figure 4.13 Compile-time metaprogramming generates code through macro expansion. Note that we're still in the compilation phase when the code is generated. This technique doesn't have any runtime overhead, unlike the earlier one in figure 4.12.

Let's try to implement the allocation process that generates the client trade from an execution. In reality there's a many-to-many relationship between orders, executions, and trades. For the purpose of this example, let's assume that there's a one-to-one relationship between execution and the client trade. We'll use the power of Clojure duck typing to model our use case.

> **ℹ Clojure tidbits you need to know**
> - *Prefix syntax and functional thinking*. Clojure uses prefix notation and is based on s-expressions. Clojure is uniform in syntax throughout, there's no order of operations, and it boasts absolute consistency. Clojure is a functional language in which you organize your modules as functions.
> - *Maps in Clojure* are used as a ubiquitous data structure to model objects.
> - *Macros* let you define syntactic extensions for your DSL. They make your DSLs concise through compile-time code generation.

4.5.2 Implementing the domain model

Here's how we define a trade and an execution in Clojure. Trade and execution essentially contain the same information. The difference is that an execution contains a *broker account,* but a trade is done on a *client account,* based on the order that the client places. The following snippet defines a sample trade and a sample execution.

```
(def tr1                                           Clojure keyword ::trading  ❶
  {:ref-no "tr-123"
   :account {:no "cl-a1" :name "john doe" :type ::trading}    ◁┘
   :instrument "eq-123" :value 1000}})

(def ex1
  {:ref-no "er-123"
   :account {:no "br-a1" :name "j p morgan" :type ::trading}
   :instrument "eq-123" :value 1000}})
```

An account is a separate structure embedded within the trade structure. An account contains an attribute :type that indicates whether it's a trading account or a settlement account. The type is modeled as a Clojure keyword that's nothing but a symbolic identifier that evaluates to itself ❶. Clojure keywords provide fast equality checks and are used as lightweight constant strings. For more information about client accounts and the various types that it supports, read the sidebar *Financial brokerage systems: client account* in section 3.2.2.

Let's define two functions in listing 4.14: one that checks whether an account is a trading account, and another that allocates an execution to a client account generating a client trade. The latter is the main domain problem use case that we'll focus on. We'll start with a function definition and see how you can make the implementation of the function more succinct when macros are generating repetitive boilerplates for it.

Listing 4.14   Allocation function for execution

```
(defn trading?
  "Returns true if the account is a trading account"
  [account]
  (= (:type account) ::trading))

(defn allocate
  "Allocate execution to client account and generate client trade"
  [acc exe]
  (cond
    (nil? acc) (throw (IllegalArgumentException.
               "account cannot be nil"))
    (= (trading? acc) false) (throw (IllegalArgumentException.    ❶  Validation
               "must be a trading account"))    ◁┘
    :else {:ref-no (generate-trade-ref-no)
           :account acc
           :instrument (:instrument exe) :value (:value exe)}}))
```

Look at what's going on in the allocate function in this listing. The core business logic that allocate handles is in the :else clause of the cond statement. The first two condition clauses ❶ perform two validations that we need to do for every operation that we carry out within the trading subsystem. For any method on trade, we need to validate that the trading account is a non-null entity and that it's indeed a trading account and not a settlement account. That's what comprises the main explicit surface area in the `allocate` method. The `allocate` method contains accidental code complexity that needs to be factored away from the core API implementation.

4.5.3 *The beauty of Clojure macros*

Because the validations that we do in the `allocate` method are generally applicable to all trade functions, why not refactor them into a reusable entity? Then we'd have a validate function that can be invoked for all accounts like we did for `trd_validate` when we defined the Ruby module `TradeClassMethods` earlier in section 4.4.1. But macros provide distinct advantages, which I discuss in the callout.

> Clojure supports macros you can use to generate code *during the compilation phase*, then the macro is expanded into the normal Clojure forms. The advantage is twofold:
>
> 1 You avoid the overhead of the function call through inline expansion of the macro during the compilation phase.
> 2 The code is more readable because you don't use the lambdas that would have been required if you used higher-order functions.

The next example will make all this clearer. In the following snippet, I define a macro that can be used as a control abstraction, much like the normal Clojure form, but that encapsulates all the validation logic within it.

```
(defmacro with-account
  [acc & body]
  `(cond
     (nil? ~acc) (throw (IllegalArgumentException.
                          "account cannot be nil"))
     (= (trading? ~acc) false) (throw (IllegalArgumentException.
                                        "must be a trading account"))
     :else ~@body))
```

Note how the body can consist of a variable number of forms that get inserted into the generated code via the splicing unquote `~@`. (For more details about how the splicing unquote works, refer to [3] in section 4.7.) If we implemented a function for the validation logic, we'd have to use lambdas instead. Using `with-account`, this is how our allocate function looks:

```
(defn allocate
  "Allocate execution to client account and generate client trade"
  [acc exe]
  (with-account acc
    {:ref-no (generate-trade-ref-no)
     :account acc
     :instrument (:instrument exe) :value (:value exe)}))
```

Now the implementation is more concise and succinct because it needs to focus only on the core domain logic. All exception handlings and accidental complexities are

Key takeaways from this section

The focus of this section was to *make your DSL implementation concise yet expressive*. This idea has been the recurring theme for all the sections in this chapter. The difference is in the implementation itself.

With Clojure macros, you make your DSL concise *without having any impact on the runtime performance*. You can bend the language itself to express the exact syntax and semantics that your DSL asks for. The Lisp family offers this awesome power as a natural way to model the real world.

being factored away to the macro, without incurring any overhead on the runtime performance. The macro `with-account` is not only coupled with the implementation of `allocate`; it's a general control structure, looks like a normal Clojure form, and is reusable across all the APIs that need trading accounts to be validated.

Generative DSLs write code for you. But as an observant reader, you must've already figured out the differences that language implementations offer with respect to when the code is generated. Section 4.4 discussed *runtime* code generation; in this section, you saw how Clojure implements *compile-time* code generation using the power of macros. Both strategies have their advantages and disadvantages, and you need to weigh your options before deciding on one specific implementation.

4.6   Summary

You've ridden with me for a long time in this chapter. You deserve kudos for being a part of this journey. We covered almost the entire range of internal DSL implementation patterns, with problem snippets from our domain of financial brokerage systems.

Key takeaways & best practices

When you design an internal DSL, follow the best practices for the language concerned. Using the language idiomatically always results in the optimal mix of expressiveness and performance.

A dynamic language like Ruby or Groovy gives you strong metaprogramming capabilities. Design your DSL abstractions and the underlying semantic model that rely on these capabilities. You'll end up with a beautifully concise syntax, leaving the boilerplates to the underlying language runtime.

In a language like Scala, static typing is your friend. Use type constraints to express a lot of business rules and use the compiler as the first-level verifier of your DSL syntax.

When you're using a language like Clojure that offers compile-time metaprogramming, use macros to define custom syntax structures. You'll get the conciseness of Ruby with no additional runtime performance penalty.

Dynamic languages like Ruby and Groovy offer powerful reflective metaprogramming paradigms that you can use to make your DSL implementations both concise and expressive. Such languages let you manipulate their meta-model during runtime, which makes them great tools for implementing more dynamic structures.

In this chapter, you saw how to make more dynamic builders and decorators that harness the power of metaprogramming. You also saw how you can use static typing to express domain constraints declaratively and how to implement generative DSLs that generate code during compile time or runtime.

Because you've read this chapter, you can now think in terms of mapping your DSL implementation to the idioms and best practices that your language offers. We talked about lots of patterns that you can easily map to appropriate contexts of your DSL model. In previous chapters, you heard about the virtues of DSL-based development, but you never got to see how a particular scenario of your problem domain maps to a specific implementation structure. The following list contains the main features that this chapter adds to your DSL landscape:

- You can now improve the conciseness of your DSL by using the power contained in your implementation language.
- If you're using a statically typed language, you can build your DSL models around typed abstractions.
- If your language offers metaprogramming, you can use it to reduce the surface syntax of the DSL and let the language runtime or the compile-time machinery generate the code for you.

Now it's time to look at more examples from the real world. In the next chapter, we'll discuss the dynamically typed family of languages and what they can do to implement expressive DSLs. So what are you waiting for? Grab your coffee mug, get a refill, and turn the page for more DSL delights.

4.7   **References**

1   Gamma, E., R. Helm, R. Johnson, and J. Vlissides. 1995. *Design Patterns: Elements of Reusable Object-Oriented Software*. Addison-Wesley Professional.

2   Konig, Dierk, Andrew Glover, Paul King, Guillaume Laforge, and Jon Skeet. 2009. *Groovy In Action*, Second Edition. Manning Early Access Program Edition. Manning Publications.

3   Halloway, Stuart. 2009. *Programming Clojure*. Pragmatic Bookshelf.

4   Odersky, Martin, Lex Spoon, and Bill Venners. 2008. *Programming in Scala: A Comprehensive Step-By-Step Guide*. Artima.

5   Coplien, James O. *Design Pattern Definition*. http://hillside.net/patterns/222-design-pattern-definition.

5

Internal DSL
design in Ruby,
Groovy, and Clojure

This chapter covers

- Making DSLs concise using duck typing and metaprogramming
- Implementing a trade-processing DSL in Ruby
- Improving our order-processing DSL using Groovy
- Thinking differently about the trade-processing DSL in Clojure
- Common pitfalls with each language

The best way to learn new paradigms and design techniques is to look at real implementations using the best languages that support them. In chapter 4, you saw quite a few idioms and patterns that can help you develop expressive internal DSLs. For this chapter, I've selected three of today's most popular languages on the JVM. You're going to go through the exercise of building real-world DSLs using them.

Before going into the details of what we're going to do, figure 5.1 is a roadmap that I plan to follow in this chapter.

The languages I've selected for this chapter are dynamically typed. I start the chapter by discussing some of the attributes of dynamically typed languages that

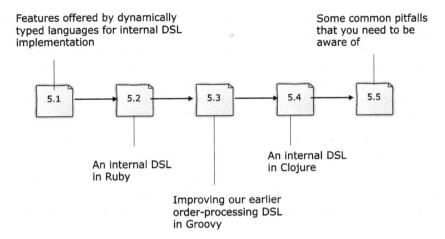

Figure 5.1   Roadmap of the chapter

make good DSLs and why I selected Ruby, Groovy, and Clojure for our discussion. Then we'll jump right into the implementation part and take you successively through the process of implementing complete DSLs using each of the three languages. We discuss the main features that these languages offer that you'll frequently use in designing DSLs and some of the rationale for when to select which pattern for your implementation.

At the end of this chapter, you'll have an overall idea of how to approach designing a DSL in languages that offer similar capabilities. Because we'll implement complete DSLs, you'll learn how to think in terms of the DSL that you design and you'll program your implementation language to fit the syntax that you want to provide to the user.

This chapter is going to be programming intensive; be prepared for lots of code coming your way and have your language interpreters handy. The examples are small and illustrative and I promise you'll have as much fun trying them out as I had writing them. The book's appendixes contain a short refresher for each of these three languages. Feel free to peek for a bootstrap in case you're unfamiliar with any of them. If you're new to the concept of development using multiple languages (also known as polyglot development), there's an introduction for bootstrapping in appendix G. But before we start in on the details, let's look at the rationale behind choosing the languages that I did.

5.1   *Making DSLs concise with dynamic typing*

One of the important attributes that an internal DSL adds on top of the underlying language is an enhanced readability of the domain semantics. The internal DSL translates the implementation to the domain user in terms of the language that he understands.

When your nonprogrammer domain expert looks at a DSL script, he should be able to understand the domain rules from it. This result is the real value that a DSL adds to improving the communication path between the developer and the domain person. I'm not evangelizing that every non-programmer domain person should be able to *write* programs using the DSL, but he should at least be able to *understand* the domain semantics from a DSL snippet.

A program written in a dynamically typed language doesn't contain type annotations; by nature it's visually less noisy and tells you what the programmer intends to do. This leads to better readability of the code, one of the prime attributes that differentiates any typical API from a DSL. In the following subsections, I'll discuss three of the most important characteristics that shape DSLs developed using dynamically typed languages:

- Enhanced readability, because there are no type annotations (section 5.1.1)
- Duck typing, which refers to the way you think of designing contracts in your DSLs (section 5.1.2)
- Metaprogramming, one way to get rid of boilerplate code from your DSL implementation (section 5.1.3)

5.1.1   Readability

As a DSL reader, you expect the language to flow smoothly, without any unnecessary complexity. The type system of a programming language can potentially add to the accidental complexity of a DSL. If you implement your internal DSL in a language that has a verbose type system like Java, there's a good chance that the resulting DSL will require you to plug many unnecessary type annotations into your abstractions. In a dynamically typed language, you don't need to provide type annotations, so the intent of the programmer is much clearer than it is in an alternative implementation in a corresponding statically typed language. Still, things won't necessarily be easier when it comes to understanding the implementation behind the intent. (You'll see more examples of this when we discuss common pitfalls of dynamic language-based DSL implementation in section 5.5.) On the whole, dynamically typed languages offer a more succinct syntax,, which results in enhanced readability of the DSL and its implementation.

Although the readability of a DSL is obvious, there's another aspect of dynamic languages that plays an important role when you design and implement internal DSLs. They're low in ceremony and rich in semantics. They're also quite a bit more concise than statically typed languages and, although you're still dealing with abstraction hierarchies, the thinking behind them is different. I'm referring to the way an abstraction responds to a message that's sent to it.

5.1.2 *Duck typing*

Dynamic typing isn't necessarily weak typing. You invoke a message on an object, and if the object satisfies the contract that the message asks for, you get a response; otherwise, the message propagates up the object hierarchy chain until one of its ancestors satisfies the contract. If it reaches the root without any handler capable of responding to the message, you get a `NoMethodError`. There's no compile-time check that statically determines whether a message invoked on an object is valid. Rather, you can change the set of methods and properties to which an object responds to during runtime. For any specific message, if an object supports the message at the time it's invoked, it's considered to be a valid invocation. This process is typically known as *duck typing*, and is implemented in languages like Ruby, Groovy, and Clojure. You can also implement duck typing in statically typed languages like Scala; we'll discuss that in chapter 6.

IMPLEMENTING POLYMORPHISM WITH DUCK TYPING

What does duck typing in dynamic languages buy you when you're implementing DSLs? Once again, the simple answer is that you get a concise implementation at the expense of static type safety. You don't need to statically declare interfaces or have inheritance hierarchies to implement polymorphism. As long as the receiver of a message implements the right contract, it can respond to the message meaningfully. Figure 5.2 shows how to implement polymorphism using duck typing.

Now let's look at an example from our domain. First, we'll do a Java implementation using interfaces and then demonstrate the conciseness that duck typing offers with an implementation in Ruby.

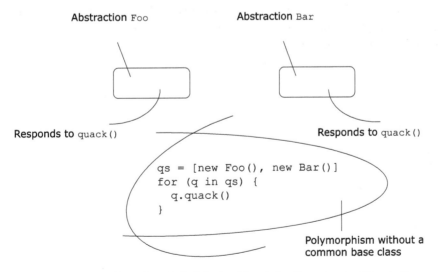

Figure 5.2   Polymorphism through duck typing. The abstractions `Foo` and `Bar` don't have any common base class, but we can treat them polymorphically in languages that support duck typing.

A TRADE DOMAIN EXAMPLE

Trades that are executed in the stock exchange can be of various types, depending on the type of instrument being traded. (I'm sure you're now familiar with trades, instruments, and executions. If you've forgotten some of the concepts, refresh your knowledge by reading the sidebars in earlier chapters.) A *security trade* involves trading equities or fixed incomes. A *forex trade* involves exchanging foreign currencies in the form of spot or swap transactions. With a statically typed language like Java, you would typically model the two abstractions as specializations of an interface, say, trade. You would also define the inheritance chain statically, as in the following snippet:

```
interface Trade {
  float valueOf();
}

class SecurityTrade implements Trade {
  public float valueOf() { //..  }
}
class ForexTrade implements Trade {
  public float valueOf() { //..  }
}
```

Now, if you have a method that needs to calculate the cash value of any kind of Trade supplied to it, you'll implement it as:

```
public float cashValue(Trade trade) {
  trade.valueOf();
}
```

Here, the argument to cashValue is constrained to the upper bound of the static type that implements the valueOf method. It's statically checked by the Java compiler. Now let's compare this implementation to one that does a cash_value with duck typing, as shown in the following listing.

Listing 5.1   Polymorphism with duck typing

```
class SecurityTrade
  ## ..
  def value_of
    ## ..
  end
end

class ForexTrade
  ## ..
  def value_of
    ## ..
  end
end

def cash_value(trade)
  trade.value_of
end
```

```
cash_value(SecurityTrade.new)
cash_value(ForexTrade.new)
```

No extras clutter up this implementation, and there's no static inheritance relationship; `cash_value` works as long you give it something that implements a `value_of` method. You might be thinking, what if I send it an unrelated object that doesn't implement the `value_of` method. It blows up during runtime, of course. That's the reason you should have a comprehensive coverage of unit tests to test your contracts.

For unit testing, you can create mocks easily too, because you don't have to jump through the hoops of ensuring static type safety. Remember, with languages that offer duck typing, you don't test for types and you don't try to emulate static typing with your dynamic language. It's a different way of thinking about abstraction design. Your test suites will test whether your abstractions implement the contract that they're supposed to provide to your clients.

Duck typing makes you write code that's free of statically checked constraints. One immediate effect is that your DSL implementation becomes much more concise, but at the same time your intentions are clear. We discussed this in section 4.2.2 when we implemented expressive decorators through dynamic mixins in Ruby. The final DSL looked like this:

```
Trade.new('r-123', 'a-123', 'i-123', 20000).with TaxFee, Commission
```

Note that we mixed in the modules `TaxFee` and `Commission` with `Trade`, and we used Ruby's duck typing to compute the total cash value of the trade.

Next up, let's revisit one technique that we saw in chapter 4. Metaprogramming is used by dynamically typed languages to save you from writing repetitive boilerplate code in your applications.

5.1.3   Metaprogramming—again!

Besides making your code free of type annotations, how does dynamic typing lead to concise DSLs? One obvious answer is by keeping you from writing repetitive code structures and instead generating them through the machinery of the language itself. Having a concise DSL API is as important to the DSL user as having a concise implementation is to you, the DSL implementer. Using their capabilities to introduce new methods and properties at runtime, both Ruby and Groovy have awesome metaprogramming facilities, which we discussed in sections 2.3.1 and 4.2. Let's return to one example to reiterate the conciseness that dynamic typing offers for DSL implementations. The following listing demonstrates how you can use runtime metaprogramming and closures to implement an XML builder in Groovy.

Listing 5.2   XML builder in Groovy: the power of dynamic metaprogramming

```
def clientOrders = //..
builder = new groovy.xml.MarkupBuilder()

builder.orders {
  clientOrders.each {ord ->
```

```
order(type: ord.getBuySell()) {
    instrument(ord.getSecurity())
    quantity(ord.getQuantity())
    price(ord.getLimitPrice())
  }
 }
}
```

Groovy's dynamic
❶ method dispatch

In this example, Groovy's `MarkupBuilder` doesn't know anything about the methods `order`, `instrument`, `quantity`, or `price` ❶. The language runtime uses dynamic method dispatch and employs Groovy's `methodMissing()` hook to intercept all undefined method calls. You can use similar techniques in Ruby. Dynamically typed languages provide an interceptor for all undefined methods. This technique makes programs much more concise and dynamic, but also preserves the expressiveness that you need.

We've just looked at the three attributes that you associate with a DSL that's implemented using a dynamic language. The first one, readability, describes the surface syntax of the DSL script. The other two attributes, duck typing and metaprogramming, have more to do with the underlying implementation techniques. Let's find out what features Ruby, Groovy, and Clojure possess that help you create and implement expressive DSLs.

5.1.4   *Why Ruby, Groovy, and Clojure?*

Ruby, Groovy, and Clojure each possess all three attributes of dynamically typed languages that make them great hosts for implementing internal DSLs. Table 5.1 contains an overview of these language features.

Table 5.1   Ruby, Groovy, and Clojure features that make them great choices for your internal DSLs

	Readability	**Duck typing**	**Metaprogramming**
Ruby	Flexible syntax, no type annotations, and strong literal support.	Supports duck typing and you can use `responds_to?` to check whether a class responds to a specific message.	Has strong support of reflective and generative metaprogramming.
Groovy	Flexible syntax, optional type annotations, and strong literal support.	Supports duck typing; you have some polymorphism without a common base class.	Has strong support for runtime metaprogramming through Groovy metaobject protocol (MOP).
Clojure	Syntax is flexible but bound by the prefix form of expressions as in other Lisp variants. You can provide optional type hints to speed up method dispatch, which avoids reflection in Java calls.	Supports duck typing as in Ruby or Groovy.	Implements compile-time metaprogramming through macros. Clojure is malleable enough to be extended as per the requirements of your DSL.

	JRuby	Groovy	Clojure
Runs on the JVM	X	X	X
Dynamically typed	X	X	X
Runtime metaprogramming	X	X	
Compile-time metaprogramming	?	?	X
Shares Java's object system		X	X
Bridges Java's object system	X		

? : Limited support through AST manipulation libraries

Figure 5.3   Ruby, Groovy, and Clojure present an interesting mix for DSL implementation

Even though Ruby, Groovy, and Clojure have some of the same characteristics, they're different enough for us to discuss them separately in the context of DSL implementation. All of them run on the JVM, have strong metaprogramming support, and are fast becoming mainstream development languages. Yet one of the areas in which they differ is the way they integrate with the JVM. Figure 5.3 summarizes some of the areas where the three languages are alike, as well as those where they differ.

In this chapter, we'll explore internal DSL implementation in all three languages. In the course of our discussion, we'll see the features that each of these languages offer and also look back at how they map to the implementation of the patterns we discussed extensively in chapter 4.

5.2   A trade-processing DSL in Ruby

We're going to develop a complete use case in this section. We'll implement a complete DSL for making new security trades and compute their cash values using pluggable business rules. After you execute the DSL, you'll get an instance of a Trade abstraction that you can use in various ways, depending on your application's functionalities. We'll start with a modest implementation and make incremental changes, making it more and more expressive and domain rich. Figure 5.4 shows a roadmap of what we'll do in each iteration as the DSL evolves.

Throughout our journey, Bob will act as our mentor, pointing out all the inadequacies and areas of improvement and helping us mold our design into the shape that fits into the glove of an expressive DSL. It's up to Ruby to help us comply with Bob's requests.

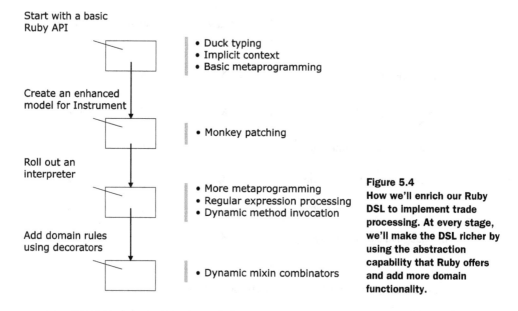

Start with a basic
Ruby API

- Duck typing
- Implicit context
- Basic metaprogramming

Create an enhanced
model for Instrument

- Monkey patching

Roll out an
interpreter

- More metaprogramming
- Regular expression processing
- Dynamic method invocation

Add domain rules
using decorators

- Dynamic mixin combinators

Figure 5.4
How we'll enrich our Ruby DSL to implement trade processing. At every stage, we'll make the DSL richer by using the abstraction capability that Ruby offers and add more domain functionality.

CODE ASSISTANCE In all of the following sections that have rich code snippets, I'll include a sidebar that contains the prerequisites of the language features that you need to know to appreciate the implementation details. Feel free to refer to the appropriate language cheat sheet in the appendixes before you proceed.

Keep our goal in mind: Bob should be able to understand the DSL and verify whether it violates any of his business rules.

5.2.1 Getting started with an API

API designs start out rather rusty. If you're working with a dynamic language, you always start with a body of clay and mold it iteratively to make it more expressive.

> **i Ruby tidbits you need to know**
>
> - *How are classes and objects defined in Ruby?* Ruby is object-oriented (OO) and follows the usual notion of any other OO language to define a class. Ruby does have its own object model that has functionalities that let you change, inspect, and extend objects during runtime through metaprogramming.
> - *How do you use the hash to implement a variable argument list?* In Ruby, you can pass a hash as an argument to a method to emulate keyword arguments.
> - *Basics of Ruby metaprogramming.* The Ruby object model has lots of artifacts like classes, objects, instance methods, class methods, singleton methods, and so on, that enable reflective and generative metaprogramming. You can dig into the Ruby object model at runtime and change behaviors or generate code dynamically.

Consider the following code snippet that our API designers came up with as the first version of the DSL:

```
instrument = Instrument.new('Google')        ⊲⌐ New Instrument
instrument.quantity = 100                        │ to be traded

TradeDSL.new.new_trade 'T-12435',            ⊲⌐ New trade
  'acc-123', :buy, instrument,                   │ to create
  'unitprice' => 200,
  'principal' => 120000, 'tax' => 5000
```

Bob saw this and yelled, "Hey! This looks too technical for me. What are those weird constructs that I need to invoke to get an instrument? That's not how I interpret an instrument when I get a trade."

Bob has a point, which I'll address shortly. But before I do, let me reiterate that a DSL never comes out right the first time. *A DSL always evolves iteratively.* That snippet is still an ordinary API with the usual readability that Ruby offers. It doesn't feel like a fluid sentence that Bob can roll off his tongue while he's tending to his usual chores in the trading business. Even so, this code gives us the baseline from which we'll move forward.

THE BASE ABSTRACTIONS

Every DSL design starts with a set of basic abstractions, on which you build your domain-friendly language. We'll call this approach bottom-up programming, where larger abstractions grow from smaller pieces and ultimately end up with the expressiveness that your domain expert wants.

We'll start our DSL design with a set of APIs for basic domain entities like Security-Trade and Instrument. The following listing provides the base Ruby abstractions that implement it.

> **Listing 5.3   SecurityTrade in Ruby (Iteration 1)**

```
class SecurityTrade

  attr_reader :ref_no,
              :account,
              :buy_sell,
              :instrument,
              :unitprice

  attr_accessor :principal,
                :tax,
                :commission
  def initialize(ref_no, account, buy_sell, instrument, unitprice)
    @ref_no = ref_no
    @account, @buy_sell, @instrument, @unitprice =
      account, buy_sell, instrument, unitprice
  end                                              ❶ Class method
                                                     to create trade
  def self.create(ref_no, account, buy_sell, instrument, h)   ⊲⌐
    tr = new(ref_no, account, buy_sell, instrument, h['unitprice'])
```

```
    [:principal, :tax, :commission].each do |m|
      tr.instance_eval("tr.#{m} = h['#{m}'] if h.has_key?('#{m}')")
    end
    tr
  end
end
```

Populate hash ❷

In this listing, notice the hash h in the create class method ❶ that's used to provide the named arguments for unitprice, principal, and tax. Using a hash to implement named arguments is a common idiom in Ruby. Another interesting trick that's employed is in ❷, where we use metaprogramming to set up the *implicit context* of the receiver and populate the trade instance with values from the hash h. We discussed how to set up an implicit context in section 4.2.1.

Listing 5.4 is the implementation of the Instrument class. There's nothing fancy about it, except that we're not making it immutable yet. For the current version of the DSL, you could've made it an immutable value object. We've kept it a mutable object for reasons that'll be clear to you in the next section when we use its mutability to come up with an expressive instrument creation DSL.

Listing 5.4   Instrument traded in Ruby

```
class Instrument
  attr_accessor :name, :quantity
  def initialize(name)
    @name = name
  end

  def to_s()
    "(Name: " + @name.to_s          +
    "/Quantity: " + @quantity.to_s  + ")"
  end
end
```

The final piece of this section is the class TradeDSL, which is just a skeleton of things to follow:

```
require 'security_trade'
class TradeDSL
  def new_trade(ref_no, account, buy_sell, instrument, attributes)
    SecurityTrade.create(ref_no, account, buy_sell, instrument, attributes)
  end
end
```

Our DSL has just started taking its first steps. As we proceed with the iterations in the following sections, you'll notice how TradeDSL evolves in expressiveness as we add more and more functionalities to it.

A DSL FACADE

The class TradeDSL also demonstrates the important technique of how you can decouple the DSL syntax from the underlying implementation. On the one hand, this class offers the surface syntax of the DSL to the user. On the other hand, it wraps the base

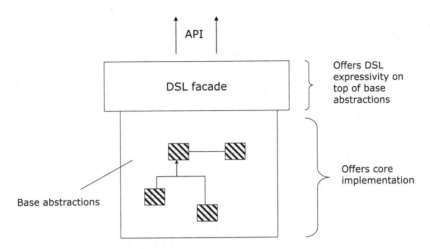

Figure 5.5   A DSL facade offers an expressive API to the user. It also keeps the core implementation structures from being exposed.

abstractions to provide a layer on top of the underlying implementation. Figure 5.5 illustrates this aspect of DSL structure.

Remember, when you design a DSL, be sure to provide a single point of interaction to the user. In this context, the `TradeDSL` class plays the role of a *DSL facade*. Currently, it only wraps the `create` method of the `SecurityTrade` class. In course of our subsequent iterations, we'll build up enough meat in this abstraction so that it becomes self-sufficient and caters to the users' requirements. But right now we need to deal with Bob's problems with the instrument creation part of the DSL. Here's where a little bit of monkey business can come in handy.

5.2.2   *A little bit of monkey-patching*

The next step in the evolution of the `TradeDSL` class is to make it easier for Bob to create an instrument. He needs to be able to ask for 100 shares of IBM the way he's used to doing on his trading desk. The result we want is something like the following, which shows the trade creation DSL that identifies the instrument being traded.

```
TradeDSL.new.new_trade 'T-12435',
  'acc-123', :buy, 100.shares.of('IBM'),
  'unitprice' => 200, 'principal' => 120000, 'tax' => 5000
```

The voodoo that Bob previously had to deal with to create an instrument using unnecessary syntactic constructs is gone, and is replaced by a more natural language that Bob speaks in his regular trading business: `100.shares.of('IBM')`. Now Bob's pretty happy! How did we achieve that?

Listing 5.5 is an implementation of the methods `shares` and `of` that we're silently introducing as methods of the `Numeric` class. `Numeric` is a built-in class in Ruby, but you can open any class and introduce new properties or methods into it. People call

> **ℹ Ruby tidbits you need to know**
>
> *Monkey patching* means introducing new properties or methods into an already existing class. In Ruby, you can open up an existing class and introduce new methods or properties that augment its behavior. This is a powerful feature; so powerful that you might be tempted to misuse it.

this *monkey patching*, and many detractors discourage this practice. As with any other superpower, monkey patching has risks and pitfalls. Any standard Ruby text (see [1] in section 5.7) will warn you when you're overstepping your limits. But when you use it judiciously, monkey patching makes your DSL flow.

Listing 5.5   Instrument DSL using monkey patching

```
require 'instrument'
class Numeric                                    ❶ Open up class
  def shares                                        Numeric
    self
  end                                               New method
                                                 ❷ shares
  alias :share :shares

  def of instrument
    if instrument.kind_of? String                ❸ New
      instrument = Instrument.new(instrument)        method of
    end
    instrument.quantity = self
    instrument
  end
end
```

This listing completes our first iteration toward shaping up our trade DSL. Note how our DSL is getting more expressive as the core abstractions evolve into larger wholes. We've removed the noise that was generated when we created the instrument in the snippet at the beginning of section 5.2.1. But we still have quite a few syntactic oddities when we consider the natural language of expression that Bob wants. With Ruby, we can push the limits even further. Our `TradeDSL` facade is lean enough to go for it. In the next section, we'll flesh it out with more syntactic sugar for the final DSL that Bob will use.

5.2.3   *Rolling out a DSL interpreter*

What is expressive enough? The answer to this question is debatable, depending on the perspective of your DSL user. To a user who's a programmer familiar with Ruby, the DSL that we came up with in iteration 1 would likely qualify as a fairly expressive one. Even a nonprogramming domain expert can figure out what's going on at the macro level, though he might be a little irritated with the additional syntax that it has. With a language as expressive as Ruby, we can push it to the limit and try to make it more aligned with the way Bob speaks at his trading desk.

> **ℹ Ruby tidbits you need to know**
>
> - *How to define multiline strings using "here" documents.* Use this technique when you want to define a string literal in place within the source code instead of externalizing it elsewhere.
> - *How to define class methods.* Class methods (or singleton methods) are instance methods of the Ruby singleton class. For more details, look at [1] in section 5.7.
> - *Using* evals *in Ruby and how they work with metaprogramming.* One of the most powerful features of Ruby is its ability to evaluate a string or a block of code dynamically during runtime. You get a number of flavors of evals that you can use in various contexts.
> - *Regular expression processing in Ruby.* Ruby has built-in support for regular expressions, which is extremely useful in pattern matching and text processing.

ADDING AN INTERPRETER

We've already developed a fairly expressive syntax for TradeDSL in section 5.2.2 that also nicely captures the domain semantics. Still, it looks too technical for Bob, who's used to a more fluid expression of the trading language in his domain.

In our second iteration, we're going to roll out an interpreter that'll interpret Bob's language, chop off the frills, and extract the essence needed to build the necessary abstractions. Here's how it'll look when we're done:

```
str = <<END_OF_STRING
  new_trade 'T-12435' for account 'acc-123'
                      to buy 100 shares of 'IBM',
                      at UnitPrice=100, Principal=12000, Tax=500
END_OF_STRING

puts TradeDSL.trade str
```

Now that we have the core abstractions in place, we're going to start adding to the syntactic sugar of our DSL. As promised earlier, the language for trade processing is steadily evolving.

What do we need to add to our TradeDSL class to make it feel like the code in the previous snippet? Listing 5.6 is another iteration of TradeDSL, the facade that we talked about in section 5.2.2. It rolls out a small interpreter that processes the user input before passing it on to SecurityTrade.

Listing 5.6 Trade DSL in Ruby, as an interpreter (Iteration 2)

```
require 'security_trade'
require 'numeric'

class TradeDSL
  class << self
    def const_missing(sym)
      sym.to_s.downcase
    end
```

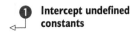 **1** Intercept undefined constants

```
      def trade(str)
        TradeDSL.new.interpret(str)
      end
   end

   def new_trade(ref_no, account, buy_sell, instrument, attributes)
     SecurityTrade.create(ref_no, account, buy_sell, instrument, attributes)
   end

   def interpret(input)                                    ❷  Implicit context
     instance_eval parse(input)                               for new_trade
   end
                                                           ❸  Process user
   def parse(dsl_string)                                      input
     dsl = dsl_string.clone
     dsl.gsub!(/=/, '=>')
     dsl.sub!(/and /, '')
     dsl.sub!(/at /, '')
     dsl.sub!(/for account /, ',')
     dsl.sub!(/to buy /, ', :buy, ')
     dsl.sub!(/(\d+) shares of ('.*?')/, '\1.shares.of(\2)')
     dsl.sub!(/(\d+) share of ('.*?')/, '\1.shares.of(\2)')
     puts dsl
     dsl
   end
end
```

Before going through the details of what this code does, let's look at a diagrammatic representation of how Bob's language is being interpreted. Figure 5.6 traces
this sequence.

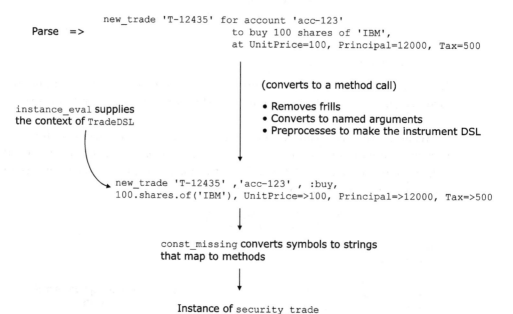

**Figure 5.6 How a sample `TradeDSL` script is interpreted by the code in listing 5.6 to generate Ruby
objects. An instance of `security_trade` is generated through the DSL interpreter.**

Try to understand the way this figure corresponds with the DSL implementation in listing 5.6. Recognize any of the techniques that we discussed in chapter 4? Well, in the listing, we have quite a few of them embedded within the code. The techniques recur from time to time in various forms and implementations. Look at the following list to discover some of them:

- Method `const_missing` ❶ uses *runtime metaprogramming* (discussed in section 4.4) to convert any undefined constants to strings.
- `instance_eval` in method `interpret` ❷ sets up the implicit context (discussed in section 4.2.1) of an instance of `TradeDSL` for executing the method `new_trade`
- Method `parse` uses regular expressions ❸ to process the user input and converts it into a form suitable for invoking the instance method `new_trade`

For a more detailed discussion about Ruby metaprogramming techniques, see [5] in section 5.7.

SPEAKING BOB'S LANGUAGE

Consider all this from a DSL user's point of view. He can use this DSL to write trade generation snippets using the same language that he does in his everyday business. We've provided some bubble words in the DSL to make it more aligned with his normal vocabulary. As a user, Bob can now enter these DSL strings into a file that he can load and process to generate instances of `SecurityTrade`. Even when he gets trade data from upstream front-office systems, he can use this DSL to generate instances of `SecurityTrade` and save it to his database.

In the next section, we'll enhance the DSL to incorporate a few business rules and make it more friendly to the users who are programmers and who want to enrich the trades that Bob generates so they can be used in the next step of the trading cycle.

5.2.4 *Adding domain rules as decorators*

Although Bob is happy with the current form that generates trades, he has some concerns about the next step of the trading cycle where we need to enrich the trades using some of the domain rules. We assured him that we're working on it and will get

---

ℹ Ruby tidbits you need to know

- *How to define and use Ruby blocks.* Blocks are used to implement lambdas and closures in Ruby.
- *How you implement mixins using Modules.* Ruby modules are yet another way to group artifacts that can be included in your classes as mixins.
- *How you chain mixins* to design decorators
- *Duck typing.* In Ruby, an object responds to a message if it implements the method by that name. Whether the object implements the method is not statically checked; you can change the object during runtime. If it quacks like a duck, it is a duck in Ruby.

back to him as soon as we've reached a level of expressiveness that he can comprehend. Let's discuss this iteration, which enhances the DSL and enriches the trade.

TRADE DSL –WHERE WE STAND NOW

We've already discussed quite a bit about our evolving DSL. Before we add to the trade enrichment part, let's step back and look at where we stand. Figure 5.7 says it all. We've developed the trade generation script that produces an instance of Security-Trade. As part of trade enrichment, we'll add business rules that are candidates for being modeled as a DSL.

When the trades reach the back office of a securities trading organization, cash values and static data need to be added so that they can be passed in to the next step in the processing pipeline. In section 4.2.2, we discussed how to compute the *cash value* of trade, also known as the *net settlement value*. After we receive trades in the back office, we need to invoke domain rules on the trades to compute their cash values. These domain rules vary across stock exchanges, the type of instruments traded, and a number of other factors. To keep our current scope simple, we're assuming a fixed set of rules. We're going to enrich our DSL to invoke those rules on the generated trades.

IMPLEMENTING DOMAIN RULES

The following rules apply to the trades that Bob generates:

- The cash value of a trade depends on the principal amount, the tax or fee amount, and the broker commission amount
- If the incoming trade stream contains any of these amounts, we'll honor them; otherwise, we need to compute them from the individual trades as per the following business rules.
- The following business rules apply to every trade:
  - The principal amount is the product of the unit price and the quantity, both of which are parts of the trade object.
  - The tax or fee is calculated as a fixed percentage of the principal amount.
  - The broker commission is calculated as a fixed percentage of the principal amount.

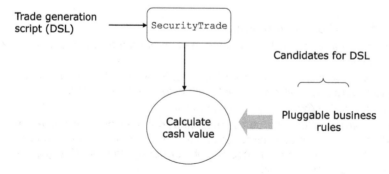

Figure 5.7 We've developed the DSL for trade generation. Now we'll add business rules as DSLs to compute cash value of the trade.

With these rules as part of the implementation, the following listing shows how the DSL is being used by the users to enrich trades.

Listing 5.7   Using the Trade DSL

```ruby
require 'trade_dsl'
require 'cash_value_calculator'
require 'tax_fee'
require 'broker_commission'

str = <<END_OF_STRING
new_trade 'T-12435' for account 'acc-123'
                    to buy 100 shares of 'IBM',
                    at UnitPrice = 100
END_OF_STRING                                                      ❶ Ruby block for
                                                                      side effects
TradeDSL.trade str do |t|

  CashValueCalculator.new(t).with TaxFee, BrokerCommission do |cv|
                                                                      Decorators
    t.cash_value = cv.value                              Side effects using mixins ❷
    t.principal = cv.p                                   in a block ❸
    t.tax = cv.t
    t.commission = cv.c
  end
  t
end
```

`TradeDSL.trade(str)` generates an instance of `SecurityTrade` that gets passed into the Ruby block ❶. In the block, the trade is enriched as a side effect of mutating the instance that it takes ❸. All this is disciplined and idiomatic Ruby programming. We're using the conciseness that Ruby offers, along with the domain semantics that we add to the language to make it more expressive.

Notice how we're making the domain rules pluggable in our DSL in this code by abstracting the computation logic of `TaxFee` and `BrokerCommission`. All the DSL user needs to do is wire up the necessary components with the `CashValueCalculator` class ❷. The technique that we use for wiring them up is called mixin-based programming, which we already discussed in section 4.2.2. Here, the mixins act as decorators of the main class `CashValueCalculator`.

To make the `TradeDSL.trade` method accept an additional block as an argument, we need to make the following small change. The rest of the DSL remains the same.

Listing 5.8   Trade DSL in Ruby: blocks for side effects (Iteration 3)

```ruby
require 'security_trade'
require 'numeric'

class TradeDSL
  class << self
    def const_missing(sym)
      sym.to_s.downcase
    end
```

```
  def trade(str)
    yield TradeDSL.new.interpret(str) if block_given?
  end
end

end
```
① Process the block as a side effect

Now let's go back to listing 5.7 and look into the implementation of the decorators that we added transparently to the `CashValueCalculator` instance.

RUBY DSL WITH DECORATORS

Listing 5.7 shows an instance of how you can add syntactic sugar on top of core abstractions like `TaxFee` and `BrokerCommission`. And unlike static languages, we can do all this dynamically through the magic of metaprogramming. The following listing implements the complete DSL that computes the cash value of a given trade.

Listing 5.9 Calculating the cash value of the trade

```
class CashValueCalculator
  attr_reader :trade

  attr_accessor :p, :t, :c

  def initialize(trade)
    @trade = trade
    @p = [@trade.principal,
          @trade.unitprice * @trade.instrument.quantity].find do |m|
      not m.nil?
    end
    @t = @trade.tax unless @trade.tax.nil?
    @c = @trade.commission unless @trade.commission.nil?
  end

  def with(*args)
    args.inject(self) { |acc, val| acc.extend val }
    yield self if block_given?
  end

  def value
    @p
  end
end

module TaxFee
  def value
    @t = @p * 0.2 if @t.nil?
    super + @t
  end
end

module BrokerCommission
  def value
    @c = @p * 0.1 if @c.nil?
    super + @c
  end
end
```
① Concise literal syntax

② Compose mixins dynamically

Table 5.2 Dynamic languages and the Ruby DSL

Attribute	Supporting Ruby features shown in listing 5.9
Readability	Malleable syntax, array literals, and optional parentheses make the code in `initialize` method ❶ clear and concise. It clearly advertises the domain rule that asks us to honor the cash value components if they come with the input trade, and to calculate otherwise. The total cash value of the trade is computed implicitly by the modules that you mix in with the `CashValueCalculator` instance. The DSL in listing 5.7 nicely abstracts away the implementation of the net cash value calculation, while explicitly telling the user which components take part in the computation. In fact, the user's going to supply the components that he wants to use in computing the final net value.
Duck typing	Note how the `value` method in `TaxFee` and `BrokerCommission` uses `super` without any static inheritance relationship. This is an example of duck typing. You can plug in any module that has a `value` method and things will be chained in magically.
Metaprogramming	The `with` method ❷ acts as the combinator that lets us compose the mixins through runtime extensions of the participating modules.

Aha! Now we have the DSL implementation ready with a friendly surface syntax that Bob can understand, and an expressive implementation that speaks the language of the domain. Table 5.2 contains a quick recap of how this Ruby implementation of the DSL embodies the three attributes of dynamically typed languages that we talked about in section 5.1.

This completes the Ruby implementation of the trading DSL. I set up one problem from a real-life use case at the beginning of the section and demonstrated how you can solve it using a DSL-based approach. Now that you've implemented it, it appears to be the most idiomatic way to implement the domain functionality that we set out to model. We used Ruby, exploited its powers of flexible syntax, duck typing, and metaprogramming, and finally arrived at a language that a domain expert can comprehend. As we completed the implementation step-by-step, I highlighted all the features that make Ruby a great language for internal DSL implementation. The idea wasn't to show off the power of Ruby, but to reiterate how a DSL-based approach can complement a powerful language to make extensible abstractions.

In the next section, we'll talk about DSL implementation in another language that, like Ruby, offers dynamic typing and has powerful metaprogramming abilities, but also has a more seamless model of integration with the JVM. You used this language in chapters 2 and 3 when we designed an order-processing DSL using it. It's Groovy, and we'll use it to improve on your earlier implementations of the same DSL.

Have you started wondering why we've been looking at so many languages when most of the time you'll be using only one for your development? In real-life application development, if you're designing DSLs, ideally you should be using the language that best fits the solution domain. Remember, it's the DSL syntax and semantics that matter the most; the language you use for implementation is only a means of getting there. The richer the set of idioms up your sleeve, the more options you have to use when you're designing your DSL.

5.3 The order-processing DSL: the final frontier in Groovy

Groovy as a language offers capabilities that are similar to Ruby's: dynamic typing and strong runtime metaprogramming power. The main difference between the two languages is that Groovy shares the object model with Java, which means that it has more seamless integration capabilities than Ruby. In fact, Groovy is often touted as a DSL for Java. For this reason, choose Groovy as the implementation language when you're designing DSLs that need to fit in the ecosystem of a Java application. Both Ruby and Groovy offer similar capabilities as hosts for implementing DSLs. But by virtue of sharing the object system with Java, Groovy offers better integration capabilities.

In this section, we'll revisit the order-processing DSL that you implemented first in chapter 2 and worked with again in chapter 3. We won't focus on the features of Groovy that we've already discussed while implementing the trade DSL in Ruby. We'll talk more about one single, stand-out feature in Groovy metaprogramming that you'll use often when you're designing an internal DSL.

We'll start with a brief recap of the earlier iterations of the order-processing DSL. Then I'll identify the drawbacks and we'll improve on our earlier attempts until we have the final version of implementation.

5.3.1 The order-processing DSL so far

We've already discussed quite a few options for Groovy implementations. Figure 5.8 offers a brief recap.

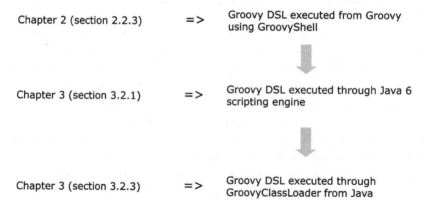

Figure 5.8 A look at the alternatives we implemented in our order-processing DSL in earlier chapters

In section 2.2.3, we did an end-to-end Groovy implementation that executed the DSL from Groovy using `GroovyShell`. `GroovyShell` takes the DSL definition as well as the script and executes it using the `evaluate` method. In section 3.2.1, we changed the DSL and used Java 6 scripting engine APIs to eval the DSL. In section 3.2.3, we explored yet another option that was an improvement over the one we used in section 3.2.1. Instead of using the Java `ClassLoader`, we used `GroovyClassLoader` from within the Java application to load the DSL for order processing.

All the options that we've explored so far have a common drawback, related to the way we used Groovy metaprogramming concepts. In this section, we'll improve our earlier attempts by implementing a better model of Groovy metaprogramming to drive your DSL.

5.3.2 *Controlling the scope of metaprogramming*

In all the earlier approaches to this DSL, we injected methods to existing Groovy classes by adding methods to their `MetaClass`.

> **ⓘ Groovy tidbits you need to know**
>
> - `ExpandoMetaClass` and how it does *metaprogramming*. A special artifact of Groovy metaprogramming that lets you dynamically add methods, constructors, properties, and static methods using a neat closure syntax.
> - *Closures and delegates*. A closure in Groovy is a lambda that can be defined in one place and executed somewhere else, much like with Ruby blocks. The delegate is usually the enclosing object of the closure, but you can change it during runtime.
> - *Class declaration* in Groovy. It's similar to Java, minus the verbosity of types. You also get that Groovy concise syntax.
> - How Groovy *categories manage the scope of metaprogramming*. Categories in Groovy are an alternative to `ExpandoMetaClass` for metaprogramming. Using categories, you can control the scope within which the changes to the meta-objects are visible within your application.

Look at this snippet from listing 3.1 where we added properties like `shares` and `of` to the `Integer` class:

```
Integer.metaClass.getShares = { -> delegate }
Integer.metaClass.of = { instrument ->  [instrument, delegate] }
```

That code lead us to write DSL scripts as follows (from listing 3.2):

```
newOrder.to.buy(100.shares.of('IBM')) {
  limitPrice   300
  allOrNone    true
  valueAs      {qty, unitPrice -> qty * unitPrice - 500}
}
```

We did this injection using Groovy's `ExpandoMetaClass`, which lets you add methods, properties, constructors, and static methods to an existing class during runtime. The problem with Groovy's `ExpandoMetaClass` is that the properties or methods that you inject to a class are available *globally*. When you're writing an application, it might not be a recommended social practice to change the behaviors of *all* instances of a class across *all* the threads of the JVM. `ExpandoMetaClass` does this, which makes your changes to a class visible to *all* other users. Global changes are also an issue with Ruby monkey patching, and can have adverse impacts on other users, introducing incompatibilities in the ways they look at the class and method definitions.

A fine-grained control over the scope of metaprogramming is a feature that you should always keep in mind when you're implementing Groovy DSLs. This is precisely the reason why we have a separate section about Groovy implementation.

THE GROOVY MOP AND CATEGORIES

The Groovy MOP gives you yet another option for making smart and controlled injections into existing classes. But instead of making these added properties visible globally, it restricts the scope to within a block of code. You define classes, called *categories*, where you define additional methods that you want to inject. Programmers use categories extensively in Groovy to produce expressive DSLs. (For a more detailed explanation of Groovy categories, see [2] in section 5.7.) Let's use categories and re-engineer our order-processing DSL to its new, improved form. The basic abstraction that captures an `Order` in Groovy is shown in the following listing.

Listing 5.10 Order class in Groovy

```
class Order {
  def name
  def quantity
  def allOrNone = false
  def limitPrice
  def valueClosure

  def Order(stockName, qty) {
    name = stockName
    quantity = qty
  }

  def limitPrice(price) {limitPrice = price}

  def allOrNone() {allOrNone = true}

  def valueAs(closure) {                          ◁┘ Ensure thread safety
    valueClosure = closure.clone()
    valueClosure.delegate =
      [qty: quantity, unitPrice: limitPrice]      ◁ Bind the free variables
  }

  String toString() {
    "stock: $name, number of shares: $quantity,
allOrNone: $allOrNone, limitPrice: $limitPrice,
```

```
➥valueAs: ${valueClosure()}"
    }
}
```

As part of our DSL, we need to give the user the flexibility of a little language for expressing the quantity of shares that he wants to buy or sell as `200.IBM.shares`. We'll do this using Groovy categories. But we need a helper class that abstracts this expression and allows the user to include the rest of the order description as a closure. Let's call this class `Stock`. Here's the class definition:

```
class Stock {
  def order

  Stock(orderObject) {
    order = orderObject
  }

  def shares(closure) {
    closure = closure.clone()        ← Ensure thread safety
    closure.delegate = order         ← Delegate to collect the information
    closure()
    order
  }
}
```

Before proceeding any further with the implementation, let me introduce the new order-processing DSL in use, so that you can follow the implementation as we move ahead. Here's the DSL script that Bob can use for ordering his stock transactions.

Listing 5.11 Order-processing DSL script

```
buy 200.GOOG.shares {
    limitPrice 300
    allOrNone()
    valueAs {qty * unitPrice - 500}
}

buy 200.IBM.shares {
    limitPrice 300
    allOrNone()
    valueAs {qty * unitPrice - 500}
}

buy 200.MSOFT.shares {
    limitPrice 300
    allOrNone()
    valueAs {qty * unitPrice - 500}
}
```

In this listing, we need to add methods to class `Integer`. We'll do that using Groovy categories this time.

THE BASIC DSL

The first category is shown in the following listing. This category will help us build instances of `Stock`.

Listing 5.12   Adding methods to `Integer` using categories

```
class StockCategory {
  static Stock getGOOG(Integer self) {
    new Stock(new Order("GOOG", self))
  }

  static Stock getIBM(Integer self) {
    new Stock(new Order("IBM", self))
  }

  static Stock getMSOFT(Integer self) {
    new Stock(new Order("MSOFT", self))
  }
}
```

You can see that 200.IBM gives us an instance of Stock using StockCategory, which is defined in the listing. On this instance of Stock, we invoke the method shares. This method takes a closure that contains the rest of the order details as an argument. When we defined the Stock class, we set the delegate of the closure that shares takes to the order instance. Doing so sets up the correct context when we specify limit-Price, allOrNone, and valueAs in the script in listing 5.11. Note that in real-life projects we can generate this code from the list of stocks in the database.

Now we've got the basic engine of the DSL ready. We need to add one last category to make the script smarter, then finish it off with a Java launcher.

5.3.3   Rounding it off

Look at listing 5.11 once again. Processing for each individual order starts with buy. This means that we need to inject a method buy to the Groovy Script class. Let's do this using another category:

```
class OrderCategory {
  static void buy(Script self, Order o) {
    println "Buy: $o"
  }

  static void sell(Script self, Order o) {
    println "Sell: $o"
  }
}
```

For this demonstration, we just want to print the order that the user has entered and check that all its attributes are set correctly. In real-life projects, you should be writing meaningful domain logic that processes the order and does other things.

This step completes the DSL implementation in Groovy. All we need to do now is write a runner that runs this DSL, and then invoke the runner code from within a Java application. Here's the Groovy code that runs the DSL using the categories that we defined above:

```
class DslRunner {
  static runDSL(dsl) {
    use(OrderCategory, StockCategory) {
```

 Use the categories

```
         new GroovyClassLoader().parseClass(dsl as File).newInstance().run()
      }
    }
}
```

In this snippet, note that the additional methods that we inject into the existing classes are available only within the scope denoted by the use {} block ❶. Finally, here's the Java application that invokes DslRunner:

```
public class LaunchFromJava {
  public static void main(String[] args) {
    DslRunner.runDSL("newOrder.dsl");
  }
}
```

Ta-da! You've just seen how a DSL implementation evolves in Groovy. Figure 5.9 depicts the translation of the DSL script through the semantic model to the execution phase.

This concludes our miniseries of DSL implementation in Groovy. In the next section, we'll implement a completely different flavor of DSL using the power of Clojure.

5.4 *Thinking differently in Clojure*

In this section, you're going to see how you can implement a use case for computing the cash value of a trade in Clojure. (If you need a reminder, section 4.2.2 contains a sidebar that discusses what I mean by the cash value of a trade.) We'll use a DSL-based approach, building smaller domain abstractions bottom up and then composing them using Clojure combinators.

We implemented this same use case in section 5.2.4 using Ruby. So why are we dealing with it again? Ruby is a language that offers a completely different paradigm

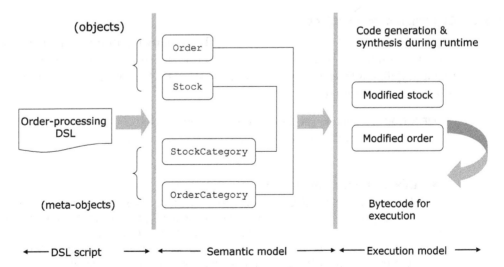

Figure 5.9 How the Groovy DSL script gets transformed into the Semantic model and finally into the Execution model

Table 5.3   Think differently when you're implementing a DSL in Clojure

DSL implementation in Ruby	DSL implementation in Clojure
Think in terms of objects and modules and how to wire them up during runtime using the power of metaprogramming.	Think in terms of the functions of the use case and how to compose them using Clojure sequences that operate on lambdas.
Use tricks like `method_missing`, `const_missing`, and other dynamic metaprogramming features to make the DSL concise and expressive.	Use macros to convert DSL syntax to normal Clojure forms—all during compile time.
A DSL implemented in Ruby or Groovy might not feel like the native syntax of the language.	A DSL implemented in Clojure looks like Clojure code because its structure is based on s-expressions.

than Clojure. Ruby is OO and uses runtime metaprogramming as the primary tool for DSL implementation. Clojure is mostly functional, with strong compile-time metaprogramming capabilities using macros. It's no surprise you need to think differently in Clojure than in Ruby or Groovy. Even when you implement a DSL for the same use case, a Clojure-based implementation might be entirely different from a Ruby-based one. Here I've intentionally picked the same use case we used for Ruby just to demonstrate how selecting another host language can influence design decisions differently. Look at table 5.3 for some of the key differentiators in Clojure that stand out with respect to Ruby. For a more detailed discussion of Clojure as a language, you can see [6] in section 5.7.

To fully appreciate the differences between the two implementations, I strongly advise you to go back and reread the information about the Ruby implementation before I take you through the Clojure one.

5.4.1   Building a domain object

To start building a DSL, we need some of the underlying abstractions that form the core of the domain model. For this reason, our first step is to design the trade abstraction and define a factory method (shown in listing 5.13) that generates trade objects from an external source.

> **DEFINITION**   A Factory method is a design pattern that provides a single point of interaction for the creation of instances of a family of objects.

> ### ⓘ Clojure tidbits you need to know
> - *Basic function definition and syntax* of the language. The syntax of Clojure is like Lisp; the prefix notation might catch you off guard. In case you're not used to it, go through the basics by reviewing [4] in section 5.7.
> - *Defining a* Map *data structure.* Map is a data structure that's used often in Clojure to implement the class-like structures of OO programming.

The source can be any data source that your system interacts with; for example, the attributes can come from a web request, flat file, or database. The factory method extracts information from the request and builds a map that represents the attributes of a trade.

Listing 5.13 Trade generation in Clojure

```
(defn trade
  "Make a trade from the request"
  [request]
  {:ref-no (:ref-no request)
   :account (:account request)
   :instrument (:instrument request)
   :principal (* (:unit-price request) (:quantity request))
   :tax-fees {}})

(def request
  {:ref-no "trd-123"
   :account "nomura-123"
   :instrument "IBM"
   :unit-price 120
   :quantity 300})
```

❶ Build trade from request

Principal value = unit-price * quantity

❷ Populate tax-fee later

❸ Sample request

Clojure is implemented on top of objects, though it presents a functional model of programming to users. In this example, we implement abstractions as name-value pairs in the form of a Clojure Map. Note that trade is a function that builds up the necessary abstraction with the relevant information from the input request. The input request ❸ is also a Map, implemented as a function of its keys. When we extract values out of the Map, we use the same syntax as we do for a function invocation ❶. As an example, the literal syntax (:account request) extracts the value of the account key from the Map.

The method trade clearly expresses the domain intents and semantics. The map literal syntax enables named arguments, which map domain concepts directly into program elements and makes the code expressive. The map tax-fees is still a placeholder ❷ that we need to fill up when we enrich the generated trade in the next section.

5.4.2 Enriching domain objects using decorators

The next step is to enrich the base abstraction with additional features that make it usable in a real-world use case of a trading lifecycle. We're going to use decorators to do this, the same way we did with the Ruby implementation in section 5.2.4 to enrich the trade with tax and fee components. But unlike the Ruby implementation, we'll use compile-time metaprogramming and macros to implement the same behavior in Clojure.

> Designing a DSL involves mapping the syntax that you want to the underlying semantics of the language. You need to change the way you think when you use a different language for implementation.

> **ⓘ Clojure tidbits you need to know**
>
> - *Higher-order functions.* Clojure supports higher-order functions where you can use functions as first-class values. You can pass functions as parameters, accept one as a return value, and so on.
> - *Macros* are the most important secret sauce for developing DSLs in Clojure. Macros are the building blocks of compile-time metaprogramming.
> - *Let binding and lexical scope.* You can define bindings at precisely the scope you need, no matter how narrow it is.
> - Understanding the Clojure *standard library functions.* A wealth of them are available at the Clojure site (http://clojure.org).
> - *Immutable data structures.* Clojure offers immutable and persistent data structures. By persistence I mean that you have access to all earlier versions, even after mutating a data structure. Look at [4] in section 5.7 for details.
> - Some *standard combinators like* reduce and ->. Combinators let you write concise and expressive code structures in Clojure. Combinators are functions that take other functions as parameters.

But how do you add behaviors to an abstraction dynamically without adding any run-time performance overhead? Clojure lets you do that using compile-time mixins. Let's see how.

USING CLOJURE COMBINATORS

Suppose we have the construct with-tax-fee that introduces additional behaviors within an already existing Clojure function to add tax and fees to our trade. In the following snippet, if we apply with-tax-fee to our trade function, we get a new function that has the additional mappings for :tax and :commission stacked on top of the existing set.

```
(with-tax-fee trade
  (with-values :tax 12)
  (with-values :commission 23))
```

In this snippet, with-tax-fee acts as the decorator to the trade function. Now you can execute trade with a request and tax and commission components will be filled up with 12% and 23% of the principal amount, respectively. (Tax and commission are usually expressed as percentages of the principal amount of a trade.)

If you're not the implementer of the DSL, you're not really bothered about what it takes to implement constructs like with-tax-fee or with-values. You can use them as combinators and develop your abstractions for the trade DSL. But in this section, we're discussing DSL implementations. So our next step is to see what it takes to implement a function that decorates another function with an additional behavior. Here's an implementation of with-values.

Listing 5.14 Wrap trade with additional behavior

```
(defn with-values [trade tax-fee value]        ←❶  Higher-order functions
  (fn [request]                                ←❷  Returns a function
    (let [trdval (trade request)                ←
          principal (:principal trdval)]             Get the
      (assoc-in trdval [:tax-fees tax-fee]     ❸  trade value    ❹  Add to :tax-fees
               (* principal (/ value 100)))))))               Map as percentage
                                                              of principal
```

The combinator `with-values` does quite a bit to augment the output of the `trade` function with additional behavior. Even though this isn't a book on Clojure, let's look into this code more closely in table 5.4 to get an idea of how it abstracts the complexity to give clients a simpler API.

But how does `with-tax-fee` integrate with `with-values` to give us the new `trade` function? That's what we'll turn to next.

Table 5.4 Dissecting a Clojure API

Clojure feature	How the DSL uses it
Higher-order functions that are an essential part of the recipe that you'll use when implementing DSLs.	The first argument that `with-values` takes is a function ❶. The `with-values` function returns another function ❷, which is also characteristic of a language that supports functions as first-class values. Because Clojure supports higher-order functions you can pass functions as parameters, get them as return values, and treat them like any other data type in the language. In ❷, `fn` denotes an anonymous function in Clojure. The anonymous function that `with-values` returns is the one that augments the input function `trade` with additional behavior to populate `:tax-fees`.
Evaluation in a lexical context to control scope	We invoke `trade` on the argument that the new function takes ❸ and augment the resultant `Map` with `tax-fee` values. The bindings in a `let` are sequential; note that we use `trdval` in the next binding for `principal`.
Immutability and the ability to implement persistent data structures	In the last step in the listing, we add `tax-fee` as the key and the `value` parameter as its value ❹. Then we add the entry to the `Map` that `trade` returned in ❸. The original `Map` doesn't get mutated. Clojure implements immutable and persistent data structures. In this case, for every invocation, `assoc-in` returns a new `Map` that augments the original `Map` with the `key` and `value` specified as arguments.

Functions that compose naturally	The fact that `with-values` returns a function helps implement chaining. So we can write code like the following:
	<pre>(with-tax-fee trade
	  (with-values :tax 12)
	  (with-values :commission 23))</pre>In this code, we chain two invocations of `with-values` with the original `trade` function. This chaining of method invocation is what we mean by composability, which is offered by languages like Clojure that implement functions as first-class values.

DECORATORS USING HIGHER-ORDER FUNCTIONS

Before we look at `with-tax-fee`, here's a little something that forms the basis of our decorator implementation. One thing is becoming clearer. Unlike the Ruby implementation, in which we focused on objects, Clojure provides you with interesting tricks to deal more with functions. The whole idea when you're implementing DSLs is to explore some of the idioms that fit the Clojure landscape more naturally. The following snippet shows an interesting trick you can do with function threading.

```
(def trade
    (-> trade
        (with-values :tax 20)
        (with-values :commission 30)))
```

The function `->` threads its first argument across the forms that are the subsequent arguments. Function threading makes implementing a decorator trivial in Clojure, because you can redefine the original function by threading it through the decorators using `->`. The implementation of a decorator shown in listing 5.15 uses this technique and is taken from Compojure, the web development framework in Clojure (go to http://github.com/weavejester/compojure for more information). If you're not familiar with Clojure, the concepts we've just been discussing will take some time to gel. But when you get the feel of how you can compose larger functional abstractions out of smaller ones, you'll appreciate the beauty that those four short lines of code can bring to your implementation.

WRAPPING IT UP WITH A CLOJURE MACRO

Instead of making the user do all this, why not wrap up the function threading stuff with a Clojure macro that reads more simply and intuitively, and at the same time abstract the same magic without any runtime overhead? That's what's happening in the following listing.

Listing 5.15   Decorator in Clojure

```
(defmacro redef
  "Redefine an existing value, keeping the metadata intact."
  [name value]
  `(let [m# (meta #'~name)
         v# (def ~name ~value)]
     (alter-meta! v# merge m#)
     v#))                                          ❶  Clojure
                                                      macro
(defmacro with-tax-fee
  "Wrap a function in one or more decorators."
  [func & decorators]
  `(redef ~func (-> ~func ~@decorators)))
```

That bit of code completes `with-tax-fee`, the Clojure version of a compile-time decorator that lets you add behaviors to existing abstractions in a completely noninvasive manner. `with-tax-fee` is implemented as a macro ❶, which gets expanded during the macro expansion phase of compilation and generates the code that it encapsulates.

Before decorating the input function, we need to redefine the root binding of the function that's preserving the metadata. The macro `redef` does this for us. This process is different from what happens in Ruby, where all metaprogramming is done during the execution phase. As we discussed earlier, during runtime we don't have any meta-objects in Clojure; they're all resolved during macro expansion.

We've done lots of stuff to our implementation and come up with a DSL that adds tax and fee calculation logic to a trade abstraction. With the decorated `trade` function, we can now define an API that computes the cash value of the trade. The features of Clojure that you've seen so far make this implementation a meaningful abstraction for the domain. The API is explicit about what it does with the trade to compute its net cash value. A person familiar with the domain and the language can understand right away what the function tries to achieve.

```
(defn net-value [trade]
  (let [principal (:principal trade)
        tax-fees (vals (trade :tax-fees))]
    (reduce + (conj tax-fees principal))))
```

❶ **Combinator increases abstraction**

This implementation is a testimony to the succinctness of Clojure. Clojure is a dense language and lets you program at a higher level of abstraction. The last expression in this snippet packs a powerful punch. `reduce` is a combinator that recurses over the sequence and applies the function (+) that's passed to it ❶.

WHAT WE'VE ACCOMPLISHED

Before we move on to the next step in running our DSL, let's step back for a moment and take stock in table 5.5 of what you've achieved so far in implementing the DSL for the cash value calculation of the trade.

Table 5.5 Evolving our DSL

Step in the evolution of the DSL	Implementation details
1 Designed the base abstraction for trade	We used a factory method `trade` that does the following: **1** Accepts data from an external source **2** Generates a trade object in the form of a Clojure `Map`
2 Injected additional behaviors into the domain object.	Changed `trade` function to one with additional behaviors for tax and fee injected for cash value calculation.
Techniques used: • Decorator pattern • Clojure macros	**How to get tax and fee to populate trade:** **1** Define the `with-values` function that augments the output of the trade function with behaviors. **2** Add tax and fee to the output of the `trade` function using the Decorator pattern **3** Define the `with-tax-fee` macro that enables the multiple application of `with-values` on an existing function. **Note:** `with-tax-fee` uses compile-time metaprogramming and has no runtime overhead.

Table 5.5   Evolving our DSL *(continued)*

Step in the evolution of the DSL	Implementation details
3 Defined the `net-value` function for cash value calculation of trade	The `net-value` function accepts the `trade` function that we modified in step 2 and also takes the following actions: **1** Gets the principal from the trade **2** Gets the tax and fees from the trade **3** Computes the net cash value using the specified domain logic

Clojure is a language with a philosophy that's different than that of Ruby, Groovy, or Java. Clojure is idiomatically functional, despite being developed on top of Java's object system. You need to think differently when you're programming in Clojure. As you saw in this section, we didn't have to do any special magic to design our DSL in Clojure. It's just Clojure's natural way of programming.

Before we go any further, let's look at figure 5.10 which illustrates the lifecycle of a DSL script written in Clojure.

Feeling tired? We still have one last bit of business left with the Clojure DSL—the instant gratification of seeing your DSL in action within a Clojure REPL (read-eval-print-loop). Get yourself a cup of coffee and a few cookies if you need caffeine and sugar to invigorate you. You might need a pick-me-up, because in the next section we're going to go interactive. You'll interact directly with the Clojure interpreter and run the DSL that you designed in this section.

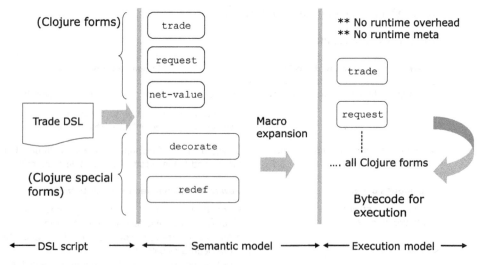

Figure 5.10   DSL script to execution model for Clojure. Pay attention to the series of steps that the DSL script goes through before it's ready for execution. As we discussed in chapter 1, the semantic model bridges the DSL script and the execution model.

5.4.3 A DSL session at the REPL

A dynamic language like Clojure gives you the pleasure of directly interacting with the language runtime through an REPL. (Read about REPL at http://en.wikipedia.org/wiki/Read-eval-print_loop.). Using the REPL, you can immediately see your DSL in action, make changes online, and feel the effect of the changed behaviors instantly. You should definitely use this feature for the seamless evolution of your DSL.

For the cash value calculation logic, our DSL looks as simple as (net-value (trade request)), which is as concise and expressive as possible. You can create a trade instantly, run your DSL in the REPL, and make changes to the trade function by adding more domain rules as decorators. Here's a look at a sample session at the Clojure REPL with the DSL we've implemented so far:

```
user> (def request {:ref-no "r-123", :account "a-123",
                     :instrument "i-123", :unit-price 20,
                     :quantity 100})
#'user/request

user> (trade request)
{:ref-no "r-123", :account "a-123", :instrument "i-123",
  :principal 2000, :tax-fees {}}

user> (with-tax-fee trade
        (with-values :tax 12)
        (with-values :commission 23))
#'user/trade

user> (trade request)
{:ref-no "r-123", :account "a-123", :instrument "i-123",
  :principal 2000, :tax-fees {:commission 460, :tax 240}}

user> (with-tax-fee trade
        (with-values :vat 12))
#'user/trade

user> (trade request)
{:ref-no "r-123", :account "a-123", :instrument "i-123",
  :principal 2000, :tax-fees {:vat 240, :commission 460, :tax 240}}

user> (net-value (trade request))
2940
```

One of the most important qualities of a DSL is the ability to hide complex implementations behind simple-to-use APIs that model the domain vocabulary. This session at the Clojure REPL demonstrates this simplicity. DSLs always make you feel like you're using a language that models the one a trader speaks at his dealing desk. In this case, it happens to have a Clojure implementation underneath.

For every new paradigm, there comes a set of pitfalls that you, as a designer, need to be aware of. So far you've seen quite a few patterns, idioms, and best practices that should guide your thought processes while you're implementing DSLs. In the next section, I'll talk about some of the pitfalls that you should stay clear of.

5.5   Recommendations to follow

So far this chapter has been a positive experience for you. We've discussed DSL implementation in three of the most popular dynamic languages on the JVM. You've seen lots of idioms and implementation techniques and actually implemented a couple of useful snippets of DSL from our domain of stock trading applications. But you always have to pay the piper, and no matter how easy all this might seem, there are some potential problems that we've got to talk about.

Instead of picking up three completely different examples, I've intentionally selected examples for this section that are broadly related to each other. The idea is to highlight the fact that even with the same problem in hand, you'll need to employ different techniques to solve it, depending on the repertoire of your language. What you can do using dynamic metaprogramming in Ruby might be better solved using a different idiom in Clojure. It's extremely important to learn to use the right tool for the right job. While you're figuring out which tool does what, you'll stumble on the most common pitfalls that might catch you off guard. Let's discuss some of them from the perspective of DSL development.

5.5.1   Honor the principle of least complexity

When you're implementing an internal DSL, select the least complex idiom of the host language that best fits in the solution model. You'll frequently see developers use metaprogramming techniques when they could've done the same thing without them. A common example of this in Ruby is the use of monkey patching. (Remember monkey patching? It's the technique in which you open up a class and make changes to methods and properties. Doing this is particularly dangerous in Ruby because these changes are always applied globally.) In many situations, instead of opening up a class and introducing new methods in it, you can instead define a new `Module` in Ruby that contains those methods and include the `Module` in the target class.

5.5.2   Strive for optimal expressivity

If you try too much for the nirvana of expressivity in your DSL, you'll introduce unwarranted complexity into your implementation. Make the language as expressive as your user requires. The Ruby DSL that we rolled out in section 5.2.2 was expressive enough for a programmer to comprehend the semantics of the domain. Here it is once again as a quick reference:

```
TradeDSL.new.new_trade 'T-12435',
  'acc-123', :buy, 100.shares.of('IBM'),
  'unitprice' => 200, 'principal' => 120000, 'tax' => 5000
```

Expressive enough! But you might be asking, why did we go for the interpreter version of the DSL? For a couple of reasons. First, I wanted to take the DSL to the next level so that it would be acceptable to the Bobs on our team. Bob was the first person who complained about the accidental complexity that our DSL had. And the interpreter version was close to what he would normally say at his trading desk. The second reason was I wanted to demonstrate how far you can stretch the dynamism that Ruby offers. But in real life when you're designing DSLs, keep in mind the level of expressivity that fits the profile of your user.

5.5.3 Avoid diluting the principles of well-designed abstractions

You'll often be in situations when you'll be tempted to make the DSL more verbose, thinking that it will make your language more acceptable to the users. One of the most common impacts of such an attempt is that it violates the principles of well-designed abstractions that we discussed in chapter 1. Introducing bubble words or frills in a language can lead to decreased encapsulation and increased visibility of the internals of your implementation. It can also make your abstractions unnecessarily mutable. Listing 5.5 showed a common example of this trade-off; we made the Instrument abstraction mutable so that we could build a nice DSL around the instrument-creation logic. Look back at listing 5.7 where we exploited this mutability property to make our DSL more expressive.

This is not to say that you should never bother with expressivity. Remember that designing a language is always an exercise of making trade-offs and compromises. Be sure to critically evaluate whatever decision you make and whatever compromises you make in your abstractions. And always keep your design principles aligned with the profile of the user who'll be using your DSL.

5.5.4 Avoid language cacophony

It's a common allegation that DSLs don't compose. A particular DSL is targeted to solve a specific problem of a domain. When you design a DSL for a trading application, you always think in terms of making it expressive with reference to the problem domain that you're modeling. You really don't think about how your DSL will integrate with another third-party DSL that does ledger accounting and maintains client portfolios.

Even though you can't know everything, always try to design abstractions that compose easily. Functions compose more naturally than objects. And if you're using a language that supports higher-order functions like Ruby, Groovy, or Clojure, always focus on building combinators that can be chained together to form little languages. Check out appendix A, where I discuss the advantages of composable abstractions and their impact on concurrency.

If your abstractions don't compose, your DSL will feel chaotic to use. Language artifacts will stand lonely and forlorn and will never feel natural to your domain users.

These pitfalls are some of the most common ones that you should be aware of while you're designing DSLs. It's extremely important to carefully select the subset of languages that you're going to use for implementing your DSL. Keep all the integration requirements of your DSL in mind and honor the principles of designing good abstractions.

5.6   *Summary*

Congratulations! You've just reached the end of our discussion about implementing internal DSLs in dynamically typed languages. I chose Ruby, Groovy, and Clojure as the three implementation languages mainly because of the variety that they offer as residents of the JVM.

JRuby is the Java implementation of Ruby that provides a bridge for it to interoperate with the Java object model. It comes with the strength of Ruby metaprogramming and adds to it the power of Java interoperability. Groovy is known as the Java DSL and shares the same object model as Java. Clojure, despite being implemented on top of the Java object model, offers the strong functional programming paradigm of Lisp.

In this chapter, we discussed how you can implement typical, real-life trading application use cases using these three languages. Ruby offers strong metaprogramming capabilities that can make your DSL dynamic at runtime, which enables you to compose and build higher-order abstractions. Groovy offers capabilities during runtime that are similar to those of Ruby, but interoperates with Java more seamlessly because it shares the same object model.

You implemented the final version of our order-processing DSL in Groovy, which we started way back in chapter 2. Through this example, you also got an idea of how a typical DSL evolves through an iterative process of incremental improvement. Clojure is the Lisp that runs on the JVM and comes with the awesome power of compile-time metaprogramming, also known as macros. You saw how to use macros to make a DSL expressive and concise, doing it all without adding any runtime overhead that the metaobject protocol incurs in many other languages.

At the end of the day, if you can always keep in mind the compromises and tradeoffs that you need to do when designing your DSL, you'll do well. After all, every language design is an exercise in how effectively you can balance your expressivity with the implementation overheads. For a DSL, the primary objective is to make your code fully reveal its intentions, which is the best way to improve the communication path between the developer and the domain expert.

Key takeaways & best practices

- Be aware of all the *metaprogramming tricks available with Ruby* when you design an internal DSL. But always remember that metaprogramming has its own costs, with respect to both code complexity and performance metrics.
- *Prefer Groovy categories* to `ExpandoMetaClass` to control the scope of metaprogramming.
- *Monkey patching* in Ruby is always tempting, but it operates in the global namespace. Use monkey patching in DSL implementation judiciously.
- *Clojure is a functional language, though it's implemented on top of Java.* Design your DSL around domain functions if you're using Clojure. Use the power of functional programming through higher-order functions and closures to design the semantic model of your DSL.

Now that you've completed this journey along the road of DSL design using the three most popular, most dynamic languages on the JVM, you must've developed a familiarity with the basic idioms that support a DSL implementation. Choosing the correct idiom of a given language is the most important aspect of development, one that shapes how expressive your DSL APIs will be. This chapter is a significant step forward for you, giving you a baseline from which to delve more into idiomatic implementation techniques in Ruby, Groovy, and Clojure.

In the next chapter, we'll look at DSL implementation from the other side of the typing fence. We'll discuss how static typing helps shape up DSL implementations. You're also going to complete a fun-filled exercise developing internal DSLs in Scala.

5.7　References

1 Thomas, Dave, Chad Fowler, and Andy Hunt. 2009. *Programming Ruby 1.9: The Pragmatic Programmers' Guide*, Third Edition. The Pragmatic Bookshelf.

2 Subramaniam, Venkat. 2008. *Programming Groovy: Dynamic Productivity for the Java Developer.* The Pragmatic Bookshelf.

3 Perrotta, Paolo. 2010. *Metaprogramming Ruby: Program Like the Ruby Pros.* The Pragmatic Bookshelf.

4 Halloway, Stuart. 2009. *Programming Clojure.* The Pragmatic Bookshelf.

5 Abelson, Harold, Gerald Jay Sussman and Julie Sussman. 1996. *Structure and Interpretation of Computer Programs*, Second Edition. The MIT Press.

Internal DSL
design in Scala

6

This chapter covers

- Scala as a language
- Developing an internal DSL in Scala
- Composing multiple DSLs
- Using monadic structures

In the earlier chapters, we've been through the pros and cons of DSL-driven development. By now you must have realized that for the parts of your application that need to model business rules, a DSL can go a long way toward improving the communication path between the development team and the team of domain experts. In the last chapter, we discussed how you can use a few of the dynamic languages on the JVM as hosts for designing internal DSLs. In this chapter, we'll look at the most promising candidate from among the statically typed ones, Scala.

Like all implementation discussions, this is going to be a programming-intensive chapter in which we'll start with the suitability of Scala as a host for implementing internal DSLs, and then dive right into real-world DSL design. Figure 6.1 is a roadmap of our journey through this chapter.

Sections 6.1 and 6.2 will establish Scala as a host for internal DSLs. After that, we get into the details of implementing real-world use cases from our domain of securities trading back-office systems. You'll see lots of idioms, best practices, and

166

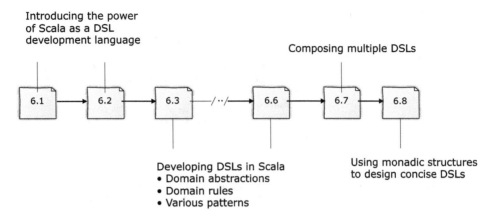

Figure 6.1 Our roadmap through this chapter

patterns in action in sections 6.3 through 6.6. In section 6.7, we'll discuss how you can compose multiple DSLs to evolve larger ones. We'll conclude the chapter with a discussion about how monads can make your DSLs concise, functional, and more expressive.

At the end of the chapter, you'll have comprehensive knowledge of how to design DSLs using Scala as the host language. You'll learn the idioms and best practices of how to model domain components and how to create easy-to-use and expressive language abstractions with them. Sounds exciting, doesn't it? Let's get started.

I used Scala 2.8 to produce the code listings and snippets. For those of you not familiar with the Scala syntax, there's a Scala cheat sheet for you in appendix D at the end of the book.

6.1 Why Scala?

Scala offers a host of functional, as well as OO, abstraction mechanisms that help you design concise and expressive DSLs. A DSL can't stand on its own; in case you missed it before, a DSL is layered as a facade on top of an implementation model. In this section, we'll take a look at how Scala shapes up as a host language, both for designing the underlying model as well as the DSL layer on top of it. Table 6.1 shows some of the features of idiomatic Scala that you'll use regularly to design your DSLs.

The confluence of the features listed in table 6.1 makes Scala one of the most powerful languages on the JVM for designing internal DSLs. But it's still a new language that makes you think differently. Introducing a new language to a team is always a big change, both technologically and culturally. Your company might already have made a big commitment to the JVM as a platform, a number of your clients' applications run on Java, and you have a whole lot of programmers trained in myriad Java frameworks. Are you going to forego all the benefits that you've accrued in order to embrace a new programming language? Fortunately, with Scala, you can afford to take an incremental step toward this transition. The next section discusses how.

Table 6.1   Idiomatic Scala in DSL design

Feature	How Scala does it
Flexible syntax	Scala has a concise surface syntax, with many features that help morph your DSL to use the more natural dialect of the domain. **Examples:** - Optional dots in method invocation - Semicolon inference - Infix operators - Optional parentheses
An extensible object system	Scala is object-oriented. It shares Java's object model and extends it on many fronts through its advanced type system. **Scala's object semantics:** - Traits for mixin-based implementation inheritance (see [12] in section 6.10) - Orthogonal extension capabilities of classes through abstract type members and generic type parameters (see [13] in section 6.10) - Constrained orthogonality of abstractions through self-type annotations (see [14] in section 6.10) - Case classes for implementing value objects[1]
Functional programming capabilities	Scala is a multi-paradigm programming language. It combines the power of OO and functional programming features. **Why object-functional?** - Functions in Scala are first-class values; higher-order functions are supported at the type-system level. You can define custom DSL control structures as closures and pass them around just like any other data type. - With a pure OO language, you need to design everything as classes, whether it is a verb or a noun in your domain. Scala's OO functional mix allows you to model closer to the semantics of your problem domain.
Statically checked duck typing	Scala supports duck typing through *structural types* (see [2] in section 6.10). **Difference with Ruby duck-typing:** Duck typing in Scala is *statically checked*.
Lexically scoped open classes	Scala offers the power of open classes through its `implicit` construct, as we discussed in the *Scala* implicits sidebar in section 3.2. **Difference with Ruby monkey patching:** Scala `implicits` are *lexically scoped*; the added behavior via implicit conversions needs to be explicitly imported into specific lexical scopes (see [2] in section 6.10).

---

[1]   The main differences between ordinary classes and case classes are simpler constructor invocation, availability of default equality semantics, and pattern matching (see [2] in section 6.10).

Table 6.1 Idiomatic Scala in DSL design *(continued)*

Feature	How Scala does it
Implicit parameters	Allow the compiler to infer some of the arguments implicitly without your having to specify them as part of your API invocation. Doing so leads to concise syntax and improved readability for your DSL script.
Modular composition	A distinct notion of an *object*, which you can use to define a concrete module of your DSL. You can define DSL constructs in terms of abstract members and defer committing to a concrete implementation until late in your abstraction design lifecycle.

6.2 *Your first step toward a Scala DSL*

The fact that Scala makes a good host for an internal DSL isn't enough to convince your manager to introduce it as one of the technologies in your development ecosystem. Any new technology needs to be introduced gradually or the risk of introducing chaos increases. Typically you can roll out this adoption slowly by using it in a noncritical line of business.

With Scala, the big plus is that it is on the JVM and interoperates with Java. You can preserve all your Java investments and still try to adopt Scala in your enterprise. You can get into using Scala DSLs in quite a few ways; you can even design a few of your own while keeping your base Java abstractions. Figure 6.2 shows some of the strategies you can use with your own development team.

As you can see from this figure, your mainstream delivery can continue in Java, while some members of your team get inducted into Scala by working in auxiliary activities of your project. Let's look at each of these ways of introducing Scala in detail in the following sections.

6.2.1 *Testing Java objects with a Scala DSL*

Testing is one of those activities that forms the core of your development practice. At the same time, it gives you plenty of flexibility in choice of technology and frameworks. Test suites need to be treated as artifacts of equal importance to your code base. You'll see lots of development going on in the industry that attempts to make test suites more expressive and exhaustive.

(Main project delivery line in Java)

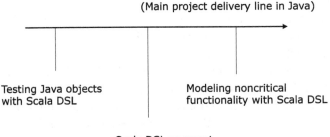

Testing Java objects with Scala DSL

Scala DSL as smart wrappers on Java objects

Modeling noncritical functionality with Scala DSL

Figure 6.2
You don't need to start doing Scala in production code from day one. These are some of the baby steps that you can start with, in no specific order, during the lifetime of your project.

DSLs have become an integral part of testing frameworks. Choose a Scala DSL-based testing framework and you can begin your journey to learning DSL designs in Scala today. ScalaTest (see [8] in section 6.10) is one such framework that lets you write DSLs to test Java as well as Scala classes. You don't need to be able to write Scala classes from the get go. You can reuse all your Java classes with these testing frameworks and get the feel of working in a DSL-based environment.

6.2.2   *Scala DSL as a wrapper for Java objects*

As we've discussed many times in this book, Scala integrates quite seamlessly with Java. You can dress up Java objects with Scala wrappers to make them more smart and expressive. In case you're not convinced, go back to section 3.2.2 where we implemented lots of smartness on top of Java objects using Scala power. This approach can be a prudent way to learn how to make DSLs on top of your Java object model using Scala.

6.2.3   *Modeling noncritical functionality as a Scala DSL*

In a large application, there are often areas that aren't so critical. You can negotiate with the client regarding their deliveries. You can select some of these as hotspots for learning to design Scala DSLs. If you don't want to get away from your main Java compile mode, you can even script your Scala DSL and run it using the `ScriptEngine` that comes with Java 6.

   Let's get down to the next level of detail and discuss how you can use these features in Scala to build domain models that help you make good DSLs.

> **CODE ASSISTANCE**   In all of the following sections that have rich code snippets, I've included a sidebar that contains the prerequisites of the language features that you need to know in order to appreciate the implementation details. Feel free to navigate to the appropriate language cheat sheet that's in the appendixes as you encounter this code.

We'll continue using the same domain of financial brokerage solutions and build examples of how these features combine to form the wholeness of a complete DSL ready to run. It is going to be an exciting journey.

6.3   *Let's DSL in Scala!*

You have enough of a background now to get into what we're here for. We'll study real-life use cases from the domain of securities trading and see how they translate to expressive DSLs using Scala as the implementation language.

   We'll be examining use cases similar to the ones I selected for the discussions about designing DSLs in Ruby and Groovy. That way, you'll see how you need to think differently, even with the same problem domain, when you're designing DSLs in both statically typed and dynamic languages. But first let's look at some of the features that Scala offers that make the syntax of your DSL expressive to users.

> **ℹ Scala tidbits you need to know**
>
> - *OO features* of Scala. You need to know the various ways you can design Scala classes and inheritance hierarchies.
> - *Type inference* in Scala, use of operators as methods, and flexible syntax, including optional parentheses and semicolons.
> - *Immutable variables* that help you design functional abstractions.
> - *Case classes and objects* in Scala and the features they offer for designing immutable value objects.
> - *Traits* in Scala and how they help you design mixins and multiple inheritance.

6.3.1 Expressive syntax on the surface

When you talk about the syntax of a language, there's always a fine line between expressiveness and verbosity. A syntax that's expressive to a nonprogramming user might seem extremely verbose to a programmer. We discussed this issue when you designed an interpreter in Ruby for the trading DSL in section 5.2.3. Remember how Bob complained about the nonessential syntactic complexities that Java forced on us in the order-processing DSL that we designed in section 2.1.2? Despite being statically typed like Java, Scala offers a more concise surface syntax, which makes the DSL less noisy. Consider the following listing, which shows typical Scala code that adds a `ClientAccount` to an already existing list of accounts.

Listing 6.1 Expressive and concise syntax in Scala

```
val a1 = ClientAccount(no = "acc-123", name = "John J.")        ◁─┐  Named and default
val a2 = ClientAccount(no = "acc-234", name = "Paul M.")     ① arguments

val accounts = List(a1, a2)                                  ◁─┐  Type
                                                          ② inference
val newAccounts =
  ClientAccount(no = "acc-345", name = "Hugh P.") :: accounts ◁─┐ Operator ::
                                                          ③ is a method
newAccounts drop 1                    ◁─④ Optional parentheses
```

Even if you're not familiar with Scala, this listing makes perfect sense. Table 6.2 shows some of the features that make this snippet so concise.

The items that we discussed in this section are purely syntactical issues on the surface. Other features also contribute to readable syntax in Scala, including powerful literal syntax for collections, use of closures as control abstractions, and advanced features like implicit parameters. We're going to look at them separately later in this chapter when we discuss the roles that each of them play in designing an internal DSL.

Let's start by designing some of the domain abstractions that form the base on which you'll build your DSLs. We'll use our trusty domain of securities trading and the same abstractions that I relied on in earlier chapters using other languages. Not only

Table 6.2   Features that make Scala syntax concise, with reference to listing 6.1

Conciseness in Scala	Impact on your DSL design
Semicolon inference	Unlike in Java, you don't need to put in semincolons as delimiters between Scala statements. Less noise is the immediate result when you design DSLs in Scala.
Named and default arguments	We instantiate a `ClientAccount` class ❶ using named arguments. The class declaration is implemented as a *case class*, which gives you a light-weight syntax for construction. The class declaration can also contain default values for arguments that don't need to be repeated during instantiation. Using these arguments provides valuable support toward improved readability of your DSL script.
Type inference	When you construct a list with the accounts, you don't need to specify the type of the resulting list ❷. The compiler infers that for you.
Operators as methods	The list `accounts` is augmented with another `ClientAccount` using the operator syntax `::` ❸. This is actually another way to do a method dispatch on the `List` instance `accounts.::(ClientAccount(no = "acc-345", name = "Hugh P."`). Note how the operator syntax and the optional dot (`.`) for method invocation make the code fragments much more readable to the user.
Optional parentheses	We drop the first account from the list using the `drop` method on `List` ❹. The parentheses are optional here, making the code fragment more aligned to natural flow.

does this approach help you connect to domain concepts that you've already learned, it also makes a good comparative study of implementation idioms across all the languages that you've seen so far.

6.3.2   *Creating domain abstractions*

When you design a DSL in Scala, it's mostly an object model that serves as the base abstraction layer. You implement specializations of various model components using subtyping, and form larger abstractions by composing with compatible mixins from the solution domain. For the actions within your model, you create functional abstractions, then compose those using combinators. Figure 6.3 explains the ways you can achieve extensibility in Scala abstractions with the dual power of OO and functional capabilities.

To build your implementation of the trading DSL, let's look at some of the base abstractions from the problem domain.

THE INSTRUMENT

Listing 6.2 is an abstraction of an `Instrument` that you trade in a stock exchange. It starts with the general interface for an `Instrument`, then specializes into `Equity` and various forms of `FixedIncome` securities. (If you need an introduction to the various instrument types, read the sidebar accompanying section 4.3.2.)

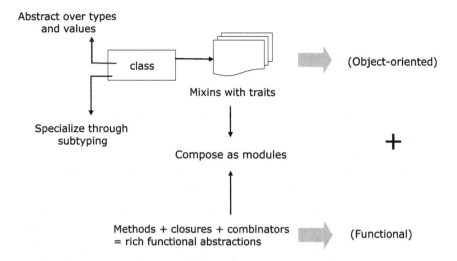

Abstract over types and values

class

Mixins with traits

(Object-oriented)

Specialize through subtyping

Compose as modules

+

Methods + closures + combinators = rich functional abstractions

(Functional)

Figure 6.3 With Scala you can use the dual power of OO and functional programming to evolve your domain model. Using the OO features of Scala, you can abstract over types and values, specialize a component through subtyping, and do composition using mixins. You can also use the functional features of Scala through its higher-order functions, closures, and combinators. Finally, you can compose all of this using modules and get your final abstraction.

Listing 6.2 Instrument model in Scala

```
package api

import java.util.Date
import Util._                                              ❶ Singleton
                                                             objects
sealed abstract class Currency(code: String)
case object USD extends Currency("US Dollar")
case object JPY extends Currency("Japanese Yen")
case object HKD extends Currency("Hong Kong Dollar")

trait Instrument {
  val isin: String
}                                                          ❷ Mixin
                                                             inheritance
case class Equity(isin: String, dateOfIssue: Date = TODAY)
  extends Instrument

trait FixedIncome extends Instrument {
  def dateOfIssue: Date
  def dateOfMaturity: Date
  def nominal: BigDecimal
}

case class CouponBond(
  override val isin: String,
  override val dateOfIssue: Date = TODAY,
  override val dateOfMaturity: Date,
  val nominal: BigDecimal,
  val paymentSchedule: Map[String, BigDecimal])
    extends FixedIncome
```

```
case class DiscountBond(
  override val isin: String,
  override val dateOfIssue: Date = TODAY,
  override val dateOfMaturity: Date,
  val nominal: BigDecimal,
  val percent: BigDecimal)
    extends FixedIncome
```

The domain vocabulary is explicit in the implementation and we don't have much noise from accidental complexities polluting the essence of the domain model. (For more about accidental complexity, see appendix A.) Because this is the first of the domain models that we'll carve out in this chapter, let's look at some of the Scala features that make this model expressive yet concise.

- *Singleton objects,* implemented as specializations of the Currency class ❶, which are instantiated exactly once. This is the Scala way of implementing the Singleton pattern (see [3] in section 6.10). It avoids all the evils of *statics* in Java.
- *Extensible object hierarchies* through traits that can be extended through inheritance ❷.
- *Simplified constructor invocations* for case classes.

Let's look at a couple more abstractions before we start building some DSL scripts out of them.

ACCOUNT AND TRADE

The following listing is the Account model in Scala. Account is the domain entity against which clients and brokers trade securities.

Listing 6.3 Account model in Scala

```
package api

abstract class AccountType(name: String)
case object CLIENT extends AccountType("Client")
case object BROKER extends AccountType("Broker")

import Util._
import java.util.Date

abstract class Account(no: String, name: String, openDate: Date) {
  val accountType: AccountType

  private var closeDate: Date = _
  var creditLimit: BigDecimal = 100000        ◁── Sets up the default
                                                   credit limit
  def close(date: Date) = {
    closeDate = date
  }
}

case class ClientAccount(no: String, name: String,
  openDate: Date = TODAY)
  extends Account(no, name, openDate) {
    val accountType = CLIENT
  }
```

```
case class BrokerAccount(no: String, name: String,
  openDate: Date = TODAY)
  extends Account(no, name, openDate) {
    val accountType = BROKER
  }
```

Now that we have the `Account` and `Instrument` models ready, we can define the base abstraction for security trade.

Listing 6.4   Trade model in Scala

```
package api

import java.util.Date

trait Trade {
  def tradingAccount: Account
  def instrument: Instrument
  def currency: Currency
  def tradeDate: Date
  def unitPrice: BigDecimal
  def quantity: BigDecimal
  def market: Market
  def principal = unitPrice * quantity

  var cashValue: BigDecimal = _
  var taxes: Map[TaxFee, BigDecimal] = _
}

trait FixedIncomeTrade extends Trade {
  override def instrument: FixedIncome
  var accruedInterest: BigDecimal = _
}

trait EquityTrade extends Trade {
  override def instrument: Equity
}
```

❶ Override methods to specialized return types

We define two types of trades, depending on the class of instrument being traded. As you'll see later, the two types of trades have different characteristics with respect to how their cash values are calculated. (For what I mean by the *cash value of trade*, see the sidebar accompanying section 4.2.2.) Also note that we override the `instrument` method ❶ in listing 6.4 to reflect the correct type of security that the trade deals with.

Well, that was quite a bit of coding to do only to set up the context for taking your first shot at writing a trade creation DSL. You'll get your chance to do that in the next section, where there's also a discussion of some of the Scala features that help you build it.

6.4   Building a DSL that creates trades

I'm a firm believer in looking at concrete things first and exploring how they evolve. Without going into any of the implementation specifics, here's how our trading DSL creates new trades for you:

```
val fixedIncomeTrade =
  200 discount_bonds IBM
➥     for_client NOMURA on NYSE at 72.ccy(USD)

val equityTrade =
  200 equities GOOGLE
➥     for_client NOMURA on TKY at 10000.ccy(JPY)
```

The first definition, fixedIncomeTrade, creates an instance of FixedIncomeTrade to buy 200 discount bonds (DiscountBond) of IBM for client account NOMURA at 72 USD per unit traded on the New York Stock Exchange.

The second definition, equityTrade, creates an instance of EquityTrade for sale of 200 equities of GOOGLE for client account NOMURA at 10000 JPY per unit traded on the Tokyo Stock Exchange.

ℹ Scala tidbits you need to know

- *Implicit parameters* are automatically provided by the compiler if they're not specified explicitly. Makes a great case for designing concise syntax of a DSL.
- *Implicit type conversions* are the secret sauce for lexically scoped open classes (similar to, but a much improved version of, Ruby monkey patching).
- *Named and default arguments* help implement the Builder pattern without a lot of fuss.

Now let's look at the regular API version of a trade-creation process that uses the constructor of one of the concrete classes. The following listing shows the concrete implementation of FixedIncomeTrade, followed by a sample instantiation.

Listing 6.5 `FixedIncomeTrade` implementation and instantiation

```
package api

import java.util.Date
import Util._                                        Implementing
                                                     FixedIncomeTrade trait
case class FixedIncomeTradeImpl(
  val tradingAccount: Account,
  val instrument: FixedIncome,
  val currency: Currency,
  val tradeDate: Date = TODAY,
  val market: Market,
  val quantity: BigDecimal,
  val unitPrice: BigDecimal) extends FixedIncomeTrade
                                                     Sample
val t1 =                                             instantiation
  FixedIncomeTradeImpl(
    tradingAccount = NOMURA,
    instrument = IBM,
    currency = USD,
    market = NYSE,
    quantity = 100,
    unitPrice = 42)
```

The difference between the DSL and the more typical API is obvious. The DSL version looks more natural and readable to a domain user, but the API has the feel of a program fragment. You've got to take care of quite a few syntactic nuances in the second version: commas as argument separators, usage of the class name for instantiation, and so on. As you'll see later, implementing a readable DSL version also imposes quite a few constraints as far as sequencing operations are concerned. You can opt for flexible sequencing using the Builder pattern (see [3] in section 6.10), but then you have to deal with two additional issues: the mutability of Builder objects and the finishing problem (see [4] in section 6.10).

Now let's dig into the implementation aspects of the DSL script that I showed you at the beginning of this section.

6.4.1 Implementation details

Before looking at the details, take a hard look at the DSL script at the beginning of section 6.4 and the normal constructor invocation in listing 6.5. The most salient difference between them that you'll notice is the absence of any (well, almost any) additional nonessential syntactic structure in the DSL version. As I mentioned earlier, syntaxes like the dot operator for method invocation or parentheses for method arguments are optional in Scala. But you still need to wire them up with enough flexibility so that everything makes sense in the final script. What do you think is the secret sauce for this wiring?

IMPLICIT CONVERSION

It's Scala `implicits`! Let's start with the creation of the `FixedIncomeTrade`:

```
val fixedIncomeTrade =
  200 discount_bonds IBM
    for_client NOMURA on NYSE at 72.ccy(USD)
```

If we take the sugar out of this statement and put back the dots and parentheses to make it more canonical, it becomes:

```
val fixedIncomeTrade =
  200.discount_bonds(IBM)
    .for_client(NOMURA)
    .on(NYSE)
    .at(72.ccy(USD))
```

With all the method invocations and arguments decorated with their honored symbols, it looks similar to the Builder pattern that we used in section 2.1.2 to build our order-processing DSL in Java. For the current implementation, you can say we're using an *implicit* form of the Builder pattern. Yes, we're literally using the *implicit* conversion feature of Scala to do the conversions so that each individual piece gets wired up in the right sequence to render the final form of the DSL.

Let's look at how `200 discount_bonds IBM` makes sense. When you understand the mechanics that build this stuff, you'll be able to figure out how the rest of the things fall in place by looking at the complete code. Look at the following code snippet:

```
type Quantity = Int
class InstrumentHelper(qty: Quantity) {
  def discount_bonds(db: DiscountBond) = (db, qty)
}

implicit def Int2InstrumentHelper(qty: Quantity) =
  new InstrumentHelper(qty)
```

We define a class `InstrumentHelper` that takes an `Int` and defines a method
`discount_bonds`. The method takes an instance of `DiscountBond` and returns a
`Tuple2` of the bond and the quantity. Then we define an `implicit` conversion from
`Int` to the class `InstrumentHelper`. This conversion converts an `Int` *implicitly* to an
instance of `InstrumentHelper` on which we can invoke the method `discount_bonds`.
Because Scala has optional dots and parentheses, you can use the *infix* form `200
discount_bonds IBM` to make it look more natural.

After you define this conversion, the Scala compiler takes care of the rest at use-
site by adding the necessary call semantics to your script. This same mechanism
works for the rest of the script and ultimately results in a method that can generate
an instance of a `FixedIncomeTrade` with all necessary arguments. We'll look at the
complete code and see some of the idioms that you need to follow to use implicit
conversions. But first, look at figure 6.4, which traces the execution of the script to
generate the trade.

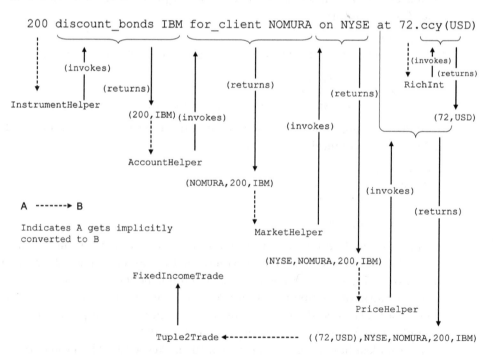

**Figure 6.4 Sequence of implicit conversions that leads to the construction of the
`FixedIncomeTrade` instance. Read the figure from left to right and follow the arrows for implicit
conversions and the subsequent creation of helper objects.**

To understand the figure, you need to look at the complete source code of the object that does this implicit magic behind your API.

A BAG OF IMPLICIT CONVERSIONS

If you look closely at figure 6.4, you'll realize that it's really a seesaw of implicit conversions that plays the role of an implicit builder. These conversions evolve the final `FixedIncomeTrade` object. The code in the following listing defines the helper functions that do the conversions.

Listing 6.6 `TradeImplicits` **defines the conversion functions**

```
package dsl

import api._
object TradeImplicits {

  type Quantity = Int
  type WithInstrumentQuantity = (Instrument, Quantity)
  type WithAccountInstrumentQuantity =
    (Account, Instrument, Quantity)
  type WithMktAccountInstrumentQuantity =
    (Market, Account, Instrument, Quantity)
  type Money = (Int, Currency)

  class InstrumentHelper(qty: Quantity) {
    def discount_bonds(db: DiscountBond) = (db, qty)
  }

  class AccountHelper(wiq: WithInstrumentQuantity) {
    def for_client(ca: ClientAccount) = (ca, wiq._1, wiq._2)
  }

  class MarketHelper(waiq: WithAccountInstrumentQuantity) {
    def on(mk: Market) = (mk, waiq._1, waiq._2, waiq._3)
  }

  class RichInt(v: Int) {
    def ccy(c: Currency) = (v, c)
  }

  class PriceHelper(wmaiq: WithMktAccountInstrumentQuantity) {
    def at(c: Money) = (c, wmaiq._1, wmaiq._2, wmaiq._3, wmaiq._4)
  }
  //..
}
```

The next listing continues with the same object `TradeImplicits` and defines the conversion functions shown in listing 6.6 as `implicit` definitions in Scala.

Listing 6.7 **The implicit definitions in** `TradeImplicits`

```
object TradeImplicits {

  // .. continued from listing 6.6

  implicit def quantity2InstrumentHelper(qty: Quantity) =
    new InstrumentHelper(qty)
```

```
  implicit def withAccount(wiq: WithInstrumentQuantity) =
    new AccountHelper(wiq)
  implicit def withMarket(waiq: WithAccountInstrumentQuantity) =
    new MarketHelper(waiq)
  implicit def withPrice(wmaiq: WithMktAccountInstrumentQuantity) =
    new PriceHelper(wmaiq)
  implicit def int2RichInt(v: Int) = new RichInt(v)

  import Util._
  implicit def Tuple2Trade(
    t: (Money, Market, Account, Instrument, Quantity)) =
    {t match {
      case ((money, mkt, account, ins: DiscountBond, qty)) =>

      FixedIncomeTradeImpl(
        tradingAccount = account,
        instrument = ins,
        currency = money._2,
        tradeDate = TODAY,
        market = mkt,
        quantity = qty,
        unitPrice = money._1)
    }
  }
}
```

The object `TradeImplicits` is in a package named `dsl`, but all the domain model abstractions are in a package named `api`. This isn't as unnecessary as it might seem. Remember when we talked about the underlying domain model that forms the base on which you build the DSL facade? In this example, all domain model abstractions are in the package `api`, while the linguistic layer is kept in `dsl`. Also, you need to keep these two layers decoupled so you can have multiple DSLs from the same domain model. Always maintain this convention when you're designing your DSLs.

In Scala, *implicits* give you the power of *open classes*, similar to monkey patching in Ruby or `ExpandoMetaClass` in Groovy. At the same time, Scala gives you a way to control the visibility of the class you open up for modification. Import the specific module only within the lexical scope that uses these additional methods and the compiler will take care of the rest. The global namespace isn't polluted, like it is in the Ruby counterpart.

IMPLICITS AND LEXICAL SCOPE
Using implicits, we added a method named `ccy` to `Int` through an implicit conversion to the `RichInt` class. If we keep this implicit conversion at the global namespace, all threads will be able to see this change. We already discussed the obvious drawbacks of this arrangement when we talked about Ruby monkey patching earlier. Make this your golden rule: *implicits must be scoped appropriately.* In this case, do an explicit `import TradeImplicits._` and make the implicit conversion available *only* to *your* lexical scope, without impacting any other thread of execution.

Still, when all's said and done, implicit conversions aren't visible explicitly within your code and might give off a magical vibe when you're debugging. To help demystify things, Scala has compiler switches that let you check implicit conversions as a post-compilation debugging tool (see [2] in section 6.10).

This example is the first Scala DSL that you've written. Aren't you excited about the expressiveness it has? If you're not comfortable yet with the ins and outs of the implementation of the DSL, go back and re-examine figure 6.4. Make sure your understanding of the code base flows in the same path as the progression shown in the figure.

OK. Now it's time to settle down after almost being swept away by the wave of Scala excitement. Let's compose ourselves and think about some of the key issues that you need to be aware of when you're deciding in favor of creating a Scala DSL.

6.4.2 *Variations in DSL implementation patterns*

If you look carefully at the code that we developed as the layer that's on top of the domain model for building the DSL, you'll notice a pattern. This pattern is also explicit in the diagram that I presented in figure 6.4. Move from left to right in the diagram as the DSL script gets interpreted. You'll notice how we build an n-tuple *cumulatively* through a successive application of implicit conversions in Scala. This phenomenon is effectively the Builder pattern that I mentioned in section 6.4.1. But unlike the traditional builder approach in which we have a separate *mutable* abstraction that builds the entity, here we're using an immutable variant of the same pattern. In the imperative version of the Builder pattern, the builder object is updated with successive method invocations, each of which returns an instance of the *self*. In this case, the methods don't belong to the same class and the implicit conversion of Scala acts as the glue that binds the invocations together. One invocation generates a tuple; that tuple gets converted implicitly to the next stage of the pipeline, which takes the earlier tuple and generates the next one.

You could have just as easily used the other pattern. Would it have made any difference? The traditional Builder pattern gives you the convenience of flexible sequencing of the method calls. The problem is that you have to invoke the finishing method to complete the build process (see [4] in section 6.10). In the current implementation, the sequence is fixed in the DSL and the compiler will complain if you finish the sequence prematurely without building the complete trade. As usual, it's a trade-off, like many other design decisions.

The traditional Builder pattern uses a *mutable* builder object. You invoke method chaining through fluent interfaces that mutate the builder object. In the form of the Builder pattern that you just saw, which evolves through implicit conversions, every object is *immutable*, which is one of the recommended idioms in abstraction design.

Before we conclude this section, let's look at the key aspects of some of the Scala features that you learned in order to build the DSL facade on top of your domain model abstractions. Table 6.3 contains a summary of this information.

You've completed the DSL for creating trade objects. In the next section, you'll build more DSLs for business rules, each of which can be verified by the domain experts. Remember that the main value-add of DSL-based development is to foster

Table 6.3   Scala features checklist for trade-creation DSL

Scala feature	Used for
Flexible syntax, optional dot (.) and parentheses leading to infix notation	Making the DSL readable and more expressive to the user
Implicit conversion	Lexically scoped open classes that add methods to built-in classes like `Int` Object chaining
Named and default arguments	Making the DSL readable

better communication with the domain experts and help them verify the business rules that you've implemented. Before you develop the DSL, you need to have some more domain abstractions that serve as the underlying implementation model.

6.5   *Modeling business rules with a DSL*

Business rules are the hotspots for using DSLs. They form the configurable sections of your domain model and are the most important things that you need to verify through your domain experts. It's an added benefit if your DSL is friendly enough for your domain experts (like our friend Bob) to be able to write a few tests around them. For our DSL, the business rule that we need to model is that the tax and fees for a trade must be calculated. See table 6.4 for how that takes place.

Table 6.4   Business rule to model with DSL: calculate tax and fees for a trade

Step	Description
1 Execute trade	Trade takes place on the exchange between the counterparties.
2 Calculate tax and fee	The tax and fee need to be calculated on the trade that takes place. The calculation logic depends on the type of trade, the instruments being traded, and the exchanges where the transaction takes place. The tax and fee form a core component of the net cash value of the trade that needs to be settled between the counterparties.

The DSL that you'll design needs to be readable enough for Bob, our domain expert, to understand the rules, check for the comprehensiveness of implementation, and certify its correctness. What do you need to do first? You guessed it! You need to create the domain model abstractions for tax and fee components before you try to add the DSL layer on top of them.

I suspect that some of my more astute readers are getting a bit impatient at the prospect of having to sit through another session of domain modeling before getting a peek at the next serving of DSL implementation. Let's do something more interesting. Let's digress and build a small DSL that implements a business rule that's based on the domain model that we've already implemented. This exercise will both

> **Scala tidbits you need to know**
> - *Pattern matching* helps implement functional abstractions and an extensible Visitor implementation.
> - *Higher-order functions* promote functional programming features in Scala. They also help implement combinators that are useful for functional programming.
> - *Abstract val and abstract type* help design open abstractions that can be composed later to form concrete abstractions.
> - *Self-type annotations* for easy wiring of abstractions.
> - *Partial functions* are expressions that can produce values for a limited domain.

perk you up and demonstrate one of the functional features of Scala that's used extensively to make a better implementation of one of the most commonly used OO design patterns.

6.5.1 *Pattern matching as an extensible Visitor*

Besides offering a simplified constructor invocation syntax, case classes in Scala use pattern matching over deconstructed objects, a feature typically used by algebraic data types in functional languages like Haskell. (For more information about algebraic data types, go to http://en.wikipedia.org/wiki/Algebraic_data_type. For more details about how pattern matching works in Scala, see [2] in section 6.10.) The reason for using pattern matching over case classes is to implement a generic and extensible *Visitor* pattern (see [3] in section 6.10).

In DSL design, you can use the same pattern to make your domain rules more explicit to users. Although with a typical OO implementation such rules tend to be buried within object hierarchies, you can use this functional paradigm over your case classes to achieve a better level of expressiveness and extensibility. For more details about how pattern matching over case classes in Scala leads to more extensible solutions compared to a traditional OO *Visitor* implementation, see [5] in section 6.10.

Consider another business rule that we'll implement as a DSL in our application: Increase the credit limit of all client accounts that were open before today by 10%.

Listing 6.3 is the `Account` abstraction of our domain model with two concrete implementations for `ClientAccount` and `BrokerAccount`. (Remember that we discussed client accounts in a sidebar in section 3.2.2. A broker account is an account that the broker opens with the stock trading organization.) The implementation of the proposed rule needs to abstract over all client accounts that are present in the system and that are affected by this change in the credit limit. Let's look at the Scala snippet that implements this rule in the function `raiseCreditLimits`.

```
def raiseCreditLimits(accounts: List[Account]) {
  accounts foreach {acc =>
    acc match {
      case ClientAccount(_, _, openDate) if (openDate before TODAY) =>
```

1 Pattern matching

```
            acc.creditLimit = acc.creditLimit * 1.1
        case _ =>
      }
    }
}
```

Note how the rule is *explicitly published* through pattern matching over case classes. Under the hood, the case statements ❶ are modeled as *partial functions*, which are defined only for the values mentioned in the case clauses. Pattern matching makes modeling the domain rule easy, because we care only about ClientAccount instances in the current context. The underscore (_) in the second case clause is a don't-care that ignores other types of accounts. Refer to [2] in section 6.10 for more details about pattern matching and partial functions in Scala.

Why is this a DSL? It expresses a domain rule explicitly enough for a domain expert to understand. It's implemented over a small surface area, so that the domain person doesn't have to navigate through piles of code to explore the semantics of the rule. Finally, it focuses only on the significant attributes that the rule specifies, blurring the nonessential parts within a don't-care clause.

A DSL needs only to be expressive *enough* for the user

It's not always necessary to make DSLs feel like natural English. I reiterate: make your DSLs expressive *enough* for your users. In this case, the code snippet will be used by a programmer; making the intent of the rule clear and expressive is sufficient for a programmer to maintain it and for a domain user to comprehend it.

Now that you have an early taste of yet another DSL fragment that models a sample business rule for our solution, let's get into the domain model of tax and fee that we promised earlier. The next section is going to be exciting. You'll learn lots of new modeling techniques that Scala offers. So grab another cup of coffee and let's get going.

6.5.2 *Enriching the domain model*

We built Trade, Account, and Instrument abstractions earlier. Those were the basic abstractions from the problem domain. Now let's consider the tax and fee components that need to interact with the Trade component to calculate the cash value of the trade.

When we talk about tax and fee, we need a separate abstraction that's responsible for their calculation. Calculating tax and fee is one of the primary business rules of the model that'll vary with the country and the stock exchange where you'll deploy your solution. And as you must've figured out by now, for business rules that can vary, a DSL makes your life easier by making the rules explicit, expressive, and easier to maintain.

Figure 6.5 shows the overall component model of how the tax and fee abstractions interact with the Trade component in our solution model.

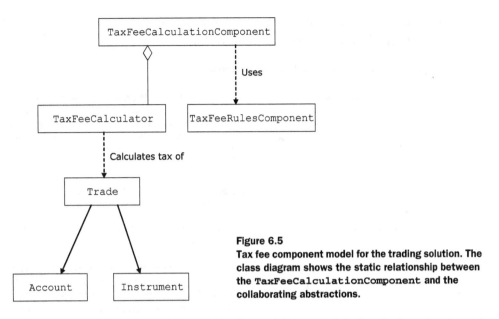

Figure 6.5
Tax fee component model for the trading solution. The class diagram shows the static relationship between the `TaxFeeCalculationComponent` and the collaborating abstractions.

Note that all of abstractions depicted in figure 6.5 are modeled as Scala traits. As such, they can be wired together flexibly, and composed with suitable implementations to generate the appropriate concrete object during runtime. Let's look at the TaxFee-Calculator and TaxFeeCalculationComponent in the following listing.

Listing 6.8 Tax and fee calculation components in Scala

```scala
package api

sealed abstract class TaxFee(id: String)         ❶ Singleton
case object TRADE_TAX extends TaxFee("Trade Tax")    objects
case object COMMISSION extends TaxFee("Commission")
case object SURCHARGE extends TaxFee("Surcharge")
case object VAT extends TaxFee("VAT")             ❷ Calculates
                                                    tax and fee
trait TaxFeeCalculator {                            for a trade
  def calculateTaxFee(trade: Trade): Map[TaxFee, BigDecimal]
}                                                 ❸ Self-type
                                                    annotation
trait TaxFeeCalculationComponent { this: TaxFeeRulesComponent =>
  val taxFeeCalculator: TaxFeeCalculator          ❹ Abstract
                                                    val
  class TaxFeeCalculatorImpl extends TaxFeeCalculator {
    def calculateTaxFee(trade: Trade): Map[TaxFee, BigDecimal] = {
      import taxFeeRules._                        ❺ Object
      val taxfees =                                 import
        forTrade(trade) map {taxfee =>              syntax
          (taxfee, calculatedAs(trade)(taxfee))
        }
      Map(taxfees: _*)
    }
  }
}
```

Let's look into this code listing and try to understand how the entire component model gets wired up. Table 6.5 has the details.

Table 6.5   Dissecting a Scala DSL implementation model

Abstraction	Role in the DSL implementation
`TaxFee`	This abstraction is the *value object* (see [6] in section 6.10) that corresponds to the individual tax and fee types. The various tax/fee types are modeled as singleton objects in Scala **❶**. **Note:** As value objects, all individual tax/fee types are immutable.
`TaxFeeCalculator`	Abstraction that calculates all the taxes and fees applicable to a trade **❷**.
`TaxFeeCalculationComponent`	This is the overarching abstraction that wires up a couple of other abstractions and forms the core that does the actual calculation of taxes and fees for a trade. `TaxFeeCalculationComponent` collaborates with `TaxFeeRulesComponent` through a self-type annotation **❸**, and `TaxFeeCalculator` through an abstract val **❹**. **Design benefits:** • The abstraction is decoupled from the implementation. You're free to provide implementations for both of the collaborating abstractions of `TaxFeeCalculation-Component`. • Implementation can be deferred until you create concrete instances of `TaxFeeCalculationComponent`.

Self-type annotations in Scala

You can use self-type annotations to specify additional types that the self object `this` can take within the component. It's almost like saying `trait TaxFee-CalculationComponent extends TaxFeeRulesComponent`, but saying it implicitly.

We're not actually creating this compile-time dependency now. Using *self-type annotation*, we're indicating a promise that `TaxFeeCalculationComponent` will be mixed in with `TaxFeeRulesComponent` during any concrete instantiation of the object. We'll fulfill this promise in listing 6.13 and in the subsequent creation of the object in listing 6.14.

Note that within `TaxFeeCalculatorImpl#calculateTaxFee`, we use an import on `taxFeeRules` **❺**, which is just another abstract val within `TaxFeeRulesComponent`.

By specifying `TaxFeeRulesComponent` as a self-type annotation, we're declaring it as one of the valid types of `this` to the Scala compiler. For more details about how self-type annotations work in Scala, refer to [2] in section 6.10.

It looks like we've achieved a lot of wiring without much coding. Limited coding is the power that Scala brings to you; you can program at a higher level of abstraction. In the next section, we're going to complete both the implementation of TaxFeeRules-Component and a DSL for defining domain rules for calculating tax and fee.

6.5.3 *Calculating tax and fee business rules in a DSL*

Let's start the domain model of the rules component with a trait that publishes the main contracts for tax and fee calculation. For brevity, we'll consider only a simplified view of the world here; in reality, things are way more detailed and complex.

```
package api

trait TaxFeeRules {                                               ❶ TaxFee applicable
  def forTrade(trade: Trade): List[TaxFee]          ◁┘              to the trade
  def calculatedAs(trade: Trade): PartialFunction[TaxFee, BigDecimal]   ◁┐
}                                                                 How to calculate  ❷
```

The first method, forTrade ❶, gives a list of TaxFee objects that are applicable to the specific trade. The second method, calculatedAs ❷, does the calculation for a specific TaxFee valid for the particular trade.

Now let's look at the TaxFeeRulesComponent, which, along with building the DSL for calculating the tax and fee, provides a concrete implementation of TaxFeeRules. This component is shown in the following listing.

> **Listing 6.9 DSL for tax and fee calculation business rules**

```
package api

trait TaxFeeRulesComponent {
  val taxFeeRules: TaxFeeRules

  class TaxFeeRulesImpl extends TaxFeeRules {
    override def forTrade(trade: Trade): List[TaxFee] = {
      (forHKG orElse
         forSGP orElse                                    ❶ List of TaxFee
           forAll)(trade.market)           ◁┘               using combinators
    }
                                                           ❷ Specific list
    val forHKG: PartialFunction[Market, List[TaxFee]] = {   ◁┘  for Hong Kong
      case HKG =>
        List(TradeTax, Commission, Surcharge)
    }
                                                           ❸ Specific list
    val forSGP: PartialFunction[Market, List[TaxFee]] = {   ◁┘  for Singapore
      case SGP =>
        List(TradeTax, Commission, Surcharge, VAT)
    }
                                                           ❹ Generic list for
    val forAll: PartialFunction[Market, List[TaxFee]] = {   ◁┘  other countries
      case _ => List(TradeTax, Commission)
    }

    import TaxFeeImplicits._
    override def calculatedAs(trade: Trade):               ❺ Tax calculation
        PartialFunction[TaxFee, BigDecimal] = {      ◁┘      domain rules
```

```
      case TradeTax    => 5.  percent_of trade.principal
      case Commission  => 20. percent_of trade.principal
      case Surcharge   => 7.  percent_of trade.principal
      case VAT         => 7.  percent_of trade.principal
    }
  }
}
```

TaxFeeRulesComponent abstracts over TaxFeeRules and provides an implementation
of it. You can supply your own implementation if you want, but TaxFeeRules-
Component is still an abstract component because it contains an abstract declaration of
taxFeeRules. We'll provide all the concrete implementations when we compose our
components together, building a concrete TradingService. But first let's take a
detailed look at the implementation shown in the listing to see how the DSL gets the
tax and fee types, then goes on to calculate the tax and fee amount.

GETTING THE LIST OF APPLICABLE TAX AND FEE HEADS

Let's look first at the implementation of the DSL in TaxFeeRulesImpl. The method
forTrade is a single-line method, which is a functional composition using Scala combinators. As you read in appendix A, combinators are a great way to compose higher-
order functions. (If you haven't read appendix A, you're missing out.)

Combinators play a role in making DSLs expressive. They shine as one of the most
useful areas of functional programming. Scala offers you the power of functional programming; feel free to use combinator-based language construction whenever you
think it's appropriate. The business rule for finding the set of taxes and fees for a
trade stated in English is as follows:

> *"Get the Hong Kong-specific list for trades executed on the Hong Kong market OR Get the*
> *Singapore-specific list for trades executed on the Singapore market OR Get the most generic*
> *list valid for all other markets."*

Partial functions in Scala

Partial functions are those defined *only* for a set of values of its arguments. Partial
functions in Scala are modeled as blocks of pattern-matching case statements.
Consider the following example:

```
val onlyTrue: PartialFunction[Boolean, Int] = {
  case true => 100
}
```

onlyTrue is a PartialFunction that's defined for a limited domain. It's defined
only for the Boolean value true. The PartialFunction trait contains a method
isDefinedAt that returns true for the domain values for which the Partial-
Function is defined. Here's an example:

```
scala> onlyTrue isDefinedAt(true)
res1: Boolean = true
scala> onlyTrue isDefinedAt(false)
res2: Boolean = false
```

Now read the single statement in forTrade ❶, which implements this rule. You'll see an exact correspondence to the most natural way of expressing the rule and you get it all within a small surface area of the API. We used the combinator orElse, which allows you to compose partial functions in Scala and select the first one that defines it.

In listing 6.9, the composed abstraction in method forTrade returns the generic list of TaxFee objects only if the market is neither Hong Kong nor Singapore. When you understand how forTrade works and how you can compose partial functions in Scala, you'll know how the specific higher-order functions forHKG ❷, forSGP ❸, and forAll ❹ work.

CALCULATING THE TAX AND FEE

It's now time to look at how the taxes and fees are calculated. This calculation is the second part of the business rule that we're addressing in our DSL. Look at the method calculatedAs ❺ in listing 6.9. Can you figure out what rule it implements?

Once again, we see Scala pattern matching making domain rules explicit. For each case clause, the return value is once again sugared with the magic of implicits that adds a method percent_of to the class Double. The result is the infix notation that you see in listing 6.9. And here's the TaxFeeImplicits object that you need to import to bring all implicit conversions to the scope of your DSL:

```
package api

object TaxFeeImplicits {
  class TaxHelper(factor: Double) {
    def percent_of(c: BigDecimal) = factor * c.doubleValue / 100
  }

  implicit def Double2TaxHelper(d: Double) = new TaxHelper(d)
}
```

After you import the TaxFeeImplicits object, you get the domain-friendly syntax in the method calculatedAs, which your business user will like a lot.

A DSL AND AN API: WHAT'S THE DIFFERENCE?

In section 6.5, you've learned how to make DSL scripts for creating domain entities on top of an underlying implementation model. You learned how to build DSLs for your business rules. I described some of the techniques that Scala gives you to implement expressive APIs over an OO domain model. In both of the implementations we worked through, I went a bit overboard and tried to make our little language more expressive using the open classes that implicit conversions offer. But even without the added sweetness of implicits, you can make your domain model implement sufficiently expressive APIs using the combination of OO and functional programming features.

This fact brings to mind a question that has surely crossed your mind as well: what's the difference between an internal DSL and an API? Frankly speaking, there's not much of a difference. An expressive API that makes the domain semantics explicit to its users without the burden of additional nonessential complexities is an internal

DSL. In all the code snippets that I've branded as DSLs, the driving force is domain expressiveness for the user. The implementer of the DSL needs to maintain the code base, the domain expert needs to be able to understand the semantics; you can achieve both of these without going overboard. But you can do that only if you're using a language that enables you to build higher-order abstractions and compose them together. Maybe it's time now to take another look at the virtues of well-designed abstractions that I point out in appendix A.

As mentioned earlier, all the components I've described so far in figure 6.5 are abstract, in the sense that we've designed them as traits in Scala. You've yet to witness the real power of composing traits to form concrete instantiable domain abstractions. Let's compose the trade abstractions in the next section and build some concrete trading services. After we have the services, they'll serve as the base for developing the linguistic abstractions of our DSL.

6.6   *Stitching 'em all together*

Now that you've built a DSL that addresses the business rule for calculating the tax and fee, let's build some new abstractions that'll be the spice for the next serving of DSL.

> **ℹ Scala tidbits you need to know**
> - *Modules* in Scala. The object syntax that lets you define concrete abstractions by composing abstract ones.
> - *Combinators* like `map`, `foldLeft`, and `foldRight`.

In this section, you'll learn how to compose traits through *mixin-based* inheritance in Scala. You'll also see another form of abstraction that Scala supports: *abstracting over types*. When you have more options to use when you're composing your abstractions, you can make your domain model more malleable, and your DSL syntax can evolve more easily out of it.

6.6.1   *More abstraction with traits and types*

When you design a domain model, one of the abstractions that you publish to your end clients is a *domain service*. A domain service uses entities and value objects (see [6] in section 6.10) to deliver the contracts they expose to clients. Let's look at a typical domain service, called `TradingService`, in the following listing, much simplified compared to a real-world use case.

Listing 6.10   Base class for `TradingService` in Scala

```
package api

trait TradingService
  extends TaxFeeCalculationComponent
  with TaxFeeRulesComponent {
```

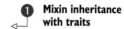 ❶ **Mixin inheritance with traits**

```
type T <: Trade

def taxes(trade: T) =
  taxFeeCalculator.calculateTaxFee(trade)

def totalTaxFee(trade: T): BigDecimal = {
  taxes(trade).foldLeft(BigDecimal(0))(_ + _._2)
}

def cashValue(trade: T): BigDecimal
}
```

2 Abstract type

3 Combinator-based programming

4 Abstract method

Let's make a quick run down of the service contracts and some of the new Scala features that they use in table 6.6.

Note that we haven't yet made any abstraction concrete; they're still abstract, with traits having abstract types that we'll define in the next section. Scala as a language offers a variety of options to design your abstractions. Choose the ones that best fit the problem at hand and make your design aligned to the idioms of well-designed abstractions that I discuss in appendix A.

Table 6.6 Dissecting the domain service `TradingService` in listing 6.10

Feature	Description
Power of mixins—composing with existing abstractions	`TradingService` mixes in with two of our earlier components `TaxFeeCalculationComponent` and `TaxFeeRules-Component` **1**. **Note:** With mixins we get inheritance of the interface as well as optional implementations. This is multiple inheritance, done right.
Abstraction over the type of trade	The trait `TradingService` abstracts over the trade type **2**. This kind of maneuver is intuitive because we need to specialize the trading service, depending on the type of trade it handles. But there's an upper bound on the constraint of our base class for security trade, `Trade`. **When do you concretize T?** When we concretize `TradingService` later, we'll supply an implementation for the abstract trade type T
The core logic of the tax fee calculation is `totalTaxFee`	The service defines a concrete method `totalTaxFee` **3** that sums over the component tax and fee items using the `foldLeft` combinator. For more details about how `foldLeft` works with the placeholder syntax (_) of Scala, read appendix D at the end of the book. **Tip:** Always prefer combinators to explicit recursion or iteration.
Abstract method for deferred implementation in subclasses	`cashValue` is an abstract method **4** that we'll define in subtypes, because the actual logic depends on the type of trade that the service handles.

6.6.2 *Making domain components concrete*

`EquityTradingService` provides the trading service for equity trades. It's a concrete component that needs to be instantiated once for all services that it renders. You model it using the *singleton object notation* of Scala (see [2] in section 6.10) in the following listing.

Listing 6.11   A concrete trading service for equity trades

```
package api

object EquityTradingService
  extends TradingService {                              ❶ Concrete type
                                                            supplied
  type T = EquityTrade

  val taxFeeCalculator = new TaxFeeCalculatorImpl       ❷ Concrete vals
  val taxFeeRules = new TaxFeeRulesImpl                    supplied

  override def cashValue(trade: T): BigDecimal = {       ❸ Concrete method
    trade.principal + totalTaxFee(trade)                    supplied
  }
}
```

This notation looks pretty straightforward, doesn't it? It contains the following elements:

- A concrete type `EquityTrade` ❶ for the abstract trade type we defined in the base class
- Concrete implementations for the values we left as abstract in the traits that we mixed in ❷
- A definition of how to compute the `cashValue` of an equity trade ❸

Similar to `EquityTradingService`, we also implement another concrete trading service `FixedIncomeTradingService`, the counterpart for the `FixedIncomeTrade` class, in the following listing.

Listing 6.12   Trading service for fixed income trades in Scala
---

```
package api

object FixedIncomeTradingService
  extends TradingService with AccruedInterestCalculationComponent {    ◁─┐
                                                            Add mixin for
  type T = FixedIncomeTrade                                 accrued interest ❶

  val taxFeeCalculator = new TaxFeeCalculatorImpl
  val accruedInterestCalculator = new AccruedInterestCalculatorImpl    ◁─┐
  val taxFeeRules = new TaxFeeRulesImpl

  def accruedInterest(trade: T): BigDecimal = {
    accruedInterestCalculator.calculateAccruedInterest(trade)    Concrete instance
  }                                                               for accrued
                                                                  interest calculator
  override def cashValue(trade: T): BigDecimal = {
    trade.principal +
```

```
        accruedInterest(trade) + totalTaxFee(trade)
    }
}
```

Note the additional component that we mix in with the core abstraction, `Accrued-InterestCalculationComponent` ❶, which computes accrued interest for the trade. Accrued interest is something typical to fixed-income instruments and also forms an integral part of the cash value calculation for fixed income trades. I'm sure it's obvious as well from how we define the `FixedIncomeTradingService` abstraction.

In this section, we defined service abstractions for our domain. Then we wired them up with the components that we built earlier to construct concrete Scala modules that you can directly use within your DSL.

> The real power that Scala offers you in this exercise is the ability to defer committing to a specific implementation until the last stage. *Abstract vals, abstract types,* and *self-type annotations* are the three main pillars that helped you achieve this. Add to them the flexibility of composing abstractions through *mixin-based inheritance* and you have the complete recipe for designing scalable components.

What you've done so far is construct a DSL from a set of underlying domain model components. In Scala, I defined the DSL layer as a set of abstractions that evolve based on the requirements of the user. In this way, you end up with hierarchies of abstractions that model the various use cases of our trading system. Now consider what happens when some of the market rules change and you need to integrate the new rules with a set of existing abstractions. Here we're talking about composing the existing DSL with some new ones. In the next section, I'll show you how you can do this using Scala's type system.

6.7   Composing DSLs

The domain model of your application is built out of intention-revealing abstractions. The DSL layer that you offer on top of the model as a facade becomes usable and extensible only if the abstractions are at the correct level. In this section, we'll consider the whole DSL as an abstraction and discuss how you can compose DSLs together. This technique comes in handy when you need to weave multiple Scala DSLs together and compose a bigger whole. In our domain of designing trading systems, integrating market-rule DSLs with the core business rules of trade processing is one use case that we'll be discussing.

After you have a DSL that's designed as an abstraction, you can extend it through subtyping in Scala. Subtyping can lead to an entire DSL hierarchy, with each of the specialized abstractions providing different implementations to the same core language. Sound polymorphic? Sure they are, and we'll use polymorphism to compose DSLs in section 6.7.1. We'll also look at composing unrelated DSLs in section 6.7.2; after all, DSLs tend to evolve independently of each other and of your application lifecycle. Your application architecture must be capable of hosting a seamless composition of multiple DSL structures.

6.7.1 *Composing using extensions*

When a trade has been entered into the system, it passes through a normal trading lifecycle that begins with *enrichment*. This process adds some of the derived information to the trade record that didn't originally come from the upstream system. This information includes the cash value of the trade, applicable taxes and fees, and other components that vary with the type of instrument being traded.

GROWING UP THE DSL

Consider the following DSL snippet. It doesn't look like a DSL right now, but you are going to add more meat to its bones as we move along. You are also going to define some of the trade lifecycle methods using the components that you've implemented so far.

```
package dsl

trait TradeDsl {
  type T <: Trade
  def enrich: PartialFunction[T, T]        ❶ Abstract
}                                              method
```

There's nothing semantically rich about the language at the moment. It just defines a method enrich, which is supposed to enrich a trade after it's been entered into the system ❶.

Let's define specific implementations of TradeDsl for FixedIncomeTrade and EquityTrade in listings 6.13 and 6.14. The DSL for FixedIncomeTrade uses the FixedIncomeTradingService abstraction that we designed earlier.

> **Listing 6.13   Trade DSL for FixedIncomeTrade**

```
package dsl

import api._
trait FixedIncomeTradeDsl extends TradeDsl {
  type T = FixedIncomeTrade

  import FixedIncomeTradingService._

  override def enrich: PartialFunction[T, T] = {
    case t =>
      t.cashValue = cashValue(t)
      t.taxes = taxes(t)                            Accrued interest for
      t.accruedInterest = accruedInterest(t)        fixed-income trade
      t
  }
}
                                                    Concrete instance
object FixedIncomeTradeDsl extends FixedIncomeTradeDsl   of the DSL
```

The DSL for `EquityTrade` uses the `EquityTradingService` abstraction that we defined earlier.

Listing 6.14 Trade DSL for `EquityTrade`

```
package dsl

import api._
trait EquityTradeDsl extends TradeDsl {
  type T = EquityTrade

  import EquityTradingService._

  override def enrich: PartialFunction[T, T] = {
    case t =>
      t.cashValue = cashValue(t)
      t.taxes = taxes(t)
      t
  }
}

object EquityTradeDsl extends EquityTradeDsl
```

In listings 6.13 and 6.14, we have `FixedIncomeTradeDsl` and `EquityTradeDsl` as individual concrete languages that implement the same core language of `TradeDsl`. To implement the enrichment semantics, they use the `TradingService` implementations that we designed in section 6.6. The class diagram in figure 6.6 shows how the two language abstractions are related to each other.

Because `FixedIncomeTradeDSL` and `EquityTradeDSL` are extensions of the same base abstraction, they can be used polymorphically through the usual idioms of inheritance. But consider yet another type of `TradeDSL` that's not specialized on the type of

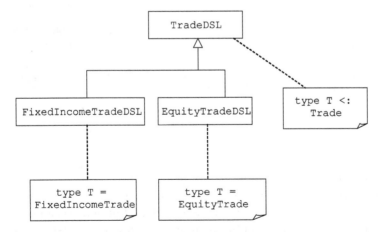

Figure 6.6 `TradeDSL` has an abstract type member `T <: Trade`, but `EquityTradeDSL` has the concrete type `T = EquityTrade` and `FixedIncomeTradeDSL` has the concrete type `T = FixedIncomeTrade`. `TradeDSL` has two specializations in `EquityTradeDSL` and `FixedIncomeTradeDSL`.

the trade. It models another business rule that needs to compose with the semantics of both `EquityTradeDSL` and `FixedIncomeTradeDSL`. Let's illustrate this composition technique in Scala using an example.

COMPOSING DSLs WITH PLUGGABLE SEMANTICS

Business rules change with changes in market conditions, regulations, and lots of other factors. Let's assume that the stock broker organization announces a new market rule for promoting high value trades as follows:

> *"Any trade on the New York Stock Exchange of principal value > 1000 USD must have a discount of 10% of the principal on the net cash value."*

Now this rule needs to be implemented when we enrich the trade, irrespective of whether its type is `EquityTrade` or `FixedIncomeTrade`. You don't want to include it as part of the core cash value calculation; it's a promotional market rule that shouldn't impact the core logic of the system. Rather, you should implement such domain rules like the layers of an onion so you can include and exclude them flexibly without intruding into your core abstractions (think decorators). Let's extend our `TradeDsl` with some new semantics that reflect these market-specific rules in the following listing.

Listing 6.15   A new semantics for `TradeDsl`—another business rule

```
package dsl
import api._

trait MarketRuleDsl extends TradeDsl {
  val semantics: TradeDsl                              ◁┐  Underlying
  type T = semantics.T                                 ❶  semantics

  override def enrich: PartialFunction[T, T] = {       ┆  Invoke contained
    case t =>                                           ┆  semantics
      val tr = semantics.enrich(t)                     ◁┘
      tr match {                                        ◁┐  Decorate with
        case x if x.market == NYSE && x.principal > 1000 =>  ┆  additional rule
          tr.cashValue = tr.cashValue - tr.principal * 0.1
          tr
        case x => x
      }
  }
}
```

This is the exciting part, where we compose the DSLs. Note the abstract `val semantics` that embeds the DSL that we want to be composed with this new domain rule ❶. Internal DSLs are also known as embedded DSLs. But in most cases, you'll find that the semantics are hardwired within the implementation of the DSL. In this particular case, we want to make the actual semantics of the composed DSL pluggable. By making them pluggable, you have the loose coupling between the composed DSLs. At the same time, runtime pluggability lets you defer your commitment to the concrete implementation. In the following listing, you define concrete objects for `Equity-TradeDsl` and `FixedIncomeTradeDsl`, composed with the new `MarketRuleDsl`.

Listing 6.16 DSL composition

```
package dsl

object EquityTradeMarketRuleDsl extends MarketRuleDsl {
  val semantics = EquityTradeDsl
}

object FixedIncomeTradeMarketRuleDsl extends MarketRuleDsl {
  val semantics = FixedIncomeTradeDsl
}
```

Later you'll look at the entire set of composed DSLs in action. But first let's add more functionality to `TradeDsl` using some of your knowledge about functional combinators. Combinators will give us compositional semantics both at the functional level and at the object level.

MORE COMPOSITION WITH FUNCTIONAL COMBINATORS

Remember we talked about the trade lifecycle earlier in this section? Before the trade is enriched, it is validated. After the enrichment is done, it is journalized to the books of the accounting system. A few more steps occur in the real-world application, but for the purpose of demonstration, let's keep it short for now. How can you model this business rule in a Scala DSL?

You will use `PartialFunction` combinators to model this sequencing, and pattern matching to make the rule explicit. The following listing enriches our original implementation of `TradeDsl` and adds a control structure that models this business rule.

Listing 6.17 Modeling the trade lifecycle in a DSL

```
package dsl

import api._

trait TradeDsl {
  type T <: Trade

  def withTrade(trade: T)(op: T => Unit): T = {        ❶ Add custom
                                                          actions
    if (validate(trade))
      (enrich andThen journalize andThen op)(trade)    ❷ Combinator-based
    trade                                                 infix operations
  }

  def validate(trade: T): Boolean = //..
  def enrich: PartialFunction[T, T]
  def journalize: PartialFunction[T, T] = {
    case t => //..
  }
}
```

You must have been wondering why you defined `enrich` as a `PartialFunction`. Partial functions in Scala use the amazing power of composition to build higher order structures.

You have defined a control structure `withTrade` that takes an input trade and lets you perform the complete sequence of lifecycle operations on it. This control structure also has an option to add custom operations to the trade lifecycle in the form of an additional argument (`op: T => Unit`) ❶. This argument is a function that operates on the trade but returns nothing. One typical use of such functions is to add side-effecting operations to the trade lifecycle. Logging, sending emails, and doing audit trails are examples of functions that have side effects but that don't alter the return value of the final operation.

Now let's look into the pattern-matching block within `withTrade`. The entire domain rule is expressed within the four lines of code that it contains. The `andThen` combinator ❷ also nicely expresses the sequence that the trade lifecycle needs to follow.

USING THE FULLY COMPOSED DSL

The following listing shows the whole composition in action. This DSL creates a trade using our trade-creation DSL, does all sorts of enrichment, validation, and other lifecycle operations, and finally composes with the market rules DSL to generate the final cash value of the trade.

Listing 6.18   The trade lifecycle DSL

```
import FixedIncomeTradeMarketRuleDsl._

withTrade(
  200 discount_bonds IBM
    for_client NOMURA
      on NYSE
        at 72.ccy(USD)) {trade =>
  Mailer(user) mail trade
  Logger log trade
} cashValue
```

You used the Decorator design pattern as your composition technique in this section (see [3] in section 6.10). We consider the `semantics` to be the decorated DSL; the wrapper provides the necessary decoration. You can use the Decorator pattern to implement dynamic inclusion and exclusion of responsibilities from an object. No wonder it turned out to be a useful tool here, when we needed to compose families of DSLs together.

What happens if the languages that you want to compose aren't related? Frequently, you'll use utility DSLs for modeling date and time, currencies, and geometric shapes that find applicability within the context of other larger DSLs. Let's see how you can manage their evolution seamlessly.

6.7.2 *Composing different DSLs using hierarchical composition*

It is quite common to use a smaller DSL embedded within a larger one. Trading solutions can use DSLs for expressing currency manipulations and conversions, date and time management, and customer balance management in portfolio reporting, to name a few situations in which you'll find them.

Now suppose you're implementing a DSL for *client portfolio* reporting. You need to report *balances* for securities and cash holdings that the client account holds as of a particular date. Note the two italicized words: client-portfolio and balance represent two important domain concepts and are candidates for DSL-based implementations. They're independent abstractions, but they often occur in close association with each other.

AVOIDING IMPLEMENTATION COUPLING

Let's find out in table 6.7 how you can make this association clean enough so that the individual DSLs can evolve as independent implementations.

`Balance` is the interface that abstracts the underlying implementation. Scala lets you define type synonyms. You can define `type Balance = BigDecimal` and happily use

Table 6.7 Composing DSLs hierarchically

Associated abstractions need to evolve independently	
Balance is:	**Client portfolio is:**
<ul><li>An amount of money or security held by a client</li><li>An important domain concept with specific semantics that can be modeled as a DSL</li><li>An amount that can be expressed as `BigDecimal` for implementation purposes only, though `BigDecimal` doesn't have any meaning to the domain user</li></ul>	<ul><li>A report of a client's balances across his holdings</li><li>An important domain concept with specific semantics that can be modeled as a DSL</li></ul>

Note:

You should always hide your implementation from your published language constructs. Not only does this method make your DSL readable, it lets you change the underlying implementations seamlessly without any impact on the client code. To learn more about how to hide your implementation, read the discussions that are in appendix A.

Modeling the association:

A snippet from the point of view of the domain user clearly shows how the two abstractions for balance and portfolio can be associated when you're designing domain APIs:

```
trait Portfolio {
  def currentPortfolio(account: Account): Balance
}
```

To Do:

You need to compose the two DSLs such that the association can be seamless across multiple implementations of each of them. You can flexibly plug in an alternative implementation of `Balance` DSL when defining an implementation of the `Portfolio` DSL.

Balance as the name to describe the net value of your client holdings in his portfolio. But what happens when you build larger families of Portfolio DSLs as specializations of your base DSL, just like the ones we made with TradeDsl in section 6.7.1? Embedding the implementation of Balance within the Portfolio DSL will couple the entire hierarchy to a concrete implementation. Even if you need to, you'll never be able to change the implementation in the future. The solution is to avoid directly embedding one DSL in the other and instead compose them hierarchically. In the end, you'll have two DSLs that fit together nicely and that are coupled loosely enough so that you can plug in your implementation of choice whenever you feel like it.

Consider the following DSL for modeling your client's portfolio in the following listing.

Listing 6.19 A DSL with implementation coupling

```
package dsl

import api._
import api.Util._

trait Portfolio {
  type Balance = BigDecimal
  def currentPortfolio(account: Account): Balance        ❶ Embedded
}                                                             implementation

trait ClientPortfolio extends Portfolio {
  override def currentPortfolio(account: Account) =      ❷ In real life, this is
    BigDecimal(1200)                                        complex logic
}
```

Ugh! By the time you get down to the first specialization of the Portfolio DSL, you see that the Balance abstraction ❶ has already been broken through ❷. Try to compose them *hierarchically* and keep the implementation of the Balance DSL outside the Portfolio DSL. Composing hierarchically means that one needs to be within the other. The difference between composing hierarchically and the code in listing 6.19 is that you are going to embed the DSL *interface* and NOT the *implementation*. I can almost hear the murmur of abstract vals coming across from my readers. You guessed it! The Portfolio DSL needs to have an instance of the Balance DSL, which we'll call Balances.

HOW DO YOU MODEL BALANCE?

To get a true understanding of a DSL, we can't deal with examples that are too trivial. After all, you can appreciate the expressiveness of a DSL only when you realize how it abstracts the underlying complexities in a readable syntax. Initially we talked about modeling a balance with a BigDecimal. But if you're a domain person familiar with the securities trading operations, you know that for a client account, the balance indicates the *client's cash position in a particular currency as of a specific date*. I'm not going into the details of how you compute balance from a client portfolio. Modeling a balance with only a BigDecimal is an oversimplification. The Balances DSL contract is shown in the following listing, followed by a sample implementation BalancesImpl.

Listing 6.20 DSL for modeling account balance

```
package dsl

import java.util.Date
import api._
import api.Util._
import api.Currency._

trait Balances {                                          Abstract
  type Balance                                            type

  def balance(amount: BigDecimal,
      ccy: Currency, asOf: Date): Balance
  def inBaseCurrency(b: Balance): (Balance, Currency)
  def getBaseCurrency: Currency = USD
  def getConversionFactor(c: Currency) = 0.9
}                                                     ❶ Concrete
class BalancesImpl extends Balances {                    implementation
  case class BalanceRep(amount: BigDecimal,
    ccy: Currency, asOfDate: Date)
  type Balance = BalanceRep

  override def balance(amount: BigDecimal,
      ccy: Currency, asOf: Date)
    = BalanceRep(amount, ccy, asOf)

  override def inBaseCurrency(b: Balance)
    = (BalanceRep(b.amount * getConversionFactor(getBaseCurrency),
        b.ccy, b.asOfDate), getBaseCurrency)
}

object Balances extends BalancesImpl
```

A client balance can be reported in a specific currency, depending on the client's preference. But for auditory regulations, it's often required to be converted to a *base currency*. A base currency is one in which the investor maintains its book of accounts. In the forex market, the US dollar is usually considered to be the base currency. In the DSL shown in listing 6.20, the method inBaseCurrency reports the balance in the base currency. In the sample implementation ❶ of Balances, we commit to an implementation of the abstract type Balance as a tuple of three elements: the amount, the currency, and the date (a balance is always calculated as of a specific date).

COMPOSING THE BALANCE DSL WITH THE PORTFOLIO DSL
In order to compose with the Portfolio DSL, you need an abstract val of Balances ❶ as a data member within it, as shown in the following listing.

Listing 6.21 The Portfolio DSL contract

```
package dsl

import api._

trait Portfolio {             ❶ Abstract val for
  val bal: Balances                Balances DSL
  import bal._                              ❷ Object import
                                               syntax
```

```
    def currentPortfolio(account: Account): Balance
}
```

Note the *object import* syntax of Scala ❷ that makes all members of the object `bal` available within the class body. Now let's look at a specialized implementation of `Portfolio` that computes the balance of a client account in the next listing.

Listing 6.22   A DSL implementation of `Portfolio`

```
trait ClientPortfolio extends Portfolio {
  val bal = new BalancesImpl                          ◁─┐  Committed to an
  import bal._                                           │  implementation

  override def currentPortfolio(account: Account) =
    val amount = //..                                 ◁─┐  Implementation
    val ccy = //..                                       │  details elided
    val asOfDate = //..

    balance(amount, ccy, asOfDate)
}

object ClientPortfolio extends ClientPortfolio
```

We've committed to a specific implementation of `Balances` in our `ClientPortfolio` DSL. Now we need to ensure that when we compose `ClientPortfolio` with other DSLs that use `Balances`, those other DSLs will also use the same implementation.

Let's look at another implementation of `Portfolio` that acts as the decorator of other `Portfolio` implementations. In the following listing we look at `Auditing`, an implementation of `Portfolio` that adds auditing features to other `Portfolio` implementations.

Listing 6.23   Another implementation of the `Portfolio` DSL

```
trait Auditing extends Portfolio {                ❶  Portfolio DSL
  val semantics: Portfolio                        ◁┘  embedded

  val bal: semantics.bal.type                     ◁─┐  Singleton
  import bal._                                     ❷  type of Scala

  override def currentPortfolio(account: Account) =    Report balance in
    inBaseCurrency(                                     base currency
      semantics.currentPortfolio(account))._1     ◁┘
}
```

`Auditing` not only composes with another `Portfolio` DSL ❶, but it also ensures that the DSL it embeds within itself (`semantics`) uses the *same implementation* of the embedded `Balances` DSL ❷. (`Balances` is embedded within `Portfolio`, which is the superclass of `Auditing`.) We enforce this constraint by declaring `bal` in `Auditing` to be `semantics.bal`, which defines it as a Scala *singleton type*. Now we can specify the concrete implementation values of `semantics` and `bal` to create an abstraction for `ClientPortfolio` that supports `Auditing`. Look at the following snippet:

```
object ClientPortfolioAuditing extends Auditing {
  val semantics = ClientPortfolio
  val bal: semantics.bal.type = semantics.bal
}
```

When you use hierarchical composition to compose multiple DSLs, you get the advantages listed in table 6.8.

Table 6.8   Advantages of using hierarchical composition for DSLs

Advantage	Reason for the advantage
Representation independence	The DSLs you compose don't contain any embedded implementation details
Loose coupling	Loose coupling between the composed DSLs, which means all of them can evolve independently
Static type safety	Scala's powerful type system ensures that all the constraints can be enforced by the compiler

The subject of DSL composition is well explained in the paper *Polymorphic embedding of DSLs* (see [7] in section 6.10). Read the paper if you want to get into the details of other ways to compose DSLs in Scala.

In earlier sections of this chapter, you've seen lots of techniques you can use to compose abstractions using the object-functional power of Scala. The discussion of composition is still incomplete, because we haven't talked about monadic abstractions. Monadic abstractions are used extensively to build composable computations. Monads have their origin in category theory (don't worry, I'm not going to discuss the mathematics behind monads; you can look into that on your own if you're interested). In the next section, you're going to see how you can put some syntactic sugar on top of monadic structures in Scala. This additional magic will help you design sequencing of DSL operations.

6.8   *Monadic structures in DSL*

I've probably put enough emphasis on how abstractions that compose well make readable DSLs. When we talk about abstracting a computation, functional programming gives you more composing power than the OO programming model. You get this added boost because functional programming treats computations as applications of pure mathematical functions, without the side effects of mutable state. The moment you decouple functions from mutability, all you're left with are abstractions that you can verify independently, without any dependence on external context. Functional programming offers mathematical models that let you compose computations as functional compositions. I'm not going into the depths of category theory or any similar formalism that makes this promise. The only thing you need to remember is the fact that compositionality of functions gives you a way to form complex abstractions out of simpler building blocks.

WHAT'S A MONAD?

You can think of monads as *function composition,* and *binding on steroids.* When you build abstractions that obey the monad laws, you can use them to construct higher-order abstractions by using beautiful composition semantics

> A monad is an abstraction in which you structure your computation into values and sequences of computations that use them. You can use them to *compose dependent computations* to form larger computations. Monads have their theoretical basis in category theory, which might be something you don't want to contemplate right now. If, on the other hand, you're not scared of category theory, go read [11] in section 6.10. For the rest of you, relax. We're not going to get into the guts of that theory here.

We're going to examine monads only in terms of what you need from them to design a Scala DSL. You'll see a lot more monadic structures when we discuss parser combinators

---

Monads for you

A *monad* is an abstraction that binds computations. Instead of giving generic definitions, let me define all monadic attributes in terms of what you'll find in Scala. (The classical approach would've been to use either category theory or Haskell to explain the first-order principles; using Scala as the basis for the explanation seems more useful).

A monad is defined by the following three things:

1 *An abstraction* M[A]*, where* M *is the type constructor.* In Scala, you define the abstraction as class M[A] or case class M[A] or trait M[A].
2 *A* unit *method* (unit v)*,* which in Scala is the invocation of the constructor new M(v) or M(v).
3 *A* bind *method, which allows you to sequence computations.* In Scala, it's implemented by the flatMap combinator. bind f m is equivalent to m flatMap f in Scala.

List[A] is a monad in Scala. The unit method is defined by the constructor List(…) and bind is implemented by flatMap.

Does this mean that you can define any abstraction that has these three things and it becomes a monad? Not necessarily. A monad needs to obey the following three laws:

1 *Identity.* For a monad m, m flatMap unit => m. With the List monad in Scala, we have List(1,2,3) flatMap {x => List(x)} == List(1,2,3).
2 *Unit.* For a monad m, unit(v) flatMap f => f(v). With the List monad in Scala, this implies List(100) flatMap {x => f(x)} == f(100), where f returns a List.
3 *Associativity.* For a monad m, m flatMap g flatMap h => m flatMap {x => g(x) flatMap h}. This law tells us that the computation depends on the order, but not on the nesting. Try verifying this law for Scala List as an exercise.

in Scala in chapter 8. In this section, we're going to talk about some of the monadic operations in Scala that can make your DSLs compose more beautifully than when you use an OO counterpart.

The accompanying sidebar gives a brief introduction to monads. For more details about monads, refer to [9] in section 6.10.

HOW MONADS REDUCE ACCIDENTAL COMPLEXITY

Consider the Java example in listing 6.24 of a typical operation in your web-based trading application. You have a key that you use to get the value from `HttpRequest` or `HttpSession`. The value that you get is the reference number of a trade. You need to do a query for the trade from the database to get the corresponding `Trade` model.

Listing 6.24 Handling alternate routes in computation using Java

```
String param(String key) {
  //..
  return value;                        ⟵  Fetch value from
}                                          request or session

Trade queryTrade(String ref) {
  //.. query                           ⟵  Do query from
  return trade                             database
}
public static void main(String[] args) {
  String key;
  //.. set key

  String refNo = param(key);
  if (refNo == null) {                 ⟵
    //.. exception processing
  }                                        ❶ Null check
  Trade trade = queryTrade (refNo);
  if (trade == null) {                 ⟵
    //.. exception processing
  }
}
```

This code shows some nonessential complexity ❶, plaguing the surface syntax of your abstraction. All the null checks have to be done explicitly and at every step in this computation of a domain model from a context parameter. Now consider the following equivalent Scala code that does the same thing as the previous code using its *monadic for comprehension* syntax.

Listing 6.25 Scala monadic for comprehensions

```
def param(key: String): Option[String] = {
  //..                                  ⟵
}                                          ❶ Monadic return value
def queryTrade(ref: String): Option[Trade] = {
  //..                                  ⟵
}
```

```
def main(args: Array[String]) {
  val trade =
    (
      for {
        r <- param("refNo")
        t <- queryTrade (r)
      }
      yield t
  ) getOrElse error("not found")
//..
}
```

for comprehensions

Let's look more into how the monadic structures in this listing chain together to create the `trade` object within the `main` method.

`param` returns a monad `Option[String]` . `Option[]` is a monad in Scala that you can use to abstract a computation that might not produce any result. `queryTrade` returns another monad, `Option[Trade]` , which has a type that's different from `Option[String]`. We need to chain these computations such that if `param` returns a null value, `queryTrade` must *not* be invoked. We did this check explicitly in listing 6.24. Using monadic structures, the underlying implementation of the monad `Option[]` takes care of this plumbing so that your code remains clean and free of accidental complexity .

How does a monad take care of this chaining? It's through the `bind` operation that we discussed in the monad laws in the sidebar earlier in this section. In Scala, `bind` is implemented as `flatMap`; the for comprehension is just syntactic sugar on top of `flatMap`, as you can see in the following snippet.

Here's the unsweetened version of the for comprehensions that makes this bind explicit.

```
param("refNo") flatMap {r =>
  queryTrade(r) map {t =>
    t}} getOrElse error("not found")
```

`flatMap` (equivalent to the `>>=` operation in Haskell) is a combinator that serves as the glue for this snippet. It's the overarching `bind` operator that injects the output of `param` into the input of `queryTrade`, handling all the necessary null checks within it. For comprehensions offer a higher level abstraction on top of the `flatMap` combinator to make your DSL more readable and expressive.

A detailed discussion of monads, `flatMaps`, and for comprehensions is beyond the scope of this book. What you need to know is that monadic structures and operations give you an easy way to implement DSLs. We've just looked at one of the most common uses of monads as a means of sequencing dependent computations without introducing nonessential complexities. Apart from this, monads are also used extensively as a mechanism to explain side effects in pure functional languages, handle state changes, exceptions, continuations, and many other computations. Needless to say, you can use all of these ways to make your DSLs appear more expressive. For more details about monads in Scala, see [10] in section 6.10.

To tie a nice big bow on our discussion about how monads help make expressive language abstractions, let's build one variant of the trade lifecycle DSL that we implemented in listing 6.20. Instead of using partial functions to sequence operations, we'll use monadic comprehensions of Scala. Doing this exercise will give you an idea about how to think in terms of monads when building your own DSL. We'll keep the example simple just to demonstrate how you can build your own computations that can be chained using for comprehensions.

DESIGNING A MONADIC TRADE DSL

Without much ado, let's define a variant of the `TradeDSL` that we discussed in listing 6.17. Each of the lifecycle methods now returns a monad (`Option[]`) instead of `PartialFunction`.

| Listing 6.26 | Monadic `TradeDsl` |

```
package monad

import api._
class TradeDslM {
  def validate(trade: Trade): Option[Trade] = //..
  def enrich(trade: Trade): Option[Trade] = //..
  def journalize(trade: Trade): Option[Trade] = //..
}

object TradeDslM extends TradeDslM
```

We can use that DSL within a for comprehension to invoke the sequence of lifecycle methods on a collection of trades:

```
import TradeDslM._

val trd =
  for {
    trade <- trades
    trValidated <- validate(trade)
    trEnriched <- enrich(trValidated)
    trFinal <- journalize(trEnriched)
  }
  yield trFinal
```

This snippet has the same functionality as listing 6.20 but it uses monadic binds to chain operations. In the case of our earlier implementation that was based on partial functions, we could only chain operations that matched exactly in types. In this for comprehension, there are sequenced operations that don't have the types that match exactly. `trades` is a `List` of `Iterable` that generates a `Trade` for every iteration of the comprehension execution. We don't have to check for the end-of-sequence explicitly because `List` is implemented as a monad; just like `Option[]`, the `flatMap` combinator within `List` takes care of such boundary conditions. `validate` returns an `Option[Trade]`, which can be `Some(trade)` or `None`. When we pipeline the output of `validate` into `enrich`, we don't do any explicit null checks or any explicit conversion from `Option[Trade]` -> `Trade`. So long as you pipeline using monadic structures like

List[] or Option[], all binds are done automatically through the flatMap combinator. In this sense, chaining operations using monadic binds is more powerful than what we achieved using partial functions in listing 6.17. When they're designed correctly, monadic operations can lead to expressive DSLs, especially if you use the syntactic sugar that for expressions provide in Scala (or the do notation in Haskell).

In case you're curious, the previous snippet boils down to the following flatMap expression:

```
trades flatMap {trade =>
  validate(trade) flatMap {trValidated =>
    enrich(trValidated) flatMap {trEnriched =>
      journalize(trEnriched) map {trFinal =>
        trFinal
      }
    }
  }
}
```

Obviously, this looks more programmatic and less readable to the domain user than the earlier version that uses for expressions.

As you saw in this section, monads in Scala are yet another way to compose abstractions. They're subtly different from partial functions and offer a truly mathematical way to chain dependent abstractions. Scala offers quite a few built-in monadic structures. Be sure to use them appropriately when you implement DSLs in Scala.

6.9   *Summary*

The Scala community is abuzz with DSLs and not without reason. Scala is one of the most potent forces among the programming languages today. It offers first-class support for designing expressive DSLs.

In this chapter, you've taken a thorough tour of all the Scala features that help you design internal DSLs. We started with a summary of the feature list of Scala, then carefully dug deep into each of them by examining snippets of DSLs designed from the domain of securities trading. A DSL is architected as a facade on top of an underlying implementation model. In this chapter, we switched back and forth between the domain model and the language abstractions that are on top of it.

DSLs need to be composable *at the contract level*, without exposing any of their implementation details. You have to design them this way because every DSL evolves on its own and you might need to change an implementation without impacting other DSLs or your core application. You saw how internal DSLs in Scala compose together statically using the power of the type system. Finally, we took a tour of how monadic operations can help construct composable DSL structures. Scala doesn't make monads as explicit as Haskell does in its programming model. But you can still use Scala's monadic comprehension to sequence domain operations without introducing a lot of nonessential complexities.

> **Key takeaways & best practices**
> - *Scala has a concise syntax with optional semicolons and type inference.* Use them to make your DSL surface syntax less verbose.
> - *Design your abstractions in Scala by using multiple artifacts* like classes, traits, and objects to make your DSL implementation extensible.
> - *Scala offers lots of functional programming power.* Use it to abstract the actions of your DSL. You'll escape the object-only paradigm and make your implementation more expressive to the user.

Internal DSLs are hosted within a specific language and are sometimes limited by the capabilities of the host language. You can get around these limits by designing your own external DSL. In the next chapter, we're going to look at some of the building blocks of external DSLs. We'll start with some of the basic theories of compilers and parsers, and then move on to higher-order structures like parser combinators that are widely used today. Stay tuned!

6.10 *References*

1 Odersky, Martin, and Matthias Zenger. 2005. Scalable component abstractions. *Proceedings of the 20th annual ACM SIGPLAN conference on object-oriented programming systems, languages, and applications, pp 41-57.*

2 Wampler, Dean, and Alex Payne. 2009. *Programming Scala: Scalability = Functional Programming + Objects.* O'Reilly Media.

3 Gamma, E., R. Helm, R. Johnson, and J. Vlissides. 1995. *Design Patterns: Elements of reusable object-oriented software.* Addison-Wesley Professional.

4 Ford, Neal, *Advanced DSLs in Ruby,* http://github.com/nealford/presentations/tree/master.

5 Emir, Burak, Martin Odersky, and John Williams. Matching Objects With Patterns. *LAMP-REPORT-2006-006.* http://lamp.epfl.ch/~emir/written/MatchingObjectsWithPatterns-TR.pdf.

6 Evans, Eric. 2003. *Domain-Driven Design: Tackling complexity in the heart of software.* Addison-Wesley Professional.

7 Hofer, Christian, Klaus Ostermann, Tillmann Rendel, and Adriaan Moors. Polymorphic Embedding of DSLs. *Proceedings of the 7th international conference on generative programming and component engineering,* 2008, pp 137-148.

8 ScalaTest. http://www.scalatest.org.

9 Wadler, Philip. 1992. The essence of functional programming. *Proceedings of the 19th ACM SIGPLAN-SIGACT symposium on principles of programming languages.* pp 1-14.

10 Emir, Burak. Monads in Scala. http://lamp.epfl.ch/~emir/bqbase/2005/01/20/monad.html.

11 Pierce, Benjamin C. 1991. *Basic Category Theory for Computer Scientists*. The MIT Press.

12 Ghosh, Debasish. Implementation Inheritance with Mixins—Some Thoughts. *Ruminations of a Programmer*. http://debasishg.blogspot.com/2008/02/implementation-inheritance-with-mixins.html.

13 Venners, Bill. Abstract Type Members versus Generic Type Parameters in Scala. http://www.artima.com/weblogs/viewpost.jsp?thread=270195.

14 Ghosh, Debasish. Scala Self-Type Annotations for Constrained Orthogonality. *Ruminations of a Programmer*. http://debasishg.blogspot.com/2010/02/scala-self-type-annotations-for.html.

External DSL implementation artifacts

This chapter covers

- The processing pipeline of an external DSL
- Parser classification
- Developing an external DSL using ANTLR
- The Eclipse Modeling Framework and Xtext

External DSLs, like the internal ones, have a layer of abstraction on top of an existing domain model. Where they differ is how they implement the layer. External DSLs build their own language-processing infrastructure: the parsers, the lexers, and the processing logic.

We're going to start with a discussion of the overall architecture of the processing infrastructure of an external DSL. The internal DSLs get this infrastructure free from the underlying host language, but the external DSLs need to build them from the ground up. First, we're going to look at hand-written parsers, and then move on to develop your first custom external DSL using the ANTLR parser generator. In the final section of the chapter, we'll look at a different paradigm of DSL development: the model-driven approach of the Eclipse Modeling Framework (EMF), using Xtext, as a comprehensive environment for external DSL development. Figure 7.1 provides a roadmap of our progress through the chapter.

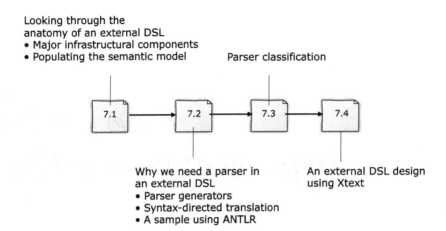

Looking through the
anatomy of an external DSL
• Major infrastructural components
• Populating the semantic model

Parser classification

7.1 → 7.2 → 7.3 → 7.4

Why we need a parser in
an external DSL
• Parser generators
• Syntax-directed translation
• A sample using ANTLR

An external DSL design
using Xtext

Figure 7.1 Our roadmap through the chapter

In this chapter, you'll learn how to develop a language-processing infrastructure using the tools available on the market today. When you're done, you can use this infrastructure to develop your own DSL processor.

7.1 Anatomy of an external DSL

You've already seen in section 1.5 how an external DSL is structured on top of a custom language infrastructure. In this section, we'll look at the details of how the architecture of the DSL evolves along with the model of the domain that it describes. I'll also describe some of the implementation options and the trade-offs that you need to make as a DSL designer.

7.1.1 The simplest option first

Let's start with the simplest of options that you have when designing an external DSL. Your DSL has a custom syntax that you've developed a parser for. The parsing engine first lexicalizes the input stream, converting them to recognizable tokens. These tokens are also known as the *terminals* of the grammar. The tokens are then fed on to the production rules and parsed as valid sentences of the grammar. This process is shown in figure 7.2.

The *parsing infrastructure* is the only processor that does everything required to process the input DSL script and generate the necessary output.

> The parsing infrastructure doesn't need to be very sophisticated for every instance of the DSL that you want to process. It's not uncommon to have simple data structures like string manipulators or regular expression processors as the parsing engine for simple languages of the domain. In most of these cases, you can bundle together the steps of lexicalization, parsing, and code generation into a consolidated set of actions.

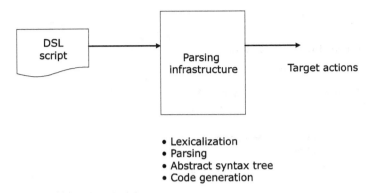

- Lexicalization
- Parsing
- Abstract syntax tree
- Code generation

Figure 7.2 The simplest form of an external DSL. The parsing infrastructure does everything necessary to produce the target actions. The phases of processing the DSL script (lexicalization, parsing, generating the AST, and code generation) are all bundled in one monolithic block.

The design shown in figure 7.2 doesn't scale when it becomes more complex. If you have a simple requirement that's not likely to scale up in complexity, you can choose this implementation of a do-all kind of language processing infrastructure. But not all problems in the world are simple. As you'll see next, the only way to address complexity is to modularize concerns and introduce a suitable level of abstraction.

7.1.2 *Abstracting the domain model*

In figure 7.2, the do-all box of the *parsing infrastructure* handled all the processing that needed to be done to generate the target output. As I mentioned earlier, this approach doesn't scale with the growing complexity of the language. Even if you consider a moderately complex DSL, the single box needs to perform all the following tasks within one monolithic abstraction:

- Parse the input, based on a set of grammar rules.
- Store the parsed language into a form of AST. For simpler use cases, you can skip the AST generation phase and embed actions to execute directly within the grammar.
- Annotate the AST, enriching it in the form of intermediate representations for generating target actions.
- Process the AST and perform actions like code generation.

That's a lot of work for one abstraction. Let's see if we can make this a little simpler.

MODULARIZING THE BIG BOX

Let's try to separate some of these responsibilities to make the design of the big box more modular. Figure 7.3 shows one way to do that.

In figure 7.3, parsing is one of the core functionalities that you can identify as a separate abstraction. One of the natural side effects of parsing is the generation of

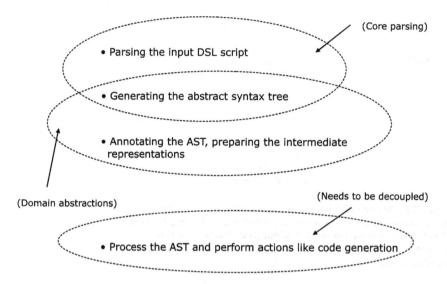

Figure 7.3 Separation of concerns for the four responsibilities that the single box in figure 7.2 was doing. Each dotted region can now encapsulate the identified functionalities.

an AST. The AST identifies the structural representation of the language in a form that's independent of the language syntax. Depending on what you want to do from the AST, you have to augment it with additional information like object types, annotations, and other contextual notes that you'll need in the next phase of processing. Your AST becomes much richer and starts accumulating the semantic information of your language.

THE SEMANTIC MODEL

When you're working on a DSL for a specific domain, the enriched AST becomes the semantic model for the domain itself. The reason the top two regions overlap in figure 7.3 is that the core-parsing process needs to generate some sort of data structure.

The next process in the pipeline will enrich this data structure with the domain knowledge. The completion of this process leads to figure 7.4, where we identify the semantic model of the domain as one of the core abstractions of the DSL processing pipeline.

The semantic model is a data structure that's enhanced with domain semantics after the DSL scripts are processed through the pipeline. Its structure is independent of the DSL syntax and is more aligned to the solution domain model of the system. It's the perfect abstraction that decouples the input syntax-oriented scripting structure from the target actions.

As part of the target output, the DSL processor can do quite a few things. It can generate code that becomes part of the application. It can generate resources that are

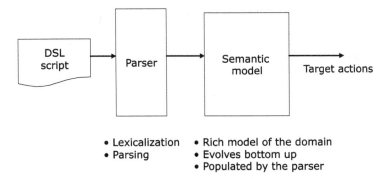

- Lexicalization
- Parsing

- Rich model of the domain
- Evolves bottom up
- Populated by the parser

Figure 7.4 We've split the parsing infrastructure box of figure 7.2 into two separate abstractions. The parser takes care of the core parsing of the syntax. The semantic model is now a separate abstraction from the parsing engine. It encapsulates all the domain concerns that are ready to be fed into the machinery that generates all the target actions.

consumed and interpreted by the application runtime, like the object-relational mapping files in Hibernate that generate the data model. (Hibernate is an object-relational mapping [ORM] framework. For more information, go to http://www.hibernate.org.) The semantic model keeps you isolated from both sides and serves as the independent repository of all the necessary domain functionalities.

One other major benefit of having a well-designed semantic model is that your application is more testable. The entire domain model of your application can be tested independently of the syntax layer of your DSL. Let's look at the semantic model in more detail and see how the model evolves during the development cycle of an external DSL.

POPULATING THE SEMANTIC MODEL

The semantic model serves as the repository of the domain model. The parser populates the semantic model as it consumes the input stream of the DSL script. The design of the semantic model is completely independent of the DSL syntax and evolves bottom-up from smaller abstractions, as with internal DSLs. Figure 7.5 illustrates how the semantic model evolves bottom-up as the repository of the domain structure, attributes, and behavior.

The difference with external DSLs lies in the way you populate the semantic model in the course of the parsing process. When you're using internal DSLs, you populate smaller abstractions in the host language. You use the compositional features of the host language to build the larger whole. With external DSLs, you populate smaller abstractions as you parse the syntax of your language. As your parse tree grows up, the semantic model is fleshed out into a concrete representation of the domain knowledge.

After you've populated the semantic model, you can use it to generate code, manipulate databases, or produce models to be used by other components of your

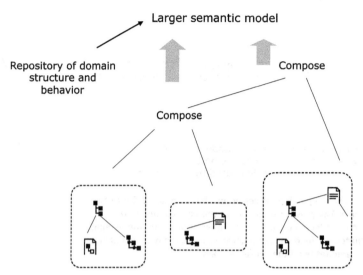

Figure 7.5   The semantic model evolves bottom-up as a composition of smaller domain abstractions. You develop smaller abstractions for domain entities, as indicated by the dotted rectangles. You then compose them together to form larger entities. In the end, you have the entire domain abstracted in your semantic model.

application. Now look again at figure 7.4. Are you convinced of the benefits that separating abstractions brings to the architecture of your DSL system?

Architecturally speaking, both internal and external DSLs form a layer on top of the semantic model. With an internal DSL, you use the parser of the host language; the contracts that you publish to the user take the form of a thin veneer on top of the semantic model. With external DSLs, you build your own infrastructure that parses the DSL script and executes actions. These actions lead to the population of the semantic model.

The parser that you implement as part of the infrastructure recognizes the syntax of the DSL script. Some important aspects of implementing external DSLs that you need to master are the techniques you can use to implement the various forms of parsers and lexical analyzers.

In the next section, we're going to discuss parsing techniques. Rather than provide a detailed treatise on parser implementations, I'll give a brief overview of the landscape and discuss parsing techniques and the class of grammars that each addresses. When you use the most appropriate set of tools to develop your external DSLs (like parser generators), you might not need a detailed exposition of how parsers are implemented. But, depending on the class of language that you design, a fair knowledge of parsing techniques always comes in handy. The references at the end of the chapter can point you to relevant information about this topic.

7.2   *The role of a parser in designing an external DSL*

The DSL script that you execute is fed into a lexical analyzer. The analyzer then tokenizes the stream into identifiable units that are recognized by the parser. When the parser has consumed the entire stream of input and has reached a successful terminal stage, we say that it has recognized the language. Figure 7.6 shows a schematic diagram of the process.

When I talk about lexical analyzers and parsers, I'm not assuming that they're complex. Their complexity depends on the language that you design. As I mentioned earlier, if your DSL is simple enough, you might not need separate stages for lexicalization and parsing. Your parser might simply consist of a string processor that manipulates input scripts, based on regular expression processing. In such cases, you can get away with a handcrafted parser, as opposed to a more complicated one that you'd need to design when you're using a more sophisticated infrastructure. Let's see how you'd build a parser for a nontrivial DSL, using such an infrastructure that generates the parser for you.

7.2.1   *Parsers and parser generators*

The parser that you design is an abstraction for the grammar of your language. If you choose to implement the entire parser by hand, you'd need to:

- Develop the BNF syntax for the language
- Write the parser that mirrors the syntax

Unfortunately, when you develop a parser manually, the entire grammar gets embedded within the code base. Any change in the grammar means that you'll have to make a significant change in the code that implements it. This kind of problem is typical when you're programming at a lower level of abstraction (appendix A provides a more detailed explanation).

A better alternative to writing nontrivial parsers by hand is to use a parser generator. A parser generator lets you program at a higher level of abstraction. You simply have to define two things:

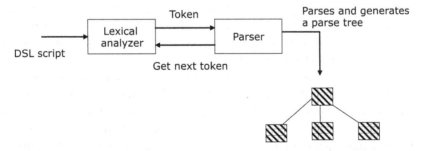

Figure 7.6   The process of parsing. The language script is fed into the lexical analyzer that tokenizes and feeds them into the parser.

- The grammar rules, in Extended Backus Naur Form (EBNF) syntax
- Custom actions that you want to execute on recognition of grammar rules

With a parser generator, the infrastructure code for implementing the parser for your grammar will be encapsulated within the generator itself. Standard procedures for error handling and parse-tree generation become part of the generator; they work the same way for every parser that you create out of it.

As with any technique that offers a higher level of abstraction, you have to write, manage, and maintain less code. Another big advantage of using parser generators is that many of them are capable of generating the target parser in multiple languages. Table 7.1 contains information about some of the commonly used parser generators.

Table 7.1   Parser generators available today

Parser generator	Associated lexical analyzer	Details
YACC	LEX	Part of the UNIX distribution (originally developed in 1975) that generates parsers in C.
Bison	Flex	Part of the GNU distribution with almost similar functionality as YACC and LEX, but can generate parsers in C++.
ANTLR (go to http://antlr.org)	Packaged with ANTLR	Implemented by Terrance Parr. Capable of generating parsers in a host of target languages like Java, C, C++, Python, and Ruby.
Coco/R	Generates a scanner	Coco/R is a compiler generator, which takes an attributed grammar of a source language and generates a scanner and a parser for that language.

Besides the list in table 7.1, there are a few other parser generators like Java Compiler Compiler (JavaCC), developed by Sun Microsystems (go to https://javacc.dev.java.net/) and IBM Jikes Parser Generator (http://www10.software.ibm.com/developerworks/opensource/jikes/project/). Both Jikes and JavaCC generate Java parsers and offer functionalities similar to YACC and Bison.

Whether you use a hand-written parser or one constructed by a generator, it's the syntax of your language that directs the parser. When the parser recognizes the language, it generates a parse tree that encapsulates the whole process of recognition into a recursive data structure. If you've added custom actions to your grammar rules, the parse tree that's generated is augmented with that additional information, forming your semantic model. Let's see how the parser generator does this translation from custom syntax to the semantic model of your domain by looking at an example of a language that's processed using ANTLR.

7.2.2 Syntax-directed translation

When your external DSL implementation processes a piece of DSL script, it starts with the recognition of its syntax. You parse the syntax and translate it to generate the semantic model. The semantic model acts as the repository for the next action that you execute. But how do you recognize the syntax? Table 7.2 shows the two sets of artifacts that you need for this recognition to be successful.

Table 7.2 Recognizing the DSL syntax

Artifact	What it does
A context-free grammar that identifies the set of valid productions	The grammar specifies the syntactic structure of the DSL. DSL scripts that obey the rules defined in the grammar are the only ones that are considered to be valid. **Note:** I'm going to use the ANTLR parser generator for all examples in this section to specify the grammar.
A set of semantic rules that you apply to the attributes of the symbols that your grammar recognizes. These rules are then used to generate the semantic model.	Along with each grammar rule, you can define actions that are executed when the rule is recognized by the parser. The action can be the generation of the parse tree or any other trigger that you want to generate, as long as the action is related to the rule being recognized. Defining an action is easy. Every parser generator allows foreign code to be embedded, along with the DSL-based production definitions of the grammar. For example, ANTLR lets you embed Java code, YACC lets you embed C.

Figure 7.7 illustrates how the grammar rules that you supply along with the custom actions get processed by the parser generator to generate the semantic model.

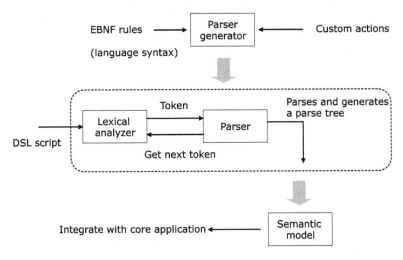

Figure 7.7 The parser generator takes the grammar rules and the custom actions as input. It then generates the lexical analyzer and the parser, which accept the DSL script and generate the semantic model. Then you can integrate this model with the core application.

Let's do a sample exercise of language interpretation for a small order-processing DSL using the ANTLR parser generator. We'll define the lexical analyzer and the grammars and embed a few custom actions that'll populate the semantic model of our language.

SETTING UP THE ANTLR EXAMPLE

The language is similar (albeit simpler) to the order-processing DSL that we developed in chapter 2 using Groovy. This example will teach you the steps you need to perform to use a parser generator to develop an external DSL. You'll develop the syntax of your DSL and generate the semantic model that produces a custom abstraction of all the orders that are being placed.

Consider the following snippet as the series of orders that a client can place with the trading organization:

```
buy IBM @ 100 for NOMURA
sell GOOGLE @ limitprice = 70 for CHASE
```

The entire order placement instruction consists of repeating lines of the same format. You'll design an external DSL using ANTLR that processes these scripts. Then, you'll generate data structures as the semantic model. To keep things simple, we'll consider each line as a separate order and the entire collection as a list of orders placed by the client. The first step is to design the lexical analyzer that'll preprocess the input script into a sequence of symbols that our grammar can recognize.

DESIGNING THE LEXICAL ANALYZER

The lexer reads the input stream and converts the characters into tokens as per the token definitions specified in the lexical analyzer. With ANTLR, you can specify lexer rules either inline with the grammar specification or as a separate file. In our example, we'll put all the token specifications in a separate file that we'll call OrderLexer.g; ANTLR specifications live in a file with a .g extension (for grammar). Note that the specification given in the following listing uses a DSL structure that's readable and expressive as a token language.

Listing 7.1   OrderLexer.g: The lexer for your DSL in ANTLR

```
lexer grammar OrderLexer;

EQ    : '=';
BUY   : 'buy';
SELL  : 'sell';
AT    : '@';
FOR   : 'for';
LPRICE  : 'limitprice';
ID      : ('a'..'z'|'A'..'Z')+;
INT     : '0'..'9'+;
NEWLINE : '\r'? '\n';
WS      : (' '|'\t')+ {skip();};          ⏎ Skip whitespaces
```

The lexer rules are matched in a greedy way. When the lexer tries to match rules with the input stream, it uses the rule that has the maximum match. In case of a tie, it picks up the rule that appears first in the order within the specification file.

The next step is to jump into the syntax of your language. That syntax is identified by grammar rules that you design.

DESIGNING THE GRAMMAR RULES

In this step, you define the grammar rules, which are based on the syntax of your DSL. It's a pretty simple DSL, and is for illustration purposes only. We're going to skip over a lot of the error processing functionalities and focus on the architecture of the grammar rules. For a detailed treatment of how ANTLR defines grammar rules and the various options that it offers to the user, refer to [2] of section 7.6.

The grammar rules in listing 7.2 are defined in a separate file, OrderParser.g. That file follows the EBNF notation, which is incredibly expressive to a language designer. Later, when you integrate the lexer and the parser along with the processor code that drives the parser, you'll see how ANTLR generates the actual parser code from these EBNF specifications. Note that the generator does all the heavy lifting of implementing the actual parser. You, as the developer, get to focus on the task of defining the specific syntax.

Listing 7.2   OrderParser.g: Grammar rules for your DSL in ANTLR

```
parser grammar OrderParser;

options {                                    ❶ The lexer
  tokenVocab = OrderLexer;                      reference
}
                                             ❷ All orders
orders     : order+ EOF;
order      : line NEWLINE;
line       : (BUY | SELL) security price account;   ❸ order has a line
security   : ID;
limitprice : LPRICE EQ INT;
price      : AT (INT | limitprice);
account    : FOR ID;
```

For anyone familiar with the EBNF notation, these grammar rules look expressive. We want to build a collection of orders ❷. Each order consists of a line that specifies the order placement details ❸. We're keeping a reference to the lexer class at the beginning of the grammar file within the options block ❶.

ANTLR comes with a GUI-based interpreter environment (ANTLRWorks; go to http://www.antlr.org/works)) in which you can run sample DSL scripts interactively through the specified grammar. It builds the parse tree for you. You can also debug your rules, in case there are any parsing exceptions.

Now you must be wondering why the grammar that we specified in listing 7.2 doesn't have any custom action for the necessary syntax-directed translation. The reason is because I want to give you a feel for the lightweight DSL syntax that the grammar specification for ANTLR gives you. The grammar rules themselves are sufficient for the successful recognition of a valid DSL script; you don't need anything else! In the next section, we'll discuss how to embed Java code as custom action definitions within each of the grammar rules.

EMBEDDING FOREIGN CODE AS CUSTOM ACTIONS

As you saw in listing 7.2, the ANTLR grammar lets you build a default parse tree through the parser that it generates. If you want to augment the parse tree with additional information or generate a separate semantic model by parsing the DSL script, you can do it by defining custom actions with embedded foreign code. In this section, we'll add custom actions to the grammar rules that we defined in listing 7.2 and generate a collection of custom Java objects by parsing the DSL script.

We begin by defining a plain old Java object (POJO) `Order`. When the script is parsed, it generates a semantic model consisting of `List` of `Order` objects. The following listing shows the resulting actions embedded in our grammar rules.

Listing 7.3 OrderParser.g: Action code embedded in the grammar rules

```
parser grammar OrderParser;

options {
  tokenVocab = OrderLexer;
}

@header {
  import java.util.List;
  import java.util.ArrayList;
}

@members {
  private List<Order> orders = new ArrayList<Order>();
  public List<Order> getOrders() {
    return orders;
  }
}

orders : order+ EOF;
order  : line NEWLINE {orders.add($line.value);};

line returns [Order value]
  : (e=BUY | e=SELL) security price account
    {
      $value = new Order($e.text, $security.value,
                $price.value, $account.value);
    };

security returns [String value]: ID {$value = $ID.text;};

limitprice returns [int value]
  : LPRICE EQ INT {$value = Integer.parseInt($INT.text);};

price returns [int value] : AT
  (
    INT {$value = Integer.parseInt($INT.text);}
    |
    limitprice {$value = $limitprice.value;}
  );

account returns [String value] : FOR ID {$value = $ID.text;};
```

Annotations in the right margin:

Custom imports and package specifications ←┘ (points to `@header` block)

Code that parser class shares ←┘ (points to `@members` block)

① **Form collection of Order objects** ←┘ (points to `order` rule)

② **Rule return values** ←┐ (points to `line returns [Order value]`)

If you're not familiar with the EBNF style of writing grammar rules and how to embed action code within them, you can look at [2] in section 7.6. Note that the rules you define can have return values ❷ that get propagated upward as the parsing continues. Computations bubble up and you end up forming the collection of Order objects ❶.

The next listing is the abstraction for the Order class. I've made this pretty simple for illustration purposes.

Listing 7.4 Order.java: The Order abstraction

```java
public class Order {
  private String buySell;
  private String security;
  private int price;
  private String account;

  public Order(String bs, String sec, int p, String acc) {
    buySell = bs;
    security = sec;
    price = p;
    account = acc;
  }

  public String toString() {
    return new StringBuilder()
      .append("Order is ")
      .append(buySell)
      .append("/")
      .append(security)
      .append("/")
      .append(price)
      .append("/")
      .append(account)
      .toString();
  }
}
```

In the next section, we'll write the main processor module that integrates the ANTLR generated lexer, the parser, and any other custom Java code. Let's see how you can parse your DSL script and generate necessary output.

BUILDING THE PARSER MODULE

Now you can use ANTLR to build the parser and integrate it with the driver code. Before we do that, we need to write the driver that takes character streams from input, feeds them to our lexer to generate tokens and to the parser to recognize our DSL script. The following listing shows the driver code, the Processor class.

Listing 7.5 Processor.java: The driver code for our parser module

```java
import java.io.*;
import java.util.List;
import org.antlr.runtime.*;
import org.antlr.runtime.tree.*;
```

```
public class Processor {

  public static void main(String[] args)                    ◁┘  Main driver
    throws IOException, RecognitionException {
    List<Order> os =
      new Processor().processFile(args[0]);
    for(Order o : os) {                                      ◁┐  Print the
      System.out.println(o);                                    order list
    }
  }

  private List<Order> processFile(String filePath)          ◁┐  Read DSL script
    throws IOException, RecognitionException {                   from file
    OrderParser p =
      new OrderParser(
        getTokenStream(new FileReader(filePath)));          ◁┐  Parser reads from
    p.orders();                                             ❶  token stream
    return p.getOrders();
  }

  private CommonTokenStream getTokenStream(Reader reader)
    throws IOException {
    OrderLexer lexer =                                          Token stream
      new OrderLexer(new ANTLRReaderStream(reader));            generated by lexer
    return new CommonTokenStream(lexer);                    ◁┘
  }
}
```

We use the tokenization support that ANTLR provides and its built-in classes for reading from the input stream. In the listing, after we construct the parser ❶, we invoke the method from the start symbol of the grammar, orders(), which is generated by ANTLR. All the classes that are referred to in the listing (like OrderLexer, CommonTokenStream, and OrderParser) are either generated by ANTLR from our grammar rules or are part of the ANTLR runtime. We're assuming that the DSL is in a file whose path is specified as the first argument of the command-line invocation.

As a sample action of what you can do with the semantic model, the program in listing 7.5 prints the list of Order objects that's generated by the parsing process. If this were a real program, you could feed these objects directly into other modules of your system to integrate the DSL with your core application stack.

We've done a lot of work in this section. Let's look back at all we've been through.

HOW FAR WE'VE COME

ANTLR has classes like org.antlr.Tool that work on your grammar files to generate the Java code. Then your build process can compile all Java classes, including the ones that form parts of your custom codebase. Table 7.3 contains a summary of what we've done so far to build the entire infrastructure for processing our external DSL.

Now you have a basic idea of the entire development lifecycle for building and processing an external DSL using a parser generator. This approach is pretty common. When you want to design an external DSL by building a language that's based on a custom infrastructure, this is the process that you'll follow.

Table 7.3 Building an external DSL with the ANTLR parser generator

Step	Description
1 Identify lexicons and pre-pare the lexer for ANTLR	In listing 7.1, we built the lexer OrderLexer.g. We used the token defi-nitions for our order-processing DSL. **Note:** Your lexer definition file should always be separate from the parser. Keeping it separate makes your lexer reusable across parsers.
2 Build grammar rules in EBNF notation	In listing 7.2, we defined the syntax of our DSL in OrderParser.g, based on ANTLR syntax. The grammar recognizes valid syntax for the DSL and flags an excep-tion for any invalid syntax.
3 Populate the semantic model	In listing 7.3, we enriched the grammar definition with custom Java code that injects semantic actions into the parsing process. We're building our semantic model using these code snippets.
4 Wrap it up	In listing 7.5, we have custom Java code that models an `Order` abstraction and a driver process that uses ANTLR infrastructure to invoke our DSL script into the parsing pipeline.

ANTLR is a great parser generator. It's used extensively to build custom parsers and DSLs. But there's still more that ANTLR can do. So far, we haven't talked about the class of grammars that ANTLR can handle. Theoretically, you can parse any language if you don't have any constraints on the efficiency of the parser that's generated. But in real life, we need to make compromises. When you're developing a DSL, you want to have the most efficient parser that can parse *your* language. You don't want a generic parser that can parse many other languages but has a low efficiency coefficient for your language. ANTLR is just one tool that can generate a parser capable of recogniz-ing a specific class of languages.

As a DSL designer, you need to be aware of the general classification of parsers, their implementation complexities, and the class of languages that each of them is capable of handling. The next section provides an overview of parser taxonomies and their complexities.

7.3 *Classifying parsers*

When a parser recognizes the input stream that you give to it, it generates the com-plete parse tree for the language script. Parsers are classified based on the order in which the nodes of the parse tree are constructed. The parser might start construct-ing the parse tree from the root; these parsers are called *top-down* parsers. Con-versely, the parse tree might be constructed starting from the leaves and moving up towards the root. We call these *bottom-up* parsers. Top-down and bottom-up parsers vary in the complexity of their implementations and the class of grammars that they recognize. As a DSL designer, it's worthwhile to make yourself familiar with the gen-eral concepts associated with both of them. Look at figure 7.8, which illustrates how parse trees are constructed by each type of parser.

Top-down parsing   Bottom-up parsing

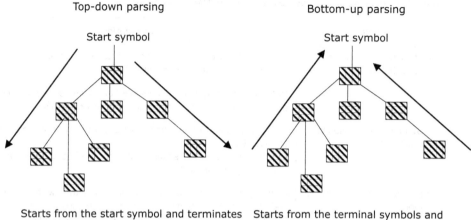

Starts from the start symbol and terminates   Starts from the terminal symbols and
at the language terminal symbols   terminates at the start symbol

Figure 7.8   How top-down and bottom-up parsers construct their parse trees.

In this section, we'll discuss how you can classify parsers based on the way they construct the parse tree and derive the language out of the production rules. Within the two classes of parsers (top-down and bottom-up), there are quite a few variations that add to the class of languages that they recognize at the expense of a little complexity in implementation. I assume a basic familiarity with parsing techniques, look-ahead processing, parse trees, and other fundamental language-processing concepts. If you need background on these topics, see [3] in section 7.6.

Let's start with top-down parsers and look at some of the implementation variations within them.

7.3.1   Simple top-down parsers

As I mentioned earlier, a top-down parser constructs the parse tree starting *from the root* and proceeds with a *leftmost derivation* of the input stream. This means it starts processing the input from the left symbol and moves toward the right symbol.

The most general form of top-down parser is the recursive descent (RD) parser. You might be asking yourself, what does recursive descent mean? Recursive means that these parsers are implemented in terms of recursive function calls (see [1] in section 7.6). The descent part refers to the fact that the parse tree construction starts at the top (which also explains the top-down category).

We're going to start with the simplest RD parser and gradually work our way through the complex variants that are powerful enough to recognize a broader class of languages as long as you use an efficient implementation. First, we're going to discuss LL(1) and LL(k) RD parsers. These two classes of top-down parsers are the basic implementations that cover most of what you'll need to design external DSLs.

LL(1) RECURSIVE DESCENT PARSER

An LL(1) RD parser is a top-down parser that can parse the syntactic structures of a language based on a *single* look-ahead token. What does LL(1) mean? The first *L* denotes that the parser processes the input string from left-to-right. The second *L* denotes that when the parser constructs the parse tree from the root down to the leaves, it descends into the children from left to right. As you might've guessed from the definition, the 1 indicates the number of look-ahead tokens. Because there's only one look-ahead token, the parser selects the next production rule to apply based on the match of this single token.

What if the parser can't find an exact matching rule based on the single look-ahead token? This might happen because your grammar can have multiple production rules that start with the same symbol. Remember the LL(1) parser can look-ahead *only one* token. In order to resolve this ambiguity of multiple rules matching the same look-ahead token, you can either use an LL(k) parser where $k > 1$, or you can use left-factoring to change your grammar definition to make it acceptable to an LL(1) RD parser (see [1] in section 7.6 for details).

Sometimes you might want a top-down parser to handle left recursion. If your language has a grammar rule of the form A : A a | b, then your top-down parser goes into an infinite loop. Remember that I mentioned earlier that RD parsers are implemented using recursive calls. A left recursion in the production rule makes it recurse forever. There are rule-rewriting techniques you can use to convert left-recursive rules. See [3] in section 7.6 for details.

LL(*k*) RECURSIVE DESCENT PARSER

The LL(k) is a more powerful variant of LL(1) in the sense that it has a larger look-ahead set. It uses this set to determine which production rule to apply on the input token. Yes, a larger look-ahead set means that this parser is more complex than the LL(1). But it's worth investing in that complexity, considering the benefits of generating more powerful parsers.

How much more powerful is this parser than the LL(1)? Because LL(k) parsers have such an enhanced look-ahead set, they can parse many computer languages. It's still limited in the sense that the parser can disambiguate grammar rules that are disjoint in only the first k tokens. But you can augment an LL(k) parser with more sophisticated features. One feature is *backtracking*, which makes the parser recognize languages that have arbitrary look-ahead sets. We'll discuss backtracking parsers in section 7.3.2.

ANTLR generates LL(k) parsers with an arbitrary look-ahead set and is the most suitable for implementing DSLs in real-life applications. Many large software applications like Google App Engine, Yahoo Query Language (YQL) and IntelliJ IDEA use ANTLR for parsing and interpreting custom languages.

You know the basics, so we can jump right into a discussion of some of the advanced top-down parsers. You might not use them very often, but it's always useful to know about them and appreciate the techniques that they employ to make efficient implementations. In fact, we'll be using one of these techniques in chapter 8 when we discuss how to design external DSLs using Scala parser combinators.

7.3.2   *Advanced top-down parsers*

The advanced parsing techniques give more power to your parsers, but at the expense of added complexity to the implementation. Keep in mind that you'll usually use parser generators or parser combinators that abstract the implementation complexities within them. As a developer, you'll use the published interfaces of those abstractions.

RECURSIVE DESCENT BACKTRACKING PARSER

This parser adds backtracking infrastructure to an LL(k) RD parser, which gives it the power to process arbitrary-sized look-ahead sets. With backtracking infrastructure in place, the parser can parse ahead as far as it needs to. If it fails to find a match, it can rewind its input and try alternate rules. This capability makes it quite a bit more powerful than the LL(k).

OK, so it can backtrack and choose alternate rules, but is there any order to this process? You can specify hints for ordering in the form of syntactic predicates, as in ANTLR (see [2] in section 7.6). You can declaratively specify the ordering so that the parser can select the most appropriate rule to apply on the input stream.

With this kind of parser, you get much more expressive grammars, called parsing expression grammars (PEGs). PEG is a more expressive form of grammar that extends ANTLR's backtracking and syntactic predicates (see [4] in section 7.6). PEG adds operators like & and ! that you specify within the grammar rules to implement finer controls over backtracking and parser behaviors. They also make the grammar itself way more expressive. You can develop parsers for PEGs in linear time using techniques like memorizing.

MEMOIZING PARSERS

With a backtracking RD parser, partial parsing results can be evaluated repeatedly when the parser backtracks and tries alternative rules. A memoizing parser makes parsing efficient by caching partial results of parsing.

That sounds great, but because the memoizing process means that previously computed results need to be stored, you're going to need additional memory. But the efficiency you gain over conventional backtracking parser implementations will more than outweigh the pain of needing additional infrastructure. You'll also be pleased to know that our old friend ANTLR supports memoization.

You can avoid this need for more memory by implementing a *packrat parser*, which, in addition to having a catchy name, also happens to be a functional pearl (see [6] in section 7.6). You implement this parser by using the natural laziness that functional languages like Haskell have. We're going to discuss packrat parsers more when we talk about Scala parsers in section 8.2.3.

PREDICATED PARSERS

In some cases, an RD parser can't determine the alternative rule to apply based on syntax alone. To help it make decisions, you can annotate the parser using Boolean expressions. A particular alternative matches only if the Boolean expression evaluates to true.

Typically, you would use a predicated parser when you want a single parser that can parse multiple versions of a language. The core language can be recognized by the base parser, and additional semantic predicates are used to handle extensions and other versions. For more information about predicated parsers, see [1] in section 7.6.

Top-down parsers can be extremely simple, like the LL(1) that we discussed in section 7.3.1. But for complex language parsing, you need sophisticated ones, like the backtracking parsers, memoizing parsers, and predictive parsers that we talked about. Each of these advanced variants makes the parsers recognize a wider class of languages, along with reducing the time and space complexity of implementation. In the next section, we're going to see another class of parsers that are possibly more versatile than top-down parsers in the sense that they can recognize *any* deterministic context-free language.

7.3.3 *Bottom-up parsers*

A bottom-up parser constructs the parse tree starting from the leaves and moving toward the root. It reads the input stream from left to right and constructs a rightmost derivation through successive reduction of grammar rules, proceeding toward the start symbol of the grammar. It's the opposite direction of what a top-down parser follows.

The most common technique in bottom-up parsers uses what is known as *shift-reduce* parsing. When the parser scans the input and meets a symbol, it has two alternatives:

- *Shift* the current token aside (usually to an implementation stack) for subsequent reduction.
- Match the current *handle* (the substring of the input string that matches the right-hand side of a production rule), and replace it with the nonterminal on the left-hand side of the production. This step is commonly known as the *reduction* step.

We're going to talk about two of the most commonly used shift-reduce bottom-up parsers: operator precedence parsers and LR parsers. Operator precedence parsers have limited capability, but are extremely simple to implement by hand. On the other hand, LR parsers are used extensively by most of the parser generators.

OPERATOR PRECEDENCE PARSER

This bottom-up parser can recognize only a limited set of languages. It's based on a static set of precedence rules that are assigned to the terminal symbols.

An operator precedence parser is simple to implement by hand, but it's of limited use because it can't handle multiple precedence of the same symbol and it can't recognize a grammar that has two nonterminals side by side. For example, the following snippet doesn't use operator precedence grammar because `expr operator expr` is a rule with more than one adjacent non-terminal:

```
expr : expr operator expr
operator : + | - | * | /
```

Let's now look at the most widely used class of bottom up parsers that can implement a large class of languages and are used by popular parser generators like YACC and Bison.

LR(K) PARSER

An LR(k) parser is the most efficient bottom-up parser. It can recognize a large class of context-free grammars. The L denotes that the parser processes the input string from left-to-right. The R denotes that it constructs the rightmost derivation in reverse during parsing. And as you might have guessed from the definition, the k indicates the number of look-ahead tokens. The parser uses this number to determine which production rule to apply.

An LR parser is table driven. The parser generator constructs a parse table that contains the action that the parser needs to take on recognition of an input symbol. As you saw earlier, the action can be a *shift* or a *reduce*. When the whole string is recognized, the parser is said to be reduced to the start symbol of the grammar.

This kind of parser is difficult to implement by hand, but it's strongly supported by parser generators like YACC and bison.

VARIATIONS OF THE LR PARSER

The LR parser has three variations: the simple LR (SLR), the look-ahead LR (LALR), and the canonical LR. SLR parsers use a simple logic to determine the look-ahead sets. The parsing process results in lots of conflict states. LALR parsers are more sophisticated than SLR ones and have better look-ahead processing and fewer conflicts. Canonical LR parsers can recognize more language classes than LALR.

WHAT YOU'LL REALLY BE USING

Parsers form the core foundation of external DSLs. You need to have a basic idea of how parsers are related to the class of languages that they recognize. I've given you a lot of nifty information in this section that'll help you choose the right kind of parser for your DSL. But when you're out there developing in the real world, except for when you're dealing with trivial language implementations, you'll never be implementing parsers by hand. You'll choose parser generators.

When you use a parser generator, you can think at a higher level of abstraction. You can specify grammar rules (or the language syntax), and the generator will construct the actual parser implementation for you. But remember, that implementation consists only of the language recognizer and a simple form of the AST. You still have to transform this AST into the semantic model that suits your processing requirement. For this, you need to write action code, embedded within the grammar rules.

In the next section, you'll learn how to take this approach up another level of abstraction by adding support for rich tooling to the process of DSL development.

7.4   *Tool-based DSL development with Xtext*

Parser generators like ANTLR are a big step forward toward developing external DSLs at a higher level of abstraction. But you still need to embed your target actions directly within the grammar rules. The EBNF rules and the logic for generating your semantic model are still not sufficiently decoupled. If you need to implement multiple semantic models for a single set of grammar rules, you might even end up duplicating the code for the parser itself; either that, or you'll have to derive your semantic models from a common base abstraction that the grammar rules offer.

Xtext is a framework for developing external DSLs that leverages the Eclipse platform. With Xtext, you get a complete toolset for managing the entire lifecycle of your DSL. It's integrated with the Eclipse Modeling Framework (EMF) and it maintains all the artifacts of your DSL development process in the form of managed components. (For more information about EMF, go to http://www.eclipse.org/emf.)

To use Xtext, you'll have to write an EBNF grammar for your language. The EMF uses this grammar to generate all the following goodies:

- An ANTLR-based parser
- A metamodel for your language, which is based on the Ecore metamodeling language of EMF
- An Eclipse editor that offers syntax highlighting, code assist, code completion, and a customizable outline view of your model

Figure 7.9 shows a snapshot of the postprocessing that Xtext does with the EBNF grammar rules that you define.

Xtext also has composable code generators that generate semantic models that you set requirements for. In this section, we'll implement the same order-processing

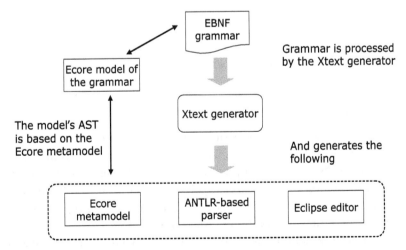

Figure 7.9   Xtext processes the textual grammar rules and generates lots of stuff. Chief among the important stuff is the Ecore metamodel that abstracts the syntax that the model of the grammar uses.

DSL that we implemented with ANTLR in section 7.2.2. You'll see how the comprehensive tooling support and model-based development of Xtext makes it easier to manage the evolution of your DSL. Let's start with the definition of your language: the EBNF-based Xtext grammar rules.

7.4.1   *Grammar rules and the outline view*

The grammar that you specify for your DSL uses the EBNF form with some of the additional adornments that Xtext supports. I'm not going to go into the details of the grammar-rule specifications that Xtext supports. The *Xtext User Guide* has all the juicy details (see [5] in section 7.6). For now, look at the Xtext grammar rules for the order-processing DSL from section 7.2.2 in the following listing.

Listing 7.6   Xtext grammar rules

```
grammar org.xtext.example.Orders                          ❶ Reusing the
  with org.eclipse.xtext.common.Terminals                    default lexer

generate orders http://www.xtext.org/example/Orders       ❷ Derived
                                                             metamodel
Model :
  (orders += Order)*;                                      ❸ Multivalue
                                                             assignment
Order :
  line = Line;                                             ❹ Simple
                                                             assignment
Line :
  buysell = ('buy' | 'sell') security = Security
  price = Price account = Account;

Security :
  name = ID;

Price :
  '@' (
      (value = INT)
      |
      ('limitprice' '=' (value = INT))
    );

Account :
  'for' value = ID;
```

This code is similar to what we used with ANTLR. Some of the newer stuff asks Xtext to generate the metamodel for the language ❷. If you have an existing Ecore metamodel, you can also ask Xtext to import it to your workspace and synchronize with the textual representation of the grammar rules that you write. You'll see more of the internals of the metamodel in section 7.4.2. Another interesting thing is that you can reuse an existing grammar by mixing it in with your rules ❶.

Xtext generates the default parse tree (AST) from your grammar rules. You can make inline assignments within the grammar to connect the various elements of the AST that the parser generates ❸, ❹.

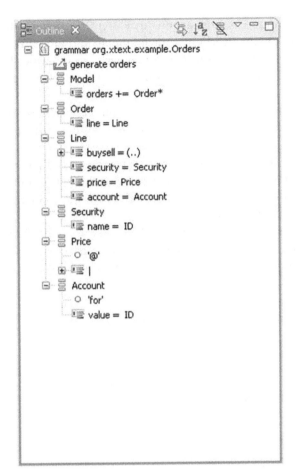

**Figure 7.10
Hierarchical, or outline view of the model.
The outline view shows the structure
associated with each rule. You can sort
the elements alphabetically and select an
element to navigate to the corresponding
one in the text editor.**

Along with the textual version of the grammar rules, Xtext also displays an outline view that shows the structure of your model as a tree. You can use the outline view to navigate to the various model elements. Figure 7.10 shows the outline view for the grammar we defined in listing 7.6.

What you see in the figure is the default view of the model. What's uber-cool is that Xtext allows you to customize almost every aspect of this view. You can customize the outline structure, let users selectively filter contents, and register custom context menus, as well as other things. You only have to override the default implementations. The outline view is part of the toolset for visualizing the model of your language. It works in collaboration with the textual representation of your grammar and gives the process of DSL development a richer feeling.

7.4.2 *The metamodel for your grammar*

After you define the grammar rules in the text editor and ask Xtext to generate the language artifacts, it generates the complete Ecore metamodel from the grammar.

(Ecore contains the core definition of abstractions in EMF.) The metamodel is an abstraction that represents the textual form of your grammar in a model that Xtext can manage easily. The metamodel uses the Ecore metatypes to describe the components of your grammar rules. Figure 7.11 shows the metamodel of our grammar in Xtext.

In this metamodel, notice that the AST of the grammar is being represented by metatypes like `EString` and `EInt`, which are some of the abstractions provided by Ecore.

Along with the metamodel, the generator also generates the ANTLR parser, which instantiates the metamodel. It's the metamodel that controls the entire tooling support offered by Xtext. For more details about the internals of the metamodel, refer to the *Xtext User Guide* (see [5] of section 7.6).

After the generator has generated the required artifacts, all the wonderful plug-ins are installed. You use the plug-ins to write your DSL scripts in an editor that offers the smartness of syntax highlighting, code assist, and constraint checks. Xtext has the

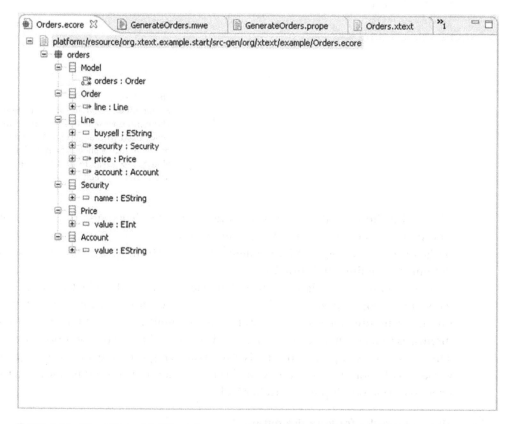

Figure 7.11   The metamodel of the order-processing DSL. Every production rule from our grammar returns an Ecore model element like `EString` and `EInt`.

entire language of the DSL in its repository as a model based on EMF; it can add smart-ness to the way the script is rendered for you. Figure 7.12 shows an editing session for our DSL.

Now we've embedded our language within Xtext's repository. Xtext gives us a tool-ing interface for manipulating the syntax of our DSL and automatically updates its own Ecore model. It also gives us a default AST in a representation as per the parser that it generates. But when you use a DSL, you need to generate a more refined abstraction—the semantic model. As a DSL designer, you want to generate your semantic model through custom code development and you'd like it to be decoupled from the core model of your language. Xtext can do this through code-generating templates that you can use to integrate the grammar rules with the generation of your model. Let's explore more of Xtext's capabilities and see what facilities the generator uses to generate code that will construct your semantic model.

Figure 7.12 The Xtext metamodel provides you with an excellent editor for writing DSLs. See how the code completion suggests alternatives for you? You can also see the syntax highlighting feature, which is quite handy.

7.4.3   *Generating code for the semantic model*

After you have the grammar rules and the metamodel defined as I've described, it's time to write a code generator that'll process the models that you created and generate a semantic model for you. You might want to generate multiple semantic models from one grammar. For example, for our order-processing DSL, we might want to generate a Java class that creates a collection of all orders that the user has entered. We could also generate a set of JSON (JavaScript Serialized Object Notation) objects with those orders for transporting them to a data store. Ideally, both these models should be decoupled from the core grammar rules. Figure 7.13 shows how the overall architecture should look.

Let's generate the Java code using the Xpand templates that Xtext offers.

CODE GENERATION USING THE XPAND TEMPLATE

The Xpand template walks through the AST of your grammar rules and generates the code for you. The first input that it needs is the metamodel, which we'll specify as <<IMPORT orders>>. Here's the main template that serves as the entry point and dispatches to all other templates:

```
«IMPORT orders»
«DEFINE main FOR Model»
  «EXPAND Orders::orders FOR this»
«ENDDEFINE»
```

In this snippet, orders is the name of the metamodel we need to import. Every template consists of a name and a metatype on which the template is invoked. In this example, the template is named main and the metatype is specified as Model (Model was an element in our grammar rule that's represented by Xtext as a metatype in the Ecore metamodel). Our main template is simple. All it does is dispatch to the Orders::orders subtemplate on recognition of the symbol Model. The following listing shows our template definition for Orders::orders.

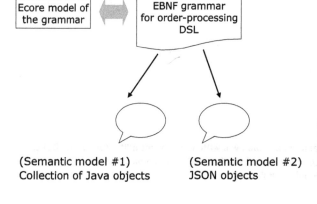

(Semantic model #1)
Collection of Java objects

(Semantic model #2)
JSON objects

Figure 7.13
The semantic models need to be decoupled from the grammar rules. For one set of grammar rules, you can have multiple semantic models.

Listing 7.7 Template for generating the semantic model for `orders`

```
«IMPORT orders»                                    ⟵  Import metamodel

«DEFINE orders FOR Model»
  «FILE "OrderProcessor.java"»                     ⟵  Generate Java file
    import java.util.*;
    import org.xtext.example.ClientOrder;          ⟵  Custom Java class
    public class OrderProcessor {                               ⟵  Class to be
      private List<ClientOrder> cos = new ArrayList<ClientOrder>();      generated
      public List<ClientOrder> getOrders() {
        «EXPAND order FOREACH this.orders»          ⟵  Templates for
        return Collections.unmodifiableList(cos);       substitution
      }
    }
  «ENDFILE»
«ENDDEFINE»

«DEFINE order FOR Order»
        cos.add(new ClientOrder("«this.line.buysell»",
          "«this.line.security.name»",
          «this.line.price.value»,
          "«this.line.account.value»"));
«ENDDEFINE»
```

When the grammar has recognized the language and has reduced to the start symbol (Model), this template will generate the code as it's specified in the listing. Table 7.4 shows in detail some of the features of the code generation template.

Table 7.4 Xtext code generation template

Feature	Explanation
Can generate any code. In our example, we're generating a Java class.	The class exposes one method that returns a collection of all orders parsed from the DSL script. The collection that's returned contains a POJO (`ClientOrder`) that we defined separately from the grammar.
Inline expansion of the `order` template within `orders`.	We access the elements from within the production rules and use templates for textual substitution of inline elements. Look at how `«this.line.price.value»` serves as the placeholder for the price value when it's parsed within the DSL script.

When the templates are ready, you can run the generator once again from the context menu of the project.

PROCESSING THE DSL SCRIPT

Let's say that this is the DSL script that we need to process:

```
buy ibm @ 100 for nomura
sell google @ limitprice = 200 for chase
```

For that script, the class shown in the following listing will be generated by Xtext in the file OrderProcessor.java.

Listing 7.8 Class generated by the template in listing 7.7

```java
import java.util.*;
import org.xtext.example.ClientOrder;
public class OrderProcessor {
  private List<ClientOrder> cos = new ArrayList<ClientOrder>();

  public List<ClientOrder> getOrders() {
    cos.add(new ClientOrder("buy", "ibm", 100, "nomura"))
    cos.add(new ClientOrder("sell", "google", 200, "chase"))
    return Collections.unmodifiableList(cos);
  }
}
```

With Xtext, defining the grammar rules and building the semantic model are sufficiently decoupled. The grammar rule definitions are managed by the smart textual editor that is complemented with the customizable outline view. The semantic model implementation is controlled through the code generators linked with the parsers through the metamodel.

Let's take a final look at the pros and cons of a hybrid textual and visual environment like Xtext when you're developing external DSLs.

THE GOOD AND THE BAD (BUT IT'S MOSTLY GOOD)

Xtext offers a novel approach to external DSL development. It augments the traditional textual representation of your DSL with a rich toolset. You still have to write your grammar rules in EBNF notation. But behind the scenes, Xtext not only generates the ANTLR parser for you, but also abstracts your grammar rules within a metamodel. The architecture, which is based on the metamodel, manages the entire toolset. You get some powerful editing capabilities for your DSL. Using Xtext-based development, you can also decouple your semantic model from the grammar rules and use Xpand template facilities to generate custom code.

Overall, Xtext gives you a powerful experience when you develop external DSLs because you have the EMF available to you. The only thing you need to keep in mind is that you're basically dependent on the Eclipse platform. Even so, only the IDE integration in Xtext is Eclipse-dependent. You can use the runtime components like the parsers, the metamodel, the serializers, and the linkers, as well as the Xpand templating in any arbitrary Java process. All this makes Xtext the framework to use when you're developing an external DSL.

7.5 *Summary*

In this chapter, you learned some of the design principles of external DSLs. An external DSL needs to have its own language-processing infrastructure. If your DSL is low enough in complexity, you can use a hand-written parser to process the syntax of the language. If your DSL is more complex, you need to use a full-stack parser generator like YACC, Bison, or ANTLR. We discussed ANTLR-based language construction in detail and you developed your own custom, order-processing DSL using it. You saw how the various components of the implementation engine like

> **Key takeaways & best practices**
> - When you're designing a DSL, you need to have a *clean separation of the syntax and the underlying semantic model.*
> - In an external DSL, the *semantic model can be implemented by host language structures.* For syntax parsing, you need to have a parser generator that integrates with the host language. ANTLR is a typical parser generator that integrates well with Java.
> - *Choose the appropriate parser class* for what you need *before* you design external DSLs that need moderate language-processing capabilities. Making the correct choice will help you moderate the complexity of your implementation.
> - *Choose the right level of complexity* that does the job. For an external DSL, you might not need the full complexity of a general language design.

the lexical analyzer, the parser, and the semantic model coordinate to generate the final DSL processor.

When you design a nontrivial external DSL with a fairly rich syntax, it's the parser that forms the core of it. Parsers are classified based on the way they process the input stream and construct the parse tree. There are two main types of parsers: top-down and bottom-up. As a language designer, you need to be aware of the class of languages that each of these implementations can handle. You also need to know the implementation complexity and trade-offs that a specific type of parser implies. We discussed all of these in this chapter when we talked about parser classification.

Judging from the DSL that you designed, you know how to select the right kind of parser for your language. In the final section of this chapter, we moved on to a different paradigm of DSL development that mixed in a rich toolset along with the standard textual model that you're already familiar with. Using the model-driven approach of the EMF, Eclipse offers Xtext as a comprehensive environment for external DSL development. We developed the same order-processing DSL using Xtext. The process demonstrated how the richness of a model-driven approach complemented with a full toolset can lead to a richer experience of language development.

In the next chapter we'll look at an entirely different paradigm for developing external DSLs using Scala. Scala offers functional combinators that you can use as building blocks to develop parsing techniques. They're called *parser combinators*, and we'll use them to develop sample external DSLs from our domain of securities trading.

7.6   *References*

1   Parr, Terence. 2009. *Language Implementation Patterns: Create Your Own Domain-Specific and General Programming Languages.* The Pragmatic Bookshelf.

2   Parr, Terence. 2007. *The Definitive ANTLR reference: Building Domain-Specific Languages.* The Pragmatic Bookshelf.

3   Aho, Alfred V., Monica S. Lam, Ravi Sethi and Jeffrey D. Ullman. 2006. *Compilers: Principles, Techniques, and Tools*, Second Edition. Addison Wesley.

4 Ford, Bryan. 2004. Parsing Expression Grammars: A Recognition Based Syntactic Foundation. *Proceedings of the 31st ACM SIGPLAN-SIGACT symposium on principles of programming languages*, pp 111-122.

5 *Xtext User Guide.* http://www.eclipse.org/Xtext/documentation/latest/xtext.html.

6 Ford, Bryan. 2002. Packrat parsing: simple, powerful, lazy, linear time, functional pearl. Proceedings *of the seventh ACM SIGPLAN International Conference on Functional Programming*, pp 36-47.

Designing external DSLs using Scala parser combinators

This chapter covers

- What are parser combinators
- The Scala parser combinator library
- Using packrat parsers
- Designing external DSLs using Scala parser combinators

With basic background information about external DSL implementations already served up in chapter 7, we're going to jump directly into parser combinators. Parser combinators are one of the most beautiful applications of functional programming. They offer an internal DSL to use for designing external DSLs so you don't have to implement your own language infrastructure as you do with other techniques of external DSL design. When we designed an external DSL for processing client orders in chapter 7, remember that we used ANTLR as the parser generator. We designed our grammar for the DSL and ANTLR generated the parser for us. To design our own DSL, we had to use an *external* tool that provided us with the necessary language implementation infrastructure. Using parser combinators, you don't have to step out of the host language for a second. This makes the implementation succinct, expressive, and completely free of any external dependency.

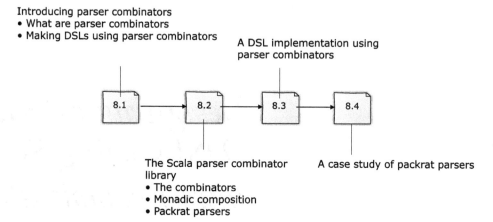

Introducing parser combinators
• What are parser combinators
• Making DSLs using parser combinators

A DSL implementation using
parser combinators

The Scala parser combinator
library
• The combinators
• Monadic composition
• Packrat parsers

A case study of packrat parsers

Figure 8.1   Our roadmap through the chapter

We'll start off with an introduction to what parser combinators are and how Scala implements them as a library on top of the core language. Then we'll go into every detail of the Scala implementation, highlighting the features that make them exemplary for DSL design. After that, we're going to design two external DSLs based on Scala parser combinators. Finally, I'll introduce packrat parsers, which let you implement a class of grammars not possible with ordinary recursive descent parsers. Figure 8.1 is a roadmap of how the chapter progresses on our gradual journey to the world of designing DSLs using Scala parser combinators.

At the end of the chapter, you will have a solid understanding of how to use the techniques of functional programming in general and parser combinators in particular to implement an extensible external DSL of your own.

8.1   *Parser combinators*

In chapter 7, I defined a parser as an engine that works on an input stream and consumes a collection of tokens. It can either recognize the stream of tokens as part of a valid language identified by the parser, or it can reject the input as soon as it encounters an invalid symbol. In either case, the parser returns a result (success or failure), along with a truncated stream containing the rest of the input not yet consumed.

When the parser returns a success, you can feed the truncated input stream to yet another parser that can potentially consume the rest of the input. In the case of a failure, you can rewind to the beginning of the stream and try parsing with another parser. Because parsers work this way, you can chain them in a variety of ways to parse a complete input stream. Figure 8.2 demonstrates how parsers can be combined to consume an input stream.

In this section, you'll see how you can use a parser as a functional abstraction of the language that it recognizes. Because it's a function of its input, a parser can compose with other parsers and evolve the syntax of our DSL in a piecemeal way.

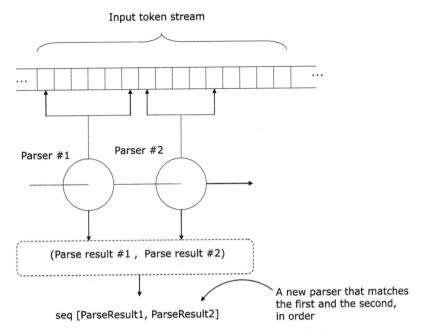

Figure 8.2   Chaining parsers. Parser #1 parses a part of the input stream. Parser #2 matches the part left over by parser #1. The combination returns a parser that combines the two results. The combination parser succeeds only if both parser #1 and parser #2 match their inputs.

Such compositions are done using higher-order functions that we formally call parser combinators.

8.1.1   *What are parser combinators?*

Let's look at the problem of composing parsers in a functional way. In functional programming, a parser is a function that takes input and produces a result. Parser combinators allow you to use higher-order functions (also known as combinators) in a purely compositional way to construct grammar structures such as sequencing, repetitions, optionality, and choice. If your language of implementation supports infix operator notation, then a grammar rule written using parser combinators resembles an EBNF production.

The biggest advantage of parsing with combinators is improved *composability*; you take primitive parsers and compose them functionally to generate larger ones (I explain the virtues of composability in appendix A). Composing with combinators is like building with LEGOs—we start with smaller pieces and build higher-order structures out of them. Figure 8.2 demonstrates a sequence combinator in action.

In the world of DSL design, you can use parser combinators to compose smaller language fragments that model parts of your DSL syntax and build the whole DSL structure out of them. The sequence combinator that you see in figure 8.2 is only one such combinator, which is shown in the figure composing two DSL syntax parsers sequentially. Any standard implementation includes a variety of such combinators, much like LEGO sets. Let's start with an overview of how some of the commonly used combinators consume an input stream and recognize the grammar of your language, shown in table 8.1.

Table 8.1   Commonly used parser combinators

Combinator	How it combines
Sequence	A parser combinator for sequential composition. If two parsers P and Q are combined using the sequential combinator, the parsing succeeds if: ■ P successfully consumes a part of the input stream ■ Q following P consumes the input that P did not consume
Alternation	A parser combinator for composing alternatives. If two parsers P and Q are combined using the alternation combinator, then the parsing succeeds if either P or Q succeeds in the following way: ■ First P runs on the input stream. If P succeeds, then the parsing is successful. ■ If P fails, then the input stream is rewound to the point where P started, and then Q runs on the same stream. ■ If Q succeeds, then the parsing is successful; otherwise, it's a failure.
Function application	A combinator that allows a function to be applied on a parser, resulting in a new parser.
Repetition	A combinator that works on a parser P and returns another parser that parses one or more repetitions of what P parses. Sometimes this combinator also allows repetitions of patterns interleaved with separators to be parsed. For example, if P parses a string abc, application of a repetition combinator generates a parser that can parse repetitions of abc like abcabcabc..., or the pattern abc interleaved with a space like abc abc abc ....

Now that you've seen some of the basic combinators, we'll dig into the specific implementations. But before that, let's look at how you can use parser combinators when you're designing external DSLs.

8.1.2   Designing DSLs the parser combinator way

When you designed an external DSL in chapter 7, you built your own language processing infrastructure. Building parsers by hand is tedious, error prone, and often leads to an unmanageable bloat of code, so we decided to use external frameworks like ANTLR or XText. Using an external framework resulted in an implementation architecture like that shown in figure 8.3.

I'm not saying that the architecture in the figure is bad. In fact, it's the most common paradigm in designing external DSLs today. Developers have been using this same architectural style since language processing tools like LEX and YACC came out of the AT&T labs.

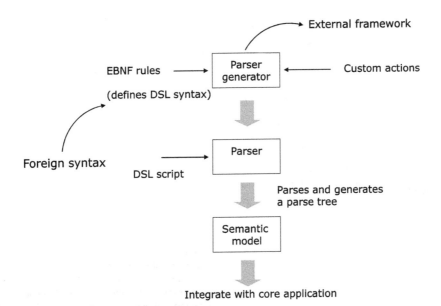

Figure 8.3 Implementation architecture of designing an external DSL using an external parser generator like ANTLR. The generator produces a parser that parses the DSL script and generates the semantic model of the application.

That doesn't mean we can't make progress by exploring newer and better ways of implementing DSLs. One obvious drawback with the architecture in figure 8.3 is the presence of external dependencies in the implementation. Parser generators are external entities and, as the figure shows, you need to use their foreign syntax when you declare EBNF rules for your DSL (see chapter 7 to refresh your memory about EBNF). This implies an extra bit of learning curve for you. The parser code that it generates has a static structure and depends completely on the underlying implementation of the generator. You can't do much tweaking to customize it.

Designing a DSL with parser combinators is an entirely different experience. You're within the abstractions of your host language when you define your grammar rules. You use higher-order functions to define your DSL syntax and to add custom actions through prebuilt combinators that the library offers. You'll see all the details in the following sections. Figure 8.4 offers a peek at how the overall architecture of your implementation is simplified when you've got parser combinators in your host language.

In this architecture, there's no dependency on external frameworks. The only constraint is that your language needs to have an implementation of a parser combinator library. Parser combinators are a relatively new entrant in the world of DSL implementation. Many modern languages like Haskell, Scala, and Newspeak offer parser combinators as libraries on top of the core language. In the course of this chapter, you'll find exciting new applications of functional programming that parser combinators espouse. You'll discover how they make your DSL design succinct, yet expressive.

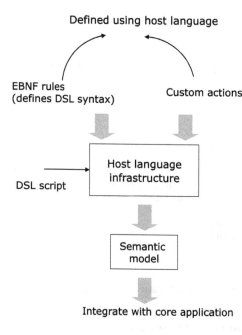

Defined using host language

EBNF rules
(defines DSL syntax)

Custom actions

DSL script → Host language infrastructure

Semantic model

Integrate with core application

Figure 8.4
Implementation architecture of an external DSL designed using parser combinators. You're completely within the confines of the host language infrastructure when you define grammar rules and custom actions.

DEFINITION   Newspeak is a programming language by Gilad Bracha in the tradition of Self and Smalltalk. For more information about this language, go to http://newspeaklanguage.org.

In the next section, we'll look at the Scala parser combinator library and the power it offers in designing external DSLs in a purely functional way. Every parser that you define serves as a building block that models part of your DSL syntax. Combinators serve as the glue that wire up these building blocks and add semantics to your language.

8.2   *The Scala parser combinator library*

Scala implements parser combinators as a library on top of the core language. You can find the library within the package `scala.util.parsing`, along with the Scala language distribution. Implementing parser combinators as a library makes it easily extensible without affecting the core language. In this section, you'll learn some of the specific combinators that the library has that help your DSL syntax to evolve. You'll learn the techniques and idioms in the Scala library through DSL snippets as we go along. For more details on the APIs, refer to [1, 2] in section 8.6 or go through the source code in the Scala distribution. (Unfortunately, there's no exhaustive coverage of Scala parser combinators in any published form. The source code is the best reference there is at the moment.)

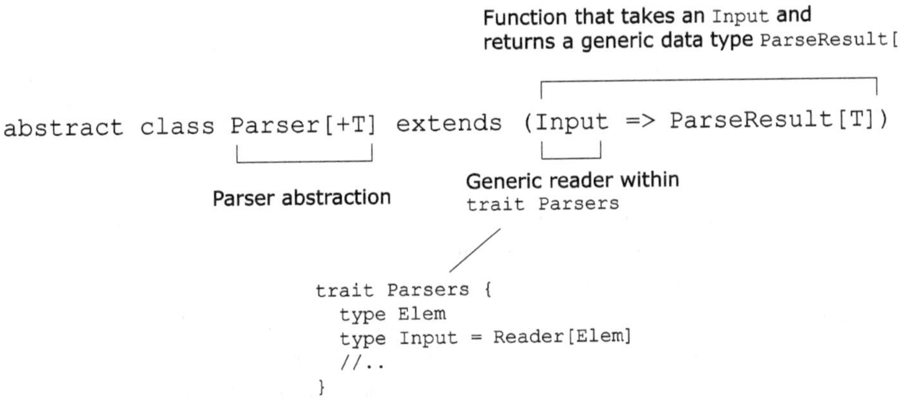

Function that takes an `Input` and
returns a generic data type `ParseResult[T]`

```
abstract class Parser[+T] extends (Input => ParseResult[T])
```

Parser abstraction

Generic reader within
`trait Parsers`

```
trait Parsers {
  type Elem
  type Input = Reader[Elem]
  //..
}
```

Figure 8.5   Modeling a parser as a function in the Scala library

8.2.1   *The base abstractions in the parser combinator library*

As you know from our discussion in the previous section, a parser is a function that transforms an input stream into a result. The Scala library models this as shown in figure 8.5.

`ParseResult` abstracts the result that a parser produces, which can be either a success or a failure. `ParseResult` also tracks the next input that hasn't yet been consumed by the current parser. The Scala library models `ParseResult` as a generic abstract class that has specialized implementations for `Success` and `Failure`. The following listing shows how Scala defines the `ParseResult[T]` type constructor and it's specialized implementations for `Success` and `Failure`.

Listing 8.1   How Scala models the parse result

```
trait Parsers {
  sealed abstract class ParseResult[+T] {
    //..
    val next: Input
  }

  case class Success[+T](result: T, override val next: Input)
    extends ParseResult[T] {
    //.. implementation
  }

  sealed abstract class NoSuccess(
    val msg: String, override val next: Input)
      extends ParseResult[Nothing] {
    //..
  }

  case class Failure(
    override val msg: String, override val next: Input)
      extends NoSuccess(msg, next) {
    //..
  }
```

❶ ParseResult tracks the next input

❷ Successful parse

❸ Base class for unsuccessful parse

❹ Failure => backtrack and retry

```
case class Error(
  override val msg: String, override val next: Input)
    extends NoSuccess(msg, next) {
    //..
  }
  //..
}
```

Fatal error, no backtracking ⑤

`ParseResult` is generic on the data type that the parser produces. In case of a `Success`, ❷ you'll get a result of type `T`. In case of a `Failure` ❸, you'll get a fail message. `Failure` can be either fatal or nonfatal. In the case of a nonfatal `Failure` ❹, you can backtrack and try other parsers supplied as alternations. The fatal case is an `Error` ⑤, in which case no backtracking is done and the process stops. No matter what happens (`Success` or `Failure`), the result specifies how much input was consumed by the parsing process and the position of the input stream that needs to be passed to the following parser in the chain ❶.

You'll see more of these alternations and backtracking in an external DSL example later in the chapter. How you're going to handle nonsuccess cases in parsing is one thing that you need to consider carefully when you design your DSL. Too many alternations can lead to performance degradation and there might be situations where you need to design parsers that don't backtrack.

 Are you wondering what role these parser combinator classes play in your DSL implementation?

Every snippet of DSL that you model needs to have a parser associated with it that checks the validity of the syntax. DSL processing continues only if it gets a valid syntax from the user. If the syntax is valid, the parser returns a `Success`; otherwise, it returns an `Error` or a `Failure`. For a `Failure`, the parser might backtrack and try alternate rules, if any are available.

So now you have parsers and various kinds of `ParseResult` implementations. But how do these parsers chain together to parse the whole of your DSL? That's the role of the *combinators*. Let's talk about some of the combinators that Scala offers and how you can use them effectively as the glue to combine multiple parsers of your DSL.

8.2.2   *The combinators that glue parsers together*

The Scala parser combinator library contains a set of combinators for wiring up parsers. When you're designing external DSLs using ANTLR or XText, you can use these combinators to design your grammar so it looks much like the EBNF notation you saw in chapter 7. The difference is that when you use combinators, you don't have to use any external environment on top of your host language. You can be within the confines of your Scala language and use higher-order functions to define your EBNF-like grammar. Just think of your DSL syntax as a collection of smaller snippets; the combinators let you plug parsers for each of them together, forming the bigger whole.

The best way to learn about the combinators that Scala has is through a real-life example. You've been through this example in earlier chapters. As a recap, consider

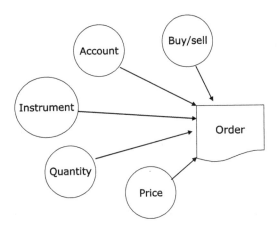

Figure 8.6
Generate an order using all the other
attributes as inputs

designing an external DSL that processes client orders from a series of inputs from the user. Figure 8.6 shows a picture form of the abstraction that you need to generate.

Now that you have a pretty good idea of what parser combinators can do for you, you have another option to think about. Instead of jumping into using an external parser generator (like ANTLR), you can now consider processing your DSL syntax as a collection of smaller parsers wired together using the combinators that Scala offers. Each of the smaller parsers parses one specific DSL structure and coordinates with the combinator to pass the input stream to the next parser in line.

You discuss the issues with the users, iterate over the syntax that they would like to have and, after a couple of iterations, come up with the version of the grammar shown in the following listing. You had a recent refresher on the Scala parser combinator library; the grammar that you've written uses it to express your DSL syntax.

Listing 8.2   A sample external DSL using Scala parser combinators

```
package trading.dsl
import scala.util.parsing.combinator.syntactical._

object OrderDsl extends StandardTokenParsers {
  lexical.reserved +=
    ("to", "buy", "sell", "min", "max", "for", "account", "shares", "at")
  lexical.delimiters += ("(", ")", ",")          ◁  Delimiters and
                                                 ❶  reserved words
  lazy val order =
    items ~ account_spec                         ◁  Sequencing
                                                 ❷  combinator (~)
  lazy val items =
    "(" ~> rep1sep(line_item, ",") <~ ")"        ◁  Repetition combinator
                                                 ❸  with separator
  lazy val line_item =
    security_spec ~ buy_sell ~ price_spec

  lazy val buy_sell =
    "to" ~> ("buy" | "sell")                     ◁  Alternation
                                                 ❹  combinator ( | )
  lazy val security_spec =
    numericLit ~ (ident <~ "shares")
```

```
    lazy val price_spec =
      "at" ~> (min_max?) ~ numericLit

    lazy val min_max =
        "min" | "max"

    lazy val account_spec =
      "for" ~> "account" ~> stringLit
}
```

The grammar shown in the listing can successfully parse this sample DSL:

```
(100 IBM shares to buy at max 45, 40 Sun shares to sell
➥ at min 24, 25 CISCO shares to buy at max 56)
➥ for trading account "A1234"
```

Congratulations! You've just designed the syntax of your first DSL using the parser combinator library. We'll add more spice that'll make it spit out the semantic model of our domain abstraction.

Now that you have an idea of what the grammar looks like and what language it can process, let's dive into the grammar rules that lead to the parsing of the DSL.

Just before doing that, note that the grammar rules begin with a set of lexical delimiters ❶ that gives you the list of characters used to separate tokens in the input. We also need to specify the set of reserved words in our language as specified by lexical.reserved in listing 8.2. In the course of the rest of this section, you'll get a good understanding of the combinators that the library offers and how you can use them to evolve your own language. For a more complete description of all the Scala combinators, look at the source code in Scala distribution.

EVERY GRAMMAR RULE IS A FUNCTION

Every grammar rule models a concept of the domain. You need to name the rule appropriately so that it represents the domain concept that it models. Use EBNF notation to model the body of the rule, just as you would when you're defining a context-free grammar in ANTLR.

Every rule returns a Parser that represents the value the function body returns. If the function body is formed through combinators that wire up multiple parsers, the end result of applying those combinators is the final Parser that the rule returns. Assume for now that every rule returns a Parser [Any]. In section 8.3.4, you'll see how to return more specific parser types by applying custom functions within the rule body.

> When you're working with the grammar rules, remember the golden rule of designing DSLs: name the grammar rules appropriately so they reflect the domain concept they model. When you're designing external DSLs using parser combinators, the grammar rules become the blueprint that you discuss with your domain experts. They're concise, expressive, and must convey information that's appropriate to the domain people.

THE SEQUENCE COMBINATOR

In Scala, the ~ symbol is the sequence combinator. You see this at ❷ in listing 8.2. The name ~ is a symbol for brevity and is simply a method defined within the class `Parsers[T]`.

Scala allows infix operator notation, so `a ~ b` is actually `a.~(b)`. When you use the sequence combinator in infix form, you get the feel of the EBNF notation. And it's made more intuitive through type inference that Scala provides.

Let's look in detail at listing 8.2 again and see how the sequence combinator works. `items` receives the original input supplied to the combined parser ❷. It tries to parse the input by invoking the body of the rule (method) named `items` ❸. If the parsing succeeds, it generates a `ParseResult r1` (for example). The next parser in the sequence, `account_spec`, starts consuming the input where `items` left off. If the parsing succeeds with `ParseResult r2`, then the combinator ~ returns a `Parser` that generates a result of type `(r1, r2)`.

THE ALTERNATION COMBINATOR

This combinator is denoted by a | in the Scala library. The alternation combinator uses backtracking when it's looking for alternate rules. This combinator works only when the previous parser had a nonfatal failure and backtracking is allowed.

Let's look at ❹ in listing 8.2. The input goes to the first alternative `"to" ~> "buy"`. An implicit conversion defined within the `Parsers` traits converts the `String` into a `Parsers[String]`. If the parsing succeeds, no other alternative is considered and the result is returned as the result of `buy_sell`. If the parsing is unsuccessful, the next alternative `"to" ~> "sell"` is tried. If that succeeds, its result is returned. The alternates you specify are always considered by the parser to be ordered choices.

THE SELECTIVE SEQUENCE COMBINATOR

These combinators are implemented as methods named `~>` and `<~`. They selectively keep either the right or the left result. Selective sequence combinators are frequently used to prune out information that doesn't form part of the semantic model; sequencing needs to be recognized, but you're interested in the result of only one of the parsers.

Look again at listing 8.2. Let's see how the selective combinator at ❸ works. The method `~>` works just like ~, but keeps only the result of the right-hand-side parser. In the example, `"("` isn't needed for future processing and can be dropped from the result. The method `<~` works just like ~, but keeps only the result of the left-hand-side parser. In the example, `")"` isn't needed for future processing and can also be dropped from the result.

THE REPETITION COMBINATOR

You use the repetition combinator to implement constructs that are repeated. Table 8.2 shows the variations of the repetition combinator.

In listing 8.2, ❸ is an example of a repetition combinator. `items` is composed of one or more occurrences of a `line_item` using `","` as the separator.

Table 8.2   Variations of the repetition combinator

Variation	Explanation
`(rep(p), p*)`	Repeat p zero or more times
`(repsep(p, sep), p*(sep))`	Repeat p zero or more times with a separator
`(rep1(p), p+)`	Repeat p one or more times
`(rep1sep(p, sep), p+(sep))`	Repeat p one or more times with a separator
`(repN(n, p))`	Repeat p exactly n times

PUTTING IT ALL TOGETHER

A common concern that haunts many developers is that all these combinators might be difficult to implement. Lots of plumbing might be required to compose the parsers. But remember that the holy grail of well-designed abstractions is abstractions that compose easily, so you can make larger abstractions out of them. With parser combinators, as you'll see in this chapter, you can create abstractions that *bind* parsers together without your having to bother too much about the plumbing code.

You've seen such abstractions in chapter 6, when we talked about monads in Scala. We're going to use the wisdom you gained there here as well and see how monadic operations make implementing the combinators easy.

8.2.3   *Monads for DSL parser composition*

Parser combinators are abstractions that use the principles of functional programming to compose primitive parsers into larger ones that can recognize a bigger language. Figure 8.7 will help you visualize how combinators compose parsers.

As you saw in the last section, combinators for sequencing and alternations thread together parsers that they get as input. How does this threading take place?

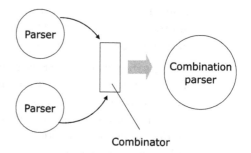

Figure 8.7   Combinators compose smaller parsers and give rise to bigger ones.

IMPLEMENTING THE SEQUENCING COMBINATOR—THE HARD WAY

Consider the sequencing combinator that Scala offers and that we've already discussed. One way to implement it is shown in the following listing.

Listing 8.3   Implementing the sequencing combinator in Scala

```
def ~ [U](p: => Parser[U]): Parser[~[T, U]] =
  new Parser[~[T, U]] {
    def apply(in: Input) =
      Parser.this(in) match {
        case Success(r1, next1) => p(next1) match {
```

❶ Parse input using current parser

❷ Success! Pass remaining input

```
      case Success(r2, next2) => Success((r1, r2), next2)
      case Failure(msg, next) => Failure(msg, next)
    }
  case Failure(msg, next) => Failure(msg, next)
  }
}
```
Final
success!

The implementation is correct and the combinator works as per the specification. The current parser consumes the original input stream and parses it ❶. If it succeeds, the result, along with the rest of the input, is passed to the argument parser ❷. If that parser also succeeds, the final result and the remaining input get returned as the final parser ~[T, U]. A class is defined for ~[T, U] in the trait Parsers.

This seems perfectly fine, doesn't it? Well, something isn't quite right. Do you see the problem with this implementation?

It's the plumbing code that takes center stage, making the core logic of the sequencing obscure to the reader of the program. This is precisely the problem that your manager was worried about. The root of the problem is that in listing 8.3 we programmed at a fairly low level of abstraction, exposing the implementation details to the user.

USING MONADS—LOOK MA, NO BOILERPLATES

In the current context, it's the plumbing for composing abstractions that gets exposed to the combinator implementation. As you learned in chapter 6, monads are a great way to overcome this problem. Monadic binds implemented in Scala using flatMap help you wire abstractions seamlessly. When you're out there designing your own combinators, you can rely on these abstractions for composing your parsers. To keep your lower-level implementation specifics from being exposed to your combinator design, the Scala combinator library makes both ParseResult and Parser monadic. This means that you can automatically chain multiple Parser and ParseResult abstractions without implementing any threading logic yourself. If we do that, our sequencing combinator implementation turns into one simple for comprehension statement:

```
def ~ [U](p: => Parser[U]): Parser[~[T, U]] =
  (for(a <- this; b <- p) yield new ~(a,b)).named("~")
```

Yes! Now you're looking at a beautiful abstraction that the developer can use in a concise way.

But what do monads have to do with our DSL implementation?

As a DSL designer, you need to be aware of the underlying implementation techniques that your library uses. The fact that parser combinators are implemented as a library in Scala implies that they're meant to be extensible. In real-life situations, you'll need to implement your own combinators. Then you'll need all the wisdom of monads when you try to compose parsers within your combinator implementation.

Look at the source code of the Scala library for all the gory details that make this possible.

Now you know that monads help you design better combinators for wiring your DSL parsers, so let's jump onto another aspect of the Scala library. There's another feature that you'll need to use to implement complex DSL structures.

8.2.4 Packrat parsing for left recursive DSL syntax

The top-down recursive descent parsers that we've looked at so far (see chapter 7) can process a fixed look-ahead set of symbols that limits the class of languages that it can recognize. Your DSL could very well have a syntax that these regular top-down parsers might either fail to handle or handle inefficiently. This problem is caused by the fact that LL(1) (see section 7.3.1) can work only with a single look-ahead symbol, and LL(*k*) works with a limited set (bounded by *k*) of look-ahead symbols when it's identifying applicable grammar rules. These parsers are called *predictive parsers* because they try to predict the rule to apply by looking ahead in the input stream.

The other class of top-down recursive descent parsers are called *backtracking parsers*. They have the ability to speculate on the next applicable rule by backtracking and trying out alternates in succession. As you saw already with the Scala combinator library, the alternation combinator can backtrack and try alternative grammar rules that you supply.

Predictive parsers are fast and use linear time parsing, but a naïve implementation of backtracking parsers can quickly degenerate to exponential time parsing. Consider this simple grammar rule for evaluating an expression with Scala parser combinators:

```
lazy val exp = exp ~ ("+" ~> term) |
               exp ~ ("-" ~> term) |
           term
```

In this exp parser, if the exp at the beginning of the first alternative succeeds but then the parser doesn't get a "+", the input rewinds and the parser tries the second alternative. Once again, it'll parse the first exp as part of executing this alternative. The reparsing continues until it gets a match from one of the full set of alternatives that you've provided. This repetition can make the running time exponential.

Packrat parsers (see [3] in section 8.6) can help solve this problem of redoing the same computation using the technique of memoization. A packrat parser caches every computation that it does, so the parser doesn't have to repeat the same computations when it needs them; it can get it straight out of the cache that it maintains, in constant time. Packrat parsers can handle unlimited look-ahead symbols through backtracking. They also use a linear-time parsing algorithm. In the following subsections, we'll talk about some of the benefits that packrat parsers give you.

> **DEFINITION**   Memoization is a technique that lets you cache earlier results so that they're not recomputed later.

MEMOIZATION MAKES PACKRAT PARSERS EFFICIENT

How do you implement memoization in a packrat parser? It depends a lot on the language you're using to implement your packrat parser. If you're using a *lazy-by-default* language like Haskell, you literally don't need to do anything to implement memoization. Haskell's default implementation of *call-by-need* semantics delays evaluation and memoizes the result for future use. Haskell provides the most beautiful implementation of a purely functional, memoizing, backtracking parser.

Scala isn't a lazy-by-default language. The parser combinator library implements explicit memoization by using a specialized `Reader` that implements caching. Here's a snippet of how the packrat parser in Scala extends the `Parsers` trait for parsing functionality and embeds within it a specialized `Reader` (`PackratReader`) that implements memoization:

```
trait PackratParsers extends Parsers {
  class PackratReader[+T](underlying: Reader[T])
    extends Reader[T]  {
    //..
  }
  //..
}
```

Now we can find out how the `exp` parser in the snippet becomes more efficient with the Scala `PackratParsers` implementation. When the first alternative fails after successful recognition of the first `exp`, the parser has the result memoized. It won't have to do any extra work to recognize the first `exp` at the beginning of the second alternative; the parse result will be available right from the cache. Because computations are reused, packrat parsing is done in linear time.

PACKRAT PARSERS SUPPORT LEFT RECURSION

Even with memoization support, the initial design of packrat parsers couldn't handle left recursion of grammar rules. In fact, no top-down recursive descent parsers can handle left recursion. Consider the same parser you saw earlier that evaluates an expression:

```
lazy val exp = exp ~ ("+" ~> term) |
               exp ~ ("-" ~> term) |
               term
```

What happens when the parser gets an expression like 100 – 20 – 45? The `exp` parser first looks up the memo table to check whether it has been evaluated before. Because this is the first attempt to parse it, the memo table is `Nil`. The `exp` parser tries to evaluate the body of the rule, which again starts with another `exp`. Soon your unfortunate `exp` parser is going around in circles in an infinite recursive loop!

Any left-recursive rule can be converted to an equivalent non-left recursive one through a process of transformation. Some packrat parsers can do this for directly left-recursive rules. But transforming the rules makes them more obscure to the reader and makes the process of generating an AST more complex.

Now packrat parsers support left recursion (direct and indirect) through a new technique of memoization, first implemented by Warth, et al. (see [4] in section 8.6).

`PackratParsers` in the Scala library implements this form of memoization and supports direct and indirect left recursion in grammar rules. You'll see examples of how to implement left recursion with Scala parsers in the next section. For more details on the implementation technique, look at the source code for implementing packrat parsers in the Scala source distribution. Besides offering linear time parsing by using backtracking with unlimited look-ahead, packrat parsers have even more features that can be useful for implementing external DSLs.

PACKRAT PARSERS PROVIDE SCANNERLESS PARSING

Typical parsers have separate scanners for tokenization of input. Packrat parsers don't need a separate scanner; they use a single formalism to express the lexical and context-free syntax of the language.

You might be asking what the benefits of scannerless parsing are. Well, these parsers don't need a separate abstraction called `lexer`; you're dealing with a single syntax. Because there's a single abstraction for the entire parsing phase, grammars that use packrat parsing are easier for you to compose. If you need to compose multiple external DSLs, you're composition is going to be improved.

The drawbacks (you knew there'd be some, didn't you?) are that you need to augment the grammar with extra disambiguation information for distinguishing between reserved words and identifiers. Extra disambiguation is also required for identifying the delimiter set in the language.

SUPPORT FOR SEMANTIC PREDICATES

In addition to the syntactic match capability that packrat parsers offer, you can add semantic predicates to the grammar rules. These predicates can determine whether the parse was a success or failure, depending on the semantic values of other syntactic entities.

ORDERED CHOICE

Unlike parsers that use context-free grammars, packrat parsers support only ordered choice in the alternation combinator. When you specify alternates in the combinator that have an overlapping prefix, be sure to list the one with the longest possible match before the other ones.

With ordered choice, packrat parsers eliminate the possibilities of shift/reduce and reduce/reduce conflicts that you can get with an LR parser.

Now you understand what parser combinators are and how you can design efficient parsing techniques by using packrat parsers. We're going to talk more about packrat parsers and you're going to design a DSL that uses packrat parsers in section 8.4. Don't go away!

 Is it mandatory for me to make all my parsers in a DSL implementation packrat parsers?

Usually only some parts of your DSL need to handle complex left-recursive rules. You can use packrat parsers to design those parsers. The others can still remain ordinary recursive descent parsers. In the Scala library, you can freely mix ordinary parsers with the packrat parsers.

We've covered all the basics of parser combinators and how you can use them in designing your next external DSL in a functional language. We've also looked at a sample grammar implementation of an order-processing DSL (listing 8.2), using the combinators available in the Scala library. You must have realized by now that you need to think differently when you use a functional technique like parser combinators to design a DSL. When you decide on an implementation strategy to use in your application, you need to be aware of the pros and cons and the relative capabilities that all the techniques offer. In the next section, I'm going to summarize everything we've talked about regarding DSL design. I'm going to focus on highlighting the differences between internal DSLs and external DSLs using parser generators and parser combinators.

8.3 *DSL design with parser combinators: step-by-step*

Parser combinators combine the succinctness of an EBNF grammar system with the power of composition that you get with pure functions. We've talked a lot about the features that parser combinators offer. Let's look at how these features stack up from a DSL designer's perspective and lead to the development of a complete language for our order-processing DSL.

You've designed internal DSLs using host languages like Ruby, Groovy, and Scala. You've been through the various techniques for designing external DSLs using parser generators and workbenches. Now you're going to see how you can use parser combinators as yet another tool in your toolbox. Before we jump into the design, look at the comparison matrix in table 8.3 that compares designing internal DSLs and the two techniques for designing external DSLs.

I hope that comparison helps you to see what's what. Now let's start with the grammar that we designed in listing 8.2 as the foundation and follow the steps that lead to the evolution of the complete model of our language. As the first step, we

Table 8.3 DSL implementation techniques

Features	Internal DSL	External DSL	
		Parser generator	**Parser combinator**
Completely built within a host language.	Yes, can be purely embedded (as in Scala) or generative (as in Ruby or Lisp).	No, usually needs an external infrastructure for the parser generator (for example, LEX and YACC, ANTLR).	Yes, the host language has to support higher-order functions and offer a parser combinator library as in Scala and Haskell.
The end-user DSL is directly runnable host language code.	Yes, DSL constructs are host language method calls.	No, the parsing infrastructure parses the DSL and executes the functions associated with every symbol.	No, every token gets converted to a `Parser` instance, all of which are then wired using the combinators as operators.

Table 8.3   DSL implementation techniques (continued)

Features	Internal DSL	External DSL	
		Parser generator	**Parser combinator**
The end user needs to know the host language.	Mostly yes, because all exceptions and error handling use the host language infrastructure. The DSL also has to be a valid program in the host language.	No, the DSL is a new language built ground-up using the parser generator.	No, the DSL is a new language that you build using the language-processing infrastructure that your host language offers.

need to verify that the grammar indeed recognizes our language and generates a parse tree.

8.3.1   Step 1: Executing the grammar

If you look at the grammar that we designed in listing 8.2, you'll see it defines the complete syntax of our order-processing DSL. It successfully parses the DSL snippet that I included immediately after the listing. The program in the following listing processes our DSL script and generates the output for a successful parse.

Listing 8.4   Running the DSL processor

```
val str = """(100 IBM shares to buy at max 45, 40 Sun shares
  to sell at min 24, 25 CISCO shares to buy at max 56)
  for account "A1234""""

import OrderDsl._

order(new lexical.Scanner(str)) match {        ❶ Invoke parser
  case Success(order, _) =>                           order
    println(order)
  case Failure(msg, _) => println("Failure: " + msg)  ❷ Successful
  case Error(msg, _) => println("Error: " + msg)        parse
}
```

We invoked the parser order ❶, which is the topmost abstraction for our DSL grammar (see the grammar in listing 8.2). If the DSL script that we provide produces a successful parse, we print the output ❷; otherwise, we print whatever error message the parser generates. Printing only the default output of the parser looks too trivial and not meaningful for processing in our application. In the next section, I'll show you how you can generate a semantic model of your choice from the process of parsing the language. But for now, can you guess what'll be the output of the print statement ❷?

To figure that out, let's first look at the parse tree that is generated from the parsing process. See figure 8.8.

The parsing process is the same as the one we discussed earlier when we talked about external DSL development using ANTLR in chapter 7. At each step of the parsing

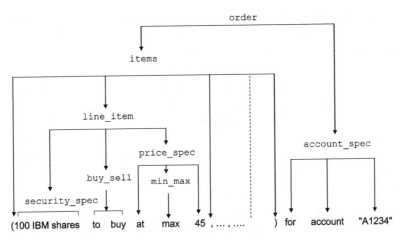

Figure 8.8   The parse tree that's generated from the parsing process of the grammar in listing 8.2. The dotted portion represents repetition of `line_item`, which ultimately reduces to the `order` node of the tree.

process, we output the result as a string. The output is determined by the combinators that we use while building up the grammar. For example, look at the DSL script portion *100 IBM shares* that gets reduced by the grammar rule `lazy val security_spec = numericLit ~ (ident <~ "shares")`. By using the combinator `<~`, we prune the phrase *shares* from the output. The result of parsing the snippet will be the result of sequencing `numericLit` and `ident`, which will come out as (`100~IBM`). Note that the `rep1sep` combinator generates a `List` of all the `line_item` abstractions that it contains. The optionality combinator (`?`) generates a Scala `Option[]`.

Proceeding similarly across all the nodes of the parse tree in figure 8.5, you get the final output for a successful parse of the earlier DSL script:

```
(List((((100~IBM)~buy)~(Some(max)~45)),
  (((40~Sun)~sell)~(Some(min)~24)),
  (((25~CISCO)~buy)~(Some(max)~56)))~A1234)
```

As you look at this output, you must be wondering what use it could have in a real application. You're right; we can't do anything meaningful with such an unstructured representation of our DSL script that contains an aggregate of tuples and lists. Let's build up a semantic model of our `Order` abstraction and see how we can use more combinators to populate it as we go along with the parsing process.

8.3.2   *Step 2: Building the semantic model for the DSL*

Now that we know that the default parsing output is useless, we need to work toward making it more meaningful and usable within the context of an application. How can we do this? The answer is simple: we need more powerful abstractions for the semantic model of our DSL.

Building a semantic model for the `Order` abstraction isn't a problem. But how do we integrate the model with the parsing process?

The Scala library has a few combinators for function application that you can use to transform the result of a successful parse. These function application combinators help you integrate your semantic model with your parsing rules. With these combinators, you can parse your DSL script and also build up the domain model incrementally by applying one of these combinators. Instead of the default return values of your DSL parsers (which I provided in listing 8.2), your parsers can return attributes of your semantic model. This way, when you complete the parsing process, you've effectively built the whole semantic model as the AST.

Let's look at these combinators in detail.

COMBINATORS FOR FUNCTION APPLICATION

Scala has two function application combinators: `^^` and `^^^`. Like all other combinators, `^^` and `^^^` are methods in the `Parsers` trait. For a parser p and function f, p `^^` f produces a parser that recognizes what p does. If p parses successfully, the combinator applies the function f to the result of p. Consider this example from our grammar:

```
lazy val order: Parser[Order] = items ~ account_spec ^^
  { case i ~ a => Order(i, a) }
```

The `^^` combinator applies the pattern-matching anonymous function to the result of the parse defined by `items ~ account_spec`. Instead of a default return value, the parser returns a `Parser[Order]`. Note that the `Order` abstraction that the function returns is lifted into its `Parser` through an *implicit* definition in `Parsers` trait of the library. Look at figure 8.9 and its subsequent explanation for more details.

Just as the combinator `^^` takes a function f and applies it to the result of the parser p, the combinator `^^^` takes a value r and replaces the result of parser p with it for a successful parse of p.

COMBINATOR FOR PARTIALFUNCTION APPLICATION

Scala's `PartialFunction` application combinator is `^?`. For a parser p and partial function f, p `^?` (f, error) produces a parser that recognizes what p does. If p parses successfully and f is defined at the result of p, the combinator applies the parser f to the result of p. If f isn't applicable, then error gives the appropriate reason.

Remember that our ultimate objective is to process the DSL script and build a domain model that the core application can use. For the order-processing DSL, one of the core domain artifacts will be the `Order` abstraction. Let's build that up in the next section using the grammar that we developed in listing 8.2 and the combinators that we just talked about.

8.3.3   *Step 3: Designing the Order abstraction*

We'll build our `Order` abstraction bottom-up so the various stages of the parsing process can construct an appropriate AST node out of the individual building blocks. The most intuitive way to do this is to model the building blocks as Scala *case classes* that can be directly plugged into the grammar rules using the function application combinators. (For more information about Scala case classes, see appendix D.)

First let's look at the Order model in the following listing. Order is the semantic model or the AST that the parser generates.

Listing 8.5 Semantic model for the order-processing DSL

```
package trading.dsl

object AST {
  trait PriceType
  case object MIN extends PriceType
  case object MAX extends PriceType

  case class PriceSpec(pt: Option[PriceType], price: Int)

  case class SecuritySpec(qty: Int, security: String)

  trait BuySell
  case object BUY extends BuySell
  case object SELL extends BuySell

  case class LineItem(ss: SecuritySpec,
    bs: BuySell, ps: PriceSpec)

  case class Items(lis: Seq[LineItem])

  case class AccountSpec(account: String)

  case class Order(items: Items, as: AccountSpec)
}
```

This is plain old Scala stuff, which we used repeatedly when we designed internal DSLs in chapter 6. Now we need to plug the various classes into the grammar rules to actually generate the AST in the form that we want.

8.3.4 Step 4: Generating the AST using function application combinators

Now that we have the underlying semantic model, let's use the Scala combinators in every stage of our parsing process and build a rich AST that we can use in our application. As always, when you're processing a DSL, irrespective of what technique you use, your ultimate aim is to come up with an abstraction that your application can use elsewhere.

The following listing shows the earlier grammar from listing 8.2, but now it's annotated with all function application combinators.

Listing 8.6 AST for the order-processing DSL

```
import scala.util.parsing.combinator._
import scala.util.parsing.combinator.syntactical._

object OrderDsl extends StandardTokenParsers {
  lexical.reserved +=
    ("to", "buy", "sell", "min", "max", "for", "account", "shares", "at")
```

```
lexical.delimiters += ("(", ")", ",")                       Make semantic model
                                                            available to parser
import AST._

lazy val order: Parser[Order] =
  items ~ account_spec ^^ { case i ~ a => Order(i, a) }     Function application
                                                            combinator ^ ^
lazy val items: Parser[Items] =
  "(" ~> rep1sep(line_item, ",") <~ ")" ^^ Items

lazy val line_item: Parser[LineItem] =
  security_spec ~ buy_sell ~ price_spec ^^
    { case s ~ b ~ p => LineItem(s, b, p) }

lazy val buy_sell: Parser[BuySell] =
  "to" ~> "buy" ^^^ BUY |                                  Function application
  "to" ~> "sell" ^^^ SELL                                  combinator ^ ^ ^

lazy val security_spec: Parser[SecuritySpec] =
  numericLit ~ (ident <~ "shares") ^^
    { case n ~ s => SecuritySpec(n.toInt, s) }

lazy val price_spec: Parser[PriceSpec] =                    1  Partial function
  "at" ~> (min_max?) ~ numericLit ^?                           combinator ^?
    ({ case m ~ p if p.toInt > 20 => PriceSpec(m, p.toInt) },
     ( m => "price needs to be > 20" ))

lazy val min_max: Parser[PriceType] =
  "min" ^^^ MIN | "max" ^^^ MAX

lazy val account_spec: Parser[AccountSpec] =
  "for" ~> "account" ~> stringLit ^^ AccountSpec
}
```

When you've become familiar with the individual combinators, this code will be self-explanatory. In most of the rules, we're using the combinator ^^ to deconstruct the tuple returned by the parser and to thread it into the anonymous pattern-matching function that follows. Figure 8.9 is a schematic representation of what goes on behind the scenes when you reduce through a sample grammar rule.

One exception to flow shown in figure 8.9 is the following rule:

```
lazy val items: Parser[Items] =
  "(" ~> rep1sep(line_item, ",") <~ ")" ^^ Items
```

In this snippet, I'm using the constructor `Items` directly instead of using the pattern-matching anonymous function. I can do that because the parser produces a single value of type `Seq[LineItem]` that directly feeds into the constructor of `Items`. The same technique is also used for the rule for `account_spec`.

In listing 8.6, notice the use of the partial function application combinator ^? **1**. Here we can use a context-specific error message in case the partial function isn't defined at the result value of the parser. Consider what happens when you give a price specification as *at max 10*; the parser returns a success. But the partial function specification adds more semantics to validate the input. In this case, we use a guard in pattern matching to state that the minimum allowed value for a price has to be greater

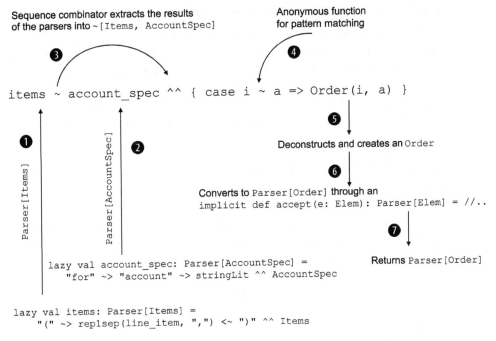

Figure 8.9   A detailed run-down of how a sample grammar rule returns a `Parser[Order]`. `items` and `account_spec` each flow in as a `Parser` ❶, ❷ to the rule. The sequence combinator runs `Parser[Items]` and `Parser[AccountSpec]` and passes the results as an instance of `~` to the function application combinator ❸. Pattern matching is done ❹ and an `Order` instance is created ❺. Through an implicit conversion, `Order` is lifted into a `Parser` ❻ and is returned ❼.

than 20. (There's more about Scala pattern matching in appendix D.) At ❶ in list-ing 8.6, though the parser reports a success, the `PartialFunction` isn't defined at that value. You can use this technique to report a context-specific error message for input validation.

Now your parser returns a structured AST as per the specifications of your semantic model. It's an instance of `Order`, which you can directly use in your application.

> Did you ever wonder why I've been declaring each method as a `lazy`
> val instead of `def`? It's because the evaluation of a `lazy val` is *deferred*
> until its *actual* use; the order in which you define the rules doesn't matter.

Congratulations! You've completely implemented an external DSL using parser com-binators. The DSL implementation is concise and uses the familiar EBNF style nota-tions for defining the syntax of the language. You implemented the semantic model using vanilla Scala abstractions and the model is totally decoupled from the syntax definition. As a designer, could you ask for more?

I think you're ready to try a more advanced DSL implementation that needs a pack-rat parser.

8.4   *A DSL that needs a packrat parser*

In the previous section, we developed one complete DSL using parser combinators, but I never mentioned a word about packrat parsers. Packrat parsers are special, in the sense that they can do cool stuff that regular top-down recursive descent parsers can't. In this section, you'll develop a new DSL that needs a packrat parser for its implementation. If the earlier DSL gave you an idea of the functional power of parser combinators, this one will focus more on the specific power that Scala's implementation of `PackratParsers` offers.

8.4.1   *Introducing the domain problem*

We're getting out of our order-processing domain. Now we're going to use a post-trade business use-case that'll form the core of our DSL.

A financial organization that has custody business does safekeeping of securities on behalf of its customers. As a customer, you can open an account with them and they'll safekeep your securities after the trade is made. Our new DSL will allow investment managers to publish the set of rules that determines the settlement bank and account where securities and cash need to be safekept after the trade is completed. In

---

📇 Financial brokerage system: settlement standing instructions

When trades take place, securities and currencies are exchanged between counterparties. This process, which takes place after the trade is done, is called the settlement of trade. Settlement involves transferring funds and securities between the accounts of the counterparties. There can be multiple accounts, depending on the trade type, the security traded, the counterparty involved, and a number of other factors.

To facilitate a smooth transfer of funds, the investment manager maintains a database of *standing rules* that need to be looked up when a trade is made. These rules are the *SSIs*. They need to be published to the brokers and custodians from time to time.

The settlement of a trade usually has two components: the security side and the cash side. You might have the same settlement instructions for both the security and cash side, or they might be settled differently. The SSI has to be explicit in case you want to settle security and cash separately.

As an example, an investment bank might state: *An equity trade executed in the Japan market has to be settled with us internally at account A-123.* This rule needs to be applied to all the customers that the investment bank is safekeeping. The rules can be organized in a hierarchy and looked up from specialized to generalized form. There can be one more rule, as in *an equity trade for Sony has to be settled externally with BOTM at account BO-234.* This means that all Sony trades will be settled via BOTM, but all other equity trades will be settled internally by the investment bank.

the terminology of the domain, we say that the DSL describes how safekeeping firms manage the *settlement standing instructions (SSIs)* for their clients. Check out the accompanying sidebar for a brief introduction to the domain problem.

In real-life, who'll use this DSL? The investment managers are potential users, as are all the business people working in the settlement of securities in an investment bank. Entering the SSI into a trading system would be a boon; it would be an expressive way to abstract the domain problem clearly for the business user. Before we dive into the DSL itself, let's look at how SSIs fit into the trading and settlement process.

UNDERSTANDING THE BUSINESS PROCESS

To have a more complete understanding of the roles that the SSIs play in a trading and settlement process, look at figures 8.10 and 8.11. Figure 8.10 shows the basic trading and settlement processes that take place between the involved counterparties.

Figure 8.11 shows why we need to have SSIs to complete the process of trade and settlement.

Now that you have an idea of what SSIs are, let's look at some representative SSI rules that an investment manager wants to publish.

SAMPLE SSI RULES THAT WE'LL IMPLEMENT

For brevity, we're considering only a simple subset of the rules that you would find in real-life implementations: .

- Settle trades for customer *chase* in *JPN* market of *ibm* internally with us at *a-345*.
- Settle trades for customer *chase* in *JPN* market internally with us at *a-123*.
- Settle trades for customer *nri* in *US* market externally at *CITI c-123*.
- Settle trades for customer *chase* of *sony* internally with us at *n-234*.
- Settle trades for customer *chase* on account *ch-123* internally with us at *n-675*.

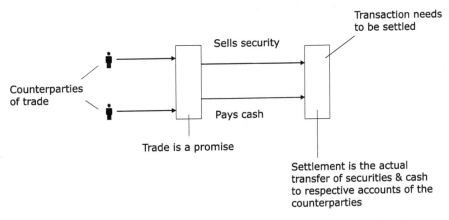

Figure 8.10 The trade and settlement processes. Trade is a promise made between two counterparties for exchange of securities and cash. The settlement is the actual commitment that transfers securities and cash between the counterparty accounts to change positions.

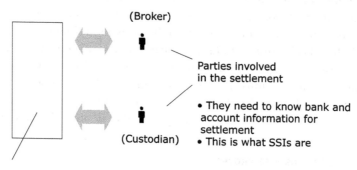

Settlement process

Figure 8.11   The SSIs are needed to complete the process of settlement. The brokers and the custodians need to know the bank and account information where the securities and cash need to be transferred.

- Settle trades for broker *icici* in *JPN* market safekeep security internally with us at *us-123* settle cash externally at *BOJ b-954*. (In this rule there are separate cash and security SSIs.)

We'll start with the grammar as we did earlier. If you went through the last DSL that we designed using parser combinators in Scala in section 8.4, the grammar in listing 8.7 will be perfectly clear to you.

8.4.2   Building the grammar

The entire grammar is a bit long, though most of it will be familiar to you. I'm not going to describe the whole thing; rather, I'll focus on some of the special aspects of it. The entire grammar is shown in the following listing.

Listing 8.7   Grammar rules for `SSI_Dsl`

```
package trading.dsl
import scala.util.parsing.combinator._
object SSI_Dsl extends JavaTokenParsers
               with PackratParsers {                ◁─┘ Use PackratParsers here

  lazy val standing_rules = (standing_rule +)

  lazy val standing_rule =
  "settle" ~> "trades" ~> trade_type_spec ~ settlement_spec

  lazy val trade_type_spec =
    trade_type_spec ~ ("in" ~> market <~ "market") |
    trade_type_spec ~ ("of" ~> security) |
    trade_type_spec ~ ("on" ~> "account" ~> account) |
    "for" ~> counterparty_spec

  lazy val counterparty_spec =
    "customer" ~> customer | "broker" ~> broker
```

❶ Left recursion and ordered choice

```
lazy val settlement_spec =
  settle_all_spec | settle_cash_security_separate_spec

lazy val settle_all_spec = settle_mode_spec

lazy val settle_cash_security_separate_spec =
  repN(2, settle_cash_security ~ settle_mode_spec)

lazy val settle_cash_security =
  "safekeep" ~> "security" | "settle" ~> "cash"

lazy val settle_mode_spec =
  settle_external_spec | settle_internal_spec

lazy val settle_external_spec =
"externally" ~> "at" ~> bank ~ account

lazy val settle_internal_spec =
"internally" ~> "with" ~> "us" ~> "at" ~> account

lazy val market = not(keyword) ~> stringLiteral
lazy val security = not(keyword) ~> stringLiteral
lazy val customer = not(keyword) ~> stringLiteral
lazy val broker = not(keyword) ~> stringLiteral
lazy val account = not(keyword) ~> stringLiteral
lazy val bank = not(keyword) ~> stringLiteral

lazy val keyword =                                        ◁⎯  Keywords modeled
  "at" | "us" | "of" | "on" | "in" | "and" | "with" |        as parsers
  "internally" | "externally" | "safekeep" |
  "security" | "settle" | "cash" | "trades" |
  "account" | "customer" | "broker" | "market"
}
```

From this grammar, can you figure out why we need to use packrat parsers? Look at the rule for `trade_type_spec` ❶. Yes, there's left recursion and ordered choice, which, as you've seen before, is one of the strengths of a packrat parser. A packrat parser uses specialized memoization techniques (see section 8.2.3) to reduce parsing complexity for left recursive rules from exponential to linear time.

To implement your parser as a packrat parser in Scala, you need to do a few specific things that I'll tell you about in table 8.4.

All of the other stuff in the grammar looks similar to what we discussed in the context of designing our order processing DSL. It'll be a straightforward (yet useful) exercise to write a driver program and run some of the DSL snippets in table 8.4 using the parser.

Now let's take a look at how you develop the semantic model that implements the domain abstraction for an SSI.

Table 8.4   Making your parser a packrat parser in Scala

Step	Description

1 Mix in with `PackratParsers`	Our SSI parser in listing 8.7 does the following:
	
	`object SSI_Dsl extends JavaTokenParsers with`
	`PackratParsers {`

Table 8.4   Making your parser a packrat parser in Scala *(continued)*

Step	Description
2 Provide the input that your parser processes as type `Input` defined in `Reader[Elem]`	A packrat parser in Scala is implemented on top of a specialized `Reader`, the `PackratReader`, which is defined as: `class PackratReader[+T](underlying: Reader[T]) extends Reader[T] {` The `PackratReader` wraps an underlying `Reader` for implementing memoization on top of it. The type of element that the `Reader` accepts is defined to be `Char` in the `Parsers` trait that you extend.
3 Explicitly specify the return type as `PackratParser[…]`	It's not mandatory for all of the parsers to be packrat parsers. For those that need memoization for backtracking or left recursion, specify the return type explicitly as `PackratParser`. You'll see examples of this when we implement the semantic model.

8.4.3   Designing the semantic model

As with the earlier case in section 8.3.4, we're going to develop domain-level abstractions in Scala that you can plug directly into the grammar rules using the function application combinators. I'm going to call the whole abstraction an SSI_AST because this is the form of the AST that we want to compute after parsing our DSL script. The following listing contains the complete semantic model.

Listing 8.8   The semantic model (or AST) for the SSI DSL

```
package trading.dsl

object SSI_AST {
type Market = String
type Security = String
type CustomerCode = String
type BrokerCode = String
type AccountNo = String
type Bank = String

trait SettlementModeRule
case class SettleInternal(accountNo: AccountNo)
  extends SettlementModeRule
case class SettleExternal(bank: Bank, accountNo: AccountNo)
  extends SettlementModeRule

trait SettleCashSecurityRule
case object SettleCash extends SettleCashSecurityRule
case object SettleSecurity extends SettleCashSecurityRule

trait SettlementRule
case class SettleCashSecuritySeparate(
  set: List[(SettleCashSecurityRule, SettlementModeRule)])
    extends SettlementRule
case class SettleAll(sm: SettlementModeRule) extends SettlementRule
```

```
trait CounterpartyRule
case class Customer(code: CustomerCode) extends CounterpartyRule
case class Broker(code: BrokerCode) extends CounterpartyRule

case class TradeTypeRule(cpt: CounterpartyRule,
  mkt: Option[Market], sec: Option[Security],
  tradingAccount: Option[AccountNo])

case class StandingRule(ttr: TradeTypeRule,
  str: SettlementRule)

case class StandingRules(rules: List[StandingRule])
}
```

The listing is self-explanatory and is pure and simple Scala code. The only reason I'm presenting it here is so you can refer to it when we use the classes in the function application combinator to process parser results.

The next listing shows the complete grammar, annotated with combinators for processing the AST and generating the StandingRules as the final data structure of our semantic model.

Listing 8.9 The complete DSL that generates our semantic model

```
object SSI_Dsl extends JavaTokenParsers                        Make AST
              with PackratParsers {                            available

  import SSI_AST._

  lazy val standing_rules: Parser[StandingRules] =
    (standing_rule +) ^^ StandingRules

  lazy val standing_rule: Parser[StandingRule] =
    "settle" ~> "trades" ~> trade_type_spec ~ settlement_spec
      ^^ { case (t ~ s) => StandingRule(t, s) }

  lazy val trade_type_spec: PackratParser[TradeTypeRule] =       Return type as
    trade_type_spec ~ ("in" ~> market <~ "market")             ❶ PackratParser
      ^^ { case (t ~ m) => t.copy(mkt = Some(m)) } |
    trade_type_spec ~ ("of" ~> security)
      ^^ { case (t ~ s) => t.copy(sec = Some(s)) } |
    trade_type_spec ~ ("on" ~> "account" ~> account)
      ^^ { case (t ~ a) => t.copy(tradingAccount = Some(a)) } |
    "for" ~> counterparty_spec
      ^^ { case c => TradeTypeRule(c, None, None, None) }

  lazy val counterparty_spec: Parser[CounterpartyRule] =
    "customer" ~> customer ^^ Customer |
    "broker" ~> broker ^^ Broker

  lazy val settlement_spec =
    settle_all_spec |
    settle_cash_security_separate_spec

  lazy val settle_all_spec: Parser[SettlementRule] =
    settle_mode_spec ^^ SettleAll

  lazy val settle_cash_security_separate_spec: Parser[SettlementRule] =
    repN(2, settle_cash_security ~ settle_mode_spec) ^^ { case l: Seq[_] =>
      SettleCashSecuritySeparate(l map (e => (e._1, e._2))) }
```

```
lazy val settle_cash_security: Parser[SettleCashSecurityRule] =
  "safekeep" ~> "security" ^^^ SettleSecurity |
  "settle" ~> "cash" ^^^ SettleCash

lazy val settle_mode_spec: Parser[SettlementModeRule] =
  settle_external_spec |
  settle_internal_spec

lazy val settle_external_spec: Parser[SettlementModeRule] =
  "externally" ~> "at" ~> bank ~ account
    ^^ { case b ~ a => SettleExternal(b, a) }

lazy val settle_internal_spec: Parser[SettlementModeRule] =
  "internally" ~> "with" ~> "us" ~> "at" ~> account ^^ SettleInternal

//..                            ⟵  Remainder is same as listing 8.6
}
```

For the left-recursive rule `trade_type_spec` ❶, we return a `PackratParser[Trade-TypeRule]`. This ensures that when the alternates are parsed, backtracking will be done using memoization and left recursion will also be processed using the optimizations we discussed in section 8.2.3.

Wow! We've got the entire DSL along with an abstraction for its semantic model. The grammar looks expressive and the `Order` abstraction is a faithful representation of the domain entity. All the individual parsers are now wired together using function application combinators that incrementally build up the domain model.

As I mentioned earlier, the roots of parser combinators are based on functional programming. The extensibility of the paradigm is also based on function combination. In the next section, you'll see some of the compositional aspects of Scala parsers that can make your DSL design extensible.

8.4.4   *Parser composition for extending DSL semantics*

As you saw in section 8.2, you can define a parser as a pure function that takes an input and produces a parse result. In the Scala library, we express this as `(Input => ParseResult[T])`. The combinators that we define are nothing but higher-order functions that implement parser composition using sequencing, alternation, repetition, and so on. But how do parsers and parse results compose?

MONADS FOR CUSTOM EXTENSION

If you go through the source code of the parser combinator library in Scala, you'll find that both `ParseResult[T]` and `Parser[+T]` are monadic. This means that they implement the standard methods `map`, `flatMap`, and `append` that help you design individual combinators like `~` (sequence) without explicitly plumbing the actual threading of inputs in combining the parsers. You saw this same example in listing 8.3 where a monadic `Parser` and `ParseResult` implementation led to a succinct implementation of `~` using for-comprehensions.

When the parser compositional semantics is glued into the basic abstractions, you can always follow the rules that help us play. You can chain combinators, you can transform a parse result using your own transformation function, and you can decorate an already existing parser with additional semantics. Consider an example where you want to log how the parsing proceeds for one of your parsers in the order-processing DSL. Here's how you can do it using the `log` combinator defined in the `Parser` abstraction:

```
lazy val line_item: Parser[LineItem] =
  log(security_spec ~ buy_sell ~ price_spec ^^ { case s ~ b ~ p =>
    LineItem(s, b, p) })("line_item")
```

`log` is defined in the `Parsers` trait as a decorator that wraps an existing parser and adds logging information around its execution. Look at the Scala source code for more details.

DESIGNING YOUR OWN PARSER AS A DECORATOR

You saw in listing 8.6 how you can add context-sensitive validations to a parser by using the partial function application combinator. If you need to add more semantics to the parsing process, you can define your own parser that can be used to decorate an existing parser. Consider the example in the following listing.

Listing 8.10 A validating parser that can add domain semantics to a parser

```
trait ValidatingParser extends Parsers {
  def validate[T](p: => Parser[T])(
    validation: (T, Input) => ParseResult[T]): Parser[T] = Parser (
      in => p(in) match {
        case Success(x, in) => validation(x, in)
        case fail => fail
      }
    )
}
```

`ValidatingParser` wraps an existing parser and can add arbitrary domain semantics to it. Note that the `validate` method takes a closure `validation` as an argument where you can specify additional domain semantics specific to the implementation of your DSL. You'll see an application of this in our `SSI_Dsl` parser (shown in listing 8.7) a bit later.

Remember I told you in a sidebar earlier in this chapter that an SSI can contain separate instructions for settlement of cash and security? We modeled this with the following parser that was in listing 8.8:

```
lazy val settle_cash_security_separate_spec: Parser[SettlementRule] =
  repN(2, settle_cash_security ~ settle_mode_spec) ^^ { case l: Seq[_] =>
    SettleCashSecuritySeparate(l map (e => (e._1, e._2))) }
```

Note that the execution of the parser results in a `SettlementRule` that we design as the following case class in our semantic model:

```
case class SettleCashSecuritySeparate(
    set: List[(SettleCashSecurityRule, SettlementModeRule)])
    extends SettlementRule
```

The parser uses a `repN(2, ..)` to validate that we have exactly *two* legs coming out from the DSL script. But in order to qualify as a valid set of rules, we need to ensure that one of the two rules *must* be for security settlement and the other one for cash settlement. How do we do this?

PLUGGING IN THE DECORATOR

One way is to plug in our `ValidatingParser` with the additional domain validation logic that we want it to execute to qualify as a valid standing rule. The following listing shows how to do this in the relevant rule of the grammar.

Listing 8.11   ValidatingParser as a decorator

```
lazy val settle_cash_security_separate_spec: Parser[SettlementRule] =
    validate(
      repN(2, settle_cash_security ~ settle_mode_spec)
          ^^ { case l: Seq[_] =>
          SettleCashSecuritySeparate(l map (e => (e._1, e._2))) }
    ) { case (s, in) => {
          if ((s hasSettleSecurity) && (s hasSettleCash))
            Success(s, in)                                          ❶ Validation
          else Failure(                                               passed
            "should contain 1 entry for cash and
security side of settlement", in)                              ❷ Validation
        }                                                             failed
    }
```

If we have a `Success` on the original parsing and the resultant `List` contains one `SettleSecurity` and one `SettleCash` entry, we return the `Success` as the final result ❶; otherwise, we convert the earlier `Success` into a `Failure` ❷ because a domain validation has failed. Of course, in order to use the `ValidatingParser` within our grammar rules, we need to mix it in with our original `SSI_Dsl` parser:

```
object SSI_Dsl extends JavaTokenParsers
               with PackratParsers
               with ValidatingParser {
    //..
```

This technique of composing multiple parsers is an application of the Decorator design pattern. It helps you keep your basic abstraction (the core parser, in this case) cleaner and lets you plug in additional domain logic wherever you need it.

8.5   Summary

If you've gotten this far in the chapter about parser combinators, you've really learned a lot about one of the most advanced applications of functional programming in language design. Parser combinators offer the most succinct way to design an external DSL. You don't need to design an infrastructure on your own to implement the DSL. The parser combinator technique gives you an internal DSL for building your own external DSL. You can use the underlying language infrastructure for the basic services like modularity, exception handling, and so on, and still design a new language for your users.

Key takeaways & best practices

■ Parser combinators are the most functional way to design external DSLs without going out of your language syntax.

■ An external DSL designed using parser combinators *tends to have a succinct implementation*, because the combinators offer a declarative syntax through infix notation and type inference.

■ Before you use the parser combinator library offered by your language, be aware of *the special features the library offers like memoized parsers, packrat parsers*, or other goodies. Being familiar with its features will help you design the most optimally performing grammar possible for your DSL.

In this chapter, you learned how Scala implements parser combinators as a library on top of the core language. You can define your grammar rules in an almost-EBNF notation by composing plain old Scala functions. The Scala library offers a rich set of combinators that allows you to process your semantic model and evolve the parsing process into your own AST. Finally, we discussed packrat parsers that let you do things that ordinary top-down recursive descent parsers don't let you do. You also used Scala in an exercise that showed you what an efficient implementation of packrat parsers Scala provides.

8.6   References

1 Wampler, Dean, and Alex Payne. 2009. *Programming Scala: Scalability = Functional Programming + Objects.* O'Reilly Media.

2 Odersky, Martin, Lex Spoon, and Bill Venners. 2008. *Programming in Scala: A Comprehensive Step-By-Step Guide.* Artima.

3 Ford, Bryan. 2002. Packrat parsing: simple, powerful, lazy, linear time, functional pearl. *Proceedings of the seventh ACM SIGPLAN International Conference on Functional Programming,* pp 36-47.

4 Warth, Alessandro, James R. Douglass, and Todd Millstein. 2008. Packrat parsers can support left recursion. *Proceedings of the 2008 ACM SIGPLAN Symposium on Partial Evaluation and Semantics-based Program Manipulation,* pp 103-110.

5 Newspeak. http://newspeaklanguage.org.

Part 3

Future trends
in DSL development

Chapter 9 contains a short discussion of future trends we're seeing in DSL-based development. Functional programming is becoming more popular, because functional abstractions offer better composability than the corresponding OO ones. I expect lots of DSL development to mature in the functional programming world. Techniques like parser combinators will become more popular as developers start appreciating their real power. Another area that's expanding is DSL workbenches, which offer a complete development and maintenance stack for DSLs. In this part of the book I also discuss the important topic of DSL versioning and some of the practices that you can adopt to ensure a smooth evolution of the DSL syntax for your users. The main thrust of part 3—chapter 9—is to touch base on these developing trends in the DSL world.

DSL design: looking forward

This chapter covers

- Overview of our journey together
- Expanding support for DSL development
- Increasing tool support for writing DSLs
- The continuing evolution of DSLs

Congratulations! You've reached the last chapter of the book. We've covered a lot of ground as I've told you about the paradigms of DSL-based development. We've discussed all the aspects of DSL design using quite a few languages, mostly on the JVM. I carefully chose a good mix of statically and dynamically typed languages, covering both OO and functional paradigms. In this chapter, we'll look at trends in DSL development that are becoming more popular and mainstream. As a practitioner, you need to be aware of these developments; some might eventually evolve and mature into useful implementation techniques.

We're going to discuss some of the areas that DSL designers are focusing on that enhance DSL-based development. Figure 9.1 shows a roadmap of the features that you'll learn about on the last leg of our journey together.

We're going to start in section 9.1 with language expressivity, where the horizon seems to be expanding by the day. Groovy, Ruby, Scala, and Clojure are way

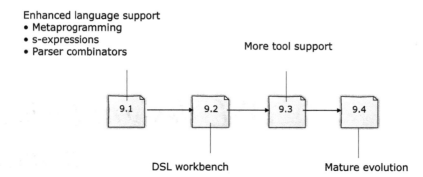

Figure 9.1   Our roadmap through the chapter

more expressive than Java and have been continuously evolving, while still keeping a human interface in mind. Of these languages, the dynamic ones like Groovy, Ruby, and Clojure already use the power of metaprogramming, which is even being added in a couple of statically typed languages. Even if you don't use metaprogramming now, as an expert in DSL development, you need to keep yourself up to date about how these features are shaping today's languages to create a better environment for DSL construction.

Another addition to the DSL implementation technique is the use of parser combinators. More languages that have functional programming capabilities will gradually offer libraries that implement parser combinators as part of their standard distribution. We're going to discuss this in section 9.1.

Next we'll step into something that has the potential to be a new norm in DSL development: the use of DSL workbenches. Section 9.3 discusses additional tool support in modern IDEs. I conclude the chapter with a section about DSL evolution where I'll discuss how to grow a DSL in a disciplined way, keeping an eye on the language's backward compatibility.

If in the earlier chapters you learned about the present of DSL design, in this chapter you'll get an idea of what to look for in the future of DSLs. You need to be prepared for tomorrow, because today is already here.

9.1   *Growing language support for DSL design*

DSLs are all about being expressive with respect to the domain that you model. When you're modeling an accounting system, you want your API set to speak in terms of debits, credits, books, ledgers, and journals. But these are only the nouns of the model, the concrete artifacts that form some of the core concepts in the problem domain. You also need to convey the verbs with the same level of expressiveness that you speak in the problem space. Remember our coffee shop example in chapter 1 that started us off? The barista could serve precisely what you ordered because you spoke in the language she understands. The whole expression needs to have a synergy with the problem domain that's being modeled. Consider the following snippet of Scala code that we discussed in chapter 3:

```
withAccount(trade) {
  account => {
    settle(
      trade using
        account.getClient
              .getStandingRules
              .filter(_.account == account)
              .first)
    andThen journalize
  }
}
```

This snippet is a DSL from the domain of securities trading system. Note how the *nouns* and *verbs* of the domain are expressively modeled through the DSL syntax. Scala's support for higher-order functions lets you treat your domain behaviors (the verbs) as uniformly as the domain objects (the nouns). This uniform treatment makes the language expressive.

You might be wondering why I'm being so emphatic about something in the last chapter of the book when the same subject has been the underlying theme throughout our discussion. I feel the need to reemphasize the fact that for a sufficiently powerful language, the expressiveness is limited only by the creativity of its users. Powerful idioms like metaprogramming, functional control structures, and a flexible enough type system let a programmer express the problem domain in a DSL that speaks the same language as the domain itself. In this section, we'll discuss how some of today's languages are extending the frontiers of expressivity to position themselves as potent forces for DSL development.

9.1.1 Striving to be expressive

With newer languages coming up pretty quickly, we'll be seeing more and more support that makes for expressive syntax design for your DSL. In the earlier chapters, we discussed all the power that Ruby, Groovy, Scala, and Clojure offer in this respect. In this section, I'll give you a brief overview of the capabilities that some of the other languages offer. I won't discuss them in detail; the main idea is to show you that now there are more languages that strive to be expressive to the human interface. Look at figure 9.2, which shows the progression of how some mainstream languages have evolved into more expressive ones in the course of time.

Expressive programming languages help close the semantic gap between the problem domain and the solution domain. In OO languages that don't support higher-order functions, you need to shoehorn objects as functors to model domain actions. Obviously this indirection manifests itself as accidental complexity (see appendix A) in the resulting DSL that you design. With support of first-class functions, your DSL becomes much cleaner and more acceptable to your users.

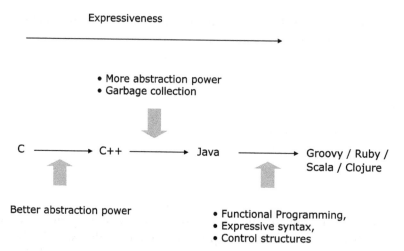

Figure 9.2   Evolution of expressiveness in programming languages

Now we're going to look at how DSL development practices have evolved over the years with increasing expressiveness of programming languages. Remember that we used to write domain rules in the days of C as well, only at a much lower level of abstraction than what we do today. Figure 9.3 shows this progression in DSL development.

Many of these features are mature today, but others are still evolving and being adopted by more and more languages. I'm going to describe three of the important features that have been gaining more ground in the ecosystem of DSL-based development. I'll start with a technique that's already become popular in the dynamic languages. Given its potential use in DSL design, metaprogramming is being introduced in more and more languages, even some of the statically typed ones.

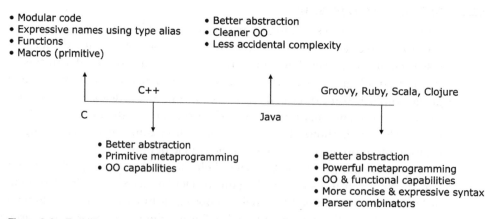

Figure 9.3   Evolution of the features in programming languages we use to develop DSLs

9.1.2   *More power with metaprogramming*

In the languages being developed today, we're witnessing an increase in metaprogramming power. Ruby and Groovy offer runtime metaprogramming, as you saw in chapters 2, 3, 4, and 5. Clojure, the Lisp on the JVM, offers compile-time metaprogramming and lets you design expressive DSLs without one bit of runtime performance overhead. If you're into DSLs, you need to master the metaprogramming techniques that your language of choice offers.

Statically typed languages like Haskell (see [10] in section 9.6) and OCaml (see [11] in section 9.6) have started to implement metaprogramming as part of the language infrastructure. Template Haskell is an extension to Haskell that adds compile-time metaprogramming facilities to the language. The traditional way to design DSLs in Haskell is to go for the embedded or the internal DSL implementation. Frequently there's a mismatch between what the DSL developer wants to write and what Haskell lets you do with its syntax. Compile-time metaprogramming lets you write concrete syntax that can be converted to appropriate Haskell AST structures. It's similar to what you can do with Lisp macros.

Developments in metaprogramming for many languages are a direct indication that DSLs are becoming mainstream. Next, we're going to look at a feature that has the potential to replace most instances of XML as the carrier of data.

9.1.3   *s-expressions instead of XML as the carrier*

An expressive language like Clojure (or Lisp) provides you with s-expressions, which can model *code as data*. In today's enterprise systems, you often see masses of XML being used as configuration data and touted as the DSL for expressive modeling. These XML structures are then parsed and processed using appropriate tools that generate executable artifacts for the application. The problem is that XML is painful to the eyes and has limited capability to express higher-order structures like conditionals. It serves as a poor alternative to s-expressions.

In one project I worked on, we were using XML for transporting entities as messages across various deployments. Consider the following XML snippet that models an Account object:

```
<account>
   <no>a-123</no>
   <name>
      <primary>John P.</primary>
      <secondary>Hughes R.</secondary>
   </name>
   <dateOfOpening>20101212</dateOfOpening>
   <status>active</status>
</account>
```

With XML as the format, we need to parse the message and transform it into an appropriate data structure. Why not use the s-expressions available in Clojure? The code becomes so much more expressive and less verbose at the same time:

```
(def account
 {no 123,
  name {primary "John P." secondary "Hughes R."},
  date-of-opening "20101212",
  status ::active })
```

The new snippet is more concise than the equivalent XML counterpart and is semantically much richer. It models data in Clojure that you can also execute. You don't have to contrive additional machinery to parse the structure and transform it into a runtime artifact; it executes directly within the Clojure runtime. I call it *executable XML*. It's a much better DSL than the XML version and is defined using only the features that your programming language offers. We'll be seeing more of such *data-as-code* paradigm as DSL-based development matures.

Another trend that's growing in popularity, mainly in functional languages, is using parser combinators. You saw in chapter 8 the power that parser combinators offer in DSL design. Let's look at them again.

9.1.4   *Parser combinators becoming more popular*

You saw in chapter 8 how parser combinators allow you to design external DSLs even within the confines of a host language library. With functional programming becoming more popular, we'll see a proliferation of parser combinator libraries. Gilad Bracha's upcoming language Newspeak (see [4] in section 9.6) has a rich parser combinator library that can decouple grammar rules from the semantic model much better than what we have in Scala. Many existing languages like F# (see [5] in section 9.6), JavaScript (see [6] in section 9.6), and Scheme (see [7] in section 9.6) are also developing their own parser combinator libraries.

Parser combinators let you develop the syntax of your DSL in a declarative way, similar to writing EBNF rules. You can write EBNF-like declarative grammar rules in parser generators too, but when you use parser combinators, you remain within the scope of your host language and get to use all its other features. With support from the host language, you can decouple your semantic actions from the grammar and get a clean implementation of the DSL.

Let's look at yet another stream of DSL development methodology. It's on a higher level of abstraction than textual DSLs. I'm talking about DSL workbenches. You saw one example of this paradigm when we discussed DSL development with Xtext. DSL workbenches could very well bring about a fundamental change in the way we think about DSLs.

9.2   *DSL workbenches*

From a high-level view, a DSL design is, in some way, an exercise in building the most expressive API you can within the confines of your environment. In the case of internal DSLs, you're limited to the host language that you use. With external DSLs, you design your own syntax, subject to the restrictions of your parser generator or combinator. In all these cases, we're talking about textual DSLs; whatever interface you present to your user, it's in the form of text-based structures. You can give very expressive APIs to your users, but if they're implemented in a specific language, the user has to abide by the rules and regulations that the language runtime mandates.

Recently a school of thought has questioned this paradigm of text-based DSL development. Suppose I, as an expert in data analytics, want to embed Excel macros within the calculation engine of my weather forecasting system. To me, a spreadsheet seems to be the most intuitive way to express the logic that the macro encapsulates. In the text-only-based world of DSL design, there's no way you can compose higher-order structures like a spreadsheet or a charting engine within the scope of your language.

Frameworks like Eclipse XText (see chapter 7) bring you a step in this direction. Instead of plain text, it stores the metamodel of the DSL, which can then be projected onto an Eclipse editor. The editor provides capabilities like syntax-highlighting and code completion. The higher the level of abstraction that such frameworks support, the easier it becomes for the end user to create, edit, and maintain her own DSL. A tool that supports end users in creating, editing, and maintaining DSLs is called a *workbench*.

9.2.1 *What's in a DSL workbench?*

In chapter 7, you saw how you can generate workbenches for your DSL using Eclipse Xtext (see [1] in section 9.6). JetBrains Meta-Programming System (MPS) ([2] in section 9.6), and Intentional's Domain Workbench ([3] in section 9.6) are similar tools in the same space. Instead of dealing with text-based programs, these tools use higher-order structures like the AST as the basic storage unit.

As a workbench user, you don't have to write text-based programs; you'll get a *projectional editor*, a special form of IDE, where you can manipulate your DSL structures. DSL workbenches usually offer seamless integration with tools like Microsoft Excel, which you can use to design your DSL syntax and semantics. The model that you build in Excel is stored in the workbench repository as metadata and corresponds to the higher-level abstractions of your DSL.

You can also generate code in specific languages from the metamodel that's stored in the workbench's repository. Wasn't this supposed to be the domain user's dream and the initial value proposition that we used to associate with DSLs? The domain workbench seems to be the ideal confluence of the domain experts and the programmers. Figure 9.4 shows how domain workbenches support the full lifecycle of a DSL implementation.

The available DSL workbenches are based on the same principle of programming at a higher level of abstraction that we've been talking about in this book. There are differences, as far as the representations of abstractions are concerned. Some of the areas where these products vary are summarized in table 9.1.

A DSL workbench can definitely be beneficial to have in your bag of tricks. Let's look at the advantages of using one.

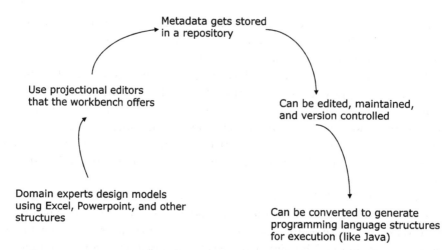

Figure 9.4   DSL workbenches support the full lifecycle of a DSL implementation. Domain experts work with higher-level structures like Microsoft Excel. The workbench stores metadata instead of program text. The metadata can be projected onto smart editors called projectional editors where you can edit, version, and manage it. The workbenches also have the facility to generate code to programming languages like Java.

Table 9.1   Feature variation in DSL workbenches

Feature	Differences between workbenches
Representation and definition of abstract syntax	The abstract syntax can be represented in terms of an abstract syntax tree or graph, and defined as a metamodel or a grammar form.
Metamodel composition	Many of the workbenches support an abstract syntax representation that's a composition of several grammars or metamodels.
Transformation capabilities	Some workbenches, like Xtext, allow template-based code transformation, while MPS supports model-to-model transformation out of the box.
IDE support	Most of the workbenches offer powerful custom IDE support out of the box. They offer syntax highlighting, code completion, and context-sensitive help to the DSL writer.

9.2.2   *The advantages of using a DSL workbench*

Even though all workbenches vary in the degree to which they offer flexibility to the user with respect to the areas mentioned in the table, all DSL workbenches offer the following advantages:

- Separation of concerns between the interface of the DSL and the implementation.
- Direct interaction between the user and higher-level structures, structures that are on a higher level than those found in textual programming languages. The workbench approach to DSL development is far more appealing to nonprogramming domain users.

- A rich end-to-end environment for DSL-driven development.
- Easier composition of multiple DSLs.

When all's said and done, DSL workbenches are still in the infancy stage, as far as adoption is concerned. The technology has promise and has been promoted for quite some time. Some concerns need to be addressed by the DSL workbench vendors before they can be positioned for mainstream adoption. The main concern is vendor lock-in with workbenches. The following attributes of a DSL workbench are the most important ones:

- Abstract representation schema
- Projectional editor
- Code generator

All of these are locked into the respective frameworks. There's always a certain level of apprehension when you're locked in a specific platform for modeling your DSL. Being locked in implies that your development team has to learn yet another specific tool set in order to implement a DSL as part of your project. Even so, workbenches are an interesting technology paradigm and we need to keep an eye on how they evolve.

Workbenches are one means to getting a complete DSL development environment. But besides workbenches, we're also looking at enhanced tool support in IDEs that can make DSL development easier than what it is right now.

9.3 *More tool support*

As you saw in the earlier section, the primary tool support for designing DSLs comes in the form of DSL workbenches. But when you're not using a workbench, how much support can you expect from the environment that you're working with?

One obvious way of getting advanced tool support for writing DSLs is from your IDE. When you program in a general-purpose programming language using the support of an IDE, you get an editor that supports syntax highlighting, code completion, and many other editing features. Now imagine getting some of these features when you program using your DSL. Consider writing an internal DSL in Groovy for the financial brokerage system, where you want to highlight every currency code that the user enters. Or you want automatic code completion for some of the financial institutions supported by your system.

Many IDEs have started offering some sort of tooling that helps you with syntax highlighting and autocompletion, even without a full-blown DSL workbench. IDEs today are extensible using a plug-in-based architecture. You can plug in your own bits to define syntax highlighting, code completion, and many other things (see [8] and [9] in section 9.6).

The blog post *Contraptions for Programming* (see [8] in section 9.6) describes a plug-in for Eclipse-Groovy-based DSL development where you implement your own custom syntax highlighter. Eclipse-Groovy components provide an extension point in the form of an interface that you can implement to customize the list of keywords that you

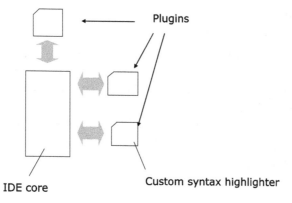

Plugins

IDE core

Custom syntax highlighter

Figure 9.5
In an IDE, besides the core part, you can implement your own plugins. For your DSL, you can design a syntax-highlighter as a plugin and introduce it alongside the rest of the IDE.

want to be syntax-highlighted. There's similar custom Groovy DSL support for IntelliJ IDEA where the plug-in implements autocompletion for methods and properties see ([9] in section 9.6). Look at figure 9.5 for an overview of how you can introduce the syntax highlighter for your custom DSL as part of IDE plug-in architecture.

So far we've talked about DSL development. Another important issue with today's DSL-based environment is the disciplined evolution of DSL versions. I'll give you a brief overview in the next section of how you can streamline the growth of a DSL so that multiple versions can coexist.

9.4 *The mature evolution of a DSL*

Many of us use DSLs in our application development. We use DSLs mainly to model the components of our system that tend to change frequently, like the configuration parameters and the business rules. One area that needs to mature further is the discipline that we follow to evolve a DSL in the face of such changes. You need to think about your DSL's evolution strategy even before you come up with the first version to be deployed.

9.4.1 *Versioning your DSL*

Depending on how your DSL is going to be used, you need to have a versioning strategy. If your DSL is going to be used solely by a closed group of users working as a cohesive unit, you might decide *not* to follow a specific versioning strategy. Whenever you need to make a change to fix a bug or to introduce new requirements, you can roll out the newer version and replace the earlier one. A simple note that points out issues of backward incompatibilities will accompany the new version.

But what if multiple groups of users are going to use your DSL? Then you'll have to plan for incremental versioning strategies. Not all your users will be interested in getting the new release, so you need to employ both of the following strategies:

- Your version management in the code base must be able to branch out to maintain multiple releases.
- You must create specific deployment scripts that can deploy multiple versions of your DSL.

Whatever strategy you use, make sure it addresses the following issues that frequently come up with respect to the evolution of any specific software module:

- Handling backward compatibility
- Catering to specific user needs that you can't roll out for general use

Many of these concerns are also applicable to software deployment in general and aren't specific to DSLs. In the following section, we'll discuss some of the practices you can follow during your design phase that will address many of these versioning issues.

9.4.2 *Best practices for a smoother evolution of DSL*

Suppose you're using a third-party DSL in your application that's been deployed in multiple customer locations. You need to add more features in your application when you discover that the new version of the DSL has exactly what you want. But the new version isn't backward compatible with the version that you've been using. What are you going to do?

Consider another scenario where your DSL models the business rules of securities trading that can vary with the stock exchange where it's deployed. It so happens that some of these rules change only for the Tokyo Stock Exchange and you need to roll out a new version that's specific to the Tokyo deployments. Yikes! The horror stories about trying to manage multiple versions simultaneously are legend.

Let's look at some of the things that you can do upfront to mitigate these teething problems and keep them from haunting you through many sleepless nights.

IMPLICIT CONTEXT FOR BETTER VERSION EVOLUTION

Consider this fluent API-based internal DSL snippet in Ruby that we discussed in section 4.2.1:

```
Account.create do
    number      "CL-BXT-23765"
    holders     "John Doe", "Phil McCay"
    address     "San Francisco"
    type        "client"
    email       "client@example.com"

end.save.and_then do |a|
  Registry.registNer(a)
  Mailer.new
      .to(a.email_address)
      .cc(a.email_address)
      .subject("New Account Creation")
      .body("Client account created for #{a.no}")
      .send
end
```

In this DSL, the account creation process uses the *implicit context* pattern of internal DSL design. This pattern makes the DSL easier to evolve when compared to the approach of making them fixed-position parameters to the create method. In the Account abstraction, you can add additional attributes without impacting existing clients.

AUTOMATIC TRANSFORMATION FOR BACKWARD COMPATIBILITY

You can use this strategy to offer an automatic transformation of the older APIs to the newer ones, with appropriate defaults. Consider this snippet of a Scala DSL for defining a fixed income trade that we discussed in section 6.4.1:

```
val fixedIncomeTrade =
  200 discount_bonds IBM
➥     for_client NOMURA on NYSE at 72.ccy(USD)
```

Users were using this DSL happily. Trades were being made using the specific currency as mentioned in the DSL (USD in the snippet). This currency is called the *trading currency*. Eventually trades get settled through a settlement process, but our DSL assumed that the settlement of the trade was also being done in the same currency. As we all know, rules change, and one day users got a notification that a trade can be settled in a currency that's different than the trading currency (called the *settlement currency*). Accordingly, the newer version of the DSL becomes:

```
val fixedIncomeTrade =
  200 discount_bonds IBM
➥     for_client NOMURA on NYSE at 72.ccy(USD)
➥     settled in JPY
```

The question is what happens to the DSLs that were written using the earlier version of your engine? Those earlier DSLs are probably going to explode, because the underlying model won't have a valid value for the settlement currency.

You can address this problem by defining an automatic transformation within the semantic model that sets up the default value of the settlement currency to the value of the trading currency. If you do this, users will have a migration path to follow and the earlier versions of the DSL will continue to run happily ever after.

A DSL FACADE CAN ADDRESS A LOT OF VERSIONING PROBLEMS

Remember the DSL facade we talked about in section 5.2.1? A facade acts as a protector of your model APIs and helps you do manipulations with the syntax that you publish for your DSL users. When you need to make changes to the DSL syntax in future versions, you can localize your changes within the DSL facade without having any impact on the underlying model. This strategy works great if you need to roll out small syntax changes as part of newer versions of your DSL.

FOLLOW THE PRINCIPLES OF WELL-DESIGNED ABSTRACTIONS

I've detailed principles of well-designed abstractions in appendix A. Read them, and then read them again. Every DSL you design must follow these principles if they're going to evolve gracefully for your users. You need to version your DSL just like you need to version your APIs. The more rigid your APIs become, the more difficult it'll be to make them evolve with newer versions.

Whatever option you choose, you need to make it possible to use multiple versions of the DSL in a single application. This area of DSL development is still evolving and needs more time to mature. You can help by carefully considering the future needs of your DSL users.

9.5 *Summary*

Here we are, at the concluding summary of the final chapter of the book. By now, you've been through all the aspects of how DSLs give you a better way to model your domain. In this chapter, we've looked at some of the future trends of DSL-based development. DSL workbenches promise more disciplined evolution of your DSL through an appropriate toolset that handles the complete lifecycle of your language. We're seeing regular programming languages getting more expressive by the day, making them more suitable for use as the host language for your DSL. Whatever language you decide to use for developing your DSL, make sure you follow the discipline that helps you grow your DSL incrementally and iteratively.

In this book, I've discussed some of the JVM languages that have great features for designing DSLs. Besides standing out individually as powerful languages for DSL design, all of them nicely interoperate with Java using the common runtime of the JVM. This is a big plus, because as a user, you're no longer restricted to using *only* one language for your DSL needs.

Besides these JVM languages, we're seeing lots of other languages that are being used extensively for designing expressive DSLs. Haskell, the pure functional language, and Erlang, the language that supports concurrency-oriented programming, are the forerunners in this development. The software development community has realized that the only way to manage the complexity of domain modeling is to use languages that offer higher-order abstractions. DSL-driven development is one of the ways that make these abstractions into beautiful and reusable artifacts. A good DSL enhances productivity, makes code more maintainable and portable, and offers a friendly interface to the users. All of the unnecessary details are hidden away. A DSL is the way you should model a domain. We've already started to see the potential of DSLs in the real world of software development today.

Key takeaways & best practices

- DSL-based application development is a relatively new topic in software. *Keep an eye on the growing trends that are developing today.*
- *Tool support in DSL-based development is rapidly improving.* Starting with IDEs and going down to native DSL workbenches, a rich set of tools always promotes the development of an ecosystem.
- *Every new language that becomes popular has something special to offer in DSL design.* Even if your favorite language doesn't offer the same feature out of the box, you can try to emulate it if the feature offers tangible value-add to the development and implementation of DSLs.

9.6   References

1 *Xtext User Guide.* http://www.eclipse.org/Xtext/documentation/latest/xtext.html.

2 *Meta Programming System.* http://www.jetbrains.com/mps/.

3 Intentional Software. http://intentsoft.com/.

4 Newspeak. http://newspeaklanguage.org/.

5 Tolksdorf, Stephan. FParsec—A Parser Combinator Library for F#. http://www.quanttec.com/fparsec/.

6 Double, Chris. Javascript Parser Combinators. *Bluish Coder.* http://www.bluish-coder.co.nz/2007/10/javascript-parser-combinators.html.

7 Pretterhofer, Lorenz. Scheme Parser Combinators. *A Lexical Mistake.* http://alexicalmistake.com/2008/06/scheme-parser-combinators/.

8 Eisenberg, Andrew. Extending Groovy Eclipse for use with Domain-Specific Languages. *Contraptions for programming.* http://contraptionsforprogramming.blogspot.com/2009/12/extending-groovy-eclipse-for-use-with.html.

9 Pech, Vaclav. Custom Groovy DSL Support. *JetBrains Zone.* http://jetbrains.dzone.com/articles/custom-groovy-dsl-support.

10 Template Haskell. *HaskellWiki.* http://www.haskell.org/haskellwiki/Template_Haskell.

11 Meta OCaml. http://www.metaocaml.org/.

appendix A
Role of abstractions
in domain modeling

You should treat this appendix as a prelude to the entire discussion on DSLs. A DSL is nothing but a layer of abstraction over an underlying implementation model. The implementation model is nothing but an abstraction on top of the problem domain model, using the technology platform of the solution domain. Unless you get it right, your domain model won't be at the correct level of abstraction, and the linguistic representation of it in the DSL won't be either. Let's see how you can make your abstractions shine.

A.1 *Qualities of well-designed abstractions*

This section focuses on the qualities of well-designed abstractions. I'll use the fields of software engineering and program design as points of reference, but I'll specifically focus on how having a well-designed abstraction makes it easier for you to design reusable domain models. As we go down this road together, you'll learn to appreciate how abstractions play a central role in designing complex domain models. As you learn to abstract more and more, you'll become increasingly proficient at distilling the core concepts of a model from the redundancies of the surrounding details. To illustrate my points, I'll discuss specific qualities that differentiate well-designed abstractions from poorly designed ones.

This section contains an informal discussion of the virtues that well-designed abstractions have. In the course of this discussion I'll present code snippets that demonstrate implementation aspects of these qualities. Depending on the aspect that I'm talking about, I've chosen the language that explains the feature in the most expressive way. Though there's a definite emphasis on OO programming paradigms, I've also used functional programming principles to implement a number of examples. If you're not comfortable with some of the languages used, this isn't the time to reach over to the bookshelves. The examples are simple enough and intuitive enough to explain the relevant design principles without your needing to dig around for more information about the specific language. You also have appendixes C through F in case you need to peek at some of the features that these languages offer.

Every abstraction has a functionality to deliver to its clients. To deliver this functionality, the abstraction publishes a set of *contracts* (also known as *interfaces*) that the clients can use. This set of contracts can vary, depending on the nature of the client. Each contract has an underlying *implementation* that's usually abstracted away from the client; the client sees only the published contracts.

In the rest of this section, I'll introduce the qualities of a well-designed abstraction. Later I'll talk about each in depth.

A.1.1 Minimalism

Depending on the nature of the client, you might decide to expose a certain amount of implementation detail. But here's the catch: all the details that you expose get published, and the client gets coupled to it. You need to be sure to expose only the essence that's required to fulfill the contract that your abstraction promises to the client. We'll discuss this issue in more detail in section A.2 when we talk about the *minimality* of abstractions.

A.1.2 Distillation

When we talk about well-engineered abstractions, it means that we've ensured that none contains nonessential details that don't belong to the core concerns of the abstraction. Abstraction implementations should be pure enough to minimize the details, yet still convey the necessary meaning. The process of creating such an abstraction is called the *distillation* of the abstraction; we'll discuss this in more detail in section A.3.

A.1.3 Extensibility and composability

Engineering is about designing things in a modular way. You can extend modular artifacts through composition. In addition to being extendable, software abstractions also need to be *extensible*. An abstraction that you design today might have to be extended with additional functionalities in the future. The important point is that this extension shouldn't break when existing clients try to use it. Section A.4 takes a detailed look at how to implement seamlessly extensible abstractions using techniques offered by current programming languages.

Extensibility is possible only through *composability*. Well-behaved abstractions can be composed to form higher-level abstractions. How do you design abstractions that compose? And what happens if your abstractions have side effects that update the global context of execution?

After you get to know the qualities to look for in well-designed abstractions, you'll be able to appreciate the role that abstractions play in designing domain models. You'll also have an idea of why you need to design abstractions at the correct level to ensure that your model speaks the language of the domain. Only then will your code be as expressive as the language of the person who's an expert in the domain.

A.2 *Minimalism publishes only what you promise*

Suppose that in your financial brokerage application, you need to design an abstraction that publishes to the external world the various prices of an instrument, based on a set of price types. Every instrument that gets traded on a stock exchange has a number of prices—opening price, closing price, and market price, to name a few. Your abstraction should have a method `publish` that accepts a specific instrument and a list of price types. It should return a Map with the price type as the *key*, and the corresponding price of that instrument as the *value*. Here's your first attempt in Java:

```
class InstrumentPricePublisher {
    public HashMap<PRICE_TYPE, BigDecimal> publish(Instrument ins,
        List<PRICE_TYPE> types) {
            HashMap<PRICE_TYPE, BigDecimal> m =
                new HashMap<PRICE_TYPE, BigDecimal>();     ❶ Populate
        //..                                                  HashMap
        return m;
    }
}
```

You intended to have the method `publish` return a Map of the price type and the price for a particular instrument. But the implementation returns a specialization of the Map abstraction—a HashMap—the method uses internally to store the data. By returning a specialization of the abstraction, it exposes the underlying implementation to the client. The client's code now becomes coupled to the HashMap ❶ that's returned from your published contract.

Suppose that later on you need to change the implementation of the underlying data structure to TreeMap. You can't do that, because it would break your client's code. Your abstraction can't evolve! How could you have avoided this problem?

A.2.1 *Evolve by being generic*

Hindsight is 20/20, and unfortunately that's what you're faced with here. You need to be sure that your initial abstraction returns the most generic type that satisfies the promise of your contract. This promise is to return a Map, a data structure that supports a key/value pair, based on lookup strategy. Here's the correct version of the abstraction, which minimizes the exposure of the implementation and returns the right level of refinement for your abstraction:

```
class InstrumentPricePublisher {
    public Map<PRICE_TYPE, BigDecimal> publish(Instrument ins,
        List<PRICE_TYPE> types) {
        Map<PRICE_TYPE, BigDecimal> m = Collections.emptyMap();
        for(PRICE_TYPE type : types) {
            m.put(type, getPrice(sec, type));
        }
        return m;
    }
}
```

Now that you've seen a concrete example, what do you think is the key symptom that lets you know that your abstraction has violated the principle of minimality of publication? Let's explore some of the fundamental concepts that can help you make this diagnosis.

A.2.2 *Subtyping to prevent implementation leak*

As we all know, inheritance is a technique used in OO to model the commonality and variabilities of an abstraction. The behavior that you define in a base abstraction can be overridden for further refinements down the hierarchy. The more you move toward the leaves in the hierarchy, the more refined the abstractions become and the more specialized the published contracts tend to be. To make successive refinements to your abstractions, you can use inheritance to model *subtyping*. In subtyping, as the term suggests, subtypes must inherit *only* the contracts from the supertype; the specific implementation of the contract is left to the subtype itself. I've created figure A.1 to illustrate this concept.

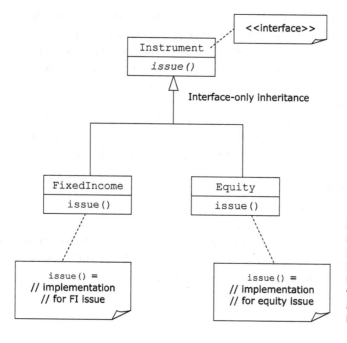

Figure A.1
Subtyping through interface inheritance. Subtypes FixedIncome and Equity inherit only the interface from the supertype Instrument and provide their own implementations.

The more specialized types are referred to as the subtypes of the more generalized ones. Subtyping doesn't imply that an implementation is shared within type hierarchies. Class-based OO languages like Java and C# implement subtyping using *interface inheritance* [2]. But in most such languages, subtyping is often used synonymously with subclassing, which results in confusing semantics and brittle abstraction hierarchies. Used correctly, interface inheritance is a useful tool that you can use to design robust hierarchies of types within abstraction families. When you extend abstractions using only subtyping, implementations can never leak out; you're left with an abstraction that is a good example of minimality.

One problem that crops up when you specialize behaviors using inheritance is that implementations are shared within the hierarchy, a situation commonly referred to as *implementation inheritance.*

A.2.3   *Implementation inheritance done right*

Implementation inheritance is a useful technique, when you use it correctly. It's easy to abuse, and when you do you get situations where your subclasses become unnecessarily coupled to the implementation of your base class. This situation is shown in figure A.2.

Now, subclasses are also clients of your base class, and in this situation implementation has leaked into them. The resulting scenario is commonly referred to as the *fragile base class* problem in OO modeling. In such situations, any change in the implementation of

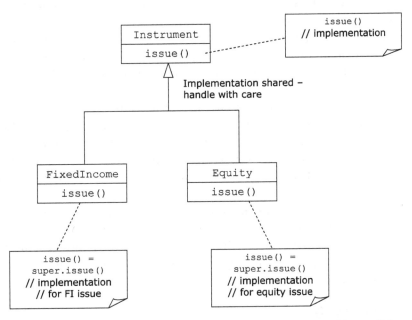

Figure A.2   Coupling in implementation inheritance. Implementation of `issue()` in `FixedIncome` and `Equity` reuses the implementation from the super class.

the base class can potentially break the contracts of the subclass, which makes the evolution of abstractions almost impossible. This situation is similar to what we faced with
`InstrumentPricePublisher` earlier. The root problem is that the base abstraction has
published its implementation to its clients.

The big thing to remember from the examples in this section is: *publish only
what you need to, and only to whom you need.* If you don't follow this advice, you risk
overexposure, your abstractions will leak implementations, and you'll violate the
minimality principle.

A.3 *Distillation keeps only what YOU need*

As we discussed in section A.1, an abstraction needs to publish only the core essence
to its clients, which makes it minimal from the outside looking in. It's also equally
important to ensure that the abstraction you design is clean in its internals as well. Distillation is the process of extracting the essence of something. In the context of
abstraction design, distillation is the process of purifying your abstractions' implementations by getting rid of all the *nonessential details.*

A.3.1 *What is nonessential?*

I sense some of you murmuring, "How do I know which part of an implementation is
nonessential? I'll repeat what the experts say: you'll know this when you have the
experience to look into your abstractions with sufficient insight and clarity. Defined
informally, a detail in an abstraction design is said to be nonessential when it doesn't
map as one of its core concerns.

Suppose you're using a word processor to draft one of your job applications for the
position of Domain Modeler. You start typing and the word processor starts highlighting words that get thrown out by its built-in spell checker as invalid. When was the last
time you bothered to check the exact version of the spell checker that the word processor came with? Or when you had to take special steps to initialize the spell checker
when you started the word processor? You always assume that the spell check function
in the word processor is set up correctly and is fully functional. If you had to bother
about its availability and do special steps to set it up every time you typed a word, that
would be a good example of you having to handle a nonessential detail as part of your
regular process.

Once again I'll take a use a common pattern in class-based OO programming to
explain the basic concepts of how to distill an abstraction out of its nonessential
details. I'll use an example from the domain of financial brokerage systems. If you're
not familiar with the domain, this might be a good time to go through some of the
concepts that I introduced in the sidebars in sections 1.2 and 1.3.

A.3.2 *Accidental complexity*

Suppose you have to design an abstraction `TradeProcessor` that processes a collection
of trades that's supplied to it. Then it computes the trade details like net trade value,

tax, fees, and commissions applicable for the trade, and other information relevant to the market in which it's being traded. The following listing shows one abstraction that you might design.

Listing A.1　`TradeProcessor` processes trade details

```
class TradeProcessor {
    private SettlementDateCalculator calculator;
    public TradeProcessor() {
        try {
            calculator = new SettlementDateCalculatorImpl(..);
        } catch (InitializationException ex) { //.. }
    }
    public void process(List<Trade> trades) {
        for(Trade trade: trades) {
            calculator.settleOn(trade.getTradeDate());
        }
        // other processing
    }
}
```

As part of trade enrichment, the `TradeProcessor` needs to calculate the settlement date, and the computation needs to consider lots of factors from the context in which the trade was executed. `SettlementDateCalculator` is responsible for providing this service. Assume for the time being that `SettlementDateCalculator` is a separate interface with an implementation `SettlementDateCalculatorImpl` that has the specific responsibility of computing the settlement date from the trade date and a host of other context information. The constructor for `TradeProcessor` creates an instance of `SettlementDateCalculatorImpl` and stores it in its context for subsequent use by the `process` method. This means that the `TradeProcessor` instance is now responsible for the lifecycle management of the service that it instantiates. `SettlementDateCalculatorImpl` might have a complex constructor that needs to collaborate with other services to instantiate successfully.

What happens if any of those services fail to instantiate? If that happens, then the `TradeProcessor` class is responsible for handling these chains of exceptions within its constructor and arranging for appropriate recovery mechanisms. Is this something that should be a concern of the domain abstraction for `TradeProcessor`?

`TradeProcessor` is a domain object. You, as the designer, should think of it only in terms of how it collaborates with the behavior of other domain objects and services to deliver what it promises to its clients. Instantiating and managing the lifecycle of services aren't things that fall under the core responsibilities of this domain abstraction. This example shows how a domain object might be designed to handle nonessential complexities that would be better handled by some lower layers of the architecture stack. Fred Brooks calls this *accidental complexity* (see [1] in A.6). Some prefer to use the term *incidental complexity*.

When you minimize accidental complexity in your abstractions, you can be sure that your abstractions will be at the proper level. As an application software designer, be sure to delegate instantiation and lifecycle management of collaborating services to lower-level frameworks like dependency injection (DI) containers.

At every step in the design process, look back to verify whether the abstraction is distilled enough and whether any lower-level details have leaked into higher-level abstractions. The class `TradeProcessor` illustrates an example where accidental complexity needs to be removed by redistributing responsibilities across the layers of the architecture stack.

A.3.3 *Removing the impurities*

The solution, as has been prescribed for many problems in computer science, is to introduce an extra level of indirection between your domain abstraction and the language of implementation. This layer acts as the insulation that protects your domain abstractions from getting polluted with accidental complexity.

Before we think about how to distill the impurities out of this abstraction, let's take a fresh look at what constitutes the impurities that we need to remove. Here's another view of the relevant section of the abstraction in the following listing, annotated to show the information that needs to be removed.

Listing A.2 `TradeProcessor` annotated with nonessential details

```
class TradeProcessor {
    private final SettlementDateCalculator calculator;
    public TradeProcessor() {                               ➊ Lifecycle
        try {                                                   management
            calculator = new SettlementDateCalculatorImpl(..);  code
        } catch (InitializationException ex) { //..  }
    }                                                       ➋ Exception handling
}                                                              for service failure
```

`TradeProcessor` manages the lifecycle of the service `SettlementDateCalculator` by instantiating a concrete implementation ➊ within the constructor. This has the following effects:

- `TradeProcessor` is now dependent on one specific concrete implementation of the service.

  When you write unit tests for `TradeProcessor`, you need to make sure that the collaborating service instance is available, along with all other dependent services. This goes against the principles of unit-testability of an abstraction, and also makes the abstraction less reusable outside this specific context of implementation.

- The constructor of `TradeProcessor` is now polluted with error handling code ➋ that arises out of the instantiation logic of `SettlementDateCalculatorImpl`.

The code is now noisy with details that shouldn't be the primary concern of `TradeProcessor`.

Do you have a better idea of what constitutes the nonessential details of an abstraction? Great! Now let's try to fix them.

A.3.4 *Keeping away implementation details using DI*

All we need to do is remove the lifecycle concerns of `SettlementDateCalculator` from `TradeProcessor`. Whenever `TradeProcessor` needs one `SettlementDateCalculator`, we'll supply an instance from outside, which is the correct way to do it. `TradeProcessor` doesn't need to bother about the exact concrete implementation of the instance that it receives, because now it's going to be insulated from the instantiation, management, and finalization of the services that it needs to collaborate with. *Dependency injection* (DI) will do this for us.

> **DEFINITION** A DI framework is an external container that creates, assembles, and wires the dependencies into an object graph through declarative configuration code. For more details on the various techniques of DI, refer to [2] in section A.6.

We're going to use Guice, the DI framework from Google, (http://code.google.com/p/google-guice/) and wire up our dependencies on specific implementations of `SettlementDateCalculator`. The following listing shows how the distilled abstraction looks.

Listing A.3 `TradeProcessor` distilled

```
class TradeProcessor {
    private final SettlementDateCalculator calculator;       Annotation
    @Inject                                                  for injection
    public TradeProcessor(SettlementDateCalculator calculator) {
        this.calculator = calculator;                        Clean
    }                                                        constructor
    //.. as in listing A.2
}
```

`TradeProcessor` is now relieved of its nonessential details and the instantiation logic is removed to an external framework. All you need to know now is how we'll tie up the implementation of `SettlementDateCalculator` with the `TradeProcessor` class. We have to configure an external `Module` in Guice that does the wiring when the application bootstraps. I won't go into the details of how Guice works. The main idea is that by introducing an external framework, we've been able to get rid of all the nonessential details in our original abstraction.

DI is only one of the techniques you can use to distill your abstractions from accidental complexities. Many language implementations offer powerful features that obviate the need to use an external framework for such purposes. We look at one such example when we discuss the powerful and extensible static type system of Scala in chapter 6. Functional programming also offers higher-order functions and closures that let you externalize functionalities that don't need to be handled within your abstraction. We explore many such capabilities in chapter 5 when we go into the details of using functional programming features in designing domain models.

A.4   Extensibility helps piecemeal growth

You've followed the principles discussed in sections A.2 and A.3, and now your abstractions have the right exposure (through minimalism) and purity (through distillation). But now your client requests that you incorporate more features in the application and you have to incorporate additional behaviors in your abstractions. It's time for you to test whether your abstractions are extensible enough.

A.4.1   What's extensibility?

Extensibility is the quality that allows your abstractions to grow in a piecemeal manner without impacting existing clients. Different paradigms of development support different extensibility mechanisms. This section will give an overview on designing extensible abstractions using the more popular techniques from the realms of OO and functional programming. We discuss other forms of extensibility when we talk about advanced language features and higher-level abstractions in chapters 5 through 8.

The `Map` abstraction in Java contains the basic functionalities of an associative data structure and provides a `Dictionary` interface to its clients. `java.util.Map` has been extended in a number of ways within the standard JDK library. On one hand, you have the concrete subclass implementations like `HashMap` and `TreeMap` that offer all the `Map` operations over different underlying storage mechanisms. On the other hand, `Map` gets richer behavioral semantics by being subtyped into `SortedMap` and `ConcurrentMap`.

How extensible is `java.util.Map`? Suppose you need to add specific behavior to `java.util.Map` that should work across all variations and implementations of the `Map` interface. Think about this, because it's not as trivial as it seems when you consider the options that Java offers as a language.

Extending any specific implementation like `HashMap` won't work, because if you do that, the additional functionality won't be available to other implementations of `Map`.

You could wrap an instance of `Map` into a decorator (see [3] in section A.6), but this solution would work only for certain specific use cases. In other use cases, wrapping `Map`s into your own classes takes away important aspects of the original `Map` instances, for example `SortedMap` or `ConcurrentMap`. Consider the following example:

```
class DecoratedMap<K, V> implements Map<K, V> {
    private final Map<K, V> m;
    public DecoratedMap(Map<K, V> m) {
        this.m = m;
    }
    //..
}
```

❶ Wrapped Map

Implementation of Map<K, V>

DecoratedMap<K, V> decorates the wrapped Map<K, V> **❶**, but can't use any of the features of the wrapped instance if the client passes a ConcurrentMap or a Sorted-Map in the constructor. Eugene discusses one such use case in [5] in A.5 where the only available option to provide an extended functionality across all Map implementations is to write a standalone utility function—not at all an OO approach from the purist point of view.

The last resort is to implement the Map interface ground-up. The problem with this is that it's going to result in lots of copy-paste code that duplicates across all such implementations.

After looking at all the alternatives, why do you think it's difficult to extend java.util.Map using a true OO approach?

In this case we have a hierarchy of abstractions and we're trying to plug in a new *behavior* across *all* implementations of the type java.util.Map. This problem is crying out for implementation inheritance, more specifically, *multiple* implementation inheritance, because we're talking about multiplicity of behaviors. What you need is the ability to compose *independent* granular abstractions that can seamlessly mix in the main abstraction additively to introduce new behavior or override existing ones. Mixins offer one such alternative, as you'll see in the next section.

A.4.2 *Mixins: a design pattern for extensibility*

Mixins let you do exactly what's needed here. They've been implemented in many languages that offer the facility of building larger abstractions out of mixable attributes.

Consider a situation where the financial brokerage house you're consulting with decides to introduce a new instrument in the market, which they call *exotic instrument*. This exotic instrument has a number of features that are common to other instruments and that have already been implemented as part of your domain model. All you need to do is assemble these existing features and extend your abstraction for exotic instrument. With mixin-based programming, you can literally do this and mix the base abstraction for exotic instrument with all the individual features, forming the whole. Look at figure A.3, which illustrates this technique. The mixin classes Coupon-Payment, Maturable, and Tradable mixes in with the parent abstraction Instrument to provide *behavior and implementation* to the whole class ExoticInstrument.

Gilad Bracha, the computational theologist, in his OOPSLA (Object-Oriented Programming, Systems, Languages, and Applications) 90 paper (see [4] in section A.6), defines a *mixin* as *an abstract subclass that can be used to specialize the behavior of a variety of parent classes.* Mixins can't be used standalone, so they're called an abstract subclass. They define uniform class extensions and can be seamlessly tagged on to a family of abstractions to add the same behavior. Scala (http://www.scala-lang.org) offers mixin implementation in the form of *traits*. Ruby calls them m*odules*. Think of traits as Java interfaces, with the difference that the method declarations in the interface can also contain optional implementation that the base can share.

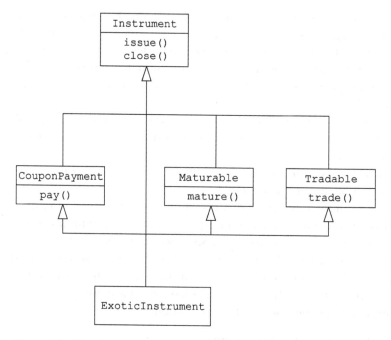

**Figure A.3   Mixin-based inheritance. ExoticInstrument gets the
implementation of issue() and close() from Instrument, then gets
composed from the mixins CouponPayment, Maturable, and Tradable.**

A.4.3   *Mixins for extending Map*

Now let's look at how you can use mixins to add a specific behavior across all implementations of the Map abstraction. Suppose you're asked to add a synchronized get method to Maps as an additional behavior overriding the existing API. First, you define a trait in Scala that provides an implementation of this behavior over the standard Map interface:

```
trait SynchronizedGet[A,B]  extends Map[A, B] {
  abstract override def get(key: A): Option[B] = synchronized {
    super.get(key)
  }
}
```

Now you can mix in this behavior with any variant of a Scala Map, irrespective of the underlying implementation:

```
val names = new HashMap[String, List[String]]
            with SynchronizedGet[String, List[String]]
```
**Mixing in with a
Scala HashMap**

```
val stuff = new scala.collection.jcl.LinkedHashMap
⟹ [String, List[String]]
            with SynchronizedGet[String, List[String]]
```
**Mixing in with a Java
LinkedHashMap**

Notice that in the final implementation, the trait SynchronizedGet is mixed in dynamically during runtime object creation.

Scala traits can also be mixed in statically as a composition of multiple attributes over an existing abstraction. Mixing in Scala traits results in a form of implementation inheritance that doesn't suffer from the drawbacks of the Java implementation. We discuss Scala traits in more detail when we talk about Scala's language features in chapter 6.

A.4.4 *Functional extensibility*

People often complain that OO programming makes them write lots of classes, often unnecessarily. Everything isn't an object, though OO sometimes would like you to feel that way. In the real world, many problems are better modeled as functional abstractions or rule-based abstractions.

Suppose you're modeling an algorithm that has a definite workflow, like in the following snippet. I've intentionally elided the arguments that the algorithm takes as input.

```
def process(...) = {
  try {
    if (init) proc
  } finally { end }
}
```

init is the initialization part of the algorithm. If init is successful, you invoke proc, which does the core processing. The end models the finalization part, which cleans up resources.

Now you're asked to extend this implementation for different variants of init, proc, and end. One option is to have separate objects for each of them wrapping the workflows as functors or function-objects. That would work, but you can do a better job by using the power of functional programming and higher-order functions. You can model init, proc, and end as functions and pass them as closures to the main process. Here's how:

```
def process(init: =>Boolean, proc: =>Unit, end: =>Unit) = {        Generic
  try {                                                             algorithm
    if (init) proc
  } finally {
    end
  }
}
def doInit = { //.. }              Initialization    Core
def doProcess = { //.. }                             processing
def doEnd = { //.. }               Finalization
```

Now let's look at an unconventional way to extend your abstraction. This technique is not supported by all languages, but it can be an effective tool, if you use it judiciously within your application.

A.4.5   *Extensibility can be monkey business too*

You don't have to build new abstractions to make what you have more extensible. Many languages offer *open classes* that let you directly extend existing structures by injecting new methods or updating existing ones. Both Ruby and Groovy support open classes and let you crack open any class and make changes to existing behavior. Doing this is typically called monkey patching. It's also frowned upon by many developers as being extremely unsafe. Even though monkey patching can be extremely powerful when you use it responsibly, there are lots of practical examples in current application development that testify against its professed virtues.

The main issue with Ruby monkey patching is that it lacks lexical scoping; anything and everything you add to an abstraction goes in the global namespace and remains visible to every other user of the same abstraction. Scala offers a much better alternative in the form of *lexically scoped open classes*. (For my own take on this Scala feature, see http://debasishg.blogspot.com/2008/02/why-i-like-scalas-lexically-scoped-open.html.) Scala calls it implicits, and they let you extend existing classes through a lexically scoped implicit conversion. This feature is unbelievably useful and strikes the perfect balance between Ruby's unsafe monkey patching and Java's strictly closed classes.

A.5   *Composability comes from purity*

Lots of studies have tried to teach limited forms of human language to other great apes. Gorillas and chimpanzees have been able to pick up and communicate through symbols and sign languages and even through a limited form of combinations of the human protolanguage. Although their vocabulary continued to grow, the area in which they failed to develop and improve was the composition of those languages into meaningful phrases. The human brain has a region known as Broca's area, which is responsible for our ability to produce grammatical sentences. This ability makes our communication meaningful, coherent, and contextual in the real world. Software abstractions that model the real world also need to define and publish contracts that enable them to interact in a similarly meaningful way.

In our daily use of computers, the operating system regularly downloads packages, updates, and newer versions. Not all these components have been developed by the same person or even at the same time. Still, all of them communicate effectively and compose seamlessly, abstracting all the implementation differences away from you.

Today we're part of a software development ecosystem where a single programming language doesn't define the layer of compatibility. We have powerful runtimes and middleware hosting multiple languages, protocols, and distribution mechanisms that can communicate with each other. When you develop an application, you use multiple languages to develop software components. These components can range from a few lines of code to hundreds or thousands of lines. You want to be able to compose them as prefabricated units of work that can plug in seamlessly with the rest of the ecosystem of your application infrastructure.

OO programming uses techniques like aggregation, parameterization, and inheritance that help you develop large abstractions from small ones. But these techniques have their own pitfalls that you need to consider every time you use them. For example, implementation inheritance in Java can lead to unnecessary coupling between class structures, making them less extensible. If you adhere to the recommended best practices of design patterns, you'll be able to avoid such pitfalls. I discussed one such pattern in section A.3 when I told you how DI can help remove unnecessary details from your component and distill it of its impurities. Now let's look at a few more ways that design patterns can help you.

A.5.1 Design patterns for composability

Consider one of the common design patterns used to abstract a set of actions from the clients. Gamma, et. al. (see [3] in section A.6) calls it the Command pattern. The intent of the Command design pattern is to encapsulate a request as an object. Then you can parameterize clients with different requests, queue or log requests, and support undoable operations. Figure A.4 illustrates the structure that the Command pattern forces on your abstraction.

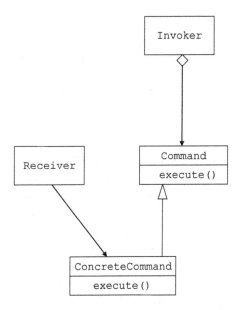

Figure A.4 Command decouples invoker and receiver from the actions. This makes the command object reusable outside the current context of execution.

The Command design pattern decouples the invoker and the receiver from the command that's being executed. This makes your individual commands *reusable* outside the context of the invoker and the receiver. You can even implement higher-level commands by aggregating individual units of commands. Commands are *composable*, by aggregation. Figure A.5 shows how you can design a `MacroCommand` using aggregation-based composability.

The Command design pattern, along with its composite variant, lets you compose at a macro level; you compose objects that are supposed to perform specific actions all by themselves. But suppose you're designing a UI and you need to be able to dynamically add and remove the individual features of your widget. You're going to need composability at a much lower level of granularity than what's possible with the Command pattern. In this case, every object you compose might have a different set of features that you assemble through the interface published by your abstraction.

Here's where you apply the Decorator pattern. You have a core object and you design a group of wrapper classes, the decorators, that share the same interface as

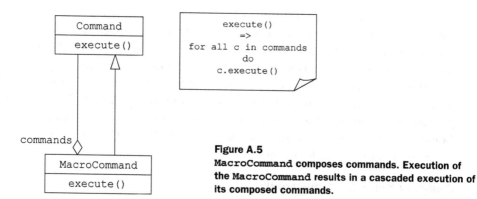

Figure A.5

`MacroCommand` **composes commands. Execution of the** `MacroCommand` **results in a cascaded execution of its composed commands.**

the core. You can dynamically attach and detach these decorators at the *object* level. The pattern provides an option for composition as an alternative to subclassing and implementation inheritance. You'll find that there are quite a few structural and behavioral patterns that are followed by the community of OO programmers for designing composable class structures. Look at [3] in section A.6 for a detailed discussion about each of these.

A.5.2 *Back to languages*

Over time, many of the design patterns that I've discussed earlier have been subsumed into modern OO and functional languages. As I discussed in section A.3, both Scala and Ruby have built-in support for mixin-based inheritance. Mixin classes are a great way to compose abstractions and are the right way to implement multiple inheritance. Scala's support for object-based mixins is an implementation of the Decorator pattern.

Besides modular mixin composition, Scala's advanced type system also supports other mechanisms that promote composability of abstractions. I discuss them in more detail when I talk about Scala as an implementation language for complex domain models in chapter 6. This section will focus on the developments on the horizon of programming languages that are becoming more and more powerful, subsuming more design patterns and best practices in the realm of language implementation.

PROTOTYPE-BASED OO

Consider another form of OO, one that doesn't have classes. Objects are the only form of abstraction that models behavior of entities. If you want to share behaviors, mark one object as the parent form of another. You don't have any static inheritance hierarchies in this model; all the problems of implementation inheritance innate to class-based OO suddenly disappear. JavaScript is based on this model, which is called the *prototype-based* model of OO, as opposed to the *class-based* model that we've already discussed. Let's see how the problem of object composition is handled by another perspective of OO that these languages take.

In the following JavaScript example, I'll define an object `instrument`, which serves as the *prototypal* object for all instruments. The term *prototypal* indicates that the object `instrument` serves as the base, which will be shared by all other objects that implement the same contract. A specialized variant of `instrument`, the `fixed_income` object, adds its own special behavior on top of the implementation provided by `instrument`. At the implementation level, `fixed_income` has a pointer to its parent object, which we call its *prototype*. In this case, the prototype is the `instrument` object.

The thought process behind this setup is simple. When you invoke a method on an object, the receiver matches the method (also called the *message*) to its own set of contracts (or messages). If the receiver doesn't find a match, it forwards the message to its prototype to see if the prototype can respond to that message. The method continues to be forwarded until one of the prototypes responds or we reach the root `Object`.

Sharing knowledge through prototypes at the object level is called *delegation*. Delegation helps you to dynamically compose abstractions at the lowest level of granularity.

```
var instrument = {
  issue: function() { //..  }
  close: function() { //..  }
  //..
}                                                    Sets the prototype
var fixed_income = Object.beget(instrument);    ←⌐   to instrument
fixed_income.mature = function() { //.. }
```

> Use the form of OO that helps you model your problem in the best possible way. Language should never be a constraint. Instead of writing boilerplate code to implement design patterns, look around at your choices. A powerful language might offer more succinct options.

When a design pattern gets subsumed in the implementation of a language, it might not be as explicit in structure as it was previously. In fact, it melds to the language itself as a natural idiom. Ruby metaprogramming is one such example.

METAPROGRAMMING (IT'S EVERYWHERE)

When you implement the Builder pattern in Java, you need to include lots of extra embellishments, but with Ruby metaprogramming, it's a natural idiom. Take a look at Jim Weirich's markup builder implementation that uses the clever trick of Ruby's `method_missing`. (To see this implementation, go to http://github.com/jimweirich/builder/tree/master.) DI similarly melds into the way Ruby usually constructs new objects. Strategy pattern can be implemented directly either through Ruby modules or by using the ability of Ruby to strip open a class and change its implementation during runtime.

A.5.3 *Side effects and composability*

Let's talk some more about the Command design pattern that I mentioned earlier. It encapsulates a user action and gives you a way to compose many of them as a higher level of abstraction. By user action I mean something the user does on an object that produces a result. But another effect of the action might be in the form of some side effect that it produces. For example, the action might also print something on the console, issue a write to the database, raise an exception, or update some global state.

Side effects depend on past history—a debit action on your bank account that updates the balance as a side effect behaves differently depending on the current balance of the account. You can't ignore the order of evaluation and compilers can't do special optimizations like composition, memoization, or lazy evaluation. A side-effected program is hard to understand, and harder to analyze.

COMMAND-QUERY SEPARATION

How can you ensure that you have side effects under control in OOP? The solution is, once again, to use the design patterns, idioms, and best practices that have evolved over the years. A good example of such a pattern is *Command-Query Separation,* a term coined by Bertrand Meyer when he was designing the Eiffel language, and subsequently promoted by Martin Fowler here: http://www.martinfowler.com/bliki/CommandQuerySeparation.html. Queries are supposed to be pure actions that produce a result without mutating any global state or producing any side effect. Commands, on the other hand, are interesting only for the side effects they produce, which usually involves some sort of mutation of state. The pattern states that every abstraction should either be a *query* or a *command,* but never both.

> Side effects never compose. Use the Command-Query Separation pattern to ensure that you've segregated queries from commands in your model. If you do, you'll have control over all the side-effecting abstractions.

Functional programming rarely uses side effects, and even when it does, some languages have special annotations that explicitly publish the exact side effect that it produces. Not all functional languages restrict side effects. Haskell does, and it does it through its static type system. You can't pass a side-effected abstraction to a function where it expects purity.

HASKELL EXAMPLES

Let's go back to our Command pattern that we modeled with objects. For a parallel in the functional world, let's apply two functions, f and g, in sequence, to every element of a collection. If we used our implementation from section A.5.1, we would've had a macro command composed of two individual commands encapsulating the functions f and g respectively (maybe as function objects). Here's how you can do something similar, but much more simply, in Haskell:

```
map f (map g lst)
```

map is a Haskell *combinator* that invokes a user-supplied function over all elements in a list. In this snippet, function g will be applied first on every element of the list lst, which generates an intermediate list structure. The outer map will apply f on every element of the intermediate list to generate the final output list. This operation is the way things usually work and is similar to the way our previous MacroCommand works.

Remember that Haskell is a pure functional language and doesn't allow effecting functions to be passed in places that expect purity. map happens to be a combinator that accepts only pure functions. Look at the type definition of map in Haskell:

```
Prelude> :t map
map :: (a -> b) -> [a] -> [b]
```

map is a function that takes another function (a->b) and a list [a] as input and generates another list [b] formed by applying the function over each element of the source list. When I invoke f or g with map, the compiler will accept it only if f and g are pure functions, without any side effects. Because f and g are guaranteed to be pure, the Haskell compiler can transform the invocation to map (f . g) lst. Instead of invoking the functions in succession, the compiler transformation invokes their composition on each element in the list. What this buys you is that the temporary data structure that was being generated in the previous case completely disappears. The guarantee of purity leads to better composability.

Now you must now be wondering how our OO Command in section A.5.1 was able to handle side effects. How can we do the same thing in the pure world of Haskell? Haskell implements the Command-Query Separation pattern at the language level. Consider the following functions:

```
f :: Int -> Int
g :: Int -> IO Int
```

The function f is a pure function that returns the same output every time it's given the same input. But g is a function that has side effects. You can determine this from the type declaration. The type g indicates that it returns an action that, when performed, might have side effects; then it returns a type of Int. For example, the function g might read from stdin or from a database, or it might modify a mutable state. Repeatedly invoking g won't produce the same results every time; the result depends on the history of actions that were already performed. Haskell's type system makes it explicit that f is a *query*, whereas g is a *command*.

Not all functional languages are as pure as Haskell. Most of them will let you use functions that have side effects without any explicit indication in the function signature. This does not negate the advantage of functional programming over OO construction with respect to composability. Functional programming is idiomatically practiced for purity and programmers find it natural to write that way. Side effects are considered aberrations in the functional world, whereas they're more natural in the OO world.

A.5.4　*Composability and concurrency*

Possibly the biggest advantage you have with composable abstractions is that they implement support for concurrent programming. Right now, you're probably using lock-based synchronization when you design concurrent abstractions that are meant to run in multithreaded environments. Designing for concurrency is hard, and it's made harder by the inherent nondeterminism in execution that thread-based models offer. Lock-based concurrency control doesn't compose; individually atomic operations synchronized on locks don't ensure atomicity when they're composed together. It's no wonder that research in computer science has been geared toward better abstractions for concurrency control.

Software transactional memory (STM) is one of the concurrency control structures that's been implemented successfully in languages like Haskell and Clojure. STM is an alternative to lock-based synchronization and gives you concurrency control that's analogous to database transactions for controlling access to shared memory within your programs. The primary advantage that STM brings to you is the ability to compose atomic operations into larger atomic operations.

Let me elaborate with a small example in Haskell. The following snippet of code implements an atomic transfer operation between two bank accounts.

```
transfer :: Account -> Account -> Int -> IO ()
transfer from to amount
  = atomically (do { credit to amount
                   ; debit from amount })
```

Even if you're not familiar with the nuances of the Haskell programming language, you don't need to run to the local bookstore right now. The example is fairly intuitive for understanding how a Haskell combinator `atomically` ensures that two individually atomic operations, `deposit` and `withdraw`, compose to form a larger atomic operation, `transfer`.

Composability is one of the recurring themes we'll visit repeatedly in part 2 of the book when we discuss how to implement higher-level abstractions using combinators. When you can compose abstractions and isolate side effects, then you can hope to make your abstractions more expressive.

A.6   References

1   Brooks, Frederick P. 1995. *The Mythical Man-Month: Essays on Software Engineering*, Anniversary Edition (2nd Edition). Addison-Wesley Professional.

2   Prasanna, Dhanji R. 2009. *Dependency Injection: Design Patterns Using Spring and Guice*. Manning Publications.

3   Gamma E., R. Helm, R. Johnson, and J. Vlissides. 1995. *Design Patterns: Elements of Reusable Object-Oriented Software*. Addison-Wesley Professional.

4   Bracha, Gilad, and William R. Cook. September 1990. *Mixin-based Inheritance. Proceedings of the European Conference on Object-Oriented Programming Systems, Languages, and Applications*, pp. 303-311.

5   Kuleshov, Eugene. February 2008. *It is safer not to invent safe hash map/Java*. http://www.jroller.com/eu/entry/not_invent_safe_hash_map.

appendix B
Metaprogramming
and DSL design

Metaprogramming is a technique that's commonly associated with designing DSLs. Using metaprogramming, you can write code that generates code. When you design a DSL, you can let the language runtime or the compile-time infrastructure generate code for you. This code might seem extremely verbose or boilerplate to your users. In this appendix, I'll discuss common techniques of metaprogramming used in designing DSLs and how you can use these techniques to make your DSL expressive and succinct.

B.1 The meta in the DSL

In section 2.1, you learn that the powerful metaprogramming capabilities of Groovy can help you write a more expressive DSL than Java can. Languages like Groovy and Ruby let you inflect dynamic runtime behaviors on objects. You can add capabilities on the fly that make the resultant semantics much more malleable. These dynamic behaviors are governed by the metaobject protocol (MOP) (see [5] in section B.8) that each of these languages implements in their runtime. The metaobject protocol of a language defines the semantics of the extensibility of the language artifacts. Take a look at the accompanying callout for a gentle introduction to the concept of MOP in programming languages.

> **DEFINITION** A meta-object is an abstraction that manipulates the behavior of other objects. In an OOP language, a metaclass might be responsible for creating and manipulating classes. To do that, the metaclass needs to store all information that's relevant to the class, like type, interface, methods, and extension objects.
>
> A meta-object protocol (MOP) for a language defines the semantics of the extensibility of programs written in that language. The behavior of the

program is determined by the MOP, including aspects of the program that can be extended by the programmer during compile time or runtime.

Metaprogramming is the ability to write programs that generate new programs or that change the behavior of existing programs. In an OO language like Ruby or Groovy, metaprogramming implies capabilities that extend existing object models, add hooks to alter the behaviors of existing methods (or even classes), and synthesize new methods, properties, or modules during runtime through introspection. Languages like Lisp use macros as the metaprogramming tool that let you syntactically extend the language during the compilation stage. Although the primary form of metaprogramming that's supported by Groovy or Ruby is runtime, Lisp metaprogramming is compile time, and doesn't incur any runtime overhead. (Both Groovy and Ruby have library support for compile-time metaprogramming through explicit manipulation of the ASTs. But it's nowhere near as elegant as Lisp. See section B.2 to see why.) Java also offers metaprogramming capabilities through *annotation processing* and *aspect-oriented programming* (AOP); it also defines all its extensibility mechanisms through its MOP.

Does your code generate code? This question is possibly the most important one to ask yourself when you're trying to determine whether your language is effective enough to implement a DSL. You can use metaprogramming to grow your host language toward the domain syntax; it's considered to be a potent force in DSL design. Statically typed languages like Haskell and OCaml that have traditionally relied on pure embedded semantics for designing DSLs now offer type-safe compile-time metaprogramming through extensions like Template Haskell and MetaOCaml respectively. For more information, see http://www.haskell.org/th/ and http://www.metaocaml.org/.

In this section, let's review the basic metaprogramming capabilities in some of today's languages that make them useful for designing a DSL. Part 2 of this book discusses each of these capabilities in greater detail, with lots of examples from the real world.

B.1.1   *Runtime metaprogramming in DSL implementation*

Why is metaprogramming support such an important feature for a language to host a DSL? The answer is that because metaprogramming support makes a language extensible, the DSL that you've implemented in an extensible language also becomes transitively extensible. OK, I'll admit that was a mouthful. Let's dig into an example so you can grasp this concept of extensibility when it comes to a DSL.

Consider figure B.1, which illustrates the execution model of a DSL in a language that supports runtime metaprogramming. If the MOP of the language supports extensibility of core language features, the DSL implementation can leverage this feature; programmers can alter or extend core behaviors on the collaborating objects. In this way, the DSL surface syntax remains concise, and the underlying implementation does all the heavy lifting in collaboration with the MOP of the language. Figure B.1 illustrates this behavior as a sample DSL snippet gets interpreted by the underlying

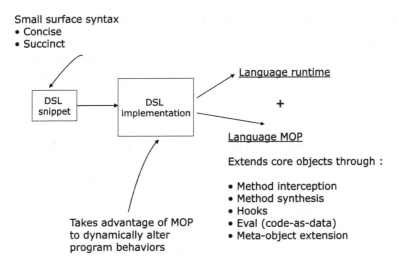

Small surface syntax
• Concise
• Succinct

DSL snippet

DSL implementation

Language runtime

+

Language MOP

Extends core objects through :

• Method interception
• Method synthesis
• Hooks
• Eval (code-as-data)
• Meta-object extension

Takes advantage of MOP to dynamically alter program behaviors

Figure B.1 The role of the language metamodel in DSL execution

implementation and finally processed through the combination of the core language runtime and the language metaprogramming behaviors.

Now that you've seen an abstract model of the role that metaprogramming plays in the DSL execution context, let's revisit our order-processing DSL and check out how the Groovy MOP plays a central role in adding to the expressivity of the language. See figure B.2 for a diagrammatic representation of the inflection points.

All the annotated parts in figure B.2 indicate points at which core language abstractions are dynamically altered or extended through metaprogramming support that Groovy's MOP defines. These extensions have been implemented as part of the DSL implementation, so the client contracts are concise and free of any incidental complexity.

Dynamic method injection into `Integer`

```
newOrder.to.buy(100.shares.of('IBM') {
    limitPrice 300
    allOrNone true
    valueAs {qty, unitPrice -> qty * unitPrice - 500}
}
```

Method synthesis using `methodMissing`

Dynamically invoke `call()` method of closure

Figure B.2 Groovy metaprogramming inflection points in our order-processing DSL

B.1.2 *Compile-time metaprogramming in DSL implementation*

As you see in chapter 2, the Groovy MOP extends the core language semantics to implement dynamic program behaviors during runtime. All code generation, method synthesis, and message interception take place when the program is being executed, which means that all meta-objects in Groovy and Ruby are the runtime artifacts of the language. Compile-time metaprogramming lets you construct and manipulate programs during compile time. You can define new constructs and interact with the compiler to perform syntactic transformations and application-specific optimizations. Isn't this in perfect harmony with Steele's vision (see [6] in section B.3) that "*a main goal in designing a language should be to plan for growth?*" Truly, with compile-time metaprogramming, you can grow a language seamlessly toward your domain syntax.

To use the most common form of compile-time metaprogramming you implement syntactic macros. Macro implementations vary in complexity and power, from the textual macros offered by C preprocessors to the sophisticated AST-based ones offered by variants of Lisp and some statically typed languages like Template Haskell and MetaOCaml. In this section, we'll take a detailed look at some of the capabilities that macros and compile-time metaprogramming add to the power of designing succinct DSLs.

Besides macros, some languages offer other preprocessor-based capabilities for compile-time metaprogramming, like the templates in C++, AOP, and annotation processing. Some languages like Groovy and Scala also have implementations of explicit compiler plugins, which provide some metaprogramming capabilities in the form of AST manipulation. We'll discuss these features later, though our main focus will be on macro-based implementations like those in the Lisp family of languages.

C++: TEMPLATES

C++ offers templates as one of the most dominant protocols for metaprogramming. C++ templates support powerful code-generation mechanisms through manipulation of data structures during compile time. This form of compile-time metaprogramming has been used quite successfully in scientific and numerical applications for generating inline versions of algorithms that employ techniques like loop unrolling for optimizing performance.

Another useful application of C++ metaprogramming is in techniques like expression templates (see [1] in section B.3) that can serve as a useful alternative to C-style callbacks. Instead of incurring the overhead of function calls associated with callback functions, expression templates let you put logical and algebraic expressions directly inline in the function body. The C++ array-processing library Blitz++ (see [2] in section B.3) uses this technique by creating parse trees of array expressions that are used to generate customized kernels. By generating code during compile time, these techniques have also been used to design DSLs that let programmers write code of the following form on higher-order data structures like vectors and matrices:

```
Vector<double> result(20), x(20), y(20), z(20);
result = (x + y) / z;
```

Besides generating code through template instantiation, C++ offers operator overloading as another primitive form of metaprogramming. As a follower of the C programming language, C++ also inherits the macro system processed by a preprocessor to the compiler. Languages belonging to the Lisp family make use of macros to provide support for compile-time metaprogramming. Let's look at those now.

LISP AND CLOJURE: MACROS

Lisp has the most sophisticated and complete support for compile-time metaprogramming, through its system of macros. Unlike C macros that have limited expressive power and that operate based on textual substitution, Lisp macros are powered by the full extensibility of the language.

When you have a macro call in your Lisp expression, the Lisp compiler doesn't evaluate the arguments. Instead, it passes them unevaluated to the macro code. The macro code is processed and returns a new Lisp form that's evaluated in place of the original macro form. This entire transformation of macro calls runs at compile time, generating code that consists of valid Lisp forms that are integrated with the AST of the main program. Look at figure B.3 for an illustration of the compile-time metaprogramming support that Lisp offers.

Besides the support of syntactic macros, the Common Lisp programming language has lots of other features that make it a natural fit for metaprogramming purposes. Its uniform representation of code and data, the recursive evaluation model, and the fact that it uses expression-based semantics as opposed to statement-based ones are some of the features that you'll enjoy using.

Clojure (http://www.clojure.org) is a Lisp implementation on the JVM that was written by Rich Hickey. Clojure offers metaprogramming through syntactic macros, much like Common Lisp does. Because Clojure is implemented on the JVM, it integrates seamlessly with Java and offers interoperability with Java objects. In the following sections, I'll use Clojure code snippets to demonstrate the Lisp way of DSL design. I'll be using the term Lisp for general reference to the paradigm that we're talking about. After all, Clojure *is* a Lisp. In section B.2 you'll find more details about how the

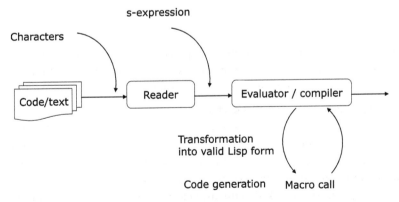

Figure B.3   Lisp uses macros to provide compile-time metaprogramming support

Lisp language design is aligned to expressive DSL implementation. If you want, look at figure B.3 again. It provides an abstract visualization of how Lisp macros generate code in the precompilation phase.

Let's go through the macro expansion process and how the final Lisp form that's evaluated by the compiler is generated. Suppose you've got the following DSL snippet that processes client orders and, based on some criteria, submits the order to the trading engine:

```
(when (and (> (value order) 1000000)
           (is-premium-client? client))
 (make-trade order broker)
 (update-journal client))
```

In that snippet, when is a macro that has the following form:

```
(defmacro when [test & body]
 (list 'if test (cons 'do body)))
```

When the Lisp compiler encounters the call to the macro, it doesn't have a runtime parameter to evaluate the arguments with. All that the compiler has is the source code. What it does is pass the following Lisp lists that represent the source code, unevaluated:

```
(and (> (value order) 1000000) (is-premium-client? client))
(make-trade order broker)
(update-journal client)
```

The compiler then runs the macro with these three list forms as the arguments. The parameter condition is bound to the list form (and (> (value order) 1000000) (is-premium-client? client)) and the forms (make-trade order broker) and (update-journal client) are bound to the &rest body parameter. The macro expansion takes place and is replaced with the following code, which is generated from the backquote expression in the macro body:

```
(if (and (> (value order) 1000000)
         (is-premium-client? client))
  (do
    (make-trade order broker)
    (update-journal client)))
```

Like the Groovy MOP, code generation takes place with Common Lisp macros as well, but unlike Groovy, it takes place during the precompilation phase. The Lisp runtime never sees any of the meta-objects; it works only on valid Lisp forms.

JAVA: ANNOTATION PROCESSING AND AOP SUPPORT

Java also supports a limited form of compile-time metaprogramming through annotation processing and support for AOP (see [4] in section B.3). You can use annotations in a Java program that get processed during build-time. These annotations generate code that can supplement or alter existing program behavior.

AspectJ (see [3] in section B.3) is the aspect-oriented extension to Java that offers a small set of powerful constructs that let you inject additional behavior into existing programs through bytecode instrumentation. You can specify well-defined points in the execution of a program, known as *join points*, at which you can inject *advices* to define additional behaviors. A collection of join points is referred to as a *pointcut*. Pointcuts, advices, and Java member declarations make modular units called *aspects*. Aspects are used to generate code at specific pointcuts and define one form of MOP for Java. You can use aspects to implement a limited form of DSLs in Java. They've been used quite successfully in Java EE frameworks like Spring (http://www.spring-framework.org) to offer concise little languages to the developer.

B.2   Lisp as the DSL

In section 2.3, we look at the role of metaprogramming and code generation in designing successful DSLs. One of the ways you can make your DSL acceptable to users is to have a concise surface syntax and yet be sufficiently expressive with the domain vocabulary. What this implies is that the host language has rich program-transformation semantics, whether at the compilation level or at the runtime level.

In section 2.3.1, you see how languages like Groovy offer runtime MOPs to generate code that alters program behavior through method synthesis, method interception, and other forms of meta-object manipulation. Runtime metaprogramming does have performance issues, because the transformation structures are being manipulated through the reflection and introspection of the meta-objects.

Languages like Lisp offer compile-time metaprogramming using macros, which we discuss in section B.1. It's the power of syntactic macros that make the Lisp runtime completely free of any metastructures; a Lisp program execution has to deal only with the valid Lisp forms that are defined as part of the core language runtime. This makes Lisp metaprogramming special and syntactic macros the bedrock of DSL implementation in Lisp. In this section, we'll go into further detail about the structure of Lisp programs and try to understand the differences between them and other language implementations.

> When you write a program in most languages, what you're writing is being represented as the concrete syntax tree (CST). The CST is the faithful representation of your program, including the white spaces, comments, and any metainformation you generate. Your program is then passed through scanners, lexical analyzers, and parsers to generate what we call the abstract syntax tree (AST). The AST is the syntactic essence of your program that gets pipelined into the next phases of the compilation process. It goes through the usual steps of transformation, optimization, and code generation. The parser of your language is primarily responsible for all such transformations that lead to the generation of the AST from the CST.

B.2.1   What's so special about Lisp?

What makes compile-time metaprogramming difficult in languages like Java or C++? In order to work effectively with compile-time metaprogramming, you need to make transformations on the AST of the program. Read the sidebar in this section for a brief outline of abstract and concrete syntax trees.

In most languages like Java or C++, a program is represented as a string of characters. The only way the AST can be generated from the CST is through the language parser, which can parse only *valid* syntax for that language. The parser isn't available as a separate module during the precompilation phase of the program. (Well, this isn't strictly true. Now there are languages like Template Haskell and MetaOCaml that implement compile-time metaprogramming using macros. I talk about them briefly in chapter 9.) Because the parser isn't available during this time, new syntax processing or precompile-time program transformation in these languages is restricted to one of the following primitive techniques:

- Macros based on textual substitutions through a compiler preprocessor as in C
- Selective preprocessing during the precompiler phases through annotations (as in Java) or templates (as in C++)
- Instrumentation of bytecodes as in AOP using AspectJ in Java

If your background is in C, you're probably ruminating on the extremely messy, painful, and error-prone artifacts that preprocessor macros gave you as part of that language. This is where Lisp shines. Lisp has been designed ground-up with an infrastructure that supports syntactic extensibility. The first step toward this outcome was decided when John McCarthy, the father of Lisp, decided that the language should have access to its abstract syntax.

So far I've mostly been talking about macros that process the AST and transform new syntax to original Lisp forms. Macros are what make Lisp extensible, but the real reason behind the power of macros lies in the design of the language itself. Let's look at some of the philosophies of Lisp language design that make it significantly different from what you see in Java or C++.

B.2.2   Code as data

In Lisp, every program is a list structure, which is the AST of the code itself. As a result, code is seen as having the same representation and syntax as data. By standardizing on this simple protocol, the language publishes the abstract syntax to the programmer. This abstract syntax is simple—it's a list. Any metaprogram that you generate using Lisp needs to conform only to this simple, standard representation.

B.2.3   Data as code

By using the QUOTE special form, data syntax can be embedded easily into the code syntax. Lisp macros are good examples of this philosophy. In fact, Lisp extends this paradigm of *data as code* and offers a full-blown template mechanism for writing metaprograms. In Common Lisp, we call this *quasiquotation*. In Clojure, the same feature is implemented through *syntax quote, unquote,* and *splicing unquote.* Here's the definition of the macro `defstruct` in Clojure:

```
(defmacro defstruct
  [name & keys]
  `(def ~name (create-struct ~@keys)))
```

The syntax quote character, represented by a backquote (`` ` ``) causes the form that follows it to be interpreted as Lisp data and works like normal quoting. But within the syntax quoted form, the unquote character (~) turns off quoting and lets Lisp compute that form. A similar technique in Common Lisp, the quasiquotation, lets you write templates of data in which some parts of the data are fixed, but the others are computed. It's pretty much a complete template sublanguage embedded within the syntax of Lisp.

We'll take a detailed look at this Lisp feature when I talk about metaprogramming in detail in chapter 5. If you're not used to the paradigms of Lisp programming, now might be a good time for you to take a break and think about the awesomeness and dynamism that this feature can bring to your code generation capabilities.

B.2.4 *A simple parser that parses only list structures*

Lisp is a language with minimal syntax. The Lisp parser is so simple because all it needs to parse are lists! Both the data and code syntax are represented uniformly using list structures. The Lisp macro body is also a list structure.

Lisp is a homoiconic language, and as you now know, it has powerful compile-time metaprogramming abilities. You might be wondering how this relates to the awesomeness of Lisp in implementing DSLs. The answer is simple: stick to the Lisp philosophy of representing your DSL as a list structure and organize repeatable constructs and patterns as macros. If you design your DSL this way, you won't need a separate parser for your DSL. You can use the Lisp parser to parse something that isn't even a valid Lisp form and extend the language with new syntax and semantics that speak the vocabulary of your domain. Look at figure B.4 for a visual of the *Lisp-as-the-DSL* metaphor.

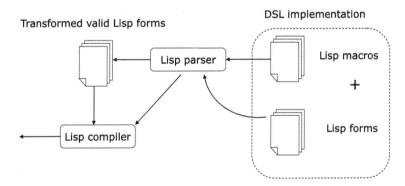

Figure B.4 Lisp as the DSL. Lisp macros get transformed into valid Lisp forms and get submitted to the compiler.

DEFINITION   Homoiconic is a five-dollar word that describes a language in which a program can be represented using a data structure that the language can process. In the case of Lisp, it's a list that makes a uniform representation for code and data.

By looking at figure B.4, can you figure out how Lisp unifies the differences between external and internal DSLs? On one hand, there's *external* syntax in our DSL, also known as macros. Macros aren't valid Lisp forms. At the same time, we don't need an external parser to process those external forms. The ubiquitous list data structure unifies them all and the native Lisp parser serves as the universal processor for our DSL. All these capabilities that I've discussed make Lisp almost a perfect language for implementing custom DSL structures.

Metaprogramming is a technique that lets you write programs that write programs. You just saw how Lisp achieves this through compile-time macros. Section B.1 gives you a general overview of compile-time metaprogramming. This section describes a concrete implementation in one of the earliest metaprograming-powered languages. When you have a solid understanding of the power of meta, you'll appreciate how you can exploit this paradigm in real-life implementations of DSLs. In chapters 4 and 5, you'll find lots of examples of compile-time and runtime metaprogramming using dynamic languages like Ruby, Groovy, and Clojure.

B.3   References

1   T. Veldhuizen. Expression templates. *C++ Report*, 7 (5) pp. 26-31, June 1995.

2   Blitz++, http://www.oonumerics.org/blitz/.

3   AspectJ, http://www.eclipse.org/aspectj/.

4   Kiczales, G., J. Lamping, A. Mendhekar, C. Maeda, C. Lopes, J.-M. Loingtier, and J. Irwin. 1997. Aspect-Oriented Programming. *Proceedings of the European Conference on Object-Oriented Programming*, pp. 220-242.

5   Kiczales, Gregor, Jim des Rivieres, and Daniel G. Bobrow. 1991. *The Art of the Metaobject Protocol.* The MIT Press.

6   Steele, Jr, G.L. Growing a language. *Higher-Order and Symbolic Computation* 12 (1999), pp. 221-236.

appendix C
A cheat sheet for Ruby's
DSL-friendly features

This appendix will assist you as you become familiar with the DSL-friendly features of Ruby. Please don't treat this information as a comprehensive language overview. For a more complete and detailed discussion of the language and its syntax, see the references in section C.2.

C.1   DSL-friendly features of Ruby

Ruby is a dynamically typed OO language with strong features of reflective and generative metaprogramming. Ruby's object model lets you change the behaviors of objects at runtime through reflection into its metamodel. You can also generate code during runtime through metaprogramming, which means that your DSL surface syntax is always concise. Table C.1 gives you a brief overview of the features of Ruby that make it a great language for designing DSLs.

Table C.1   Ruby feature overview

Classes and objects	

Ruby is OO. You can define classes that have instance variables and methods.
A Ruby object has a set of instance variables and an associated class.
A Ruby class is an instance of the class `Class`. It has everything that an object has, plus a set of method definitions and a reference to the superclass.
When you design a DSL using Ruby, it's common to model the entities of your domain as classes.
	``ruby
	class Account
	  def initialize(no, name)
	    @no = no
	    @name = name
	  end
	  def to_s
	    "Account no: #{@no} name: #{@name}"
	  end
	end
	``
	
	`initialize` is a special method that's called when you invoke `Account.new`. It's used to set the state of your object after the initial memory allocation.
	`@no` and `@name` set up the instance variables of the class. You don't have to declare variables before using them.

Singletons	

You can define a method specific to a particular object.
The set of method definitions within a Ruby class (as I've already mentioned) are nothing but *singleton* methods that are defined for the instance of the class `Class`. Singletons are also known as *class methods* in Ruby.
	``ruby
	accnt = Account.new(12, "john p. ")
	def accnt.do_special
	  ##
	end
	accnt.do_special ## runs
	acc = Account.new(23, "peter s. ")
	acc.do_special ## error!
	``
	
	`do_special` is a method that's defined only for the instance `accnt`. It's an example of a *singleton* method in Ruby, where self refers to the instance `accnt`

Metaprogramming	

Metaprogramming is the secret sauce behind Ruby DSLs. Ruby is a reflective language that lets you peek into the runtime meta-objects and change their behaviors.	```ruby
	class Account
	  attr_accessor :no, :name
	end
	``
	
	`attr_accessor` is a *class method* that uses reflective metaprogramming during runtime. It generates accessor methods for the attributes that are supplied as parameters. Note how concise the surface syntax is; the boilerplates are generated during runtime.
	
	``ruby
	class Trade < ActiveRecord::Base
	  has_many :tax_fees
	end
	``
	
	This example is from the `ActiveRecord` library of Rails. The *one-to-many* relation between entities is expressed through a class method in Ruby and used with reflective metaprogramming.

Table C.1 Ruby feature overview (continued)

Open classes	

Ruby lets you open any class and add or change attributes, methods, and properties during runtime.
This feature is popularly known as monkey patching, and is considered to be one of Ruby's most dangerously powerful features. Because monkey patching works in the global namespace, you need to use this feature judiciously.
	<pre>class Integer
	  def shares
	    ##
	  end
	end</pre>You can design DSL-friendly features using Ruby's open classes. For example, you can open the class `Integer` and add a method named `shares`, so that your DSL user can write code like `2 shares`. On the down side, all users who'll be using the class `Integer` are affected by this monkey patching. Be careful!

Evals	

In Ruby, you can evaluate a string or a block of code on the fly. This is one of the most powerful features of Ruby metaprogramming.
In designing DSLs, you can use the evals to set up the appropriate context. Then you can pass a block that invokes methods, without explicitly specifying the context. This makes your DSL syntax less verbose.
You can set up a different context in which to evaluate the code by using one of the following flavors of evals that are available:
 	
• `class_eval`—evaluate a string or a block of code in the context of a class or a module
• `instance_eval`—evaluate a string or a block of code in the context of a class instance
• `eval`—evaluate a string or a block of code in the current context
	<pre>class Account
	end
	Account.class_eval do
	  def open
	    ##
	  end
	end</pre>The context is the class `Account`. `class_eval` creates an instance method for the class `Account`.<pre>Account.instance_eval do
	  def open
	    ##
	  end
	end</pre>The context is the singleton class of `self.instance_eval` produces a singleton method (or class method) for `Account`.

Modules	

Modules offer a way to group related artifacts like methods, classes, and so on, so that they can be included in your class as a mixin component.
Modules also offer a namespace facility in Ruby.
	<pre>module Audit
	  def record
	    ##
	  end
	end</pre>The module defines a new namespace for grouping together all the audit-related methods. Now you can use it as a mixin and include it in your class to make it auditable:<pre>class Account
	  include Audit
	  ## can use the method record here
	end</pre>

Table C.1   Ruby feature overview *(continued)*

Blocks	

Ruby blocks are chunks of code, somewhat similar to anonymous methods, that can be reified for later execution. Just like methods, a Ruby block can take parameters.
A block is used synonymously with lambdas, which can implement higher-order functions in Ruby.
	``ruby
	sum = 0
	[1, 2, 3, 4].each do |value|
	  sum += (value * value)
	end
	puts sum
	``
	`|value|` in horizontal bars is the parameter that gets passed to the block.
	The method each which belongs to a Ruby array, accepts a block as a parameter

Hash as a variable-length argument list	

Ruby has a user-friendly way to implement a variable-length argument list to a method. You can simply pass a hash, then access it as key/value pairs.
Doing this adds to the readability of the DSL code and makes implementing the Builder pattern a trivial task.
	``ruby
	def foo(values)
	  ## values is a hash
	end
	``
	Calling the function:
	``ruby
	foo(:a => 1, :b => 2)
	``
	Example application of this idiom from Rails:
	``ruby
	class Trade
	  has_many :tax_fees,
	    :class_name => "TaxFee",
	    :conditions => "valid_flag = 1",
	    :order => "name"
	end
	``

Duck typing	

In Ruby, you design an abstraction NOT based on types, but based on the set of messages it responds to. If an object responds to a quack message, then it's a duck!
This kind of coding wouldn't work in Java. In Java, you need to specify the type signature of the argument when it's passed in a method.
	``ruby
	class Duck
	  def quack
	    ##
	  end
	end
	class DummyDuck
	  def quack
	    ##
	  end
	end
	def check_if_quack(duck)
	  duck.quack
	end
	``
	The method check_if_quack will work with instances of Duck as well as DummyDuck, because both of them respond to the message quack.

C.2   References

1   Thomas, Dave, Chad Fowler, and Andy Hunt. 2009. *Programming Ruby 1.9: The Pragmatic Programmers' Guide,* Third Edition. The Pragmatic Bookshelf.

2   Perrotta, Paolo. 2010. *Metaprogramming Ruby: Program Like the Ruby Pros.* The Pragmatic Bookshelf.

appendix D
A cheat sheet for Scala's
DSL-friendly features

This appendix will assist you as you become familiar with the DSL-friendly features of Scala. Please don't treat this information as a comprehensive language overview. For a more complete and detailed discussion of the language and its syntax, see the references in section D.2.

D.1 DSL-friendly features of Scala

Scala is an object-functional language that runs on the JVM. It has great interoperability with Java by virtue of having the same object model (and more). Scala has a nice, concise syntax, offers type inference, and a whole bunch of mechanisms for designing abstractions based on a combination of OO and functional paradigms.

Table D.1 Scala feature overview

Class-based OOP	

Scala is OO. You can define classes that have instance variables and methods. But besides being a class, a Scala abstraction can be of many other types, each with its own set of features and applicability. We're going to look at most of them in this appendix.
When you design a DSL using Scala, it's common to model the entities of your domain as classes or as any of the other ways to group related functionalities.
For details about class definition syntax, refer to [1] in section D.2.
	```scala`class Account(val no: Int, val name: String) {`
	`  def balance: Int = {`
	`    //.. implementation`
	`  }`
	`  //..`
	`}````
	
	A class definition can take parameters. In this snippet, `val` implies that `no` and `name` are immutable and cannot be reassigned.
	`balance` is a method that you can define. It doesn't take any argument and returns an `Int`.

Table D.1 Scala feature overview *(continued)*

Case classes	
You can add the word *case* before a class definition and get a lot of mileage out of the abstraction that the compiler generates. It's called a *case class* in Scala. For a case class, the compiler automatically does the following: • Converts the constructor arguments into immutable `val`s. You can explicitly specify `var` to decide otherwise. • Implements `equals`, `hashCode`, and `toString` methods to the class. • Lets you invoke a shorthand notation for the constructor. You don't need to specify the keyword `new` while instantiating an object of the class. The compiler gives you a companion object that contains the `apply()` constructor and an extractor on the constructor arguments. Case classes are also useful for pattern matching. They're the most idiomatic way to implement algebraic data types in Scala. Because of the built-in features of immutability that case classes offer, they're often used to build immutable value objects when designing DSLs	```scala\nabstract class Term\ncase class Var(name: String)\nextends Term\ncase class Fun(arg: String, body:\nTerm) extends Term\n``` For this case class definition, you can instantiate as `val p = Var("p")`, without having to explicitly specify `new`.

Traits	
Traits are yet another way to specify abstractions in Scala. They're similar to Java interfaces in that you can leave out the implementation for concrete classes. But unlike interfaces, you can specify partial implementations of some methods in a trait. Traits offer a way to implement mixins in Scala and can also be used to design the correct way to use multiple inheritance.	```scala\ntrait Audit {\n def record_trail {\n //.. implementation\n }\n def view_trail // open\n}\nclass SavingsAccount extends Account\nwith Audit {\n //..\n}\n``` Traits are a great way to design open reusable abstractions without committing to a specific implementation. Note how in this definition, the method `view_trail` is kept open for implementation by the abstraction that mixes in the trait.

Table D.1 Scala feature overview *(continued)*

Higher-order functions & closures

In Scala, functions are first-class values, and you can pass a function as an argument to yet another function. You can also have a function return another function. Functions as first-class values give Scala the main power for functional programming.
Higher-order functions make code less verbose and express the correct verb semantics of your DSL.
Closures let you write fewer classes and objects and more functional artifacts.
	``scala
	val hasLower =
	bookTitle.exists(_.isLowerCase)
	def foo(bar: (Int, Int)=>Int) {
	  //..
	}
	``
	In the first example, the method `exists` takes a function as an argument that it applies to each character of the string. In Java, this would've been way more verbose.
	The second example shows the literal syntax of a function in Scala.

Pattern matching

Like all functional programming languages, Scala has pattern matching. You can match arbitrary expressions with a first-match-wins policy in Scala.
Case classes and pattern matching are a potent combination for implementing functional idioms in Scala.
You can implement an extensible Visitor pattern using case classes.
As you see in chapter 6, pattern matching plays an important role in making expressive business rules
	``scala
	def foo(i: Int) = i match {
	  case 10 => //..
	  case 12 => //..
	  case _ =>
	}
	``
	The previous rendering is a more concise Scala version of Java's switch/case statement. But pattern matching has many other uses.
	``scala
	val obj = doStuff()
	var cast:Foo = obj match {
	  case x:Foo => x
	  case _ => null
	}
	``
	The earlier example is a more idiomatic way of implementing an `instanceOf` check used in Java.
	``scala
	trait Account
	case class Checking(no: Int) extends Account
	case class Savings(no: Int, rate: Double) extends Account
	def process(acc: Account) = acc match {
	  case Checking(no) => // do stuff
	  case Savings(no, rt) => // do stuff
	}
	``
	Case classes can be used directly for pattern matching. Note that earlier I said that case classes implement extractors by default.

Table D.1   Scala feature overview *(continued)*

Objects as modules	
Objects define executable modules in Scala. After you define abstractions using classes and traits, you can compose them together into a concrete abstraction using the `object` syntax. Object syntax is the closest approximation of *statics* that are used in Java.	```object RuleComponent extends Rule with CountryLocale with Calendar { // .. }``` `RuleComponent` is a singleton object created out of the specified abstractions.

Implicit arguments	
You can leave out the last argument of a function by declaring it to be `implicit`. The compiler will look for a *matching* argument from the enclosing scope of the function.	```def shout(at: String)(implicit curse: String) { println("hey: " + at + " " + curse) } implicit val curse = "Damn! " shout("Rob")``` The compiler will complain if it can't find a matching argument from the enclosing scope.

Implicit type conversions (aka Pimp My Library)	
You can extend existing libraries without making any changes to them by using implicit type conversions. It works much like Ruby monkey patching, but it's controlled within the lexical scope. Martin Odersky named this the *Pimp My Library* pattern (see [2] in section D.2). The implicit conversion function is automatically applied by the compiler. This helps you make your legacy abstractions smart with improved APIs.	```class RichArray[T](value: Array[T]) { def append(other: Array[T]) : Array[T] = { //.. implementation } } implicit def enrichArray[T](xs: Array[T]) = new RichArray[T]``` The implicit definition of `enrichArray` serves as the conversion function from `Array` to `RichArray`.

Partial functions	
A partial function is one that's defined *only* for a set of values of its arguments. Partial functions in Scala are modeled as blocks of pattern-matching case statements. `PartialFunctions` are used idiomatically to define the message receive loop in Scala actors.	```val onlyTrue: PartialFunction[Boolean, Int] = { case true => 100 }``` `onlyTrue` is a `PartialFunction` that's defined for a limited domain. It's defined only for the Boolean value `true`. The `PartialFunction` trait contains a method `isDefinedAt` that returns `true` for the domain values for which the `PartialFunction` is defined. Here's an example: ```scala> onlyTrue isDefinedAt(true) res1: Boolean = true scala> onlyTrue isDefinedAt(false) res2: Boolean = false```

Table D.1 Scala feature overview *(continued)*

Generics and type parameters	

Scala offers type parameters that you specify as part of your class and method declarations. You can also specify explicit constraints on these types that your abstraction will honor. You get an automatic level of constraint checking by the compiler without having to write a single line of validation logic.
 	
With Scala, you can abstract many of your DSL constraints within the type system.
	`class Trade[Account <:`
	`TradingAccount](account: Account) {`
	`  //..`
	`}`
	
	In this class definition, you won't be able to create an instance of `Trade` with an account that doesn't satisfy the specified constraint.

D.2 References

1 Wampler, Dean, and Alex Payne. 2009. *Programming Scala: Scalability = Functional Programming + Objects.* O'Reilly Media.

2 Odersky, Martin. Pimp My Library. *Artima Developer.* http://www.artima.com/weblogs/viewpost.jsp?thread=179766.

appendix E
A cheat sheet for Groovy's
DSL-friendly features

This appendix will assist you as you become familiar with the DSL-friendly features of Groovy. Please don't treat this information as a comprehensive language overview. For a more complete and detailed discussion of the language and its syntax, see the references in section E.2.

E.1 DSL-friendly features of Groovy

Groovy is a dynamically typed OO language with strong features of reflective and generative metaprogramming. Groovy shares the object model with Java and has strong interoperability with the Java language. Groovy can also be used as a scripting language. It has optional typing, operator overloading, strong literal syntax, and functional abstractions like closures. Table E.1 gives you a brief overview of the features of Groovy that make it a great language for designing DSLs.

Table E.1 Groovy feature overview

Class-based OOP	

Groovy is OO. You can define classes that have instance variables and methods. The syntax is similar to Java and the default visibility modifier is public. For details about class definition syntax, refer to [1] in section E.2.	```
	class Account {
	  Integer balance(Date date) = {
	    //.. implementation
	  }
	  //..
	}
	``
	This snippet shows a class declaration in Groovy.

Table E.1 Groovy feature overview *(continued)*

Optional typing	

You can declare static types just like you can in Java; these types are honored at runtime. Groovy also offers dynamic typing like Python does, where the type declaration is replaced by the `def` keyword. Formal parameters to method and closure declarations can even omit the `def`.	```String str = new String("Groovy");```
	```str = 8```
	```def dstr = "dynamic"```
	```dstr = 20```
	
	`str` will be assigned the `String` 8
	`dstr` will be assigned the `Integer` 20

Properties	

You declare properties as fields with the default visibility modifier, no matter what type you're using.	```class Foo {```
	``` String str```
	``` def dyn```
	```}```
	
	This snippet shows a class with properties.

Strings	

You can define single-line strings, multiline strings, or a `GString` with placeholders.	```def single = 'single line string'```
	```def multi = """ I am a multi line```
	``` string"""```
	```def gstring = "$single has ${single.size}```
	```characters"```
	
	This code shows various strings that are supported in Groovy.

Collection data types	

Groovy offers all common collection data types like `Range`, `List`, `Map`, and so on. All of them have a strong literal syntax that makes great DSL snippets.	```// range (half inclusive)```
	```(0..<10).each { println it }```
	```// list manipulation```
	```[1,2,3] * 2 == [1,2,3,1,2,3]```
	```[1,[2,3]].flatten() == [1,2,3]```
	```[1,2,3].reverse() == [3,2,1]```
	```[1,2,3].disjoint([4,5,6]) == true```
	```// map definition literal syntax```
	```def map = [a:0, b:1]```
	
	Examples of various collection data types in Groovy.

Closures	

A closure is a block of code that can be reified for later execution. It encapsulates some logic and an enclosing scope.	```def clos = { println "hello world!" }```
	```clos() //prints "hello world!"```
	```def mult = {x, y -> println x * y}```
	```mult(2, 5) // prints 10```
	
	These snippets show closures in Groovy.

Table E.1 Groovy feature overview *(continued)*

Builders	
Builders help you build hierarchical data models with amazingly concise syntax. The secret sauce is metaprogramming.	```def builder = new groovy.xml.MarkupBuilder(writer) builder.html(){ head(){ title("Welcome"){} } body(){ p("How are you?") } }``` Groovy builders work based on a combination of metaprogramming and closures.
Metaprogramming—ExpandoMetaClass	
The `ExpandoMetaClass` is one of the primary metaprogramming constructs that allows you to dynamically add methods, constructors, properties, and static methods using a closure syntax.	`Integer.metaClass.twice << {delegate * 2}` This snippet adds a method named `twice` to the class `Integer`. This new method is visible to all threads in unlimited scope
Metaprogramming—categories	
This concept is similar to the `ExpandoMetaClass`, but visibility is limited to the scope that you explicitly specify.	```class IntegerCategory { static Integer twice(Integer i) { return i * 2 } } use (IntegerCategory) { assert 4 == 2.twice() }``` The method `twice` is visible only within the scope specified by `use {}`.

E.2   References

1 König, Dierk, Paul King, Guillaume Laforge, and Jon Skeet, 2009. *Groovy in Action*, Second Edition. Manning Early Access Program Edition. Manning Publications.

2 Subramaniam, Venkat. 2008. *Programming Groovy: Dynamic Productivity for the Java Developer*. The Pragmatic Bookshelf.

appendix F
A cheat sheet for Clojure's DSL-friendly features

This appendix will assist you as you become familiar with the DSL-friendly features of Clojure. Please don't treat this information as a comprehensive language overview. For a more complete and detailed discussion of the language and its syntax, see the reference in section F.2.

F.1   DSL-friendly features of Clojure

Clojure is a functional programming language that's built on top of the JVM. It's dynamically typed, with optional type hints and type inference, and is targeted as a general-purpose programming language. Clojure is a dialect of Lisp and compiles directly to JVM bytecode. It's homoiconic and has strong features of concurrency control built in the language.

Besides the features described in the table, Clojure has lots of other features related to concurrency and state management, lazy sequences, sequence-comprehensions and looping, and many advanced data structures. For more on these, refer to [1] in section F.2.

Table F.1   Clojure feature overview

Functional—organize DSLs around functions	

You organize your entire DSL as a collection of functions.
In Clojure, functions are first-class artifacts with strong support for higher-order functions and closures. Anonymous functions are also supported.
In spite of the fact that Clojure is built upon Java, the language is predominantly functional. You can go down to the Java level and invoke object semantics, but idiomatic Clojure is functional.
	``
	(str "hello" " " "world")
	=> "hello world"
	(count [1 2 3 4 5])
	=> 5
	(+ 12 20)
	=> 32
	``
	Prefix notation is the normal order of the day.
	
	Note:
	Clojure is homoiconic. Note that every function invocation is a list that begins with the function name.
	``
	(filter even? [1 2 3 4])
	=> (2 4)
	``
	even? is a Clojure function that returns `true` if the input is an even number. In the previous example, we pass the function even? as a parameter to `filter`, which applies even? to every element of the passed sequence.
	``
	(filter #(or (zero? (mod % 3))
	         (zero? (mod % 5)))
	    [1 3 5 7 9 10 15])
	=> (3 5 9 10 15)
	``
	`filter` can also take an anonymous function.

Functional—function definition	

You define a function using `defn`. That's pure syntax, which I illustrate in the example. The most interesting part is that in Clojure (like any other Lisp variant), a function is also data that starts with a symbol.	```
	(defn ^String greet
	  "Greet your friend"
	  [name]
	  (str "hello, " name))
	``
	`defn` starts the beginning of a function definition. The next part is the documentation associated with the function definition, called the *docstring*. Then we have the parameter list in a vector, and finally the body of the function.
	Optionally, you can have metadata with the ^ prefix. Here it indicates the return type of the function.
	The whole function definition is also a Clojure list that contains members for every part of the definition.

Designing abstractions	
The Clojure way	**Traditional OO way**
▪ Public fields ▪ Immutable objects ▪ Polymorphism through multimethods and protocols ▪ No implementation inheritance	▪ All data is hidden inside classes through private members ▪ Objects are mutable ▪ Polymorphism through inheritance hierarchies, which can mean inheritance of interface or implementation ▪ Implementation inheritance allowed

Table F.1 Clojure feature overview *(continued)*

Sequences

| Every aggregate data type in Clojure is a sequence. You can treat sequences uniformly through a set of APIs that apply equally to every member of the sequence family. You can also treat all Java collections as Clojure sequences. Take a look at the examples. | ```(first '(10, 20, 30))```
 `=> 10`
 `(rest [10, 20, 30])`
 `=> (20, 30)`
 `(first {:fname "rich" :lname "hickey"})`
 `=> [:fname "rich"]`

 In the code snippet:

 ■ The first example invokes `first` on a `List`.
 ■ The second example invokes `rest` on a `Vector`.
 ■ The third example invokes `first` on a `Map`. |

Sequences are functions

| Clojure treats every sequence type as a function. This follows from the mathematical definitions of the sequences. Here's a list of the ways we can express Clojure's sequences mathematically:

 ■ A `Vector` is a function of its position.
 ■ A `Map` is a function of its key.
 ■ A `Set` is a function of membership. | `(def colors [:red :blue :green])`
 `(colors 0)`
 `=> :red`
 `(def room {:len 100 :wd 50 :ht 10})`
 `(room :len)`
 `=> 100`
 `(def names #{"rich hickey" "martin odersky" "james strachan"})`
 `(names "rich hickey")`
 `=> "rich hickey"`
 `(names "dennis Ritchie")`
 `=> nil` |

Creating sequences

| Clojure offers a number of functions that you can use to create sequences. Many of them offer a lazy sequence as a result and can be used to generate infinite sequences. | `(range 0 10 2)`
 `=> (0 2 4 6 8)`
 `(repeat 5 3)`
 `=> (3 3 3 3 3)`
 `(take 10 (iterate inc 1))`
 `=> (1 2 3 4 5 6 7 8 9 10)` |

Filtering sequences

| Clojure offers combinators that you can use to filter a sequence. Always prefer using these combinators instead of coding an explicit recursion. | `(filter even? [1 2 3 4 5 6 7 8 9])`
 `=> [2 4 6 8]`
 `(take 10 (filter even? (iterate inc 1)))`
 `=> [2 4 6 8 10 12 14 16 18 20]`
 `(split-at 5 (range 10))`
 `=> [(0 1 2 3 4) (5 6 7 8 9)]` |

Table F.1   Clojure feature overview (continued)

Transforming sequences	
Clojure offers lots of combinators that transform an existing sequence. They take as input one sequence and generate another sequence or value by applying some transformation.	``` (map inc [1 2 3 4]) => (2 3 4 5) (reduce + [1 2 3 4]) => 10 ```
Persistent data structures and immutability	
In Clojure, all data structures are immutable and persistent. This means that after you make changes to an object, you can access all historical versions of the same object without incurring additional overhead in storage requirements.	``` (def a [1 2 3 4]) (def b (conj a 5)) a => [1 2 3 4] b => [1 2 3 4 5] ```
Macros	
The secret sauce of DSL design in Clojure is macros. Macros are artifacts that get expanded to valid Clojure forms during the macro-expansion phase. Macros are a very potent tool to use to design custom syntax constructs in your DSL.	``` (defmacro unless [expr form] (list `if expr nil form)) ``` The macro defines a control structure like `if` or `while` that you can use just like normal Clojure forms.

F.2   References

1   Halloway, Stuart. 2009. *Programming Clojure.* The Pragmatic Bookshelf.

appendix G
Polyglot development

As you've seen throughout the book, DSLs are not limited by a single programming language. You can use the language that best fits your requirements. Even though it seems that this means that your application will become a nest of chaos between indiscriminate islands of language cacophony, that doesn't have to be the case. But how will you know when your project has entered such an unfortunate state? Simple! You'll feel like the confused programmer in figure G.1.

In this appendix, you'll see how to bootstrap yourself into a disciplined polyglot development environment. I assume that you'll be developing DSL-based applications on the JVM. In such developments, Java can play the role of the base host language where your main application is developed using Java, and you're developing DSLs in some other language to make your published APIs expressive to your clients. Just a friendly reminder—this appendix is only for entry-level users planning to start developing DSLs using a mixed-language paradigm. If you're already experienced in such development patterns, feel free to skip this appendix.

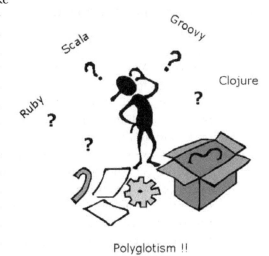

Figure G.1 Don't let this happen to you!

I'm going to discuss two examples of how to bootstrap your development environment in case you decide to develop your DSL in a non-Java language on the JVM and integrate it with your Java-based application. The first example is based on Groovy, which is a dynamic lan-

337

guage. You'll get a feel for how modern IDEs give you a seamless integration of a mixed Java-Groovy project. The second example is based on Scala, which is a statically typed language. In that example, you'll see how to set up your environment for a mixed Java-Scala project.

G.1   *What features should you look for in an IDE?*

When you're working on a polyglot project in languages on the JVM, you'll want to look for the following features in your IDE:

- Support for a mixed Java-*X* project where *X* is Scala, Groovy, Ruby, or Clojure, and any combination of Java/*X* project dependencies.
- A rich syntactic editor integrated with the IDE that provides some amount of assistance to the developer. The richness of the editor means support for syntax highlighting, inferred types, documentation on hover, code completion, and the like.
- A unified explorer view of all project artifacts, including types, packages, and views of the combined project.
- Debugging support integrated for the languages.

Additionally, there will be other features that vary across languages. Generally, statically typed languages offer better IDE support than dynamic ones because there's more meta-information available to them. But things are improving every day. Many popular IDEs are becoming more and more user-friendly, offering a better experience to the developers.

G.2   *Bootstrapping a Java-Groovy development environment*

If you've worked on any nontrivial Java project, you must've had the experience of using a modern IDE like Eclipse (http://eclipse.org) or NetBeans (http://netbeans.org). When you use multiple languages for developing DSLs, I'm sure you'll also be looking for similar user friendliness in interaction and building project artifacts from your IDE. This is something that's evolving quickly—keep an eye on your favorite platform for all the recent updates.

Groovy is a language that has good integration with Java. As I mention in chapter 3, Groovy shares the object model with Java; any IDE that works well for Java-based projects should also work equally well for Groovy-based ones. But there's a catch. Groovy is a dynamic language where you can optionally specify types. In many cases, the compile-time type information isn't present with the IDE. Code completion or other rich features that the editor offers might not be that refined in Groovy. Even so, things are improving and we're seeing lots of plugins being developed that perform these smart acts in the editor, even for dynamic languages.

To bootstrap your Groovy-based DSL development environment in a Java project, take the advice given in table G.1.

Table G.1 Steps for setting up a Groovy based DSL development environment

Do	Use it for
Download the Java Development Kit (version 5 or 6).	Regular Java development, as well as the runtime for Groovy-based development.
Download the NetBeans IDE (latest version); for exact version compatibility information, check out the documentation at http://netbeans.org.	The IDE that you'll use for hosting Java and Groovy projects.
Create a regular Java application from the NetBeans menu.	This application will be the one that can host Java and Groovy source files.
Name the project and start creating Java and Groovy source files.	The IDE that will provide an integrated view of the Java and Groovy project artifacts. The Groovy DSL scripts will appear alongside Java source files, based on the package structure that you design. Without any additional plugin, you'll be able to build your project from within Netbeans. Your DSL scripts can be happily invoked from within Java classes, using one of the methods that we discuss in chapters 2, 3, and 4.

G.3 *Bootstrapping a Java-Scala development environment*

Scala, as we've discussed earlier, is statically typed with a powerful type system. IDE support for Scala is evolving—we already have quite good support for Scala editing through Eclipse, IntelliJ Idea, and NetBeans.

Installing Scala support in Eclipse is as simple as pulling in the latest version of the plugin. Here's the complete rundown of what you need to do to bootstrap your Eclipse environment to support a mixed Java/Scala development.

Software requirements:

- Java Development Toolkit 1.6
- Eclipse Classic 3.5.2 (Check the exact version at http://eclipse.org)

After you've installed Eclipse, you need to install the plugin for Scala development. On the home page for Scala IDE (http://www.scala-ide.org/), there's a friendly video that takes you through the steps in detail.

Eclipse plugin for Scala is improving daily. Now with the plugin installed, you get a rich set of features for developing a mixed Scala/Java project:

- Support for Scala/Java project development
- Rich editor support with code completion, type inferencing, and so on
- Incremental compilation
- Debugger support
- A lot more for all the artifacts of Scala and Java

G.4   *Popular IDEs for polyglot development*

Table G.2 provides a list of some of the commonly used IDEs for developing applications that use multiple languages. With each of the IDEs, I've listed the corresponding required plugins and the common languages that they support.

IDEs are improving every day and are getting richer with new features. Please check the URL for your preferred IDE before you decide to jump on it.

Table G.2   Polyglot IDEs

IDE	Plugin support
Eclipse (http://eclipse.org)	Plugin support for: • Groovy (http://groovy.codehaus.org/Eclipse+Plugin) • Ruby • Scala (http://scala-ide.org) • Clojure (http://code.google.com/p/counterclockwise/)
NetBeans (http://netbeans.org)	Plugin support for: • Ruby (http://netbeans.org/projects/ruby/) • Clojure (http://www.enclojure.org) • Scala (http://wiki.netbeans.org/Scala) • Groovy support is native; no plugin is required
Emacs (http://www.gnu.org/software/emacs/)	Among all the JVM languages, Emacs is possibly the number one choice for Clojure editing. One point of warning though: unless you're familiar with Emacs, it takes some time to get into the mode. If you want to try out the Emacs-Clojure combination, go to http://www.assembla.com/wiki/show/clojure/Getting_Started_with_Emacs
IntelliJ IDEA (http://www.jetbrains.com/idea/)	Plugin support for: • Groovy (http://www.jetbrains.com/idea/features/groovy_grails.html) • Ruby (http://www.jetbrains.com/idea/features/ruby_rails.html) • Scala (http://confluence.jetbrains.net/display/SCA/Scala+Plugin+for+IntelliJ+IDEA) • Clojure (http://www.assembla.com/wiki/show/clojure/Getting_Started_with_Idea_and_La_Clojure)

index

RELATED MANNING TITLES

Groovy in Action, Second Edition
Creating Modular Applications in Java

by Dierk König, Guillaume Laforge, Paul
  King, Jon Skeet

  ISBN: 978-1-935182-44-3
  700 pages, $49.99
  Spring 2011

Scala in Depth
by Joshua D. Suereth

  ISBN: 978-1-935182-70-2
  225 pages, $39.99
  Spring 2011

Clojure in Action
by Amit Rathore

  ISBN: 978-1-935182-59-7
  475 pages, $49.99
  Spring 2011

The Joy of Clojure
Thinking the Clojure Way

by Michael Fogus and Chris Houser

  ISBN: 978-1-935182-64-1
  400 pages, $44.99
  January 2011

For ordering information go to www.manning.com